RADAR
FOR MARINERS

DAVID BURCH

International Marine / McGraw-Hill
Camden, Maine ■ New York ■ Chicago ■ San Francisco
Lisbon ■ London ■ Madrid ■ Mexico City ■ Milan
New Delhi ■ San Juan ■ Seoul ■ Singapore ■ Sydney ■ Toronto

The *McGraw·Hill* Companies

1 2 3 4 5 6 7 8 9 10 DOC DOC 0 9 8 7 6 5

Library of Congress Cataloging-in-Publication Data
Burch, David.
  Radar for mariners / David Burch.
      p.   cm.
  Includes bibliographical references and index.
  ISBN 0-07-139867-8
  1. Radar in navigation. I. Title.
  VK560.B85 2005
  623.89´33--dc22   2004018420

Questions regarding the content of this book should be addressed to
International Marine
P.O. Box 220
Camden, ME 04843
www.internationalmarine.com

Questions regarding the ordering of this book should be addressed to
The McGraw-Hill Companies
Customer Service Department
P.O. Box 547
Blacklick, OH 43004
Retail customers: 1-800-262-4729
Bookstores: 1-800-722-4726

Photographs by the author, unless otherwise noted.
Illustrations by Tobias Burch.

Book p/n 0-07-139868-6 and CD p/n 0-07-139869-4
parts of
ISBN 0-07-139867-8

CONTENTS

CONTENTS

The goal of this book is to teach safe, efficient use of radar for small-craft navigation in any condition of visibility. We focus on small craft because ship radars typically offer features and operations that are quite different from those available on the radars normally used on vessels less than some 80 feet or so long. Ship radar features are discussed only briefly, except for those few that are available on more elaborate small-craft radar units. Despite this small-craft focus, however, this book should serve as a solid foundation for those going on to learn ship radar.

Radar is a broad and detailed topic even when restricted to small-craft applications, and that makes learning radar rather like learning celestial navigation. Any book that asks you not to use radar on board until you have mastered all the nuances risks testing your patience and perhaps losing your attention. Too many details too soon are too distracting. Most readers want to start using radar quickly, then fill in the gaps as they go along.

Therefore, to expedite the learning process, we present in Part One the most fundamental aspects of radar use. With that information you will understand the role of radar and how to apply it for typical navigation tasks. Part One will get you underway and will also provide an excellent foundation and contextual outline for the more detailed presentation in Part Two.

We do not mean to imply that Part Two is optional; it is not. All the topics included there are important to safe, efficient, *and versatile* use of radar. The truly optional topics have been left out of the book altogether or are covered with a quick reference alone. You need the details in Part Two for special circumstances and to understand the "whys" of radar and its limitations. Using what you learn in Part One will show you what you need to extract from Part Two. Finish

Part One and you are ready to start using radar. Finish Part Two and you will be better at it. If you are reading this book before selecting your radar, Part Two also includes discussions of various options that might influence your choice.

Even if you do not have a radar at hand, you can practice your skills with the Starpath Radar Trainer software simulator for PC computers, which is on the Radar Resources CD included with this book. This practice simulator can be operated a limited number of times for no charge and includes all the functionality needed to illustrate and practice the principles of radar operation in a very realistic manner. For those who wish to pursue their training further, there is a full commercial version of the program on the CD as well, available for purchase at a discounted additional price. Purchasing instructions are on the CD. The Radar Resources CD also includes several other valuable free aids to learning radar. Among these are sample radar manuals, annotated radar screen images, plotting sheets and other aids, an e-book copy of the *Navigation Rules*, and more.

Throughout the text we cover pros and cons of various radar controls and options but make no specific brand recommendations. There are many choices and configurations on the market (see the References and the Radar Resources CD), which is good, as we all have different needs and preferences. This book will help you home in on the features you might need most. We stress now (and will again) that the most important decision is to get *some* kind of radar onto the boat and learn how to use it. Just about any modern unit, installed in any standard location, will give you some 80 percent or more of the additional safety and efficiency afforded by the use of radar—once you take the time to learn to use it. And this book is intended to help you do just that.

Please check the glossary for the finer points of definitions when new terms appear or when common terms (such as *echo*) seem to be used in an unfamiliar way. The glossary is extensive, covering most radar terminology. In this book all miles are nautical miles, equal to 1,852 meters, which is 6,076 feet, some 15 percent longer than a statute mile. All times are in the 24-hour system, wherein 13 minutes past 2 p.m. is written 1413. We will have occasion to refer to the *Navigation Rules*, as several of these make explicit reference to the use of radar. Hence the phrase *as required by Rule 7* would be a reference to Rule 7 of the International Regulations for Preventing Collisions at Sea (COLREGs), also known as the *Navigation Rules*, or just *Nav Rules*. These are discussed in detail in Chapter 12, and a complete copy of the *Navigation Rules* suitable for printing or for reading and searching from a computer screen is included on the CD.

The list of abbreviations should have all the acronyms used in this book, and the references section offers some ideas for further reading and research.

This book focuses on issues of radar operation that are not much influenced by late-breaking developments. Nevertheless, thanks to the Internet, we can keep readers up to date with the latest news in the field. Please see www.starpath.com/radarbook for updates and news related to this publication. Radar options that did not exist a few years ago are standard now, and ones on the horizon now will be standard in the future. We also use this Internet page to keep readers informed of any developments related to the CD that comes with this book. A purchase of the Radar Trainer program includes access to an interactive online course in radar usage.

This book has benefited from the help of many people, to each of whom I am most grateful. First and foremost, I would like to thank Captain Bill Brogdon, USCG (retired), for his very thorough review of the entire manuscript and for many valuable comments and suggestions throughout the various topics covered. Dennis Sethe, Simrad, Inc., and Buddy Morgan, Japan Radio Company, Ltd., provided valuable suggestions and insights into numerous functional aspects and practical applications of radar. Ron Petersen, chairman of the IEEE International Committee on Electromagnetic Safety (Standards Coordinating Committee 28), sailor and scientist, provided invaluable insights into the numerous details that contribute to an understanding of radiation safety in the vicinity of marine radar installations. And thanks to Robert H. Nicholas Jr., admiralty attorney, Baker & Hostetler, Houston, Texas, for discussions on the *Nav Rules* and for valuable comments on related sections of the book.

The photographs of radar screens throughout the book were taken with the kind assistance of several skippers and their vessels. These include: Stan Willey on M/V *Me Too*, Randy Hamblin on M/V *Saga*, Craig Campbell and Pat Sharpe on M/V *Catalyst*, Don Taylor on S/V *First Sight*, Iko Knyphausen on S/V *Bjossa*, and Chad Peterman on F/V *Aimee O.* Thanks to all of you for often "going out of your way" to help me get these pictures.

And a special thanks to Tobias Burch for rendering my rough sketches into vector drawings—then patiently redoing them numerous times as the ideas evolved—as well as creating the semitransparent overlays of radar-screen photographs onto e-chart images.

The following companies kindly provided images of their products to be included in the book as well as electronic editions of sample manuals included on the Resources CD: Furuno, JRC, Nobeltec, Raymarine, Simrad, and Xenex. Thank you all for these and for your ready help in technical support whenever questions came up.

E-chart screen captures and related navigation studies were carried out using Visual Navigation Suite (Nobeltec), The Capn Voyager (Nautical Technologies), and Navigator (Memory-Map).

PART 1
WORKING KNOWLEDGE OF RADAR

Part One contains the basics of radar function, operation, and application needed to get underway. More details and special features for expanding this knowledge are presented in Part Two.

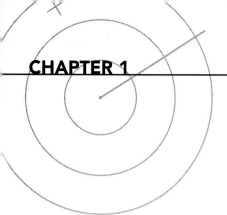

CHAPTER 1

How Radar Works

Radar (*radio detection and ranging*) is an onboard electronic navigation instrument that measures the range and bearing of landmasses and vessels in its vicinity. It works by sending out a rotating beam of microwave pulses and detecting the pulses that are reflected back from objects around it. It works like a depth sounder, pointed toward the horizon rather than the bottom. As with a depth sounder, what we see on the radar screen are only electronic blips or echoes of the targets, not realistic representations. Also like a depth sounder—or a flashlight scanning a dark room—the radar beam only "sees" what is in view of the beam at the moment. The radar's internal display electronics must paint a picture on the radar screen as the beam scans the horizon, refreshing it every 3 seconds. It takes some practice to read a radar screen and interpret what is really out there. We cover this in Chapter 3. As we shall see, some objects are better radar reflectors than others, which gives rise to the term *radar target*. A good radar target is one that sends back a strong, well-defined image to the radar screen. Figure 1-1 illustrates schematically how a radar operates.

Isolated targets such as other vessels, large buoys, islets, or drilling platforms are easier to interpret than large, irregular landmasses. At longer distances, isolated targets appear as simple dots or small line segments. As they get closer their target sizes increase, but unless an object is big and fairly close, the size of the echo on the radar screen (of a ship or buoy, for example) is not a measure of the actual size of the target. This concept is explained further in Chapter 3. The image or echo of a target seen on a radar screen is sometimes called a *blip*.

The basic components of a radar system are

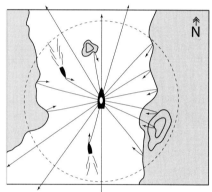

Figure 1-1. *A boat's radar at work. The top view shows the rotating radar beam reflecting from various targets. The bottom view shows how these targets might appear on the radar screen. The dark images are the targets; the gray trails mark target locations over the past 6 minutes using a plot option. The beam rotates about every 3 seconds and updates the radar screen on each rotation. This radar is set to look out to a maximum range (R) of 1.5 miles. Range rings (RR) are shown every 0.5 mile. The "heading line" from the center of the screen marks the direction your vessel is headed.*

an antenna, the radar display unit, and a power source—a typical radar consumes 30 to 40 watts when transmitting. The radar display unit includes a radar screen and a set of controls (knobs, buttons, and sometimes a track ball). There are sophisticated electronics in both the display unit and the antenna, and it is generally most efficient to have a professional electronics technician install and calibrate the system before use (installation options are discussed in Chapter 7). After proper installation it runs dependably and requires little attention as a rule, although basic performance monitoring as discussed in Chapter 13 is always prudent. Radar is a powerful broadcasting device, so an FCC (Federal Communications Commission) Ship Station Radio License (or international equivalent outside the United States) may be required in some cases (see Chapter 7). If you already have a license for a marine radio, the radar can be added to it without a new license.

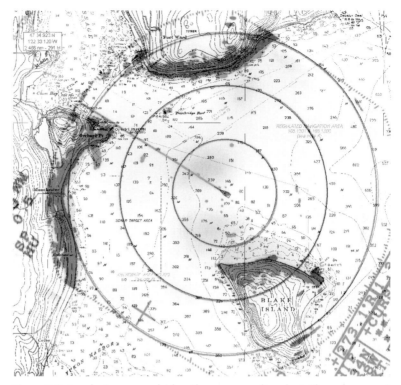

Figure 1-2. A radar image overlaid on the corresponding chart. The radar range is 1.5 nautical miles (nm) with range rings at 0.5 nm intervals. A careful study shows several rocks along the shorelines as well as numerous buoys. The buoy about 1 mile off the starboard bow seems to be located just off its charted position. One surprise in this view might be how prominent the dock at Orchard Point appears on the radar. Checking the Coast Pilot, however, we learn that this is actually a wharf that often has large ships moored alongside it, which accounts for the strong radar reflections. Notice how the steep shore of Blake Island blocks out any radar view of its other side, but the dock and buoys on the bottom right side show up nicely. This illustration was prepared by overlaying a photograph of the radar screen, made partly transparent, on top of an e-chart view of the precise vessel location at the time recorded in the radar picture, using range rings on the vessel to coordinate the two scales. Some modern electronics actually allow for this type of comparison when underway, as discussed later in the book. (Similar handmade overlays can be seen later in Figures 3-10, 3-13, 3-14, 4-6, and 4-9.)

What you see on the radar screen are your surroundings to a maximum distance equal to the selected range setting. The word *range* is used many ways in navigation, but for radar, it simply means the distance from your vessel to the radar target. Typical small-craft radars have maximum ranges of 16 to 36 miles—ship radars extend out to 72 miles or more—but we have to cover more background before we can appreciate the significance of these numbers. On the *plan view* used on radar display screens, your vessel is in the center of the screen. Dead ahead is usually straight up (at the top of the radar screen), your surroundings to starboard are in the right half of the radar screen, your port side is on the left, and aft at the bottom. Modern

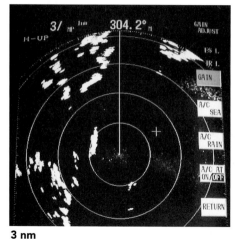

3 nm

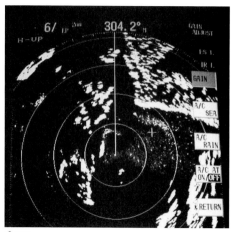

6 nm

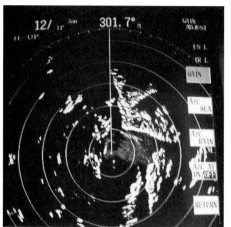

12 nm

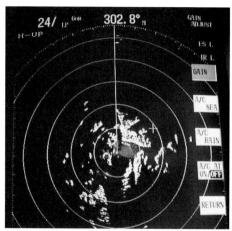

24 nm

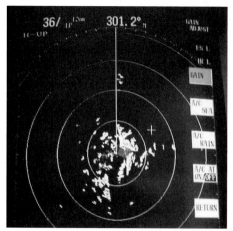

36 nm

Figure 1-3. A single location viewed on five different range scales. In this particular example, we do not learn much from scales beyond 6 miles or below 3 miles—although it is always good radar policy to periodically check larger and smaller scales than the working ones, especially when looking for traffic. In piloting waters, it is fairly rare to use scales beyond 6 miles, but contrary to this example, we often use scales lower than 3 miles. Even in this example, if we wished to study the shore on the port beam, we would switch to the 1-mile scale. As a rule, you want the area being studied to be on the outer part of the radar screen for most detail. Note, too, that with this radar model we see a full range ring farther forward than the range setting specifies. At the 3 nm setting, for example, we "see" 3 nm to the sides and aft but 4 nm forward. This is not a crucial display convention, however, because all radar models offer the option to offset the center to look farther in any direction of choice.

radars offer options to this display mode, but this *head-up* mode is the most fundamental and still the most common in small-craft radar. Head-up display is illustrated in Figure 1-2, which shows a radar image overlaid on the chart region it is viewing. It is similar to the schematic view of Figure 1-1, but with real data.

Radar units are often loosely referred to by their maximum range. A "32-mile radar" has a maximum range of 32 miles but can also be set for 24 miles, 16 miles, 8 miles, and so on. In the past (as well as in many units today), the available range options were fixed values. In some modern units, the user can choose any range desired up to the maximum range of the unit. Also in the past, radar screens were circular, so if you selected a display range of 6 miles, the circumference of the display was 6 miles away in all directions. Most modern radars screens are rectangular, with the display shifted slightly toward the bottom to show an extra ring forward. Today, a range setting of 6 miles will more likely mean that you can see 6 miles to the right, left, and aft, and approximately 7 miles dead ahead, as can be seen in Figure 1-3. In all modern units, however, there is always an Offset function that lets the user arbitrarily shift the center location for longer looks in any direction. This is covered in Chapter 8.

RANGES, BEARINGS, AND BUOYS

To navigate from what we see on the radar, we need numerical values of the ranges and bearings to the various targets shown on the radar screen. The very convenient, electronic way of measuring these values with radar is one of the primary virtues of the instrument.

Suppose we are looking for a buoy about 2 miles ahead on the starboard bow according to the chart and our GPS position. The first step in locating this buoy on the radar screen is to select the appropriate range scale. If the range scale were set to only 1 mile, we would not see the target because it is more than 1 mile away.

When we increase the Range (by just pushing a button or turning a knob) to the 3-mile scale, however, we should see a target about two-thirds of the way out from the center in the top right quadrant of the screen. If we increase the Range again, to 6 miles, the target should remain at the same relative bearing on the screen, but will now be nearer the center, just one-third of the way out, and will register as a smaller blip. If our range options were just 3 or 6 miles, the 3-mile scale would be the better choice. Generally the smallest range that shows the target of interest will give the best results for range and bearing measurements. This lowest range, however, might not offer the best overall perspective for orientation, so one of the basic things we learn in all aspects of radar usage is frequent switching of ranges to keep an eye on things up close and at a distance.

A large buoy, or one with a specially designed radar reflector on it, would show up much like a small vessel—just a little blip on the screen. The radar cannot generally tell you which of these you might be seeing—buoy or vessel—but if you were expecting a buoy, that would be your first guess of what the target is. A small buoy might not show up at all at 2 miles off because it does not have enough reflecting surface to send back a detectable signal, but larger ones will show up nicely. We cover this subject more in Chapter 3.

The first estimate of a numerical value for the actual range to the buoy comes from the range rings. Each range scale on the radar comes with a set of predefined concentric rings at specific ranges. On the 3-mile or 6-mile ranges, these rings are typically drawn 1.0 mile apart. At 12 miles they might be at 2.0 miles apart, and so on. Modern units often let the user select both the sequence of ranges as well as the ring spacing within them, so you might see a 6-mile range with either 1- or 2-mile ring spacing. A typical radar shows the active Range and Range Ring settings prominently in one corner of the display, such as R 3.0, RR 1.0. If we notice that a target is just inside the first range ring, then we know it is just less than 1 mile off. But we can do much better than that.

Every modern radar has a function called *variable range marker* (VRM). It is a range ring for which you can control the radius. The VRM is operated differently on different units, but all do the same thing. Press a button to turn it on, and then press another button to vary the range of the ring. We cover the finer points of using the VRM in Chapter 4; for now, just set the VRM ring to coincide with the closest edge of the buoy target, and then read the value numerically from the VRM readout—in this case it might read 1.89 nm. You can measure very accurate distances this way if you have *good radar targets*—a term that will become more clear as we proceed.

If you are moving toward the buoy, you can watch it move down the screen, getting closer to you. Its motion is easy to detect, because it will move off the VRM that you had set on its previous position. Readjust the VRM to see how much closer it is now. The value of the VRM cannot be overstated. It is not just for watching isolated buoys or vessels moving on the screen, but also for more general radar navigation. More specific examples are given in Chapters 5 and 12. We will also very shortly cover other ways to measure the distance to a radar target.

A bearing to the buoy is just as easy to obtain. Here the tool is called the *electronic bearing line* (EBL). Press a button to turn it on and a prominent radial line—along with its digital bearing—will appear in one corner of the radar display. Press another button (or turn a knob, depending on your model) to rotate the line to the right or left. Adjust the EBL until the line goes through the center of the buoy target and read off its bearing, such as 048 or 048 R. In head-up display mode, these bearing measurements are usually in *relative* units, meaning relative to the bow of your boat, also called *ship's heading* or *head*. In this example, the buoy was located 48° to the right of the bow at the time of measurement. Using relative units, dead ahead is 000, starboard beam is 090 R, aft is 180 R and port beam is 270 R. If the EBL had read 300 R, then the buoy would have been 60° to the left of the bow. Figure 1-4 illustrates relative bearings.

If we want a compass bearing to the buoy that we can use to look for the buoy on deck, we need to correct the relative output of the EBL for our actual heading. Do this by adding the relative bearing to your course heading. If our compass course is 200 C at the time of the reading, for example, then the compass bearing to the buoy (located 48° to the right of the bow) is 248 C. When targets are on the port side of the boat, with relative bearings greater than 180, it is best to add the relative bearing to your heading and then subtract 360 as needed. In the second example above, 200 (ship's heading) + 300 (relative bearing to buoy) = 500, and 500 − 360 = 140 degrees, which is the compass bearing to the buoy. For this and numerous other reasons, every nav station should have a simple calculator on hand at all times (large keys and a large display are assets). It will prove useful often, as in compass conversions, speed-time-distance computations, and for some special quick computations needed for radar, which we discuss later on.

(Later we discuss options in modern radars that let us read actual compass bearings or even true bearings directly from the radar without manually

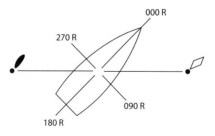

Figure 1-4. *Relative bearings are used in much of radar work. The buoy shown is at a bearing of 045 R and the light is at 225 R. Most radar units will identify a relative bearing with an "R," as opposed to a true or magnetic bearing, which requires a special heading sensor input to the radar.*

correcting for vessel heading, but this requires an optional heading sensor input to the radar.)

It is simple to get a bearing for any target we see on the radar using the EBL, but we must be mindful of several factors when we interpret the result. First, even though electronic bearings are typically specified to within a tenth of a degree, it is rare that the accuracy of the intended measurement has this level of precision. In the head-up example given above, we had to correct for our course heading of 200 degrees to get the buoy's compass bearing. But we may not have been precisely on course at the time we noted the EBL reading. The ship's heading will typically swing around a bit in a seaway, so the EBL will move on and off the target once it is set. In short, the accuracy of the bearing will depend on the accuracy of your heading knowledge at the time of the measurement. With head-up display, careful coordination with the helmsman is needed for precise bearing data; another solution is a digital heading output right on the radar screen so that you can record the EBL and heading at the same time. In Chapter 7 we cover even more convenient interface options.

When taking bearings to tangents of large radar targets (as opposed to centers of small, well-defined targets like buoys), other considerations affect accuracy as well. We cover these in Chapter 10.

Another way to measure ranges and bearings with modern radar is to use a *cursor* mode. In this mode a track ball or track pad is used to move a prominent crosshair cursor around on the radar screen while at the same time displaying the range and bearing to the cursor location somewhere on the radar screen. Want the range and bearing to a headland? Just roll the cursor over to that location on the screen and read it off digitally in a bottom corner of the screen. This is a very convenient option, which sometimes includes a further option to draw an EBL and VRM circle through the cursor location by pressing buttons.

The cursor is generally the preferred method of finding target range and bearing. It has the advantage of being quick but the disadvantage of not leaving permanent marks on the screen, as the VRM and EBL do. Underway you will have call for both types of measurements, which opens the opportunity for errors. A potentially serious error would be to set the cursor on a headland and then read the output from the VRM, which is inadvertently set on some other location. Often the outputs on the screen are very similar and just marked by different icons. It is often true with modern electronics that the more convenient our tools, the more careful we have to be in using them. Sample measurements are shown in Figure 1-5.

Bearing and range measurements are fundamental to radar usage. To a radar operator, VRM and EBL are acronyms as common as GPS or radar itself. We will use abbreviations throughout the rest of this book. VRM and EBL have several crucial applications that cannot be replaced with the cursor mode feature, but

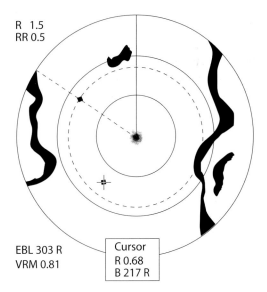

R 1.5
RR 0.5

EBL 303 R
VRM 0.81

Cursor
R 0.68
B 217 R

Figure 1-5. *The electronic bearing line (EBL), variable range marker (VRM), and cursor readouts are ways to measure the range and bearing to a target. Some units have two EBLs and VRMs. The cursor mode is often the quickest way to get range and bearing to a target.*

when just a value of range or bearing is needed, the cursor mode will generally be the first choice for the job. In Chapter 2 we cover a related tool called the *electronic range and bearing line* (ERBL). In Chapter 4 we cover ways to optimize the accuracy of the measurements.

HEAD-UP DISPLAY MODE

Until recently, small-craft radar had only one display mode available—namely, the head-up mode using relative bearings for the EBL as discussed above. This is still an option on all radar systems, and still the only option on many units in use today. It is also in many ways the most fundamental mode and the easiest to interpret. You think of your boat in the center of the screen, pointed straight up, and things you see around you on the radar screen are located relative to your vessel. Look to the right of your boat for things on the right of the screen; look back for things on the bottom of the screen, etc. The translation from radar image to the world around you is particularly direct and intuitive if your nav station faces forward. It is perhaps a bit less intuitive if your nav station faces athwartships or even aft, but in all cases this is a direct, easily interpreted radar display mode. Your heading line remains vertical, from the center to the top of the radar screen, regardless of your vessel heading or the orientation of the display unit within your vessel. No special inputs to the radar are needed.

In head-up mode, when your course changes to the left, or counterclockwise, all radar targets rotate a corresponding amount to the right, or clockwise, but no matter which way you head, the heading line remains straight up, and the top of the radar screen is the direction the bow is pointed. In head-up mode, the EBL reads out bearings to radar targets in relative units. Suppose the EBL is set on a target at 048 R (48° on the starboard bow), and then we turn away from it, 10° to the left. The heading line and the EBL will not move on the radar screen as we turn, but the target will rotate right 10°, and is now 58° on the starboard bow. This illustrates the fundamental advantage of the head-up mode—things are where they appear to be on the radar—but it also illustrates an inherent disadvantage when it comes to identifying what we see on the radar when we are moving. If our heading is swinging about as we proceed along our course, as it would in choppy water or a seaway, target positions will "smear" as they rotate back and forth in response to our heading swings. They get painted onto the screen wherever they happen to be when the radar beam passes across them.

In Chapter 7 we explore other display modes available on modern radars and the required extra inputs needed to make them work. The optional displays are called *course-up* and *north-up* modes, either of which requires a heading sensor input to the radar. In the meantime, the head-up, relative-bearing display is the best choice for getting underway with radar.

MARKING AND READING THE SCREEN BY HAND

When using radar for navigation and especially for collision avoidance, we often must know not only where the targets are at the moment, but what paths they have been following. This requires a way to record the history of target tracks on the radar screen. Modern radar offers electronic ways to measure or mark just about anything on the screen, but these electronic options may not always be the most efficient solution to a task at hand. We can, for example, use the cursor or VRM to measure a distance on the screen, or even an offset VRM (as discussed in Chapter 2) to measure a line segment on the screen. But these may take some time to set up, or your particular model may not even have the option you need. Likewise, some units have ways to electronically mark a position on the screen, and some do not.

In any event, it is good practice to do these measurements the old-fashioned way by hand, using homemade tools and the proper markers.

In nearly every example of systematic observations of a target on the radar screen, we need to somehow mark the target's position right on the screen itself and label it with the time of the observation.

The method for this job often mentioned in older references is to use a grease pencil, or china marker. These markers come in various colors and have the advantage of durability, yet they can be erased with a rag and a little elbow grease, possibly with a dab of alcohol from a small bottle kept in the nav table. Simple rubbing alcohol works well for cleaning up china markers on glass radar screens, but on plastic screens or components, be sure to check cleaning instructions first; alcohol may not be compatible with some plastics. China markers work reasonably well on some radar displays but do not show up well on others, no matter what color is tried.

China markers historically have come in a tight paper wrapper that you unpeel to expose more of the marker point as needed. They can also be sharpened as needed with a knife. Gardening shops also carry a newer model that is more like a mechanical pencil, with the wax lead in a hard plastic housing that you turn to advance.

An alternative to china markers is called an overhead projector pen. One company that makes them is Vis-à-Vis. These come in various colors and also in a fine-point version. They make sharp, clear marks and lines on a radar or glass computer screen, dry quickly, and—once dry—are very durable as long as they do not get wet. The marks come off easily with a damp cloth. This is the type of marker I find most useful for radar plotting.

You might be tempted to use dry-erase markers for this job, since they come in many colors and leave sharp, clear marks on a radar or computer screen. They clean up very easily—in fact, too easily for this job, especially when underway. If you so much as touch them, they will smear or erase. These markers are convenient

for practice at home on the Radar Trainer simulator (included on the Radar Resources CD), but they are not a good choice underway. Generally when you mark a target it is important to watch the marks over time, and you do not want to risk losing them.

When you mark a target it is important to write the time beside it (see Figure 1-6). Be sure you are using the same clock for each subsequent mark. Often there is some nav output such as position and time from the GPS next to the radar, which makes a convenient reference. Generally these times are only recorded to the nearest minute (e.g., 1247), but it is useful to wait until an exact minute for the mark—another good reason to have a time output prominently displayed next to the radar.

If you do not already have such an output in plain view next to the radar, consider purchasing a digital clock. Very slick models are inexpensive these days, with optional displays. I prefer a model with big digits showing hours, minutes, and seconds, and one that is easy to set from the front. Some come with adhesive backing that you can mount anywhere; some oven timers are good for this. A built-in stopwatch is also valuable for various navigation jobs.

In many practical applications we need to read the distance between two marks on the radar screen. These can be two sequential marks of a target's position that we made while evaluating collision risk, or they can be two landmarks (the width of a bay, for example) that we need to identify. They can be electronic marks, marks we made by hand, or simply two unmarked targets on the screen.

One way to measure the distance between marks is to turn on the range rings and interpolate the distance by inspection—e.g., just looking and estimating. If the entrance to a bay appears to be just less than one range ring interval wide, and the rings are set to 1.0 mile, then the bay is just less than a mile across. Another method is to mark the separation on a sheet of paper, or set dividers to the distance,

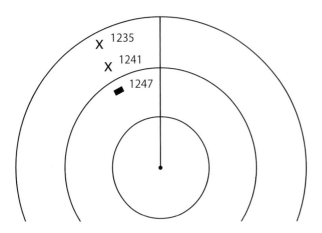

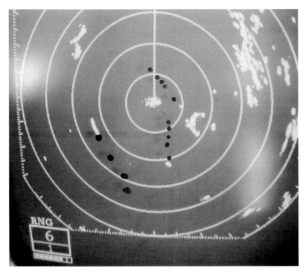

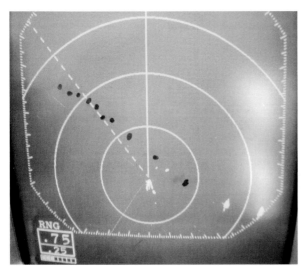

Figure 1-6. *Handmade marks on the radar screen. The marks in the top figure show the history of the target as it approaches. We can learn much from these simple marks, such as how fast the target is approaching (about 1 range ring per 12 minutes in this example), and by projecting the line forward we can see how close it will pass if everything remains the same. Marks can be made at any time or time interval, but we will later see the advantage of using 6-minute intervals. An X has been used as the mark here to emphasize the marking process, but in practice just a dot the size of the target will do the job. In this example the target's relative motion is toward the center of the screen (your boat!) along a fairly constant bearing. If nothing changes, a collision could result in 16 or 17 minutes.*

The middle screen shows three targets marked at regular intervals until the forward one passed at 1 mile off the bow. (The time interval used was noted at the time, but not saved.)

The bottom picture shows a speedboat, airborne at every wave, that crossed the bow at about 200 yards off moving at about 20 kts. The EBL was set on the target at 0.5 mile off to monitor its relative course. This radar did not have a functioning electronic plot option, so these handmade marks were used often on this trip. The two targets between last two marks are waves; the far bottom right is an island, and approaching that is the speedboat at the time of the snapshot.

and then use the VRM. Several methods are illustrated in Figure 1-7.

A convenient third method, which is more accurate than an eyeball estimation and much quicker than using the VRM, is to construct a special portable range scale that matches your radar unit. You may also want to make one for your computer to use with the Radar Trainer simulator (Radar Resources CD).

The device is simply a subdivided range scale hand-drawn onto a piece of cardboard or any flat surface. I find the tongue depressors used by nurses and doctors convenient for this purpose—a trick I learned from a riverboat captain in Biloxi. They can be purchased from any pharmacy. Just mark the scale along the edge to match the spacing of the range rings on your radar, as shown in Figure 1-8.

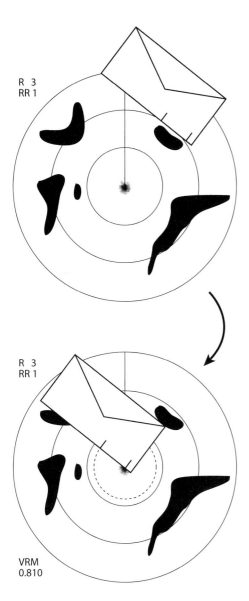

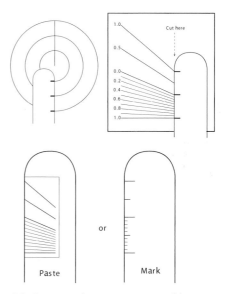

Figure 1-8. *A tongue depressor as a portable range scale. The idea is to have some object in hand that will directly measure subdivisions of your radar's range ring spacing. This calibration can be done by hand with a ruler, or more easily using some form of a proportional grid such as a Loran TD interpolator (on older charts). There are several printable versions of such a grid on the Radar Resources CD. You can cut the grid and paste it onto the portable scale or use it as a guide to mark the scale itself. You need a scale for each radar ring spacing, though several ranges usually share the same spacing.*

Figure 1-7. *Range rings and the VRM can be used to measure distances. With the range ring (RR) interval set to 1.0 nm, we can tell by inspection that the small islet on the port side is about a third of a mile offshore and that the entrance to the bay next to it is about 1 mile across. We can get more precise values by marking a card and then using the VRM to read off the distance digitally. The island on the starboard bow is 0.81 nm wide. We can also make special tools for the job as shown in Figure 1-8 and again in Figure 6-3. Modern radar units also provide a way (the electronic range and bearing line, ERBL) to make such measurements digitally on the screen (see Chapter 2).*

The scale shown in Figure 1-8 is available on the CD as a printable graphic (instructions are included). Just find where the scale matches your range ring spacing on radar or computer, cut it there, and paste or tape it onto a piece of cardboard or a tongue depressor. Loran interpolators on charts are set up in a similar way and may be useful for this—if you happen to have an older chart with Loran lines printed on it.

When using a portable range scale, remember that the meaning of a range ring changes with the scale—at a range of 6 miles, they are usually 1.0 mile apart, at a range of 12 miles they are 2.0 miles apart, and so on—but this does not affect the use of the portable scale. You need a separate portable scale for each distinct ring spacing.

As mentioned initially, this problem of distance measurement and target marking can be solved with various elegant electronic features on modern radars (see Chapter 2), but it always pays to be prepared to do it by hand. You may find, in some circumstances, that your homemade approach is a better solution.

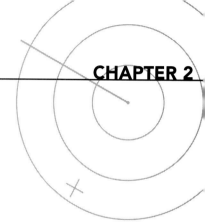

Operation and "Tuning"

Some readers will remember the days before cable television when we had to "tune" a TV to get the best picture. It was not just a matter of turning the set on to see a beautiful, sharp picture; we had to adjust various knobs on the set, then maybe on the antenna, and then maybe on the TV again. . . . Your radar unit requires roughly analogous adjustments whenever you turn it on. Rarely will you be able to avoid at least some degree of this tuning. In this chapter we cover the primary picture-quality controls of Brilliance, Contrast, Tuning, Gain, Sea Clutter, and Rain Clutter, along with the basic operational controls that help us interpret what we see. More specialized controls are discussed in Chapter 8.

Since one of the controls used to optimize the radar picture is actually called "Tuning," it is best to avoid the common use of the term referred to above, and reserve this term for that specific control to avoid miscommunication. It is rather like the mariners' common use of the word *tides*, as in "What are the tides doing?," when in fact the question intended was "What are the tidal currents doing?" A key element of good navigation is good communication. When we say "Check the tuning," we actually mean adjust the Tuning control, rather than tweak the full set of controls that influence the final picture.

First, though, we must turn the unit on and let it warm up.

WARM-UP

All radar units require a 1- to 2-minute warm-up time when first turned on. Often a countdown timer shows on the screen, perhaps with a note about the warm-up delay. This time is required primarily to thermally warm up (energize and stabilize) the key part of the electronic circuit that will actually produce the microwaves, called the *magnetron*. For safe navigation it is important to remember this delay. You cannot flip on the radar at the last minute to see what is out there. Most radars have a Standby mode, which keeps the instrument warmed up and ready to transmit while avoiding the full power consumption of actual microwave transmission.

STANDBY MODE

A radar in Standby mode is warmed up and ready to transmit, but is not actually transmitting microwaves and the antenna is not rotating. Usually if you can get near the antenna (often housed in a plastic case called a *radome*) you can hear whether the rotation motor is running or not. This mode is usually toggled on and off with a control panel button marked "Transmit." The power saving is typically about 45 percent; a radar that draws 33 watts when transmitting might require only 18 watts in Standby mode. In some models the power saving might be less. The radar screen will usually be blank in Stand-by mode, with "Standby" or "ST-BY" showing on the screen. Press "Transmit" to get the picture back. (A related power-saving mode is called "Watch" mode [Chapter 8], which runs the radar intermittently at preset intervals, rather than manually switching between Transmit and Standby.)

On sailing vessels with limited power resources, it makes sense to keep the unit in Standby mode whenever someone is not actually viewing the screen. On power-driven vessels, power consumption is not so much an issue, but judicial use of Standby mode can also extend the lifetime of radar components. It is also good policy not to transmit radar when the beam might reach people, as when motoring through a crowded marina, transiting locks, or when someone is working close to and in line with the antenna. Related issues of radar safety and etiquette are discussed in Chapters 5 and 7.

PICTURE-QUALITY CONTROLS
Brilliance

This knob or button controls the brightness of the display. The Brilliance or Brightness control does not alter radar signal and image resolution as the Gain and Clutter controls do (discussed below), but adjusting it can produce a somewhat similar effect. It is important to understand that the Brilliance control simply brightens or dims the entire display—not just the active radar images, but also all the other text and outputs on the screen. Brilliance must be changed whenever the ambient light in the nav station or wheelhouse changes: when night turns to day, bright sunlight yields to overcast, etc. Generally, you want the display just bright enough to be seen clearly, but no brighter. Brilliance must be balanced with Gain for the best picture. If the Brilliance is too high, it can mask the need for Gain adjustments that influence the resolution of the radar images.

If you cannot see the picture simply because it is too faint, try the Brilliance control first, before increasing the Gain. Likewise, when the picture appears too bright, turn down the Brilliance before reducing the Gain. Some units permit Brilliance adjustment in only one direction, so to dim the screen you may have to increase brightness to its maximum value and start again. See Figure 2-1.

Some modern radars offer the option of adjusting the brightness of the radar rings independent of the Brilliance control. After setting the Brilliance, you can use the range ring brightness control to fine-tune the display. When available, this is a useful feature for optimizing the display under various conditions.

Contrast

Modern radar displays often include a Contrast control as well as a Brilliance control. This control would be used in conjunction with the Brilliance to optimize the picture, much as you would do when adjusting a computer screen for varying degrees of background lighting or image intensity. Contrast might also be checked when making significant Gain changes. Types of radar displays (LCD and CRT) are discussed in Chapter 8.

Tuning (Tuning Bar)

As mentioned above, many people refer to the adjustment of all the various knobs or buttons on a radar as *tuning* the radar, but only one of the several adjustments is actually called "Tuning," and this control is an important one for optimizing the radar image. There is generally a manual coarse-tune control as well as a fine-tune control, which can be a manual or auto-tune control. Sometimes the manual tune control is a prominent knob on the main panel; other times it is found only within a menu of controls or setup options.

On some units you may find that once properly calibrated at installation, you will rarely interact with this control, with the auto-tune setting meeting all of your needs; on other vessels or radar units, you may find that the Tuning control is more frequently used.

The Tuning control adjusts the frequency of

Figure 2-1. Alternative Brilliance settings on a radar display. Brilliance adjustments optimize screen brightness for the ambient lighting—as opposed to Gain adjustments, which affect the radar signals and influence image resolution.

the receiver to match the frequency of the incoming echoes, which is determined by the magnetron—the source of the transmitted signals. Magnetron frequencies differ slightly from one radar to the next, even of the same model, and these frequencies drift as the unit stabilizes thermally.

When the receive and transmit frequencies are matched, the unit is "in tune," and the target images have optimum intensity and appear sharper; when out of tune, they are weaker and more poorly defined. Most modern radars have automatic tuning through a circuit called the *automatic frequency control* (AFC), but generally the manual tuning must be set first to have this function properly. The manual tuning on some units may be part of the setup controls or accessed via a menu option, rather than a more prominent control on the main panel.

Many radars, however, do have a direct access to manual tuning, and some new models that have AFC still provide a tuning bar to indicate the quality of the tuning, even when there is not a control panel knob for manual tuning. A radar tuning bar is like the tuning bar on some FM radios—you maximize the number of bars showing for the best reception. Similarly, if all is working properly, you adjust the radar tuning knob until you get the largest number of segments filled in, and this in principle should correspond to the best picture. Be aware, however, that the tuning bar display is only a guide, and it may not be the proper measure of the optimum tuning for what you want to see at the moment—or the tuning bar display itself could need calibration. It measures total image intensity only, which might not be the best measure of the optimum picture. Radar images with many bright targets on the screen may show different tuning bar behavior compared to images with just a few weaker targets on the screen, and tuning bar indications on low ranges may not be the same as on higher ranges.

To use manual tuning, the best procedure is to have the unit warmed up for 20 minutes or

more, and use a high range that employs a long pulse length (discussed below). Then select a distant target such as a large vessel, islet, or headland at least several miles away—the farther the better, and preferably not a really bright one. A weak distant target that shows consistently is best. It is also best done when not in rain or choppy seas, with the Interference Reject (Chapter 8) and the Rain and Sea Clutter controls shut off completely.

Set the Gain just high enough to barely show some speckles of noise on the screen, then watch both the radar picture and the tuning bar (if there is one) as you adjust the Tuning control slowly up and down from mid-range. The proper setting is when the image appears the sharpest and brightest. Remember the picture is only painted every 2 to 3 seconds, so you must wait to see the effect of an adjustment. Once the tuning is set properly on this high range, it should be correct for the lower ranges as well, although the peak value in the tuning bar may differ. If the sharpest, brightest image does not correlate with the maximum tuning bar readout, then make note of that to see if this behavior persists. If it does, then you can use the observed best value as your tuning bar reference point. It could also be worth discussing this with your radar technician to see if it can be adjusted. The installation settings affect the centering of this control and the Tuning indicator might need tuning!

On the other hand, if the tuning bar is fully pegged when the picture is optimized, and you have a coarse-tuning control in one of the menus, then you can likely recenter the tuning bar display yourself. Use manual control to set the tuning bar to mid-range, and adjust the picture back to optimum with the coarse control. This should return the tuning bar indicator to a useful range. (If you cannot locate a coarse control and the bar is fully pegged, it's best to ask a technician about it.)

The use of the tuning bar indication for performance monitoring is discussed in Chapter 13. Some units show a digital value for the tuning level, just as they might for all of the picture-quality controls, which offers a more quantitative way to record optimum settings.

In the worst case, without a tuning bar or an isolated target, manual tuning can be done on wave reflections in choppy water or on your own wake after a turn. Adjust Tuning as described above for maximum sea clutter.

Once the tuning setting is about right, which it likely will be after a professional installation, then in practice the most common use of tuning might be just to see if the picture at hand is optimum when looking for the most detail possible. In this case, you just watch carefully the region of the screen you care about the most as you very slowly make adjustments of the Tuning control.

Tuning may drift some when the unit is first turned on (in the first 30 minutes or so of transmitting), but should remain stable and not require adjustment after that. If you have a manual tuning knob, you should not need to adjust it very often provided it is properly set up internally. Again, some auto-tuned models do not even include this control on the main panel. If you have a tuning bar, just keep an eye on its status to get used to its behavior. Then if the picture seems off at some point, you can look at the bar to see whether manual tuning is needed. It should not change much, but if a crewmember has not read the section on radar etiquette (see the end of this chapter), they may have come by and twiddled your knobs!

As discussed in Chapter 9, the Tuning control can also be a key to removing some types of false echoes and interference from the radar screen in special cases where these might be prominent.

Gain

Gain measures how much reflected signals are amplified when received. This is the major control used to optimize the radar picture and it often must be adjusted whenever you make large changes in range or must optimize the picture under changing conditions on the same range, such as getting closer to land or when a large vessel passes. The Gain is normally adjusted with the AC Rain turned off and with a high or maximum range scale. Increase the Gain until you see a faint coverage of white specks on the background over the full radar screen. Note that full Gain can turn the screen white, and zero Gain turns it black. Most operators prefer a Gain setting that leaves just a faint coverage of white specks in the background. These specks are a combination of sea clutter (discussed below) and electronic noise.

If the Gain is too high, you will lose resolution (the ability to distinguish nearby targets), and if it's too low, you will miss weaker targets. Check the Brilliance control again if needed. If the ambient lighting around the radar screen has changed, the display brightness might need to be adjusted before setting the Gain. The key is to be sure the AC Sea is off, and then turn up the Gain until you see white specks. It is easy to set the Gain when a target is in view, but it is more difficult when no target is there—offshore without any traffic in range—hence the comfort of seeing the specks. When a target does come into view, the Gain can be readjusted.

Gain must usually be reduced when large, close targets are present and may have to be increased when looking for small targets or when using AC Rain. Sometimes better range and bearing resolution can be achieved by reducing the Gain, and sometimes reducing the Gain will help reduce clutter from rain or snow.

Remember always to return the Gain to its normal setting if it has been changed for special purposes. Gain adjustments are illustrated in Figure 2-2.

In modern units, there is usually an option for using automatic Gain control as well as manual gain control. Generally speaking, these automatic controls work very well, but it is likely that on most units you will be able to

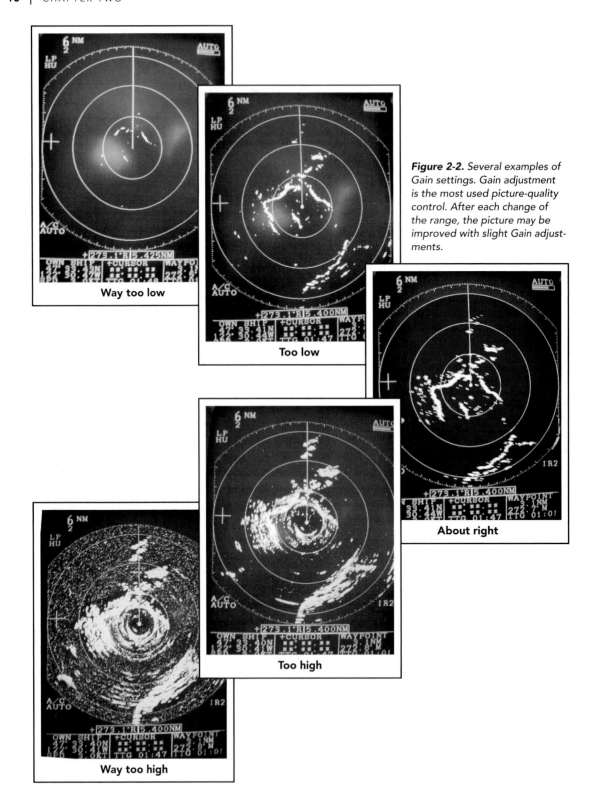

Figure 2-2. *Several examples of Gain settings. Gain adjustment is the most used picture-quality control. After each change of the range, the picture may be improved with slight Gain adjustments.*

optimize the feature you want to see best on the range you want using the manual control. I have seen an exception, however. On an older LCD model I used recently, there were three levels of automatic gain and a manual option. In this unit, optimizing the picture boiled down to selecting the best automatic level to use, which required changes with the range. I could not improve the picture at all using the manual control.

Sea Clutter (AC Sea or STC)

Radar echoes from waves are called *sea clutter*. In big seas or heavy chop this background can dominate the screen and block out smaller targets at shorter ranges. This can be an issue on inland waters as well as on the ocean. Fully developed seas in just a 10-mile fetch, for example, will generate very heavy clutter on ranges of about 1 mile or less. However, all radars include an electronic filter to remove or greatly reduce this problem. The control is called by various names: Sea Clutter, AC Sea (AC stands for anticlutter), or STC (for sensitivity time control). Since it has many names, it's useful to know its international symbol, shown in Figure 2-3.

AC Sea is a control that should be kept at Minimum or Off unless needed. If set too high, it can block out close targets. Generally it does nothing, regardless of setting, for ranges farther than about 4 miles. In

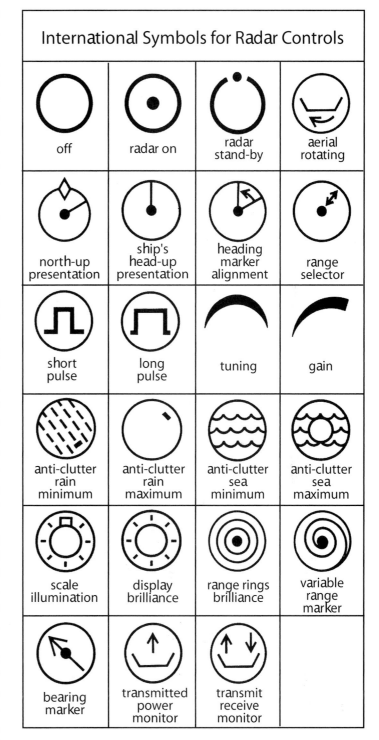

Figure 2-3. *International symbols. These are used on some units, and some units use them in the manuals but not on the actual controls.*

calm sea conditions, it should be kept off. In rough seas, the entire close-in region of the screen on the lower ranges will be nearly solid white from wave reflections. In these cases, the control should be increased until this smear is broken up into a pattern of small dots. This is easy to optimize if you have close, small targets present. Just increase the Sea Clutter until the targets stand out prominently. Without such targets, you have to estimate this. Always leave some clutter showing.

If no close target is showing on the screen but you're trying to determine if any are in the area, close concentration is required. The wave echoes are transient, showing one place on the screen and then another, whereas a real target will show repeatedly in the same place. Hand-marking suspected candidates with a Vis-à-Vis marker can help identify real targets in a maze of clutter.

On a sailboat that is well heeled over sailing to windward, you might occasionally see more sea clutter to leeward because the leeward beam sweep is pointed toward the water and the windward beam is sweeping toward the sky. Electronic adjustments cannot fix this (see Heel-Angle Adjustments in Chapter 8), and this is not the normal observation for a vessel with a horizontal radar antenna, as on a power-driven vessel or when sailing downwind.

With a level antenna, there is usually more clutter to windward, since the beam emitted in that direction reflects from the fronts of the waves, which are better reflectors than the backs of waves. In bigger seas you can be reasonably confident the Sea Clutter is correct by turning it up until you see this windward-leeward distinction clearly, while still leaving some clutter on the weaker side. Note that you need some waves causing discernible clutter to see this effect. See Figure 2-4. In many cases sailing downwind at sea, you can actually read the wind direction fairly well relative to your heading by estimating the center of the distribution of sea clutter to windward.

If you have the option to switch between long or short pulses on the range scale, use the short pulse option when looking for close, small targets in the presence of sea clutter.

Since AC Sea effectively reduces the gain at close ranges beyond what is possible with the Gain control itself, it is often used to optimize the picture when navigating in close proximity to land—an application of the control that has nothing to do with sea state at all. It is also useful when anchoring (Chapter 5) or transiting narrow channels. Some units have two or three levels of STC or auto STC. These options change how fast the gain is reduced and how far out the effect extends. Practice with different settings in different conditions to learn what works best.

What you end up calling this control ("Sea Clutter," "AC Sea," or "STC") probably depends most on how it is labeled on your own radar unit. But since it has frequent use as a low-range gain reduction in anchoring or other close-quarters navigation, as well as in suppression of sea state clutter, the abbreviation "STC" is likely the term that best represents its overall use in picture optimization.

Rain Clutter (AC Rain or FTC)

When in or near a rain or snow squall, the radar screen becomes cluttered with reflections from the precipitation. This can be so severe that it masks the presence of any target in a nearby squall or, if you are in the squall, masks the presence of approaching traffic. Reflections from precipitation are usually easy to identify from their unique appearance. A rain squall on the radar screen appears as a large patch of speckles, as if spray-painted onto the screen. Often the boundaries of a squall, or at least the part with rain content, can be clearly seen on the radar and maneuvered around. Squall maneuvering is discussed in Chapter 11.

The AC Rain filter breaks up the continuous display of precipitation echoes into a much

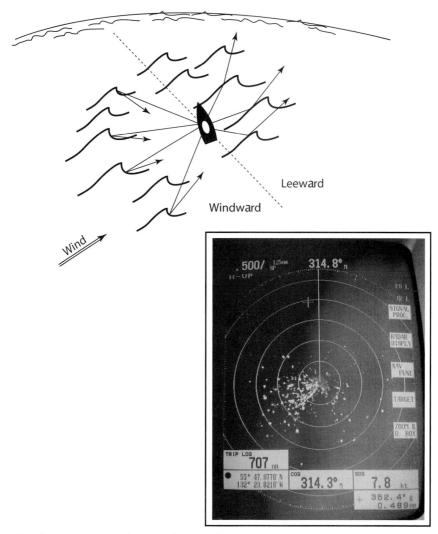

Figure 2-4. *Sea clutter. Since wave fronts are better reflectors than wave backs, we generally see more sea clutter to windward, as shown in the insert for a wind on the port quarter. (Note that the radar shown here has a shadow in the aft direction due to the temporary storage of a stack of kayaks on the aft upper deck.) The appearance of sea clutter on the radar can sometimes be masked in a heeled-over sailing vessel, because the radar is looking up over the nearby windward seas and more down toward the leeward side. The image here (from a motor vessel) shows the effect, but it can be much more pronounced with bigger waves on low ranges.*

finer speckled pattern. Often the filter is presented with two modes: a toggle to *fast time constant* (FTC) display, which is an On/Off switch used for heavy interference; or a variable control, often called Rain Clutter or AC Rain, for weaker interference. These filters generally work quite well in rain and snow and will reveal targets that might not otherwise be seen. In very heavy rain or hail, however, the radar may be effectively blocked out by this interference and these controls may not adequately solve the problem. In cases like this, if there is any probability of traffic during the blocked-out period, you must assume a safe speed consistent with the conditions. Rain and squalls are discussed further in Chapter 9.

If the FTC mode has been selected and then the precipitation stops, the filter should be shut off, because it tends to reduce the sensitivity of the receiver, often breaking up larger, continuous targets into patches that might not be interpreted as continuous targets.

FTC controls might also be used in fair weather in crowded or confined harbors or near any large target that generates bright images on the screen to improve the picture since they reduce sensitivity in a manner qualitatively different from reducing Gain. This FTC adjustment can be valuable for optimizing the picture when navigating in tight quarters, such as anchoring, or when looking for detailed features within any radar image. Sometimes distinct features of even distant targets can be enhanced by clipping the echoes with some FTC; in one case I recall revealing a breakwater along a shoreline that was not visible without this adjustment.

Unlike Sea Clutter, which works in close range, but progressively less at larger ranges, the FTC control works uniformly over the full range of the display. This

distinction between AC Sea and AC Rain is shown schematically in Figure 2-5.

If you have the option to switch between long or short pulses on the range scale, use the short pulse option when looking for targets within the rain pattern or squall itself, and use

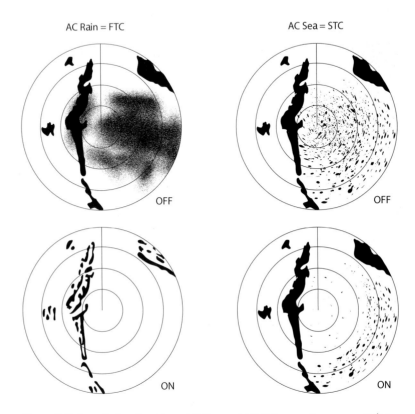

Figure 2-5. *A reminder about how AC Sea and AC Rain operate on your radar screen. AC Rain (also called fast time constant, FTC) operates over the full range showing on the screen as you increase its strength, whereas AC Sea (also called sensitivity time control, STC) operates from the center out in an increasingly larger radius of effect. Also, FTC will operate over all ranges, whereas STC is limited to a few miles of effect; looking closely you can see the active region increase on the radar screen as you adjust the control. Besides removing actual rain clutter, FTC tends to clip all echoes to some extent, leading to thinner images that can sometimes improve target interpretation by revealing identifiable structures.*

The left side shows schematically the effect of FTC on a local squall and nearby land targets. The right side is another day at the same location in the presence of a strong wind on the starboard quarter. Turning on the STC in this case reduces the sea clutter, which has been increased out to the middle of the third range ring. Both examples overemphasize effectiveness to illustrate their behaviors.

If you have the Range set below the effective extent of the STC, you will just see the Gain being quickly reduced over the full screen as you further increase the STC. STC causes a very strong reduction in the Gain for low ranges.

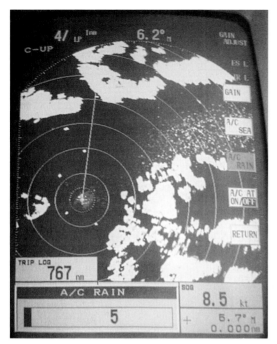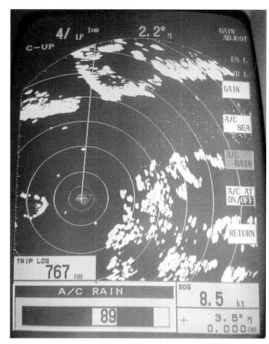

Figure 2-6. *AC Rain (also called FTC) in action. The radar is in the course-up mode, which accounts for the heading line being slightly rotated from the vertical, and the center of the radar has been offset for a better view of the region of rain 3 to 6 miles off the starboard bow. The left screen shows the view with AC Rain almost off (relative setting of "5"). The rain shows up as a sprinkle of noise on the screen. This is a rather light rain; a heavy rain would show a more solid pattern.*

In the right screen, AC Rain has been increased to "89," which was enough to remove most of the rain, showing that there was one real target just above the rain pattern, although with the target just out of the rain, we could likely have known that without this adjustment.

Notice that this AC Rain or FTC control has also broken up, or "clipped," all of the radar images, not just the rain. The closest edge of each target is not affected, but the farthest edge of each target has been clipped, which tends to break up solid images into components. Sometimes this clipping effect helps interpret the images. In this case, with FTC on we have a better idea that there is likely a mound dead ahead, about a mile inland, which indeed there is—a prominent 2,250-foot hill on the southeast corner of Mitkof Island, at the entrance to Wrangell Narrows, Alaska. Other examples are discussed in Part Two.

the long pulse option when you are in rain or looking through it for targets beyond. Radar screen captures illustrating both rain suppression and the target-clipping effects of using AC Rain are shown in Figure 2-6.

If you want to look at a squall pattern itself, this control should be shut off to enhance the squall boundaries, and you might want to even raise the Gain a bit.

As above with the STC control, the abbreviation FTC is a more generic description of the functionality than AC Rain. The table summarizes their functions.

SUMMARY OF FTC AND STC CONTROLS

FTC	STC
suppresses rain clutter	suppresses sea clutter
clips all echoes in the radial direction	offers additional Gain reduction at low ranges
applies over the full screen	applies from the center out as the control is increased

MEASUREMENT CONTROLS
Plots, Wakes, or Echo Trails

All modern radars include an option that leaves tracks on the screen that mark how the targets moved across the screen. These trails and the control that engages them are variously referred to as "plots," "wakes," or "echo trails." This is a crucial feature for evaluating risk of collision, but it has a limited application in radar position navigation. There are two basic formats or styles of trails: one leaves a trail behind the target for a user-selected duration of time (30 sec, 1 min, etc.), and the other style makes discrete marks on the screen at specific intervals (every 3 min, 6 min, etc.). There are virtues to both styles, although the former is perhaps the most versatile. There is also a Continuous mode where the trail marking stays on as long as the Trail option is engaged. In the Continuous mode, the two different trail styles look identical on the screen. These three types of trails are illustrated in Figure 2-7. The trail of fixed duration is often called a "Wake."

The length of the trails and the length of time they have been accumulating are crucial to their use. In the Wake mode, you know the time interval automatically. In the Discrete marks style or the Continuous mode, a timer is started and displayed on the screen when you turn on the trails. A glance at this digital display will instantly tell you how long the trails have been accumulating. We cover the use of this valuable feature of modern radars in Chapter 6 and beyond. For initial adjustment of the radar picture, the Trail option is best turned off until needed for evaluating risk of collision with approaching targets.

The Wake mode also generally shows a clock when initially engaged. The clock will run until the selected wake interval has been reached, and will then display the time duration of all trails. In the 3-minute Wake mode, for example, if you see a constant 3 minutes on the clock, it means that all trails on the screen represent how the targets moved during the previous 3 minutes. After that initial 3 minutes, the wakes build at the front end of the target as it moves on your screen and simultaneously erase at the back end, so you are left with a 3-minute history displayed.

In general, wakes and plots are straight patterns. If an individual trail turns or has a bend in it, it means that the target has turned or changed speed. After a target maneuvers, its trail will straighten out on the new heading. But when you turn your vessel, all trails on the screen might change. The Rules of Thumb section in Chapter 11 discusses this behavior for various radar configurations.

It is not a problem if your (older) radar does not have a trail option. In Chapter 6 we show how to use the methods for making these crucial marks yourself, either right on the radar screen with an appropriate marker, on a separate radar plotting sheet, or on a plain piece of paper.

Electronic Range and Bearing Line (ERBL)

In Chapter 1 we discussed measuring ranges and bearings to various targets on the radar screen using the VRM and EBL. These measurements were all made from our own perspective—that is, from the vessel to the target. The EBL emanated from the center of the radar screen and the VRM circle was centered on the center of the screen. If we saw two targets on the screen we could use the VRM and EBL to measure the range and bearing to each individually, but we could not use the VRM and EBL to measure the range and bearing *between* these two targets.

In standard radar applications, we have frequent occasion to measure the distance and direction between two points on the radar screen. Prior to the year 2000, most small-craft radar operators had to do this measurement by hand, using an improvised range scale. It is not difficult, as discussed at the end of Chapter 1, but most new radar units include a wonderful feature that will carry out this point-to-point measurement electronically. Readers using

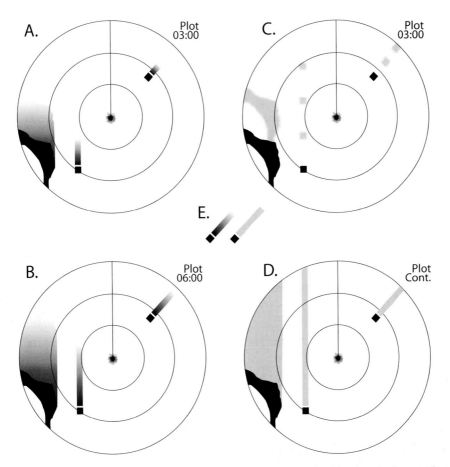

Figure 2-7. *Types of plot trails. Part A is a wake trail, set to erase all records older than 3 minutes. The wake length can be adjusted to meet your needs on the present range scale. Part B is the same type of trail with the wake time increased to 6 minutes. We see from the land wakes how far we moved relative to the land in 6 minutes, and from this we can conclude that the starboard-bow target is moving toward us at about half that speed (more on this later). Part C is an interval plot. This mode places a mark (the actual image of the target for several sweeps) at intervals selected by the user. Part D shows a plot trail in Continuous mode. Modern radars offer all options. The timed wake is often the most convenient. Part E illustrates the difference between solid-wake and gradient-wake displays (sometimes called single-tone or multi-tone) available on some models. Gradient wakes look good on the screen and are a bit less distracting, but they are not as good as the solid trails when it comes to actually measuring wake lengths, which is needed to evaluate target speeds (see Chapter 6).*

older radars will still have to do it by hand, but the next generation of radar users will soon think of this new tool as fundamental.

This feature is called a free, floating, or offset EBL and VRM, or more generically an *electronic range and bearing line* (ERBL). Push a button to active it, move the cursor to one of the points marking the segment you wish to measure, and press another button to lock the reference cen-

ter of the standard EBL and VRM to that new location. From then on, the VRM and EBL work as before, but now the line is measured from the new reference point. Different models and brands activate and apply it differently. We cover its use throughout the text, and also explain how to achieve similar measurements without this aid. Examples of the use and operation of an ERBL are given in Figure 2-8.

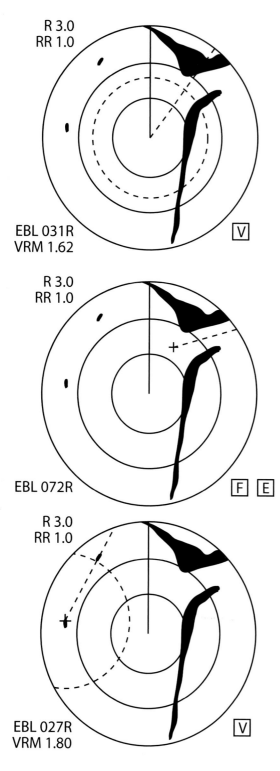

R 3.0
RR 1.0

EBL 031R
VRM 1.62

V

R 3.0
RR 1.0

EBL 072R

F E

R 3.0
RR 1.0

EBL 027R
VRM 1.80

V

Figure 2-8. *Use of an electronic range and bearing line (ERBL). For reference, the top picture shows a conventional, centered EBL and VRM, used to measure the range and bearing to a channel entrance. The entrance is 1.62 nm away, in a direction that is 31° to the right of our present heading. The V indicates that the VRM is the active function being adjusted by a single control knob. The EBL is locked onto its present setting. With this style of control, if you press the VRM button again it will lock that in place as well. Press VRM again and it will hide the ring. Or press the EBL button to switch control to the EBL and get the same options for that.*

The middle picture shows the ERBL in action to measure the course along the center of the channel. In this case, the course along the channel is 72° to the right of your heading. With this style of control, you press a button called "Float" that unlocks the ERBL reference from the center of the screen and allows it to be moved to any location on the screen with the track pad. Whenever it is in this mode, the letter F shows on the screen. Press Float again and it locks it at the new location, or press Float again and it recenters the ERBL as when you started. In this example, the VRM has been shut off, and the EBL is active. Turn the control knob and the EBL will rotate; press the track pad and the reference location will move. The measurement wanted can still be taken, even though these controls are not locked.

In the bottom picture, the ERBL is used to measure the range and bearing between two targets on the port bow. The targets are 1.80 nm apart, and the bearing from one to the other is 27° to the right of your heading. In this case, the ERBL center has been locked on the one target (no F showing) and the VRM is the active control.

This is just one convenient scheme for operating the ERBL. Every radar brand has its own user interface for these controls. Some are easier and quicker to use than others—a judgment that obviously depends on the user. How this valuable function works might be one way to compare units, since the user interface is a key selection criterion among units that offer many of the same basic features.

Pulse Length

The pulse length control affects how the picture looks, but it is probably best thought of as a measurement control. The radar beam consists of a series of pulses, and these pulses and the spacing between them change with the selected range (for a physical and electrical description of the radar beam, see Chapter 7). Many modern radars offer the option of user-selected pulse length (short, long, and sometimes medium) on some radar ranges. The short length is usually preselected for lower ranges and the long length is fixed for the larger ranges of the unit. But for the intermediate ranges, the user may have a choice. Reasons for the choice in various circumstances are discussed in the related sections below. A summary of selection criteria is given in the table.

PULSE LENGTH SELECTION CRITERIA

Task	Best Pulse Length Choice
for general use on low ranges	short
for general use on high ranges	long
to look for weak targets any range	long
to separate two close targets in line	short
to look for targets within sea clutter	short
to look for targets within rain clutter	short
to look for targets beyond rain clutter	long

Another way to think of it is this: to enhance target selectivity, use the shortest pulse length; to enhance target sensitivity, use the longest pulse length; for some compromise in these goals, use a medium length.

OTHER CONTROLS AND FEATURES

More specialized radar controls and adjustments include: Echo Stretch (ES), Interference Rejection (IR), Zoom and Offset, Guard rings, Alarms, Watch mode, and Navigation Data. All are covered in Chapter 8. Special features of radar including those that might contribute to unit selection are discussed in Chapter 7.

SUMMARY AND GENERAL ADJUSTMENT TIPS

One of the first things to do when optimizing the radar picture is to check which functions are in Auto and and which ones are in Manual mode. There can be Auto Anticlutter modes as well as Auto Gain modes and Auto Tuning modes. Generally the tips below apply to operations in Manual modes. Auto modes work quite well in many circumstances, but in special cases you will do better by shutting them off. Manual adjustments can sometimes affect the display in Auto modes. Practicing with your own unit is the only solution. Experimenting with both Auto and Manual in various conditions will soon sort out what is best for your unit. Remember that the picture redraws only every 2 or 3 seconds, so all adjustments must be made slowly. Turning a knob up and then back down within this time period will not reveal the effect of the adjustment.

Here are the basics to consider when adjusting the radar picture:

1. If there are other people using the radar, do not touch the knobs without checking with the person using the radar for navigation. They may have it set to enhance or track some particular feature. Simply changing the Range up and down could erase valuable information on the screen, such as the plot trails discussed above. This respect for your fellow operator's settings is called *radar etiquette*.

2. Often the first knob to turn is Brilliance. If you are using the radar at night and the screen is so bright that it interferes with night vision, turn down the Brilliance until the view is clear and comfortable. During the day, if the screen is

so faint it cannot be seen clearly, then turn up the Brilliance until you have a clear picture before further adjusting. You do not want to make Gain adjustments until the Brilliance is correct. After adjusting the Gain, you might want to go back and forth a bit between Gain and Brilliance (and perhaps Contrast) to get the sharpest image.

3. It is always easier to set the Gain with solid radar targets on the screen. Whenever you can, practice when there is traffic in view, so you will know how to set up the screen when there is none. For more specialized practice, watch for a case when traffic is safely passing in a rain or snow squall to see the effects of adjusting the AC Rain. Remember, while in a squall with limiting visibility, you are operating under Navigation Rule 19, so it is crucial to have the radar properly adjusted. We cover this rule in Chapter 12.

4. Do not overadjust. Some controls work against each other. As a general rule, keep all optional controls (STC, FTC, ES, IR, and possibly Auto AC) in the Minimum or Off settings. If you have a manual Tuning knob with a tuning bar, then set it for maximum scale. Set Gain to have a light background of specks when set to a higher range. Then use the other controls as needed. Adjustment of the Gain will become natural as you further your experience with large and small targets, both close and far away.

5. As a rule, Gain is the main knob you will use to micro-tweak the picture and clarify a particular target. Often when changing scales, a quick test of the Gain adjustment will help clarify any target you want to see. When a large target gets close, the Gain will always have to be reduced.

6. When no discernible targets are in view and significant waves are present, use the following directions to look for close targets. First, zero the Rain and Sea Clutter. Then set Range to a high value, and increase Gain until a light, speckled background appears. Next, lower the Range, and then increase Sea Clutter to break up the screen into a speckled pattern of dots.

7. For optimum resolution (e.g., to distinguish two close vessels or identify a landmark), use the lowest range scale that shows the target and lower the Gain to prevent distorting the display. Factors that affect the resolution are discussed in Chapter 7, and optimizing range and bearing measurements are discussed in Chapter 4.

8. When a big target gets close, reduce the Gain or the screen will smear and block out all other targets. The first indications of this appear as the target begins to smear in a radial pattern. This issue is covered under Side-Lobe Interference in Chapter 9.

9. When approaching land, and when anchoring or docking, turn down the Gain, and adjust the AC Sea (STC) and AC Rain (FTC) to break up bright patches on the screen and get better definition on the shorelines. AC Sea adjustments can help dramatically with this, as illustrated in the Anchoring with Radar section and Figure 5-7 in Chapter 5. The steps are: Turn the Gain down, if not off (depending on the unit). Very slowly, and in small increments, increase AC Sea to optimize what you are looking for. Then add some AC Rain to clip the images and further improve your vision. When finished and shutting down, you might want to reset all these adjustments to zero to minimize possible confusion the next time out. Optimizing close targets with STC and FTC is illustrated in Figure 2-9.

10. When looking for targets at maximum

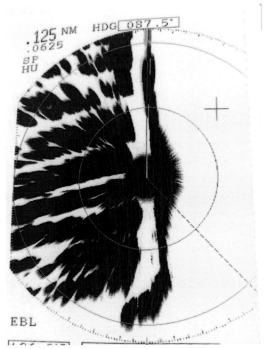

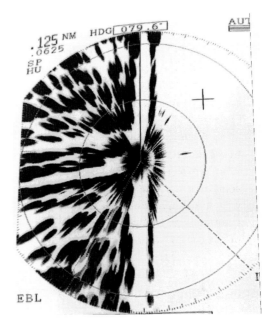

Figure 2-9. *Optimizing close targets with STC and FTC. The top left shows a radar image of close docks and a breakwater with the Gain turned all the way down. The top right has some STC (AC Sea) applied, and the bottom right has then some FTC (AC Rain) applied to clip the images and improve the picture a bit more. Too much STC can erase the picture completely on such low ranges, so it has to be carefully optimized. The setting of the FTC is not so sensitive. (See related picture adjustment example in Figure 5-7.)*

This image is also used in Chapter 7 to illustrate minimum range. The width of this channel from the end-tied boats on the left to the breakwater on the right is about 37 yards, which can also be measured from the radar images some distance ahead or astern. The sunburst pattern at the center of the screen in the top left picture is effectively a measure of the minimum radar range, which we can see is about 30 yards. In the bottom right

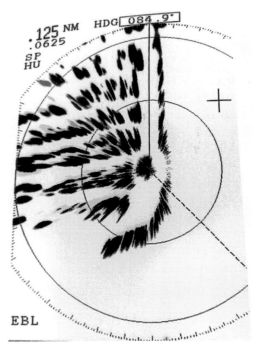

picture we have "tuned" out this pattern, but we still do not expect to see targets there, and indeed have lost view of the adjacent breakwater as well. These limits of the radar itself do not often interfere with navigation as we can clearly see here what we might care about the most in dense fog—namely, are there any other vessels in the channel at the moment and where are we within the marina. Note that in the bottom view we can actually count docks.

The top right picture shows examples of weak multiple reflection echoes on the starboard beam and bow outside of the breakwater. These and other types of false echoes are discussed in Chapter 9.

range, turn up the Gain temporarily to get a more continuous pattern of specks and watch the screen intently. When new targets first come into view, they may only show on every other sweep or possibly every tenth sweep. Mark them with a pen. You might also temporarily try Echo Stretch in this case (see Chapter 8). Try turning on the Plot option along with the Echo Stretch if you cannot consistently watch the screen.

11. If your vessel has obstructions or rigging near the antenna that cause prominent ghost targets (Chapter 9) when near land, try small adjustments of the Tuning control. This might suppress them significantly without degrading the rest of the radar image.

12. Remember that there is generally no way to walk up to a radar screen and tell at a glance that the picture is properly adjusted—even if it seems to look "OK" at first glance. Unless you know the radar has been set correctly, it pays to quickly look over the various settings.

CHAPTER 3

Interpreting the Radar Screen

The radar screen shows what is around us in all directions, and though the picture itself is not visually realistic, we can determine useful values of the range and bearings to many features, which is needed to navigate or evaluate risk of collision. The underlying task in all cases is being sure we know what is displayed on the radar screen. The more practice we get with interpreting the radar images, the more we can use what we see on the radar in conjunction with what we see by eye. The key here, as with many aspects of navigation, is practice, but a few guidelines will help. What we see on the radar screen depends on several interrelated factors. We will look at these individually and then put them together in the Three Views of the World section at the end of this chapter. Here, we are discussing what the radar looks like in a static view (a sample of a real radar image overlaid on a chart was shown in Figure 1-2). Much of our radar navigation is done from this perspective, but in Chapter 6, when we deal with traffic, we discuss how radar images change as a result of our own motion.

HOW FAR DOES THE RADAR SEE?

All radars have limits on how close and far they can see, called the minimum and maximum radar ranges. The minimum range, or the closest things you can see on radar, is discussed in Chapter 7, since it is not among the first concerns in radar operation. Antenna mounting

options and related discussion are also in Chapter 7.

Three main factors determine the answer to how far a radar can see. First, how high is your radar antenna? Radar broadcasts are essentially line of sight with a little boost from refraction, as it bends the microwaves over the curvature of the earth. The higher the antenna, the farther it sees, as shown in Figure 3-1. The range formula is:

$$\text{Geographic Radar Range} =$$
$$1.22 \text{ nm} \times (\sqrt{\text{antenna height}}) +$$
$$1.22 \text{ nm} \times (\sqrt{\text{target height}}),$$

where the heights are given in feet. If the heights are in meters, change the factor of 1.22 to 2.21.

The height of the radar antenna and the height of the target enter into the answer—we can see a tall object from farther off than we can see a short object. This line-of-sight or geographic-range formula is fundamental to many aspects of navigation. It is the one we would use for figuring the visual range of a light at night, or of a hill on an island during the day. Radar range is about 5 percent larger than normal visual range because of differences in refraction for microwaves versus light waves (change the 1.22 in the formula to 1.17 for visual range). If your antenna is 16 feet high and you are looking for a vessel that is 9 feet high, then the geographic range is 1.22 x 4 + 1.22 x 3, which is about 8.5 miles. If you are more than 8.5 miles apart, the other vessel is below your

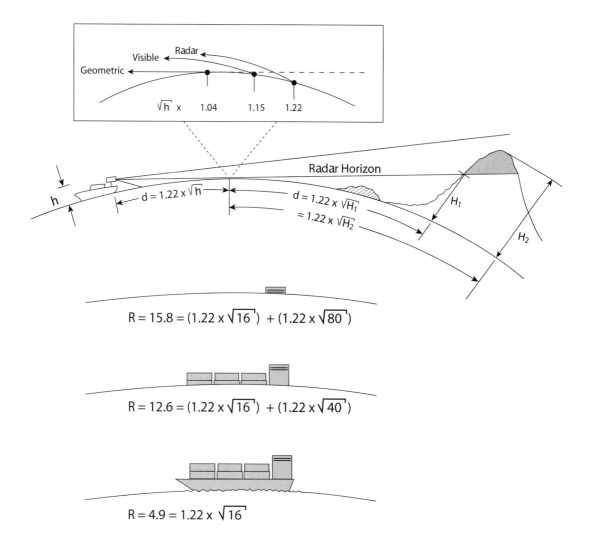

Figure 3-1. *Geographic radar range. The distance to the radar horizon depends on antenna height (h) and target height (H) as shown. It is about 5 percent farther than the visible horizon in standard conditions and about 15 percent farther than the geometric horizon, which does not take refraction into account. Objects below the radar horizon cannot be seen, and any targets that are seen beyond the radar horizon may not reflect the true range of the landmass. The prominent hill below the coastal peak would not show up on the radar at all. We must always be careful when interpreting targets seen beyond the radar horizon. Likewise, when estimating when a target might first be seen, these factors come into play again. We might guess that the ship would be seen at some 16 miles off based on its total height of about 80 feet, using an antenna height of 16 feet. But it is more likely to show a steady target image when at least half of its vertical extent (the shaded area) is above the horizon at about 13 miles off. The full vessel is above the horizon only when within 5 miles off.*

radar horizon. If the target vessel is only 9 feet tall, then at 8.5 miles off just the tip of it will be over the horizon, which will not provide enough of a surface to send back radar reflections. Also, when you are at this geographic range limit, your change in elevation with wave height or when rolling in a seaway will break up the reception so you will not get a good signal on every sweep. In short, for a good solid response on the radar, you must be well within the geographic range of the target. Chapter 9 discusses rare exceptions caused by unusual atmospheric conditions. Chapter 10 discusses the influence of geometric range on making a landfall.

The second factor in how far a radar can see is determined by the size of your target. You will see a ship much farther off than you will see a skiff or buoy, and you will see an island with a mountain on it from much farther off than you will see a ship. As discussed, the height of the object is the first factor that matters, since the target must be over the horizon to be seen at all, but once over the horizon, the shape and bulk of the target are also factors. A side view of a ship can be seen from farther off than a head-on view (see Figure 3-2). The overall exposed reflecting surface and orientation affects how well the target reflects radar waves. A steep cliff reflects radar waves much better than the sloping surface of a sand dune or rolling hill, and the front of a wave reflects better than the back of a wave.

Figures 3-3 and 3-4 shows how two objects (buoys, in this case) of about the same size can have dramatically different radar reflections. The round shape of a can buoy is an ineffective reflector, whereas the well-placed right angles of a radar reflector buoy are excellent reflectors. Note that some can buoys have radar reflectors and most lighted buoys carry reflectors, but there are no standard conventions for this. Some buoys or beacons with reflectors are marked "RaRef" on the chart, but not all reflectors are marked. As you gain experience in your own waters with radar, the range and prominence of various buoys on the radar will become valuable local knowledge for the region.

Individual radar reflectors for vessels are effective and should be standard equipment on all small craft (this is required by Canadian Rule 40 in Canadian waters). Most ocean yacht races also require radar reflectors because they have proven helpful. These reflectors can extend your visible range to other radars by a significant amount. The ideal configuration for the most basic design is called the rain catcher position, shown in Figure 3-3. Studies have shown that this basic type of inexpensive reflector works as well as more sophisticated and expensive designs. The exception might be an active reflector which works more like a racon, discussed in Chapter 4.

The actual material of the target can influence the reflection (metal is better than wood), but this influence is generally overestimated. The size, shape, orientation, and texture of

Figure 3-2. *For an object of any shape, reflection is proportional to the square of the projected area, which means that it increases roughly as the fourth power of the linear dimensions. A ship with a beam aspect (A) would give a much better return than one with head-on aspect (B), and a small vessel (C) would give a much smaller return than either A or B.*

the target are more important than its composition. A 4-foot radar antenna in good conditions will very nicely detect ducks, logs, and vessel wakes, not just small fiberglass skiffs. A small boat (without a radar detector) is usually a relatively poor target because of its small size and smooth, sleek profile, and not because it is made of wood or fiberglass rather than steel.

The physical size of the target is the dominating factor in most cases (Figure 3-2), since reflective strength is roughly proportional to the fourth power of the linear dimensions of the target. Reflection intensity also depends on the square of the wavelength, which means the same object would reflect some 10 times better with X-band radar (3 cm wavelength, used on small-craft vessels) than S-band radar (10 cm wavelength, used by ships on the high seas). Ship captains are aware of this and will therefore switch to their X-band units when looking for small, close targets such as a yacht at sea.

Reflectivity also depends on the angle of incidence as the beam strikes a surface as well as the roughness of the surface, as illustrated in Figure 3-5. When the targets are large, however, there is plenty of intensity reflected back to the antenna even when most of it is lost due to forward scattering. (The behavior of scattering radar beams is discussed in more detail in Chapter 7.)

The third factor in how far a radar can see is the power output or maximum range of the radar unit itself. A coastal

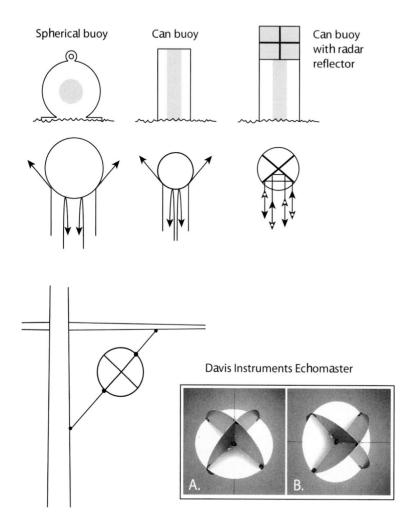

Figure 3-3. *Radar reflection from a can buoy is better than from a spherical buoy, but a buoy with a radar reflector is even better. The shaded areas show the approximate active reflecting surfaces.*

Radar reflectors designed for vessels use the same principle of (trihedral) corner reflection. The model shown is the Davis Instruments Echomaster. The optimum mounting rig is one that leaves a corner oriented toward the horizon, called the rain catcher position (A), since the top corner is pointed straight up. In practice, the mount called the double rain catcher (B) might be preferred on sailing vessels because it rotates toward rain catcher mode when heeled over. In this mode, the axis of the intersecting reflector planes runs athwartships when on an even keel.

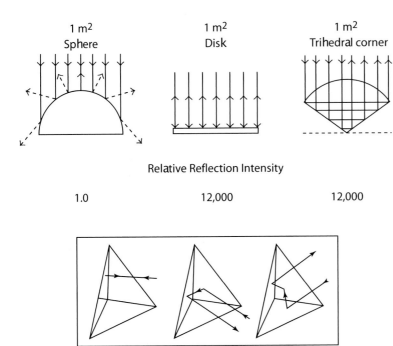

1 m² Sphere   1 m² Disk   1 m² Trihedral corner

Relative Reflection Intensity

1.0   12,000   12,000

Figure 3-4. *Shape, texture, and aspect influence radar reflectivity. A disk with projected area of 1 m² gives a radar reflection that is some 12,000 times stronger than a sphere with the same projected area. A corner or trihedral reflector with the same projected area reflects the same as a disk, but has the great advantage of being much less sensitive to the angle of incidence. Return reflections from a flat disk fall off rapidly with just a slight tilt of the disk, whereas the trihedral reflectors can tilt some 30° or so before the reflection reduces to about half their maximum values. Surfaces that are irregular or rough on the scale of the radar wavelength (3 cm) act more like corner reflectors than flat surfaces.*

higher maximum ranges, and will cost more as well. Ship radars often have maximum ranges of 72 nm or more, whereas 48 or 36 nm would be at the high end for small-craft radar, and 16 or 24 nm is typical for smaller vessels.

As far as most small-craft radar is concerned, the use of the highest ranges is mostly limited to looking for land. Even with a 36-mile radar mounted at 25 feet looking for a ship that is 81 feet tall (e.g., geographic range of about 17 miles), we should not count on seeing it at this theoretical limit. Until you get better data for your specific unit, you can use the table to get rough estimates for practical radar ranges. The table below shows guidelines for estimating maximum practical ranges in typical conditions (antenna height of 16 feet, max electronic range of 36, calm to moderate seas).

Note that the geographic radar range to the

mountain peak might be 5,000 feet high and 10 miles inland from the coast. This peak would have a geographic range of about 84 nm according to the range formula above, reaching some 74 miles out to sea. At 50 miles offshore we are well within geographic range of this peak, but if our radar unit is only rated at 36 miles for maximum range, then we will not see the peak or the coast below. The radar unit has a maximum range scale of 36 miles, so the radar signals cannot go that far and come back again.

The maximum range of radar units is much like the nominal range of a navigation light, which corresponds to the brightness of the source. Higher powered radar units will have

PRACTICAL RADAR RANGES

Target	Estimated Actual Range (nm)
large ship	9 to 12
medium ship	6 to 9
fishing vessel, large yacht	3 to 6
small yacht	1 to 3
large buoy	3 to 5
medium buoy	1 to 3
small buoy, skiff	0.3 to 1

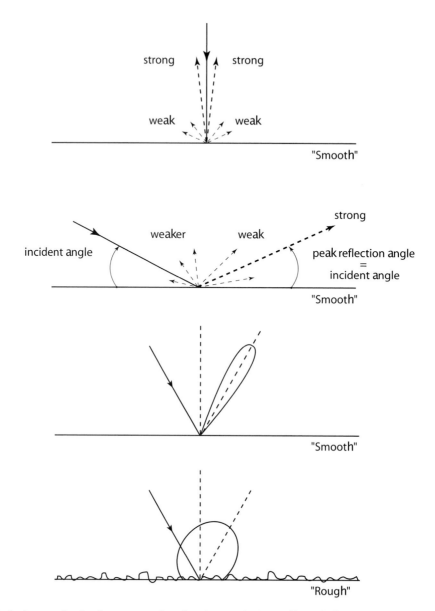

Figure 3-5. *Radar beam reflection from a smooth surface is specular (mirrorlike), which means the strongest scattering occurs at a reflection angle equal to the incident angle. When a beam hits any surface at an angle, most intensity is lost reflected forward. This is a favorable behavior since it yields strong radar reflection from a corner, but it is unfavorable when the radar beam hits an isolated plane surface. This latter behavior of the beam is the source of some ghost targets and other false images, discussed in Chapter 9, caused when the beam gets scattered off multiple targets before returning to the antenna.*

The bottom two figures illustrate the angular distribution of a radar beam reflected from smooth and rough surfaces. Rough means rocks, trees, and other irregularities that are large compared to the 3 cm wavelength. No real target is ideally smooth, because there are corners, edges, and other features that get illuminated by the radar beam, which essentially hits the target as a vertical wall (as discussed in Chapter 7). The arrows shown here are the direction the "wall" is moving. Every real target acts to some extent as shown in the bottom figure, with some intensity returning back to the antenna, regardless of what the target is.

horizon for an antenna 16 feet high is about 4.8 nm, so several of the typical targets shown in the table are well above the horizon and still not detectable. A 4-foot-wide open array antenna with a 4 kW transmitter would tend to have larger limits here, compared to an 18-inch radome antenna at 2 kW power output. Technical specifications are discussed in Chapter 7.

The section on power output in Chapter 7 and the section on rain and squalls in Chapter 9 have more discussion of maximum range. Rain can significantly reduce the maximum range of a radar when looking for weaker targets. Chapter 9 also has a section on abnormal atmospheric conditions, which can, in rare conditions, reduce or enhance the range of radar operation.

When considering radar range as a specification of a particular brand or model, remember that in typical small-craft operations you will use the lower scales more often than the higher scales. A unit with a maximum range of 16 nm may meet the needs of many operators of even relatively large vessels, because even those with ranges of 48 miles will spend most of the time on scales of 6 nm or less. The real issue in radar model selection is not the maximum range itself, but rather the rest of the perfor-

mance parameters, which improve for units with bigger antennas and longer ranges. As we see in Part Two, the main selection criterion is antenna size (or perhaps power consumption, for sailing vessels) and the right maximum range will come with that automatically. In other words, you may want a 36-mile range model simply because it has the parameters that work well on the 6-mile range. Or you may choose a unit with a 16-mile range because it is the only one that will physically fit on your boat.

Shadows

In radar terminology, a *shadow* is the region behind an obstruction that the radar beam is blocked from reaching. Isolated objects or terrain within the shadow behind the obstruction may show on the radar if they rise above the obstruction, but anything below that will not appear on the radar screen. If the terrain behind the obstruction rises above it within the range that is in view on the radar, then echoes will appear, again marking the end of that shadow. This definition of radar shadows is illustrated in Figure 3-6.

Radar is line of sight, so it cannot see over the horizon, around corners, or over the top of tall obstructions. Folding this factor into radar

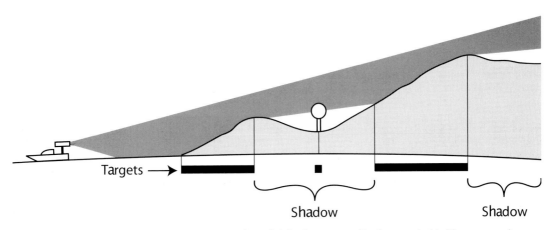

Figure 3-6. *Radar shadows. Radar transmission is line of sight. It can see taller features behind lower ones, but tall shorelines block out all that is behind them. The shadow ends when the terrain rises high enough to be back into the radar beam. Snapshots of radar screens showing this effect are presented in several figures throughout the text.*

screen interpretation can be difficult. For example, if you have a 36-mile radar and a 9-foot antenna, you would not expect to see a 100-foot-tall island 20 miles away on your radar, as it is below its geographic range of 15.6 nm. This is expected and becomes second nature early into radar usage. But if you hear on the radio that a ship is a mile or two from you, southbound in a curving channel, it will not usually be obvious when it might appear on the radar screen. It will depend on the shape and height of the land bordering the channel and your relative location to it.

Land shadows are illustrated in Figure 3-7. If a feature is to be seen over the top of an intervening landmass, then that feature must be taller and generally more conspicuous. Even with that, the shape of the inland radar target or a target behind an intervening landmass will often be difficult to interpret. The intervening land must be high enough to cast a shadow so the shape of the second feature might appear. Except for seeing over low islands or spits, radar cannot often be used to identify land features that are inland of the shoreline, and those that can be identified will rarely be usable for navigation.

A more common challenge is sorting out how radar shadows of coastal features might show up on the radar. Often a steep coastal feature will show up as a large island or as a narrow outline of the coast. Sometimes a nearby small headland or point shows up as a large vessel or islet near the beach. Examples are shown in Figures 3-8 and 3-9. Even knowing about radar shadows, you might run across puzzles to solve, one of which is explained in Figure 3-10. A valuable way to practice radar image identification as part of routine navigation with GPS is covered in Chapter 4.

Another factor to consider is the effect of the size of the rotating radar beam. The angular width of the beam itself is a few degrees wide, which means that coastal details within these few degrees cannot be discerned in the radar

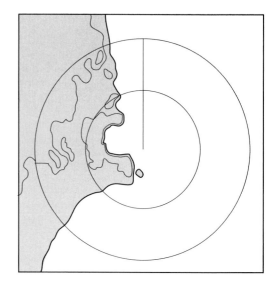

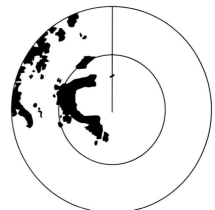

Figure 3-7. Because of shadowing, a continuous coastline often appears in large segments, as shown. We can roughly correlate parts of the radar image with inland peaks marked by contour lines on the chart, but range and bearing data would have little quantitative value. We see the small island astern very clearly, and must conclude that the target dead ahead is a vessel, since there is no land shown on the chart in that location. (Radar image and chartlet adapted from Boatowner's Guide to Radar by Jack West)

image. Features seen on the radar are spread out to some extent depending on the distance to the target. For now we just note this effect to keep it in mind when interpreting the radar picture. See Figure 3-11. We cover this important aspect of radar observation more quantitatively in Chapter 7.

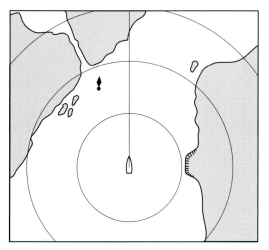

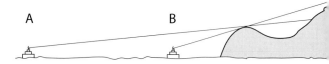

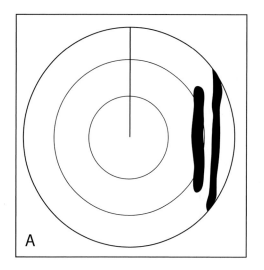

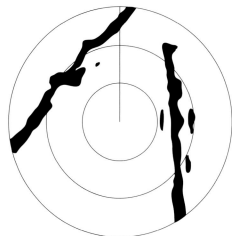

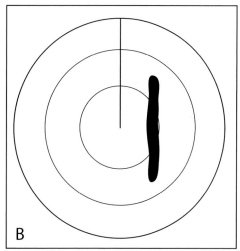

Figure 3-8. Radar shadows and beam width affect the radar view. The bottom figure represents the radar screen view from a 15-inch radar antenna with a horizontal beam width of about 6°. The top view is the chart of the region with the corresponding radar rings overlaid on it for reference.

The small island at the point on the starboard bow is lost in the image of the coastline, which is broadened out by the beam width. The channel entrance on the port bow does not show, and the group of three islands blends into one target for the same reason. With a larger radar antenna, the beam angle would be narrower (Chapter 7), and the islet groups and channel entrance might be resolved.

The steep point on the starboard side shows up as an islet or large vessel on the radar screen due to vertical shadowing, independent of horizontal beam width. We do not get reflections from the land behind it until the land has risen some elevation above the cliff. A related effect is shown in Figure 3-9.

Figure 3-9. A coastal feature can show up as one or two targets depending on distance off. The top figure shows positions of a vessel relative to the profile of the coastal land. At some distance from the land (A), we see radar reflections from both the near hill and the far one. When close to the land (B), the nearest hill blocks the radar completely from the hill behind it and we see only the nearest one. Even a relatively low point of land can show up as a separate image when close to the land, and even sometimes when rather far from it as shown in Figure 3-10.

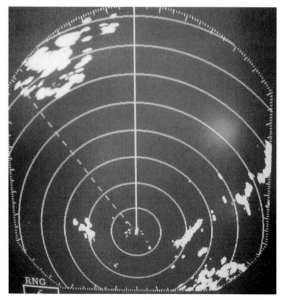

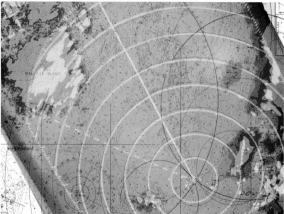

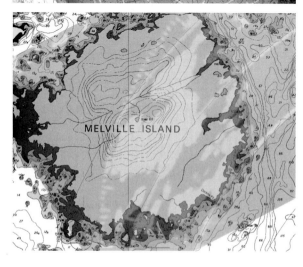

Figure 3-10. *Even knowing about radar shadows, we were puzzled by the land showing about 6 miles off on the port bow when it first came into view, as shown in the top picture. We knew from the chart that this island had a large mound in the middle, but was otherwise surrounded by a wide, flat plain, with two streams but no other structure. So we could not at first account for the prominent breakup of the image as it appeared. When we got closer the answer was obvious. The plain is thickly covered with a forest of tall trees. These trees act just like a cliff that blocks the radar beam all the way back to the base of the central mound, as shown in the bottom view.*

This view was made by overlaying a digital snapshot of the radar image on an e-chart picture of the region. Since we had not recorded our position at the time of the snapshot, we had to do traditional radar piloting to find our position so we could superimpose the pictures at the right place. This was done by intersecting several measured ranges (read from the snapshot) as discussed in Chapter 10. The digital plotting of that fix accounts for the circles showing in the middle overview.

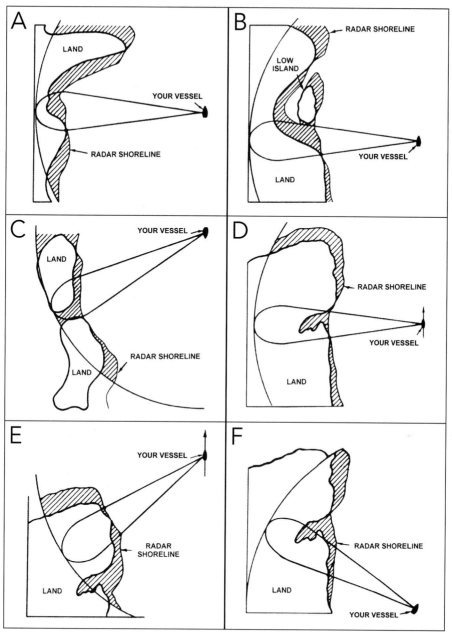

Figure 3-11. *The size of the radar beam pulses affects the target images seen. The radar beam is narrow but it still broadens all targets by half the beam width and sets the minimum target size to be about equal to the beam width, which is some 1° to 6° in bearing, depending on the size of the radar antenna. The pulse length determines the radial extent of the target size. Beam width cannot be adjusted. Pulse length changes with range setting and can also be varied on some ranges by the user. It varies from about 30 yards to over 100 yards in range, depending on the settings. Notice that the land closest to the radar (marked by dotted lines) always shows at the right range, regardless of these effects at other bearings. More details on how to work with these factors are covered in Part Two. The beam dimensions and subsequent target distortions in this figure are exaggerated to show the effects.* (Adapted from Pub. 1310, *Radar Navigation Manual*)

THREE VIEWS OF THE WORLD

One of the basic things we learn in navigation is how to correlate the two views of the world represented by what we see by looking out over the waterway and what we see on a nautical chart. Setting aside key issues of interpreting charted soundings, compass variation, and conventions in symbols, this task boils down to understanding perspective and the effects of elevation on what we see. Is that an island peeking around the corner or is it a headland on the coast? Is that headland A or headland B? The latter question comes up often, as what may appear on the chart as just a slight bend in the coastline shows up as a prominent headland when viewed from the water.

In some cases, once the sun sets, the identification of landmarks can become easier if there are lights marking the points. We can get our bearings from easily identified lights, figure relative bearings from those lights to other lights, and so on. It is standard procedure to identify all lights within sight when navigating at night.

Navigating by radar is much like navigating at night. The radar screen provides us with a number of radar targets, some of which will be easier to identify than others. Our job in learning how to read a radar is to add this third view of the world—the radar image—to the other two views in order to piece together the most complete picture of where we are relative to the track we wish to follow and the hazards we wish to avoid. One view of the "three views" is shown in Figure 3-12.

It is often a matter of educated guessing how the radar shadows will show up and guessing which aspects of the terrain might be better reflectors than others. Prominent points, islets, or any other isolated targets are the main assets in this query. Use the EBL and VRM to confirm these identifications and then take bearings to other radar targets and compare them to what is on the chart and what you can see. Figures 3-13 and 3-14 give several examples. More ex-

Figure 3-12. *Three views of the world. The navigator's job underway is to coordinate what is seen on the radar, the chart, and out the windows. Each view tells us more about what the other views show.*

amples are given on the CD included with this book. Also, revisit Figures 1-2 and 1-3 in light of these discussions. Chapter 4 offers a prescription for standard radar navigation procedure that will develop this skill in practice.

The *U.S. Coast Pilots, Canadian Sailing Directions,* and the *British Pilots* each list conspicuous radar targets to varying degrees when describing the waterways they cover. In areas with high tidal ranges, they might even state that a certain islet is a good radar target at half tide or lower, or that a certain cliff is conspicuous but eroding quickly so its range might not be accurate, and so on. It is an excellent exercise to start keeping your own log of good radar targets in the waters you frequent. When planning a repeat of the voyage, possibly a few years later, your own sailing directions might be the best reference available.

The radar view of our world adds much to our perspective and navigational skills. A broad point of land viewed head-on, for example, can be difficult to discern by eye, but on the radar screen, the shape of the land typically shows up nicely. We also stand to gain more frequent

Figure 3-13. *Radar picture from Wrangell Narrows, Alaska, overlaid onto a vector chart of the region. The radar images are the darkest patches. The range rings are at 0.5 nm spacing. A set of five buoys about 2 miles ahead and to the left of the heading line show up very nicely, and we can tell from their locations that one of the targets in that area must be a vessel (just left of the buoy on the heading line, 2.2 miles ahead). Rocks show well on Boulder Flats (2 miles off, just forward of the port beam), and we can even see a charted piling as a tiny dot on the west shore of Anchor Point, which shadows most of Blind Island. The cut into Colorado Creek is apparent, even at the edge of the screen, just aft of the port beam.*

Figure 3-14. *Radar picture from Elliott Bay, Seattle, Washington, overlaid onto a chart of the region. The radar rings are 0.25 nm apart. The heading line shows our southeast orientation at the time. Shadowing of the large cliff and the trend of the radar image around the cliff directly on the port beam are apparent, as well as the blocking of the beam 1 nm dead ahead by the turn of the shoreline. The large water tank on the hill shows up weakly, and we coincidentally had a picture taken just as the racon buoy astern has been triggered to send out a radar signal (see Chapter 4). The buoy 0.5 nm astern shows up right on the range ring, and there are two vessel targets on the starboard quarter, one much larger than the other.*

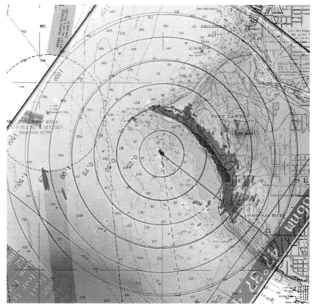

practice at judging visual ranges. Without any reference to chart or GPS, we can identify a radar target we see visually and in an instant measure its distance off with the VRM or cursor. Such an exercise is especially valuable in the fog. For example, you note that you can just discern a buoy or landmass emerging from the fog. A quick check of the radar range tells you the atmospheric visibility, and then you know for future encounters when to expect to see things (or vessels) by sight—all powerful components of better navigation. We should add for completeness, though, that atmospheric visibility can vary significantly with direction and elevation, which is something else you learn quickly with radar.

CHAPTER 4

Radar for Position Navigation

RADAR *VERSUS* GPS

Experienced navigators (whether small-craft skipper or sea captain) will often single out radar as the most important electronic navigation instrument. Even in this age of high-precision GPS navigation, radar gets such high acclaim because it aids in both position navigation and collision avoidance, and because it is a more visual tool. GPS tells us where we are, but it does not tell us where the land is, which is often the main concern on inland and coastal waters. In midocean, the location of approaching vessels is the most immediate and frequent concern of navigators. This is beautifully solved by radar, but using GPS-based electronics tied to radio communications is still in the development stage (see AIS discussion below).

A GPS directly connected to an electronic charting system that shows us precisely where we are on the chart, where we have been, and where we are going is hard to beat. But things are not that simple, and many of those who have access to all of that technology still prefer radar. The virtues of radar are its reliability and what might be called its clarity. Both radar and GPS are electronic wonders, but radar is more transparent in that you can see images you recognize—the outline of the bay, where you are located relative to a breakwater, and so on. With radar you can see ranges, meaning two objects in line, which is always the key to good piloting. You can set the VRM as a danger circle around you and watch that you do not get too close to a shoreline. We cover this use of radar in Chapter 5.

You can obtain this same information from a GPS trail on an electronic chart, but that is more of a computation than an actual picture of what is around you. Navigators are for the most part a conservative group, generally preferring reliability to convenience. Radar has more tradition and testing than GPS. As time goes by, navigation practices will certainly evolve, but for the moment, a radar picture is the assurance needed to supplement the immense convenience of GPS trails on electronic charts. We discuss the procedures for combining these two crucial tools shortly.

We might also mention that in some parts of the world, charting precision has not yet caught up with the accuracy available from GPS. There have been cases where all the boats in a harbor will agree precisely on the latitude and longitude of where they are anchored, but according to the best chart of the area, they are well inland! Radar readings do not depend on the accuracy of charts. If the radar says you are 0.35 mile from the entrance to the bay, then that is where you are, regardless of what a charted GPS position might show.

On the radar, you can also see a vessel coming out of the bay you are approaching and thus maneuver as needed to avoid a collision. Sometime in the not too distant future, GPS will also be an aid to collision avoidance. This technology, the *automated identification system* (AIS) is discussed in Chapter 13. In AIS, your GPS position, course, and speed will be automatically broadcast all around you via short-range radio signals. Any nearby vessels receiving your signal will in turn broadcast their position and motion back to you. The combined data are displayed on an electronic chart on each vessel along with an automatic analysis of the interaction and much more information. This is a very promising development and will inevitably be used by all vessels sometime in the future, and probably by highway traffic as well. But like all safety-critical technology, it will be some time before it is available to the public. For now, we have radar, long tested and dependable, for the crucial task of collision avoidance. Collision avoidance with radar is covered in Chapter 6 and in more detail in Chapters 11 and 12.

Relative Positions

All position fixes in navigation are relative positions. In any fix, we find our position on the chart relative to the location of a headland, buoy, lighthouse, depth contour, etc. Even a GPS fix is relative to the locations of satellites some 10,000 miles away. Usually the goal of these fixes is an actual latitude and longitude on a chart. Here, however, we use the term "relative" in a more generic manner. The most basic and most common application of radar for navigation is using it to see where you are relative to identifiable landmasses without actually pinpointing a position on a chart. A simple case is to note from the radar when transiting an entrance channel in the fog or at night that you are indeed in the middle of the channel. When breakwaters cannot be seen at all by sight, for example, they will still show up very nicely on the radar.

When traveling along a coastline, you might identify on the radar screen two prominent headlands seen on the chart, and then note that you are about halfway between them and about 2 miles offshore. Often that is all you need to know at the moment. There are endless examples; one is shown in Figure 4-1. You can use radar for precise charted fixes, as ex-

plained later in this chapter and in more detail in Part Two, but by far the more common application is just this type of confirmation of relative position.

Another application might be to identify and confirm the location of a buoy marking the entrance to a channel. You know from the chart that this buoy should be at the head of the channel, about half a mile out from the breakwater. You can see its light, but you cannot see the breakwaters. Both the buoy and the breakwaters show up on radar, so you can check to confirm that the buoy is indeed in the right place before heading to the channel approach. See Figure 4-2. Later in Chapter 8, we go over a wonderful feature of many new radars (the "Lollipop" or "Radar Marks" display) that lets you enter the coordinates of a buoy into the GPS, which is connected to the radar, so the buoy position is marked on the radar screen.

Radar is often used for checking your relative heading. For example, you believe, from your chart work and intentions, that you are parallel to a given shoreline, or pointed toward a gap between two islets. Usually your intended track has some relationship to the land about you that could be verified by a pilot flying overhead. In many cases, the radar serves just as that pilot's perspective would. The heading line on the radar is the way you are headed, and—barring currents, leeway, etc, that always have to be taken into account—the heading line is marking the path you will follow as you proceed. You just look at the lay of that line on the radar screen relative to the land. Is the heading line indeed parallel to the bright image of the coastline you see on the radar? Or does your heading line bisect the two islets you are headed for? There are many ways to use the third view of the world provided by radar. Examples are shown in Figure 4-3.

When yacht racing—or cruising in a group—your position relative to other vessels (within a few miles of you) can be accurately monitored using radar. Simply mark a target vessel with

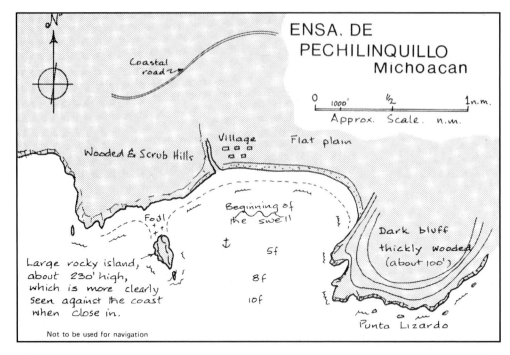

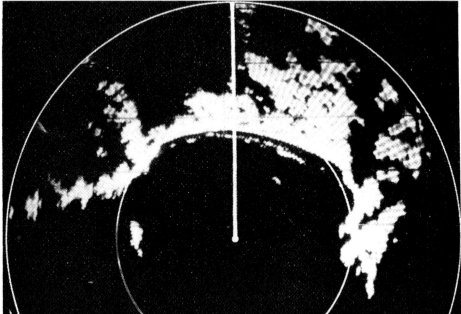

Figure 4-1. *Relative position identification from a radar image. Here we are just inside the center of the bay. In this approach we do not care about the specific Lat and Lon of our location. Indeed, the cruising guide sketch on top has the most detail available in print for this bay. The best nautical chart of the area barely shows the bay at all. The radar shows the port-side island and associated rock very nicely, as well as the breaking surf along the inside shoreline dead ahead. The small target to the right ahead is either an "uncharted" rock or another vessel. (Top: Courtesy* Charlie's Charts of Mexico, *www.charliescharts.com. Bottom: Radar image from* Boatowner's Guide to Radar *by Jack West)*

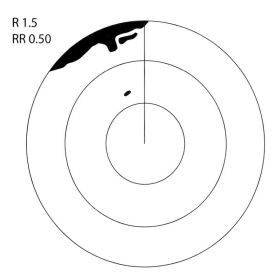

R 1.5
RR 0.50

Figure 4-2. *Radar confirmation of position. Even though we cannot positively identify the entrance protected by two breakwaters projecting into the ocean because they are not resolved, the indication of it along with a lighted buoy in the right location helps establish our destination. As we get closer, the two breakwaters will be resolved.*

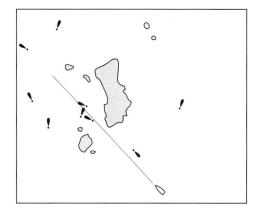

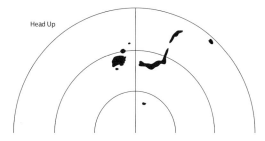

Head Up

Figure 4-3. *The heading line used as a pointer to confirm our heading. Even though the island group is not realistically represented on the radar due to shadowing, there are enough identifiable targets to confirm our heading.*

the VRM and EBL and watch how the radar target moves off that location as time goes by. How to determine the course and speed of the target vessel from this measurement is covered in Chapter 6. Of course, if the target vessel is traveling in exactly the same direction and speed as you, then its range and bearing from you will not change with time, and its radar echo will not move off the mark.

RADAR *AND* GPS: USING RADAR UNDERWAY

The reality of modern navigation is that we should all have radar *and* GPS—and a good depth sounder! Two hallmarks of good navigation are planning ahead and not relying on any single aid for crucial decisions. In some cases, radar will be our primary navigation instrument, and in other cases it will be the GPS. Generally speaking, the *course over ground* (COG) data from the GPS is its most powerful contribution to navigation. Unfortunately, GPS is so easy to use for this and other data that it can

end up being an aid we depend on too much. When this happens, our navigation suffers.

One of the main values of radar for navigation is the quick and dependable means it offers for checking the GPS position. In this application, we ultimately rely on the accuracy of the GPS, but we want a quick and easy confirmation from the radar observation that we are in the right "ballpark." Later, in Chapter 10, we will use the radar to check that we are in the right "bench." The procedure is very simple using conventional paper charts, but is even easier using electronic charting. There are other virtues of this exercise as well.

With paper charts, just after plotting your position on the chart—obtained from GPS or any other means—take a quick look at the region around you on the chart for a landmark that will show up on the radar. (Use the guidelines discussed in Chapter 3 for guessing a good target, typically a headland, islet, or corner of a bay.) Note the name of the landmark, if it has one. Then with parallel rules and dividers, measure from the chart the range and bearing to that mark from your present position. Turning to the radar, set the EBL to that bearing (correcting for your heading as discussed in Chapter 1), and then set the VRM to the measured range of the landmark. This measurement could also be done with the cursor to read out range and bearing, and sometimes that is all that is needed. Other times it easier to interpret the screen with the actual EBL lines drawn in rather than relying on the digital readout of the movable cursor. Figure 4-4 illustrates this procedure.

Most of the time, the marks will adequately line up and you can congratulate yourself for having correctly deduced a conspicuous radar target from the chart. Even if the marks do not line up as expected, you will have learned something valuable. If they are way off, then maybe you are not quite oriented, or you have made a mistake. In either case, the exercise has done its job. More likely, the landmark is simply not showing up on the radar as you guessed it would. Again, it is valuable knowledge. Study the chart to see why that might be, and choose another target to make the test.

That's it! Go from GPS position fix to range and bearing, and from there go to the radar to confirm the fix. You are not finding a fix with the radar in this process, just checking one. It is an exercise that should be done as often as possible. The main virtue of the exercise is that it gets you involved with your radar. Every time you practice, you learn more about what land looks like on radar.

In addition, this practice encourages you to note the names of prominent landmarks around you. It is a good habit for navigators to be continually aware of the names of nearby landmarks. It is valuable for orientation and safety and it can be valuable for future trips along the same route. You may not know where Point Nowhere is, but if you were to hear the follow-

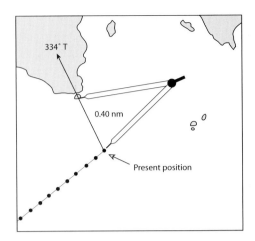

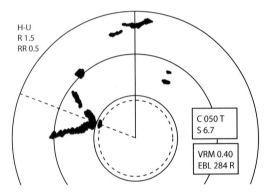

Figure 4-4. *Confirming a position with the radar. From our electronically charted GPS position shown in the top view, we note there is a prominent islet at the headland on our port beam, which should be 0.40 nm off in direction 334° T. We are steering 050, so this target should be 334 − 050 = 284° R on the radar. Checking the radar at this range and bearing, we do see the target where it should be, which is confirmation of our position. We also see several other easily identifiable targets in the region that could be used to make this check. The range and bearing to the island could also be measured with the cursor readout without having to employ the EBL and VRM.*

ing radio call on a foggy night, you would wish you did: "This is the Tanker Jonstone, southbound at 20 kts, calling the vessel dead ahead, located 6 miles west of Point Nowhere."

You can safely guess that such a broadcast was made with the VHF set to low power, so if you heard it at all, this Point Nowhere must be somewhere close to you. In cases like this, you can avoid a lot of anxiety if you keep track of landmarks around you, and of course, by keeping a good watch on your own radar. Watching for traffic on radar is covered in Chapter 6. You might also hear vessels in distress giving their location relative to coastal landmarks, so you would then know if you were in a position to help.

The process of identifying landmarks and checking them with the radar from your GPS position is especially easy with GPS connected to electronic charting. Your GPS position is shown on the chart continuously, leaving a trail of past positions. At any moment you can select the range and bearing tool from the electronic chart menu and drag a line from the boat symbol to any point on the chart for an instantaneous readout of its range and bearing. This particular option is one of the great benefits of electronic charting.

The above discussion should bring to mind one rule of thumb: Whenever possible, select your working waypoints with some prominent radar target in mind. This helps with quicker orientation when turning onto new course legs in all conditions, plus if you are stuck navigating by radar alone, your job will be easier.

Range and Radar Bearing Fix

The exercise discussed above is basically the reverse of getting a fix by range and radar bearing. We could use that process without GPS at all to find our position on a chart from radar alone, called a range and bearing fix. This process is the easiest and quickest way to get a position fix from radar, but usually not the most accurate option. Done carefully with the right targets, however, it will often meet the needs at hand. Later we will cover more precise methods.

The principle is simple. Find a well-defined, preferably isolated, radar target, measure the range and bearing to it, and then plot these on the chart for a fix. Buoys would in principle be ideal for this, but they cannot be relied on to be exactly where the charts show them. A beacon on a pile of rocks with a radar reflector or a small round islet is ideal. Using paper charts, the plotting is the same as a fix from a compass

bearing and a distance-off measurement from, for example, a vertical sextant angle, or two bow angles. These and other techniques call for the use of a draftsman's compass for drawing circles, because ranges and the position circles they provide are the key to good radar navigation. The plotting of a range and bearing fix, however, does not require the circle to be drawn because you already have the bearing. Just draw the bearing line through the target and use dividers to mark off the distance.

The plotting is even simpler and faster with electronic charting. Just draw an electronic line segment in the direction you measured on the chart near your vessel and extend it to the length of the range you measured. Then use the tool that lets you move that line segment around on the chart so it is positioned with its outward end on the landmark. Your fix is the other end of the line. It should end up on top of your vessel icon if you have GPS attached to the charting program and you are not moving quickly. To test how well you are doing, you need to mark your position on the e-chart as soon as you can after receiving the radar data, because you will have moved off that position during plotting. All charting programs have a way to set a mark or waypoint at the vessel's present position with one button click.

An alternative electronic chart plotting method would be to place a mark on the site of the radar target whose range and bearing you have measured, then electronically set a range ring on the mark with a radius equal to the range you observed. Then draw a bearing line from the mark in the observed direction. The intersection of circle and line is your fix. This procedure can actually be quicker on some e-chart programs, and might be required on those that do not let you move a bearing line once drawn. Figure 4-5 shows a range and bearing fix by both paper chart and e-chart plotting.

Electronic charts are ideal for practicing this fix method, or any method for that matter. You can do everything digitally and precisely, and then you can zoom in to see how close you

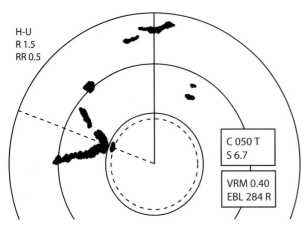

H-U
R 1.5
RR 0.5

C 050 T
S 6.7

VRM 0.40
EBL 284 R

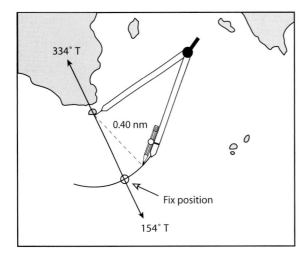

Figure 4-5. *Range and bearing fix from radar. This is the reverse of what is shown in Figure 4-4. From the radar we measure the range and bearing to a prominent isolated target to be 0.40 nm in direction 284° R (top figure), which corresponds to a true bearing of 334° T measured from our course of 050° T.*

With a paper chart (middle figure), draw a bearing line through the charted target location in the proper orientation using the compass rose and parallel rules, or similar tool. This is one line of position. Then use a draftsman's compass to swing an arc with a radius of 0.40 mile centered on the target. This arc is a circle of position. Our fix is the intersection of the line and arc. When you draw the bearing line first, you could use simple dividers to mark the distance off for the fix and not need a draftsman's compass, but the compass is valuable for other types of radar fixes (covered in Chapter 10), so if available, it makes a more intelligible plot of your fix.

With an electronic chart (bottom figure), place a mark (A) on the charted target location and set a range ring on this mark equal to 0.40 nm. Then draw a bearing line from mark A to a new mark (B), which is in direction 154° T, the reciprocal of 334° T. Again, the fix is the intersection of the range circle and bearing line. Most e-chart programs will let you start drawing the range line in the general direction you want, pause, right-click, and reverse the line direction, and then you can continue adjusting the second mark location to a proper reverse bearing of 334° T. This saves doing any arithmetic to get a reciprocal.

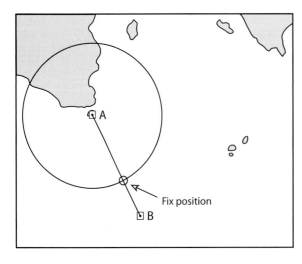

actually are to your GPS position. Use the range and bearing tool on the chart to put real numbers on your accuracy. There will always be some level of discrepancy, even if the chart is correct and your craft is dead in the water. Generally it is the radar bearing that contributes the most uncertainty or error to the measurement, because its accuracy is tied to how well you knew your vessel heading when you set the EBL on the target. Remember that without a heading input to the radar, the radar measures only relative bearings (Chapter 1). Also, unless the radar target was an isolated symmetrical landmark, the width of the radar beam itself could introduce an uncertainty of several degrees because it smears out the edges to some extent, as we explain in Chapter 7.

To do the best job for a range and bearing fix, follow these guidelines:

1. Choose a small, isolated, symmetrical radar target that you can identify on the chart.
2. Set your Range to the lowest possible setting that still shows the target. This will move it to the outer part of the radar screen, which makes it as big as possible so you have optimum angular discrimination.
3. Temporarily reduce the Gain to see if that sharpens the target image.
4. Set the VRM to align with the inside (closest) edge of the radar target image (discussed below).
5. Set the EBL to go through the center of the radar target image.
6. Read the ship's heading and the aligned EBL as simultaneously as possible. Take several readings if your heading changes and the EBL moves off the target and must be realigned.
7. Record the time of the fix—and the GPS latitude and longitude when practicing.

This method can be extended to more general landmarks and targets, but then it is crucial to take into account the corrections for radar

beam width discussed in Chapter 7. With a heading sensor attached to the radar (Chapter 7), the compass bearing to the target can be read directly from the EBL in step 6, which simplifies the process.

An extension of this technique is given below, and more precise methods of position navigation are presented in Chapter 10.

Note that step 4 in the list above calls for something unexpected. We might guess that the center of the radar blip (halfway between the closest and farthest target edges) for an isolated small target such as a buoy would be the best measure of its distance off, but this is not the case. The radial extent of the radar blip can be easily measured with the high precision of the VRM or cursor output, and when this is done, you will find that the target extent is much greater than the actual physical size of the buoy. Even the best radars have some minimum size for which they can paint a target (due to pulse length and screen resolution, discussed in Part Two), and this will often be larger than the physical dimensions of a small target object. The timing circuits within the radar display, however, store and display the right location of the leading edge of the image. Therefore, to get the most precise values, use the edge that is closest to you for the measurement, rather than the center. This is a minor point in many measurements, but there is no reason to lose accuracy in any case, and in some cases it is crucial to the interpretation of the picture, as shown in Figure 4-6.

Range and Two Radar Tangents Fix

The range and radar bearing fix can be extended to larger targets in special cases where two distinct sides of the target can be clearly discerned on the radar. An islet or two ends of a breakwater work well for this, or in some cases, two sides of a headland. It involves measuring the tangent bearings to both sides of the object along with a range to its nearest

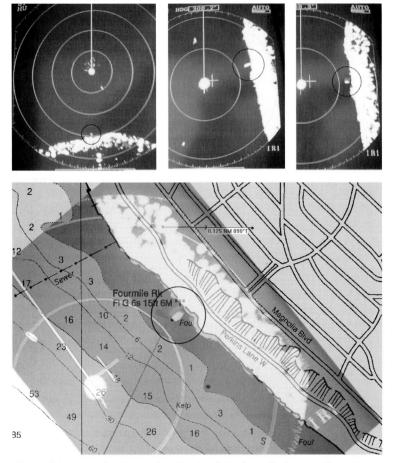

Figure 4-6. *Do not hesitate to look for details in the radar images. Here a large rock just 52 yards offshore can be clearly resolved in this radar picture. The right-side view applies some FTC to sharpen the image. The bottom shows the rock area enlarged and overlaid onto the chart. Notice that the leading edge of the rock image correlates correctly with the charted position of the target. Also note that the radial extent of the rock target (about 34 yards) is equal to the short pulse length on this radar. Had we switched to medium pulse or long pulse, we would not have seen the rock resolved from the shoreline.*

ing lines. Note we are *not* putting the fix in the center of the triangle of position-line intersections as is usually done in other types of lines-of-position fixes.

The discrepancy between the fix position on the range circle and bearing-lines intersection depends on several factors, primarily the size of your radar antenna. For small units (radome less than 2 feet in diameter) the offset could be quite large, depending on the size and distance to the target. For 4-foot antennas, the difference will be much smaller. In visual navigation we are accustomed to navigating using bearings to tangents —one edge of an island or a turn in the coastline—but in small-craft radar navigation these may not be dependable bearing targets. Practicing this method is a good way to develop a feeling for the effect with your radar unit. This is discussed more in Chapter 10.

This type of fix is essentially the same as a range and radar bearing fix, where we use the tangents to locate the effective centerline of the target, and we use knowledge of radar behavior to choose the fix location. With well-defined radar targets, radar ranges are generally more accurate than radar bearings, and this exercise illustrates part of the reason why. If the target is a poor one, however, then ranges might be questionable. A poor radar target for range measurement is one that

point. The plotted data on your chart (see Figure 4-7) should show the bearing lines intersecting somewhat inside of the range circle, because the true tangent bearings have been exaggerated on the radar screen by the horizontal width of the radar beam (see Chapters 3 and 7). This plotting requires a draftsman's compass to draw the range circle, or an improvised method. The proper choice for the fix is on the range circle, halfway between the bear-

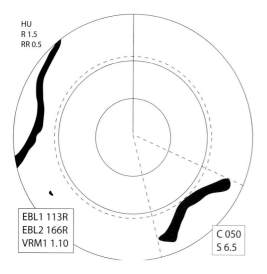

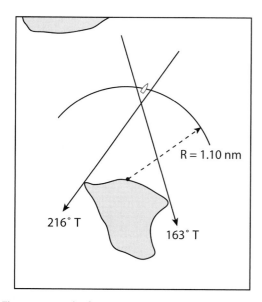

Figure 4-7. *Radar fix by range and two tangents. Use the EBL or cursor to find the bearing to each side of an isolated target as shown in the top picture. Then set the VRM or cursor on the closest point to you to find the range to the target. Then plot the fix as shown in the bottom part using parallel rules to transfer the bearing lines and a draftsman's compass to draw the range circle. For small antennas, the range ring should always end up farther out than the bearing line intersection, and the fix is on the range ring, halfway between the two bearing lines. For larger antennas, the intersections will coincide more closely.*

has a low, gentle slope affected by tides or one that is partially over the horizon.

Radar Images and Tide Height

Some parts of the world have large enough tide ranges that the lay of the land viewed visually or by radar changes dramatically with tide height. When in areas with significant tides, it is often crucial to keep in mind the state of the tide when taking radar observations and comparing with the chart. This is especially true at night and in restricted visibility. Examples are given in Figure 4-8. Remember that on a chart with blue water, green foreshore, and tan land, when the tide equals zero, the water meets the land where the blue meets the green; when the tide equals mean high water, the water meets the land where the green meets the tan. Intervening values have to be guessed. The heights of mean high water are printed on all nautical charts. A rock awash (the symbol is a simple asterisk) must be above the surface at tide equals zero and below the surface at tide above mean high water (see References on small-craft navigation for more details).

More Methods . . .

There are more accurate methods of doing position navigation with radar, which we cover in Chapter 10. Intersecting ranges is one and range and visual bearing is another. We can also make corrections to get more precise bearing lines. These are in Part Two because absolute position fixing is not the main role of radar in the presence of GPS. Radar is more frequently used to check position, as we have discussed, and to verify the orientation and location of our vessel relative to the land around us.

Racons (Radar Beacons)

When it comes to radar navigation, *racons* (from *ra*dar bea*cons*) are gold mines. They are electronic aids to navigation mounted on buoys or beacons in certain waterways worldwide, usually where there is significant ship traffic.

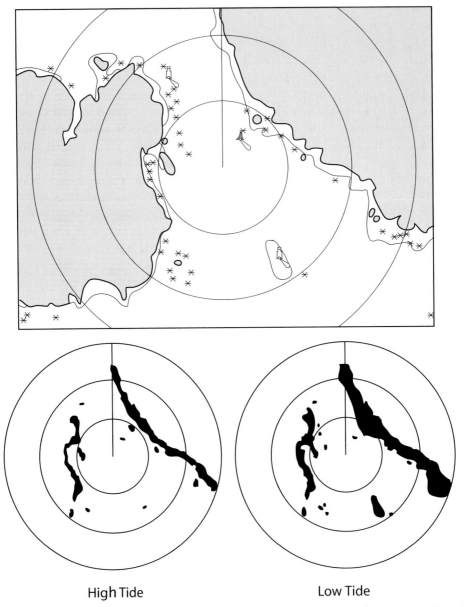

High Tide   Low Tide

Figure 4-8. *Radar images can change significantly in areas with large tidal ranges. The fictitious area shown is a composite of several radar-significant tidal observations. In the high-tide view (at or above mean high water) we see all the coastal islets very clearly and the awash rocks are all below the water. The three light beacons show up well, and we expect the radar image to follow along the high-water border on the chart, which it does fairly well. At low water (near or below zero tide height) we have a quite different view of the waterway, and some other areas might have even a more dramatic difference with large tide changes.*

The light beacons ahead of us still show as before, but the one behind us is completely masked by the tidal shoaling that is now above water. This is now behind us, but when approaching it in the fog it can be quite a puzzle if we had not had any reason to think about tide heights all day long. When looking for a buoy or light and we see an "island," it is time to think about the tides. We have also lost the coastal islets as they blend into the foreshore above water now. And we see new targets, which are the rocks awash, some of which show up prominently on the radar.

Sometimes, isolated drilling platforms, lighthouses, and center spans of bridges will be marked with racons. When a vessel's radar beam strikes one, the racon sends out a prominent radar signal, which is detected on the vessel's radar screen. And the resulting echo is not subtle. Indeed, if you saw one of these on your radar for the first time without knowing what it was, you would probably become quite alarmed.

Racons are unique radar targets. First, they do not show up on every sweep. Most sweeps show the target as a simple buoy or nothing at all, but when triggered, it shows as a bright elongated mark several degrees wide emanating outward for a distance of up to 3 miles, depending on your selected radar range. The wide mark itself is either solid or divided into dash-dot segments representing the Morse code letter that uniquely identifies the target, as shown in Figure 4-9. Racons are shown on charts along with their identifying letter, which vary along the waterway. These show positive identification of the radar target, which is reassuring for radar navigation, since all other buoys show up as small blips. When racons are on buoys, however, we have the usual concern that the buoy might not be exactly where it is "supposed" to be. But since these are typically such key aids along any waterway, such as marking the mid-channel buoys in a vessel traffic service lane, their positions are monitored carefully and frequently.

When navigating in close proximity to a racon, the racon signal might be so strong that it will interfere with other aspects of radar navigation. Typically the signals can be reduced or even shut off by using the AC Rain (FTC), but this can also distort their presentation, as shown in Figure 4-10.

AC Sea (STC) might also interfere with the detection of close targets as well; and if their images are still not looking sharp, check your Tuning control on targets in the vicinity of the racon (not the racon itself). If your radar is not properly tuned, the racon image, like all others, may not look as sharp as it should.

A racon can greatly extend the radar range of a buoy (the signal is essentially line of sight), which means you may see the racon flash before seeing the radar image of the buoy. The main reference for such aids would be Publication 117, *Radio Navigational Aids*, or an international equivalent from the United Kingdom or Canada. Racon signals should not be used for radar tuning or other picture adjustments. Racons on U.S. buoys typically operate for 20 sec and then are shut down for 20 sec to

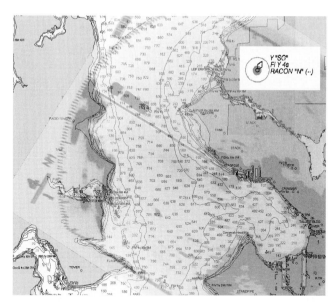

Figure 4-9. *Sample of a radar image overlaid onto a vector e-chart. The photo of the radar screen happened to catch the racon just as it fired. The racon image is made up of the two rectangular images, just to the right of the heading line, which is pointed toward the northwest. A few seconds later and this echo would have appeared on the radar as a simple buoy target. The inset shows a racon chart symbol as it might appear on a paper chart or a raster e-chart. The "RACON" part of the symbol means the Morse code letter "N" (dash, dot) is the radar image it presents. The racon radar image always emanates outward, away from the charted location of the buoy.*

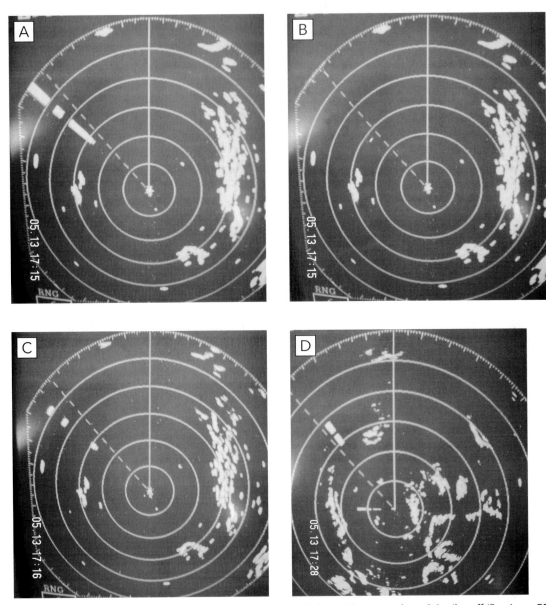

Figure 4-10. *Racon images. A is a triggered racon (dash, dot, dash = "K") seen at about 2.8 miles off (R = 6 nm, RR = 1 nm). B is the same buoy, barely visible, without the racon triggered. C shows how having too much FTC turned on can clip the racon signal and mask its true identity. A is the same image as C with less FTC applied. D is the view taken some time later when abeam of the racon seen in A, with R = 18 nm and RR = 3 nm. Notice a new racon (dash, dash = "M") clearly visible at 9 miles off, although the buoy housing the racon would not show at all at this distance.*

conserve battery power. The off time is also an asset for seeing targets behind the racon itself.

While on the topic of unusual radar targets, we might mention aircraft. It is not uncommon in Alaskan waters, for example, that in low visibility or in low stratus ceilings, seaplanes will fly low, following along a narrow waterway. It can be quite startling in the fog to see a bright, prominent radar target coming straight down the heading line at high speed—or even two of them, just to either side of the heading line. Even with the mystery resolved in a moment or two, the first exposure to this type of target is an eye-opener. A sample of an aircraft seen on radar is shown in Figure 4-11.

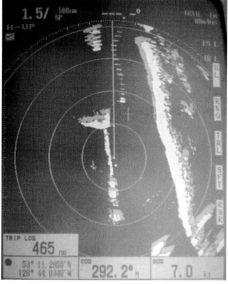

Figure 4-11. *Low-flying aircraft seen on radar. The top picture shows the plane emerging from the clouds, the bottom as it appears on radar. The screen is redrawn every 3 seconds, and the range rings are set to 0.5 nm. We see that it took the plane about 18 seconds to travel 0.5 nm, so its SRM was 0.5 x 3600/18 = 100 kts. Our speed toward it was 7 kts, so its approximate speed was 93 kts. Your first airplane sighting on radar can be an eye-opener when headed straight toward you and you do not see or hear the plane.*

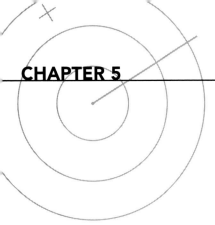

CHAPTER 5

Radar Piloting

For the sake of our purposes here, we need to distinguish between radar piloting and radar navigation, although they are not separate activities in the broadest sense. *Radar navigation* is using radar to find our actual location on a chart, a latitude and longitude, or a range and bearing from a known position, as introduced in Chapter 4 and detailed further in Chapter 10. Radar can be used to find a position on its own, as a primary means of position fixing, or to confirm a position found by GPS.

Radar piloting refers to using the radar to guide us along some desired route, without immediate concern for our exact position. In this application the concern is not finding out where we *are*, but being certain we know where we are *not*. This comes up repeatedly in routine navigation, and is the most frequent application of radar. We cover a few basic techniques here and present more sophisticated maneuvering in Chapter 10. Most of these methods rely on creative use of the VRM, EBL, and ERBL, as well as simple use of the heading line.

MAINTAINING A CHANNEL POSITION

A simple application is maintaining a specific location along a narrow channel that has nice steep sides (good radar targets) or even just one side that gives a good radar reflection. You might be transiting a channel that is just 0.3 mile wide, but because there are dangers along the edge and traffic in the channel, you want to stay just to the right of middle. In this case, just set the VRM to the distance off you wish to maintain, and then drive with the VRM skimming along the side you referenced from. See Figure 5-1. The first step in this process is referring to the chart to ensure that the distance selected is indeed a safe one. In Chapter 10 we cover methods that can be used with midchannel buoys when no shorelines are readily available for radar reference. *Guard sectors* can also be used that will set off alarms if you get too close to the shoreline. These are discussed in Chapter 8.

Sometimes there may be bends in the channel that the radar cannot see around, so a close, simultaneous monitoring of the GPS will keep you posted on where you are along the route. There can also be times when the radar will assist the depth sounder when following a depth contour along a shoreline in the fog. You then have two ways to identify your location.

In these procedures, and in any type of radar piloting, it is crucial that you know what you are seeing on the radar (Chapter 3). Here is another case where the coordination of radar and GPS is so valuable. The exercise for developing this skill is explained in Chapter 4. In Chapter 10 we cover a wider range of techniques.

ROUNDING A CORNER AT FIXED DISTANCE OFF

Figure 5-2 shows another valuable, common application that can be used for routine navigation control or for maneuvering to avoid hazards

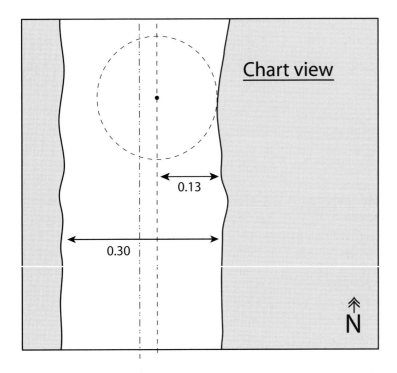

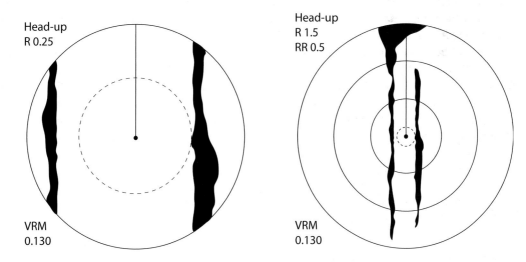

Figure 5-1. *Using VRM to maintain distance off. In the top example, we wish to stay 0.13 mile off the right side of the channel that is 0.3 mile across, so we set the VRM to 0.13 and drive with it just touching the shoreline—in this example the range rings (normally just one at 0.125) have been shut off, which often helps the display in some applications. Periodically, we expand the range and look ahead to see if the heading line is indeed parallel to the shoreline, meaning we are driving parallel to the shore. In this case we also note that the channel turns right in about one mile, and we lose radar sight of the right-hand shore as it becomes shadowed by the corner.*

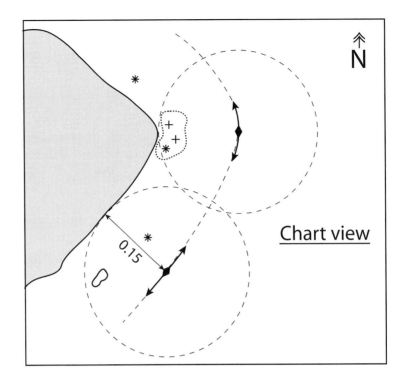

Chart view

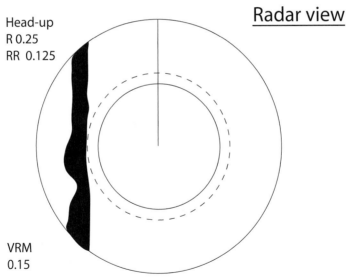

Radar view

Head-up
R 0.25
RR 0.125

VRM
0.15

Figure 5-2. *Using VRM to round a corner. The top view shows a section of an e-chart program with a temporary movable mark and associated range ring to confirm a safe distance off for rounding the corner. The mark can be dragged along the shore to check for hazards within that range. The same can, of course, be done on a paper chart with the dividers set to the chosen distance. After confirmation, set the VRM to the safe distance and steer around the corner without letting the VRM circle touch the land.*

around a corner. For example, there may be off-lying underwater rocks within 0.25 mile of a headland you must bypass, and for traffic or current reasons you wish to go around as closely as possible, or you might be in a race and looking for the shortest safe route. In cases like these, the shoreline will give a solid radar echo that you can depend on, and you can set the VRM to a safe range and then round the corner being sure the VRM circle does not touch the land.

This is a technique worth practicing as soon as possible. It is easily mastered using the Radar Trainer simulator. It is especially valuable at night or in the fog, but it is useful even in clear weather, because it is not always easy to do this visually when the terrain is changing at the corner. The visual counterpart is to choose a landmark on the corner as you approach and watch it carefully to see that it stays right on the beam as you round, but this is not as good as radar if you are being set toward the shore as you round.

With an e-chart program there is a nice way to prepare for this type of radar-assisted rounding or coastline traverse. Most e-chart programs allow you to set a range ring on any mark on the chart. One trick is to choose your safe distance off for rounding and then plot a mark near the shoreline and put a range ring on the mark with a radius equal to your chosen distance off. Then grab that mark and drag it around the corner or along the coastline you intend to follow and watch to confirm that nothing hazardous enters the ring as you proceed.

USING THE HEADING LINE TO IDENTIFY LANDMARKS AHEAD

The heading line shows which way you are headed and where you will be if you proceed in that direction. Often you can simply look at the radar targets that lie ahead on the heading line to know if you are pointed in the right direction. However, often it is difficult to discern the lay of the land ahead even in clear weather. At night and in the fog it is impossible. Usually by expanding the radar range and looking ahead along the heading line you can identify enough to confirm your course. By just steering along a shoreline, the orientation of the heading line lets you know if you are properly aligned with the coastline. Even in clear weather, it is not always easy to make this evaluation by eye. See Figure 5-3. If a landmark on the heading line is in doubt compared to one on the right or left, you can use the EBL to see how

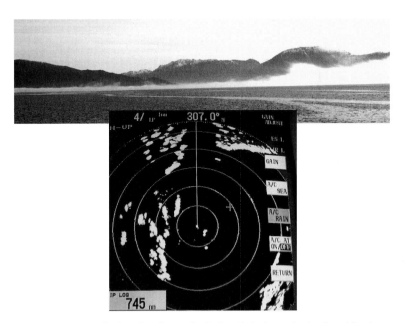

Figure 5-3. *Using the heading line to look ahead. An interplay back and forth between chart and radar will usually answer the question of what is what on the horizon. Here we see the shoreline ahead we wish to round to the left, just across from the small off-lying island (in the fog). On the radar this looks like a series of islands because of the shadowing caused by the headlands.*

far off the bow the other mark is, which might help identify it visually.

IDENTIFYING AN ENTRANCE CHANNEL

This is an ideal task for the ERBL (Chapter 2). I found this very useful when I was approaching a coastline from offshore and wanted to determine the position of the entrance buoy as early as possible. There were numerous small targets in the vicinity, which were hidden due to poor visibility. The chart showed an offshore buoy with several channel buoys marking the approach, but these could not be identified among the many targets on the screen (it turned out there were a number of fishing vessels in the region of the entrance). From the chart I learned that the entrance range was on heading 110 T. So I set up an ERBL oriented in the direction 110 T on the radar screen and moved the line around the screen until I could recognize targets in the right spacing. The spacing of the buoys could be read from the chart. See Figure 5-4.

Without an ERBL, you can improvise by using the EBL. Set it in the right direction taking into account your heading, and use some form of parallel indexing, which we discuss briefly below and more in Chapter 10.

DETECTING CURRENT SET

The GPS tells you that you are being set by current or wind whenever the course over ground (COG) is different from your compass heading. You can also see this graphically on a GPS plotter that shows your intended track and your actual track. In many circumstances, you can get the same

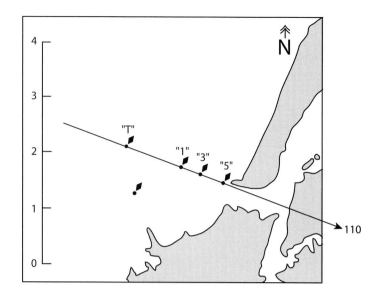

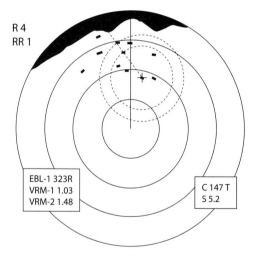

Figure 5-4. *Identifying buoys and channels with ERBL. From the chart we note that the entrance buoys lie along a bearing of 110 T, that "T" and "1" are a mile apart, and that buoy "3" is about 0.5 mile farther in. From the radar we can identify these buoys among other targets by directly measuring their orientation and spacing. We do not see buoy "5" for some reason, but have enough to go on without it. The other targets are either buoys or vessels in the area, which we could determine with a longer look at the way they move as we proceed in. Note that from 4 miles out, the entrance channel (about 0.3 mi wide) is not resolved with our radar, which has a nominal horizontal beam width of 6° (0.3 mi at 3.5 mi off corresponds to about 5°). With a heading sensor input we could read all the bearings directly, but in this head-up display we need this reasoning: I am steering 147, I see the targets in a line bearing 323 R, which means it is 360 − 323 = 37° to the left of my course, which gives 147 − 37 = 110, which is what I am looking for.*

information from the radar screen, which in some cases may be more convenient. In any event, it is a backup or further confirmation of this most important observation.

One approach is to have the heading line parallel to the coastline and the VRM set on the beach. With no current, they both stay in place, but if there is an onshore component of the current or leeway, you will note that though the heading line remains parallel to the shoreline, the VRM is creeping up onto the shore.

Another example would be to note that the radar trail of a known buoy or small islet is not moving as a stationary target should (covered in Chapter 6) but appears as a moving target. If a stationary target is not moving straight down the heading line, then you are being set. A buoy within a Lollipop display (Chapter 8) is ideal for making this observation.

OFFSET TRACKING

The above method can be applied in more general circumstances with a bit of extra plotting or use of an offset EBL. When the task is to pass an underwater danger at a given distance off and there are prominent radar targets in the neighborhood, you can often use those targets as a tracking or "index range" to mark a safe track past the danger. Exposed rocks, islets, or navigation aids marking corners of a shoaling are possible targets that could be used to define an index range. With the radar targets of the selected index range in view some distance off, turn to the course you wish to pass them on, then draw a line on the radar screen or use an offset EBL to mark the range line between the two targets. Set the VRM to the desired safe passing distance, and then steer the vessel such that *both* targets remain on the index line, which will be tangent to the VRM, as shown in Figure 5-5.

This technique is much improved in the north-up display mode discussed more in Part Two. But even using head-up mode (HU), it can—in the right circumstances—keep you

alerted to your location relative to your desired track past the hazard. In HU mode, targets rotate when you turn, so you must be vigilant when steering in the presence of current or leeway. If you let the targets get much off the index line, just steering to place one target back onto the index line might not provide the safe passage intended. Indeed, whenever you note that your heading must change to keep the target on the line, you know you are being set off course by some source. See Chapter 10 for more details of this technique, which is a basic form of parallel indexing. North-up and head-up applications are compared there.

ANCHORING WITH RADAR

Radar can contribute to all aspects of coastal piloting, so it should be no surprise that it offers support to the anchoring process. Even in clear daylight, the radar image of the region around you, including other anchored vessels, is valuable confirmation of what you would be otherwise judging by eye alone or watching on the GPS plotter. Generally the task is to locate a central position or some other location based on relative distances off of vessels or land. It is an ideal task for radar. At night or in fog, it is best to plan the approach keeping in mind available radar aids as shown in Figure 5-6. Then if GPS signals are blocked by steep cliffs or trees surrounding your anchorage, you have a safe, efficient way to navigate the approach using your radar alone.

The reason radar stands out as an aid to anchoring is simply that other aids you might rely on for position navigation are not helpful in some places. You might be in a bay that is too small to be seen on the only chart you have—a common circumstance in many remote cruising grounds—or you could be in a deep fjord without dependable GPS coverage, so the option to watch your position on a large-scale e-chart might not be possible.

In short, practicing and getting used to anchoring with radar is well worth the time and

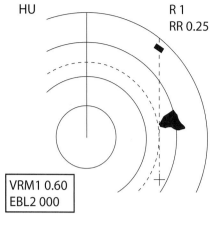

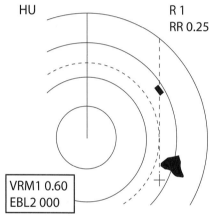

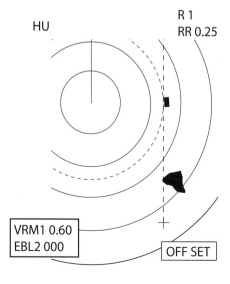

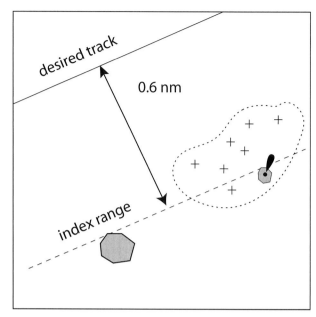

Figure 5-5. *Using an index range and an offset EBL to maintain a desired track in head-up (HU) mode. If both index targets stay on the EBL, you know you are maintaining the desired off-set and not getting set left or right. The figure top right shows a charted light marking a shoal area with underwater rocks and southwest of it a small islet that shows well on the radar. From this we decide to maintain 0.6 mile off the light as we pass. We use the VRM to set the desired distance off, then use an offset EBL to mark the line the light and islet must follow to maintain the desired course. Without an offset EBL, the line can be drawn directly on the radar screen as explained in Chapter 1. This is similar to dragging the VRM along a shoreline, where we use the line between the light and the islet to replace the shoreline. Note that as we approached the hazard (bottom radar image) the radar was offset to view backward to keep the complete index range in view on the screen.*

Another example of this method with more details on the setup and precautions is covered in Chapter 10. A key issue here is that the locations of the index range targets should be compatible with an appropriate passing range. A more versatile method, parallel indexing, is discussed in Chapter 10, but that method requires a north-up (NU) display mode.

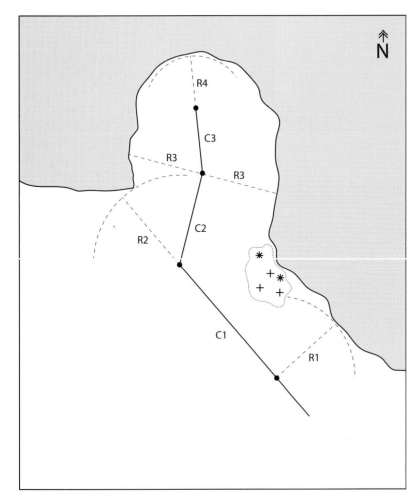

Figure 5-6. *Anchoring with radar. This is a picture of a paper chart as we might prepare it ahead of time for making an anchorage approach by radar alone. In the example, we will use course C1 to approach from the SE at distance R1 offshore to clear the rocks hazard at the corner. (During the actual approach we will set this distance on the VRM to monitor distance off.) When within range R2 of the headland, we will turn to course C2, then watch that we enter on the centerline with range R3 the same on either side, and finally turn to course C3 and approach to within range R4 to anchor. Recording crucial ranges and courses ahead of time can save last-minute scrambling at the chart, which can come up if the radar image of the area does not look as expected, or other vessels are present, and so on. The trickier the entrance or conditions, the more crucial planning becomes.*

should become a standard method, day or night.

It could be a moonless night in a remote anchorage where there is nothing to see visually and you cannot use e-charts or GPS, so you are left to do the job with radar. Such an exercise calls for careful planning. Lay out the route on the chart or plotting sheet, marking the course headings, times at waypoints, and bearings to prominent landmarks at the turning points or checkpoints. Then the entrance plan can be followed slowly, monitoring progress along the route with the radar. Once inside the bay, a safe location relative to the shorelines can be discerned from the radar. And once anchored, a VRM can be set touching the shore at one or more places to monitor drift or anchor dragging. A guard ring might also be useful until you are safely settled in. If the land image drifts into the guard ring, an alarm will go off.

In some anchoring situations, parallel indexing might be useful for navigating a long or complex entrance channel. This is covered in Chapter 10.

When close to bright land images on the radar screen, besides reducing the Gain, the AC Sea (STC) control can help with optimizing the picture, as shown in Figure 5-7. Radar picture adjustment is discussed in Chapter 2.

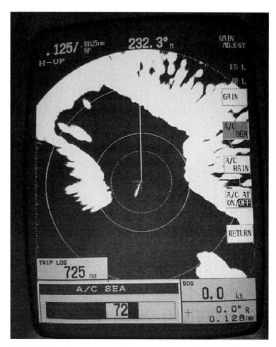

Figure 5-7. *Two radar images of a close anchorage where AC Sea helped improve the picture significantly. The left side shows the radar picture before optimization as it appeared after pulling into the cove and lowering the range scale and reducing Gain to the lowest setting. The AC Sea setting was at 24 percent of maximum. The right side shows the improvement in the picture after increasing the AC Sea to 72 percent. AC Rain might also help with this type of picture adjustment, depending on the Gain settings, what functions are set to Auto or Manual, and so on. In any event, the Gain must be greatly reduced when close to large targets. The smaller target in the top corner of the cove is an exposed rock; the larger target to the left of it is a group of logs.*

CHAPTER 6

Radar for Collision Avoidance

R adar is without doubt the most important aid we have for evaluating risk of collision and monitoring the safe passage of another vessel. It is so valuable for this application that it is the only electronic navigation aid singled out in the *Navigation Rules* with specific instructions on its use and limitations for this purpose. We cover these issues in detail in Chapter 12, but note here a segment of Rule 7b, which states that when evaluating risk of collision, " . . . proper use shall be made of radar . . . including . . . radar plotting or equivalent systematic observation of detected objects."

Just looking at the radar screen will not suffice; that is not plotting, nor is it a "systematic" observation. The Rule says "shall," not "may." You must always systematically evaluate what is taking place. It is crucial to your safety, and it is the law. The same law applies around the world, as the *Navigation Rules* are international.

If you glance at the radar and note the appearance of a new target in front of you, and then sometime later come back to the radar and see there is still a target in front of you, maybe closer than before, you know little more after the second glance than you knew after the first. Cursory observations do not help you evaluate the risk of collision and do not give you any guidelines on how to proceed. Unstructured observations add more anxiety than safety to navigation. To use radar for safe, efficient navigation you must make systematic observations with careful records. Fortunately, such procedures are easy to learn and carry out.

The key to evaluating risk of collision with radar is understanding the distinctions between true motion and relative motion, as illustrated in Figure 6-1. *True motion* is what you would see from an overhead view of the waterway, with both vessels moving. It is motion relative to the fixed earth. *Relative motion* is what you see on the radar. It is how the other vessel or land targets appear to move as you observe them from your moving vessel. Unless you are stopped (or using special options on some radars, discussed in Part Two), target motion you observe on the radar screen is always relative motion. The faster you are moving, the larger the difference between true motion and relative motion.

First we will look at moving targets as viewed from a stationary radar and then get underway to see how the picture changes when we, too, are moving. The goals in radar traffic observations are first to track the relative motions of targets seen on the screen, to evaluate collision risk, and then to figure out the true motion of any approaching target in order to decide how best to maneuver.

In other words, if you see a target approaching from dead ahead, you first note that if nothing changes you will have a close encounter. Your next step is to determine if this approaching target is a vessel headed straight toward you, or one whose stern you are about to crash into, or perhaps a navigation buoy you are about to run down!

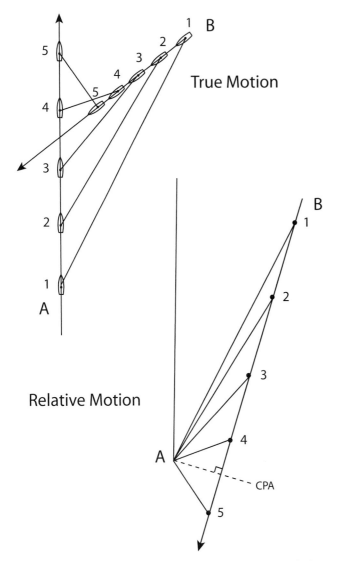

True Motion

Relative Motion

CPA

Figure 6-1. *True motion versus relative motion. Boat A, headed north, is crossing in front of boat B headed southwesterly, with snapshots of their positions every minute for 5 minutes. The true motion plot is how they would appear from overhead, with both boats moving across the water. A is moving about twice as fast as B. The bottom picture shows the motion of B relative to A. It is how B appears to move from A's moving reference frame, which is how the radar image of B would appear on the radar screen of A. The CPA, the closest point of approach, occurs in this example between minutes 4 and 5.*

The separation between boats and the bearing from one to the other is the same in both views, but the apparent speed and heading of B has changed when viewed from A. Also note that the CPA is easy to predict and measure after just 3 minutes or so in the relative plot, but is more difficult to ascertain at any time in the true motion plot.

WORKING WITH MOVING TARGETS

Consider this situation for practicing radar observations. We are tied to a mooring buoy on the edge of a waterway. We see a buoy, A, about 1 mile off on our starboard bow, and we see another buoy, B, at about the same distance dead ahead, as shown in Figure 6-2. We can see a vessel, C, headed toward buoy B from buoy A.

We are not moving, and our radar image is essentially static except for the one target moving across the screen from right to left. We can easily identify this as the vessel we see on deck by its relationship to the two buoys, which are in clear sight. Let's assume our bow is pointed due north (but this is not crucial to the exercise) and that the range scale is set to 1.5 miles. The time is 1215 and we can see the vessel on our radar screen just above buoy A headed toward buoy B. At this point we start the Plot option, which will leave trails on the radar screen behind all moving targets and also start a clock to time the duration of the trails.

Five minutes later, the target vessel, C, is just above buoy B. The locations of A and B on our radar have not changed because we and they are not moving. Since we are not moving, it is easy to figure out how fast and in which direction vessel C is traveling. The length of the plotted trail from 1215 to 1220 is how far the vessel moved in 5 minutes, and we can measure this from the plot trail on the radar image. That distance in miles divided by 5 minutes is the vessel's speed in miles per

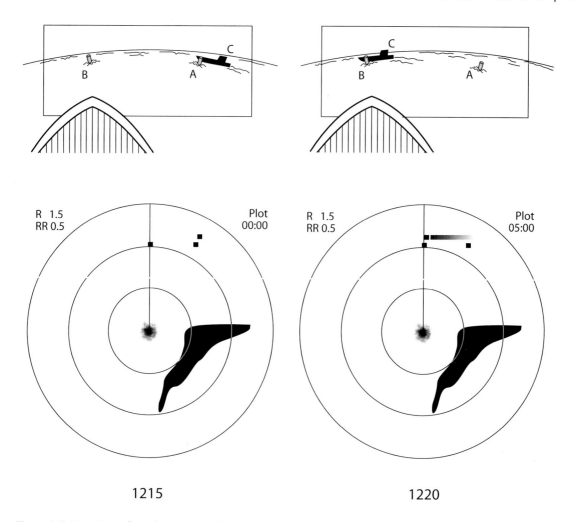

Figure 6-2. *Two views of a radar screen and waterway taken 5 minutes apart. Our vessel is not moving. The buoy we are tied to is too close to be seen on the radar. At 1215 we start the Plot option to watch the vessel headed toward buoy B. At 1220 we see the vessel approach the buoy and note its 5-minute wake trail on the radar.*

minute. Multiply that by 60 and we have the vessel's speed in knots.

The measurement of the length of vessel C's trail on the radar screen is an ideal job for the ERBL described in Chapter 2. Just engage the function, move the cursor to one end of the trail, turn on the VRM from this new location, expand the ring out until it just touches the other end, and read off the value in nautical miles.

Since not all radars have such a feature, let's do it the traditional way. Following Figure 6-3, we use any card or our navigation dividers to

record the length of the target trail from 1215 to 1220. We now have the distance we want to know and can use the radar's (traditional, center-based) VRM to measure it. We set one mark in the center of the screen, increase the VRM to the second mark, and read off the value. In this case the trail is 0.62 nm long. To compute target vessel speed, 0.62 nm/5 min = 0.124 nm/min, and 0.124 nm/min x 60 min/hr = 7.4 nm/hr = 7.4 kts. From our moored position we have discovered with our radar that the vessel we see crossing in front of us is traveling at 7.4 kts.

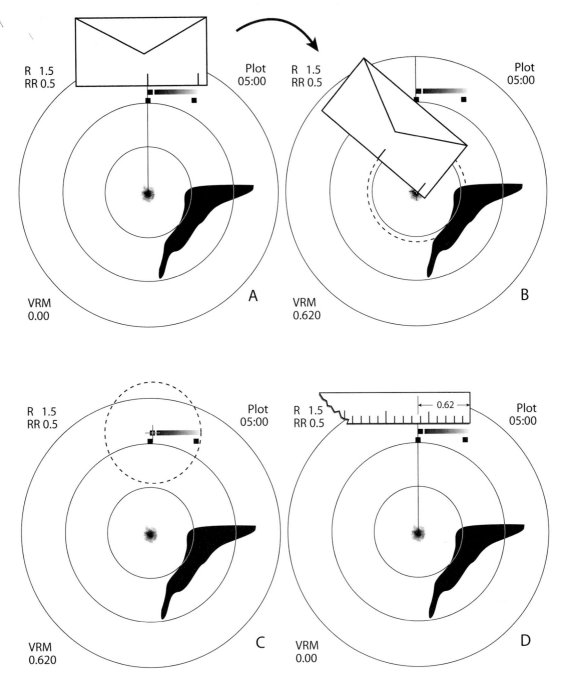

Figure 6-3. *Measuring distance on the radar screen. In A, two tick marks on an envelope record the length of the 5-minute target trail. In B, this distance is measured using the center-based VRM. In C, the same distance is measured without an aid using the floating VRM, which has been electronically moved to one end of the trail. In D, the same distance is measured using a portable range scale, which is any custom-made ruler calibrated to the range ring interval on the screen, as described in Chapter 1 and later in this chapter. In this view, the radar cannot see the mooring buoy we are tied to.*

Viewed on deck, it would not be so easy to determine a precise course for the vessel—it would be even more difficult if it were not headed perpendicular to us—but with the radar we can tell at a glance that its course is 270, based on our own heading of 000. The target's course is 90° to the left of our heading line, which is pointed toward 000.

If our heading when we did the measurement had been 330, for example, instead of 000, then we would have to conclude that the vessel's course was 90° to the left of 330, which is 330 − 90 = 240. When our own heading is magnetic, the ship's course we are finding is also magnetic. But no matter what a vessel's course or our heading, when we are stationary it is a simple matter to determine the course and speed of a moving vessel. Next time you are moored within radar sight of moving vessels, give it a try, or use the Starpath Radar Trainer software simulator that comes with this book.

RELATIVE MOTION

Our use of radar to find the course and speed of a moving target in the last example was easy because we were stationary. The speeds and directions we observed on the radar were true values, unaffected by our own motion. Once we get underway, the speeds we measure will be *speeds of relative motion* (SRM), and the trail directions we observe will be *directions of relative motion* (DRM). An extra step is required to determine a target's true motion from the relative motion observed on a radar that is itself moving. This is a fundamental aspect of radar observation since we are concerned about target motions around us more often when we are moving than when we are stationary.

To illustrate this, let us carry on with our last example. (Assume for now that we are using head-up radar display. We will generalize this to north-up when we are done.) We cast off and get underway at 1220 and head toward buoy B at a speed of 6.0 kts, while vessel C carries on at 7.4 kts on a course of 270. We reset the Plot option at 1220, which erases all prior trails, and 5 minutes later at 1225 we have another view of the radar screen, as shown in Figure 6-4.

Some things are different now. Our vessel remains, as always, in the center of the radar screen but we have pulled away from shore

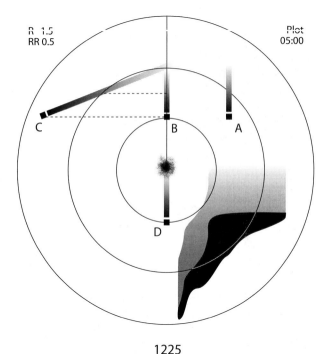

1225

Figure 6-4. *Relative motion. The radar screen is the same as in Figure 6-3, 5 minutes after resetting the Plot option when the target vessel passed buoy B. The three buoys and the land move straight down-screen (head-on targets), but the target vessel, C, now has a direction of relative motion of 240. The lengths of the trails indicate their speeds of relative motion. Target D is the mooring buoy we pulled away from. All stationary targets have the same trail lengths, which we call the buoy trail. C appears to be traveling from the northeast, but in fact it is traveling from the east, which is "aft" (with respect to our boat) of its apparent direction. The dotted lines have been added to show that buoy B would always appear on the stern of the target ship.*

after being underway for 5 minutes at 6 kts. Six knots is 1 mile per 10 minutes, so we have moved 0.5 mile farther off the shoreline. (To figure any speed in minutes per mile, just divide 60 by the speed. At 15 kts, your speed is 4 minutes per mile; at 5 kts, it is 12 minutes per mile, etc.) Use the card method described above and the range scale shown in Figure 6-4 to confirm that the distance to shore is 0.5 mile greater than before. Note that the shore itself also left a trail, so this is equivalent to measuring the length of the shoreline trail.

Note that the two buoys, A and B, have also proceeded straight down the radar screen at precisely the same 0.5 nm. This should be no surprise. They are fixed to the earth, and the reason they have moved on the radar is because we are approaching them. We moved 0.5 mile toward buoy B, so it appears on our radar screen as 0.5 mile closer to us. Likewise, the mooring buoy we left moved 0.5 nm away from us—it was too close to be seen on the radar when we were tied to it.

All motion we see on the radar screen when we are moving is relative motion, and since we are in the middle of the radar screen doing the observing, it is all motion relative to us. In any radar display, targets moving down the radar screen, whether vertically or obliquely, are called *down-screen targets*. Those moving down-screen vertically, or precisely parallel to the heading line, can be referred to as *head-on targets*, regardless of their location on the screen. They could be in front of us (at the top center of the screen), or abeam of us (on the left or right of the screen), or behind us (at the bottom of the screen). In Figure 6-4 we have five down-screen targets, but only four are head-on targets.

The essential factor to notice is this: If a radar target is dead in the water, and we are on a steady course (e.g., not set by current or wind), then even though that target (such as a buoy in our example) is getting closer to (or farther from) us as we proceed, it is not getting any closer to or farther from us in the left-right direction. That is, it is not getting closer to or farther from our heading line, which is why it moves parallel to the heading line.

> ► **Any target that is dead in the water moves straight down the radar screen parallel to the heading line.** ◄

In other words, a stationary target is always a head-on target. Not all head-on targets are stationary, but it is easy to determine which ones are. If we are moving at 7 kts, a stationary target moves down the screen at 7 kts. If we are moving at 12 kts, the target moves at 12 kts. If we stop, the target stops.

This includes all landmasses, islets, and any other land features as well as buoys, anchored vessels, or vessels that might be underway but not making way. The trails or wakes made by such objects are called *buoy trails*, and they will prove to be useful references for identifying other traffic targets. As we shall see, the observation of a target's trail length and direction is the first crucial step when identifying isolating targets on the radar screen that could be approaching traffic.

We will use the phrase *your buoy trail* to mean the trail length a buoy would make on our radar screen regardless of whether there is an actual buoy in range. In this sense, the phrase is used as a reference length for judging the speeds of all targets, moving or stationary. It is "ours" in the sense that our own speed and course determine the length and direction the trail buoys make, or would make if present. (Our vessel's central position on the radar screen does not leave a trail except in the rather specialized mode called true motion display, discussed in Chapter 8.)

When we see targets moving straight down or up the radar screen parallel to our heading line, we know immediately that they are either dead in the water or on a course exactly parallel to ours, either in the same direction or in precisely the opposite direction. If their courses were just slightly different from ours, they would be getting slightly closer or farther from our heading line in the left-right direction as they proceeded, and they would not be moving parallel to the heading line. The simplicity of this observation is one of the beauties of radar.

If a moving target vessel's average course is just a few degrees different from yours, you will eventually see a trail that is not vertical. However, the time it takes to discern the orientation of the trail depends on many factors, including relative speeds, sea conditions, radar display mode, currents, winds, and the steadiness of your own course keeping. Real radar trails are not often nice, clean straight paths, but instead are smeared to varying degrees reflecting the statistical location of the target's echoes at the time they were captured onto the screen. Nevertheless, the orientation of a target's trail on the radar screen is the most fundamental observation in radar, and it is crucial to many decisions. We cover these important details in Chapter 11.

Direction of Relative Motion

The orientation of a target's plot trail—the way it is pointed—is called its *direction of relative motion* (DRM). Go back to Figure 6-4, and review what happened to the radar trail of the target vessel C once we started moving toward it. Before we got underway its DRM was 270; once we started moving, it shifted to about 240.

Vessel C, however, is still headed due west, past buoy B. If you imagine yourself on that vessel your course would still be 270, and if you look aft you would still see buoy B directly astern. But from our moving perspective, its trail on our radar screen has bent down-screen. If we now did the same exercise as before—without accounting for our own motion—we would falsely conclude that the true course of this vessel was 240.

Thus we have this situation: we see on the radar screen a target moving in direction 240

and it is our job to determine its true course from what we see and our own known speed. We will cover the procedure shortly, but it will be easier if we first establish some terminology and analogies.

The direction (and subsequent trail) of relative motion behaves just like apparent wind behaves on your vessel. If we have wind on the beam when we are stationary, and then we start moving, the apparent wind direction (the direction the wind comes from) will move forward, toward the bow. To help remember this, think of the apparent wind direction when you put your head out a car window, driving at 60 mph. It is in your face, dead ahead. See Figure 6-5.

If you start out with moderate wind on the beam and accelerate, the apparent wind speed will increase and its direction will move forward as your speed increases. The faster you go, the more forward it moves until your speed is much greater than the wind speed, at which time it will be nearly dead ahead—in your face. Put another way (in reverse), when you are moving, the true wind direction is always aft of the apparent wind direction. If the apparent wind is on the starboard bow (045 R), the true wind is more on the beam. If the apparent wind is on the beam, the true wind is more toward the quarter. Apparent wind on the quarter means a true wind more toward the stern.

We want to use this wind analogy to determine what the true direction of a radar target is relative to what we see on the radar. We see relative motion on the radar, which is like the apparent wind. The true motion of all the targets will thus be "aft" of their apparent motion.

We can think of the radar target trail line as a wind vector, or we can take the reciprocal of the DRM for a wind direction. The apparent course of 240 (wind = 240 − 180 = 060 R) was made by a vessel with true course that is more aft relative to our heading (270 − 180 = 090 R). A wind at 60° on your bow is forward of one that is 90° on your bow, which is abeam. Whenever you see a radar trail on the screen of your

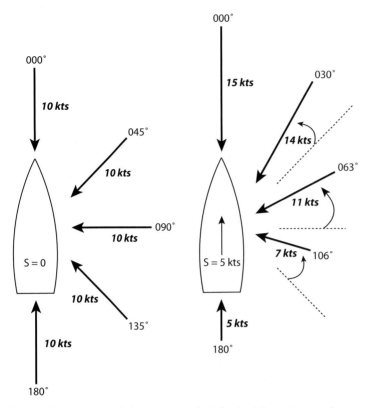

Figure 6-5. *Apparent wind versus true wind. On the left, we have various true wind possibilities, which are all the same as apparent wind because our speed is zero. On the right, once we get underway, however, each of the apparent wind arrows shifts forward by an amount that depends on its original direction. Radar target trails work the same way in that all true vessel trails are aft of their apparent trails when we are moving.*

moving vessel, you can imagine rotating it aft to get a better idea of its actual heading relative to yours.

Even if you do not care to know the precise true course of a radar target, it is often important to know its approximate heading relative to yours. You could, for example, see a radar target at night that appears to be heading straight toward you on the starboard bow. Without thinking through the relative motions involved, you might start looking with binoculars for a red and green light, which would be the lights to expect on a vessel headed toward you. But that head-on appearance on the radar is only its direction of relative motion. Its true

course will be aft of that. You should instead be looking for a red light alone, or even a white light (the stern). It all depends on your relative heading and speed. In any case, the true trail is aft (with respect to you, the observer) of the apparent trail.

The wind analogy may help you remember how the relative motion of radar targets behave on the radar screen using the target classification presented below. We will also include more examples.

For one example, look back to Figure 6-4 and imagine yourself (headed 000) in front of target C on the screen, which is moving in direction 240 R. That target would appear to be headed from your starboard bow (060 R), but its true course of 270 is from your starboard beam (090). The true motion is aft of the apparent motion. If it were night, you might guess from the radar image (without thinking) to look for a red port-side light, but knowing its true heading of due west you would instead expect to see a white stern light, because you are viewing it from more than 2 points aft of its beam.

For the sake of discussion, we will distinguish traffic targets based on their directions of relative motion, as defined and illustrated in Figure 6-6.

Parallel and Crossing Targets *Head-on targets* and *stern targets* move *parallel* to the heading line. Head-on targets move down the heading line; stern targets move up the heading line. These targets do not cross the heading line. Stern targets are easy to interpret. They

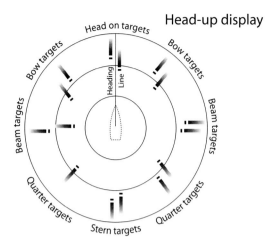

Head-up display

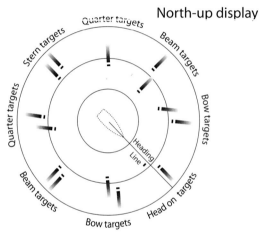

North-up display

Figure 6-6. *Radar target classifications. These are useful for discussion of radar targets and predicting target behavior following various maneuvers. The classification is tied to the orientation of the ship's heading line. The precise bearings of the targets do not matter; this is just a method of general description relative to the orientation of the heading line. Course-up display is similar to north-up display except that the operator can lock in any heading at the top of the radar screen instead of due north (000). Course-up and north-up displays are explained and illustrated in Chapter 7.*

are on the same course and overtaking you. That is the only type of traffic that will move straight up the heading line. In the next section we go over how to figure the actual speeds of stern targets and how to interpret head-on targets as well.

Crossing targets will cross or have crossed

your course line. We classify them according to their orientation to your vessel—if you imagine your vessel right in front of the target's trail. *Bow targets* approach from the forward quadrants, *quarter targets* move in a direction from your aft quadrants, and *beam targets* move perpendicular to your heading line. In other words, the classifications refer to their direction of relative motion on the radar screen, not their actual location relative to you.

Each of these target specifications and the descriptions of their behaviors apply to targets seen anywhere on the screen, but clearly the more interesting cases are those that are actually converging on you. Thus a beam target headed toward you is of more interest than a beam target passing well behind you.

We need these target classifications to develop insights and maneuvering guidelines that apply regardless of the radar display mode in effect at the time. It is not uncommon these days to switch back and forth between display modes, so we need our guidelines to follow along with us.

As we shall see below, parallel targets are quick and easy to identify, but crossing targets take more consideration. It is rather like figuring the effect of a current on your course. When the current is parallel (with you or against you), it is easy to figure its effect on your speed. But when the current is diagonal to your heading, there is a vector problem to solve. Target vessel C in the example from Figure 6-4 is a bow target, and buoys and land are always head-on targets.

A target that does not move at all on the radar screen, even though you are moving, is a special type of parallel target because it is not getting any closer to or farther from your heading line. This unique target is a vessel that is headed in the same direction and moving at the same speed as you. We refer to these targets as *buddy boats*, because if you were traveling with a buddy you might well want to match your speed and course. To be a buddy boat, however, the boat must move precisely as you do if its relative position is not to change. Radar is very sensitive to this observation. If a target's course or speed is just a little different (a few tenths of a knot or few degrees in heading), you will soon detect it, and indeed be able to measure the difference quantitatively. We will exploit this fact in the discussion of radar applications to sailboat racing in Chapter 11.

Speed of Relative Motion

A target closing in on us straight down the heading line is the quintessential head-on target. You can tell if this is a vessel headed toward you or, say, a drilling platform you are about to run into by measuring how fast it is approaching on the radar screen. If it is approaching at exactly your speed, you know its entire apparent motion is due to your actual motion, and the target is dead in the water. On the other hand, if the target is moving toward you at 16 kts and you are proceeding at only 6 kts, then it is a vessel headed toward you at 10 kts.

The speed at which a target moves across the radar screen is its *speed of relative motion* (SRM). If you stop, its speed of relative motion will turn into its true speed, but as long as you are moving, the speed of target motion on the radar screen will be affected by your own speed.

The analysis and identification of parallel targets are always a matter of comparing the target's SRM with your own speed. There are two ways to determine a parallel target's SRM. If you have a known buoy or isolated small landmass on the screen with a trail behind it, then that buoy trail length is your measuring stick. Any down-screen target trail equal to that is dead in the water, and its SRM is the same as your speed. Any parallel target trail shorter than that has a slower SRM than your speed, and anything longer than that has a faster SRM.

Even without a buoy trail in sight, you can compute what the length of the buoy trail would be. This type of speed computation is best done

using specific time intervals. A 6-minute interval is the standard in radar observations because the length of a 6-minute trail is speed in knots divided by 10. Put another way, if your speed is S miles in 60 minutes, then you are moving $\frac{1}{10}$ of S in $\frac{1}{10}$ of an hour, which is 6 minutes. This is sometimes called the *six-minute rule*, and it is used repeatedly in radar. If you are moving at 8 kts, then your buoy trail is 0.8 nm. If you are moving at 20 kts, then your buoy trail is 2.0 nm.

Likewise, it is just as easy to determine the SRM of any target on the screen by multiplying the length of its 6-minute trail by 10. If a target has a 6-minute trail of 1.2 nm, then its SRM is 12 kts, and so on.

The Wake option on modern radars is very handy for this observation. With wake trails set to 6 minutes, you see immediately the relative speeds of all moving targets on the screen. The ERBL can be used to measure the length of the trails, or you can just make a portable range scale marked off in tenths of a knot on a piece of cardboard or a tongue depressor (see Chapter 1). With a portable scale you can quickly and accurately measure the SRM of any target.

With the wake length set to 6 minutes, it is often adequate just to look at the screen and judge lengths relative to the range rings. At a range of 6 miles the rings are typically 1 mile apart. A target with a 6-minute trail of one ring spacing is therefore moving at 10 kts. Examples are shown in Figure 6-7.

For smaller range settings on your radar, the 6-minute trails may be too long. If so, switch to 3-minute trails and double the length of the 3-minute trail before multiplying by 10. A 3-minute trail that is 0.35 nm long, is 2 x 0.35 = 0.7 nm in 6 minutes, so its SRM is 7 kts. Or, carry two portable range scales, one for 3 minutes and one for 6 minutes. Generally, each radar range and each wake trail time would require a special portable scale, but a generic one marked off in tenths can often be used for all

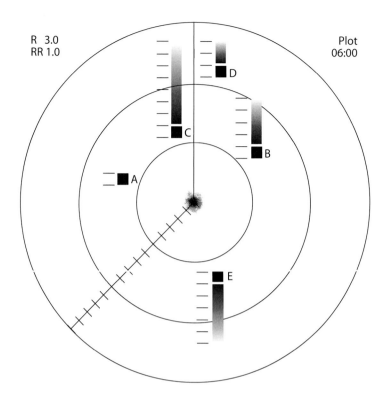

R 3.0
RR 1.0

Plot
06:00

Figure 6-7. Parallel targets. The speed of relative motion is 10 times the length of the 6-minute plot or wake trail. Here our vessel speed is 10 kts. Target A has not moved in 6 minutes, so it has the same course and speed as we do. Target B has a trail length of 1.0 nm, so its SRM is 10 kts, which is our speed, so it must be dead in the water, and its plot is a buoy trail. Target C has a trail length of 1.6 nm, corresponding to an SRM of 16 kts, so it is headed toward us at 16 – 10 = 6 kts. Target D with a trail of 0.6 nm is moving toward us at 6 kts, so we are overtaking it, and it has a speed of 10 – 6 = 4 kts. Target E is overtaking us with a trail length of 1.2 nm, so it has an SRM of 12 kts. We are moving at 10 kts, so its actual speed is 10 + 12 = 22 kts.

situations, as long as you keep in mind the scales that apply.

$$\text{SRM (kts)} = \text{6-minute trail length (nm)} \times 10$$

$$\text{Buoy trail length (nm)} = \text{your speed (kts)}/10$$

Fixed wake times of 3, 6, or 12 minutes make the analysis easier, but you can use any time interval. All such Plot functions start a timer when the trail starts. From the length of the trail and the time it has accumulated, you can figure the SRM.

$$\text{SRM} = \text{observed trail length (nm)} \times 60/\text{trail time (min)}$$

or

$$\text{Buoy trail length} = \text{speed (kts)} \times \text{time (min)}/60$$

If your radar does not have a Plot or Wake option, then you must do the job by hand. Mark a target when first seen on the screen (see Chapter 1) and label it with the time, then mark it again 6 minutes later, and carry on as discussed above. Try to do the time marks to account for the seconds—e.g., wait for 00 seconds on the clock for the first mark and mark again 6 minutes 00 seconds later.

SUMMARY FOR HEAD-ON TARGETS (parallel motion, down the heading line, anywhere on the radar screen):

If their wakes are the same length as your buoy trail, they are dead in the water.

If their wakes are longer than your buoy trail, they are on the exact reciprocal of your course. If they are on or near the heading line ahead of you, they are headed toward you, otherwise they are passing on a parallel but opposite course. Their true speeds are their SRMs minus your speed.

If their wakes are shorter than your buoy

trail, their courses are the same as yours. If they are ahead near the heading line, you are overtaking them, otherwise you are just passing them on a parallel course. Their true speeds are your speed minus their SRMs.

SUMMARY FOR STERN TARGETS (parallel motion, up the heading line, anywhere on the radar screen):

Regardless of their wake lengths, they are moving faster than you and on the same course. If astern, they are overtaking you, otherwise they are passing on the same course. Their true speeds are your speed plus their SRMs.

SUMMARY FOR CROSSING TARGETS (oblique trails, seen anywhere on the radar screen):

Figure the SRM of crossing targets precisely as you do for parallel targets, but it is not as simple to conclude what their true courses and speeds are.

If the crossing trail is almost parallel, then the results will be almost the same as for a parallel target.

When the trail is more diagonal, you must solve a *relative motion diagram* to determine the true speed and course of the target. The full answer is actually discernible in Figure 6-4, as we shall see when we cover this important part of radar observation in Chapter 11. *Hint:* How did the target move on the radar screen *relative* to buoy B?

The key to discussing and learning about target behavior on the radar screen is the target classification scheme we have been discussing. Determining the general classification of the targets we see is the first step in evaluating risk of collision. The various display options available in modern radars make this an even more important step in the process. The problem is solved as soon as we become accustomed to thinking of the top of the radar screen being at the tip of the heading line, regardless of which way it is pointed. Then we can use the term *down-screen target* to mean a target moving down the heading line, whereas *up-screen targets* are moving up the heading line. In this sense, the heading line always defines the up direction, even if, in the display mode you are using, the heading line is not pointing straight up on the screen. The heading line is always the reference line for figuring target interactions and predictions.

In the traditional head-up mode, the heading line always remains straight up and the tip of the heading line is centered at the top of the radar screen. But in north-up displays this is not usually the case, and in course-up mode it is only true immediately after engaging that mode and before any subsequent course changes are made.

In Figure 6-6, head-on targets and bow targets are down-screen targets. Stern targets and quarter targets are up-screen targets. Thus up-screen versus down-screen make up one system of target classification and parallel versus crossing targets make up another. Targets that do not move at all on the screen (buddy boats) are unique, but easy to identify.

This terminology will become increasingly valuable as we discuss Rules of Thumb for predicting target behavior in response to our maneuvers in Chapter 11. Figure 6-8 presents a target classification exercise.

To summarize DRM, SRM, and wake trails in a nutshell, a target with a very short wake must be traveling at a course and speed close to yours. If the wake is very long, then the target is moving much faster than you. To decide what is long, compare the target wake to the buoy trail of any stationary target or compute it as described above and in Figure 6-9. Using radar to interpret very short wakes is common in sailboat racing (see Chapter 11 and Figure 11-30).

EVALUATING RISK OF COLLISION

We know from Rule 7d of the *Navigation Rules* (see Chapter 12) that a vessel approaching on a constant compass bearing poses a risk of collision. This situation is illustrated in Figure 6-10.

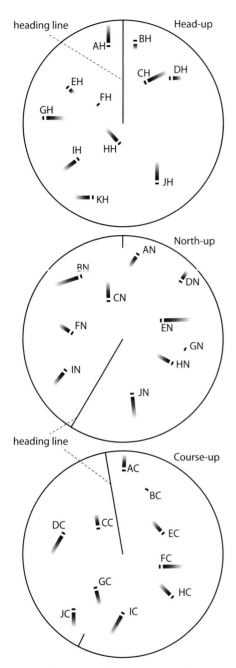

When watching an approaching target visually, we either monitor its bearing relative to some structure on our own vessel, which works as long as we do not alter our course or viewing position, or we take actual compass bearings to the target with a hand-bearing compass. The same interaction as viewed on each vessel's radar is shown in Figure 6-11. In this section we look at ways to make these collision risk observations from radar along with related procedures of systematic observations. In Chapter 12 we discuss maneuvering options in various conditions.

For close targets, radar is an invaluable addition to visual observations of vessel movements, and in low visibility radar is all you have. But in clear weather you can often evaluate the relative course of a distant vessel quicker by eye and a hand-bearing compass than by radar. Practice with the hand-bearing compass, however, is mandatory. Hand-bearing compasses may not work properly from all positions on all vessels due to magnetic disturbances, and they might not work at all from steel vessels. In these cases, bearings taken with a pelorus or similar instrument relative to the ship's heading will work. Very precise relative bearing measurements can also be made with an inexpensive plastic sextant. If magnetic disturbances are not a problem, a good pair of binoculars with an internal compass is an excellent tool for this job.

When you first see a new target appear on the radar screen, you should take immediate action. This is true regardless of where the target appears on the screen, but those dead ahead—near the heading line—will generally

Figure 6-8. *Target classification practice. Three radar display modes are shown. In the course-up display, the vessel has made a turn to the left after setting the course-up heading. In all three displays, which targets would be classified as: 1. up-screen; 2. down-screen; 3. parallel targets; 4. crossing targets; 5. beam targets; 6. bow targets; 7. quarter targets; 8. head-on targets; and 9. stern targets?*

Answers:
1. *Up-screen:* BH, EH, CN, DN, GC, DC, JC, IC. 2. *Down-screen:* AH, CH, HH, JH, IN, JN, AN, DN, CC, EC, HC. 3. *Parallel:* AH, BH, FH, JH, IN, AN, DN, DH, GH, KH, FN, HN, FC, Bow: CH, HH, JH, JN, BN, GN, CC, JC, BC. 4. *Crossing:* all but parallel 5. *Beam:* AC. 7. *Quarter:* EH, IH, CN, EN, DC, IC, DC. 8. AC. 7. *Quarter:* EH, IH, CN, EN, DC, IC, DC. 8. *Head-on:* AH, JH, IN, AN, CC. 9. *Stern:* BH, DN, JC.

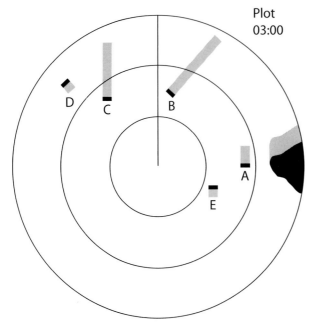

Plot
03:00

Figure 6-9. *Wake lengths show relative speeds at a glance. Target A is a buoy off a point of land, so the wake trails of the buoy and land represent our own motion in 3 minutes. Once we have identified buoy trails such as these, we can use them as a reference length and conclude that targets C and B have relative motions much faster than our own speed, and targets D and E have relative speeds much lower. If our speed, for example, was 6 knots, represented by the buoy trail A, then—judging by trail lengths—target B is moving across the screen (speed of relative motion, SRM) at about 24 kts and target C is moving at about 18 kts, whereas D and E are progressing across the screen at just 3 kts or less. Remember, by comparing wake trail lengths we are judging the speeds of relative motion of these targets, not their actual true speeds, which is typically the next step in the analysis.*

need your most urgent attention, since such a target could be a ship headed straight toward you with a high closing speed (SRM).

The following is a typical sequence of events that might occur when a new target is detected. Needless to say, procedures vary with the conditions; these are just typical steps in the process. As we shall see in the discussion of Rule 19 discussion in Chapter 12, the rules on maneuvering procedures are different in clear weather, when you can see targets visually, than in restricted visibility, when you see targets only by radar.

The Call to Action

STEP 1. When the target first appears, turn on the Plot option (or mark it by hand if your radar does not have that option). Remember, if you have selected a 6-minute wake trail, you may not be able to evaluate target SRM until the full 6 minutes has elapsed, even though a part of a trail is showing. That trail may grow in length throughout the 6-minute interval if started from scratch or if the target has just moved onto the screen. You could note from the plot clock when 3 minutes have passed and try for an earlier analysis, as described above.

A distant target on a larger radar range may have to be watched for some time in order to evaluate its wake trail; 6 minutes may be too short a wake period. You may have to set it longer or even make it continuous for an early identification. Also note that if the trail is coming out from under a bridge (on smaller ranges), you should wait until the end of the trail is clearly in sight even if the selected 6 minutes has elapsed. Otherwise the speed of the emerging target may be underestimated.

Without a Trail or Plot option, mark the target right on the screen (Chapter 1) and label it with the time. In some cases, it is preferable to mark the screen even if you have the Plot option.

STEP 2. Place an EBL on the target. This EBL is marking the relative motion collision route. Usually the EBL is set up as relative to your heading, so while you remain on constant heading, this EBL is the compass bearing that Rule 7d instructs you to monitor. In cases of special concern, you might also record the range and bearing to the target on paper, in case the EBL might be needed for some other operation or

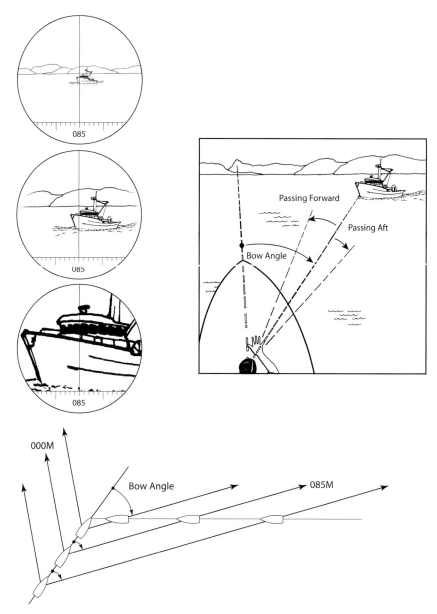

Figure 6-10. *Evaluating risk of collision without radar. A compass in a pair of binoculars is one way to monitor target bearings; in good conditions, bearing changes of just a few degrees can be detected this way. In the top left sequence of bearing observations, the vessel being watched with the binoculars has actually pulled slightly forward, since we first saw its pilothouse aft of 085 and now the pilothouse is at 085. However, this is still a risk-of-collision situation that requires special care. Rule 7d (ii) addresses this.*

If we remain on a constant heading and do not move around on deck while watching, the bearing can also be monitored by watching the bow angle relative to structures on our boat or by hand. A constant bow angle means a collision course; a target moving forward on the bow will pass ahead; a target moving aft on the bow will pass astern (top right). Bow angles are often convenient and adequate for the job, but they clearly are not as precise as compass bearings, which are not affected by our position on deck or by course changes.

If the compass bearing to a target does not change as the target approaches, that target is on a collision course with us (bottom).

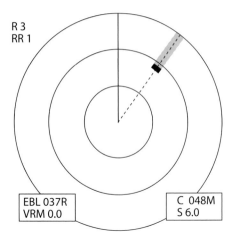

R 3
RR 1

EBL 037R
VRM 0.0

C 048M
S 6.0

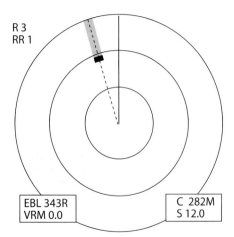

R 3
RR 1

EBL 343R
VRM 0.0

C 282M
S 12.0

Figure 6-11. *View of the interaction shown in Figure 6-10 as seen on the radar of each vessel. The bottom radar is from the vessel that is being watched in the binoculars. The vessels are clearly approaching on a collision course so an appropriate maneuver will be called for on the part of at least one of the vessels.*

you have any reason to think it might move. Modern radars have two EBLs for this purpose.

STEP 3. The radar is now set up, and the next job is to start looking for the target visually. You have its bearing and distance, which should help. If the target is distant, look for it with binoculars. Tell others in the pilothouse or cockpit about the traffic and where to look. It is always important to find the target visually as soon as possible.

STEP 4. Back to the radar. As soon as a clear trail or wake can be discerned, you can start predicting risk. If the target trail is moving off the EBL to cross the heading line, then it will pass in front of you. If moving aft of the EBL, it will pass behind you. Targets moving straight down the EBL are on a collision course, at least potentially. When a target is first observed, however, it is often difficult to determine its course precisely, so more data must be gained until its course is clear. In this step you are just noting whether the vessel is passing in front or in back, or is a potential collision risk, traveling down the EBL. See Figure 6-12.

Note that you might be tempted to adjust the Gain at this point to optimize the picture, but when watching specific trails for risk of collision this should be done judiciously. If you turn up the Gain too high, even for just a moment, the background can get bright with noise; all that random noise will paint trails across your screen and you might lose your actual target trail and have to start again.

STEP 5. For those targets that are definitely moving off the EBL, the next step is to determine how close they would pass if each held its course and speed. In other words, you need to find each target's *closest point of approach* (CPA). This is a fundamental step in radar observation. If the CPA is not a safe distance, you may need to maneuver, or stand by in anticipation of the other vessel's maneuver, depending on the situation according to the *Rules*. In any event, you must navigate with special caution.

The procedure is to project the target's wake trail forward until it crosses your heading line or passes astern. From this projected path you can determine two things: when the target will cross your course line and when it will reach its CPA. These are generally not the same, as shown in Figure 6-13, which also shows ways to

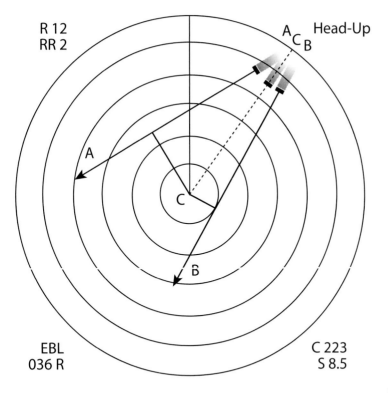

R 12
RR 2

Head-Up

EBL
036 R

C 223
S 8.5

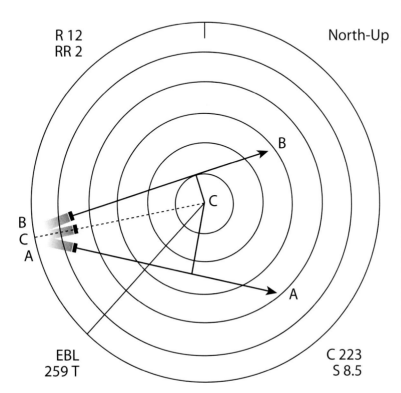

R 12
RR 2

North-Up

EBL
259 T

C 223
S 8.5

Figure 6-12. *Using EBL to evaluate risk of collision. At 11 miles off we detect a target and set the EBL on it. If it moves as shown for target A, it will pass in front of us and the closest point of approach (CPA) will be about 5 miles. If it moves as shown for target B, it will pass astern with a CPA of about 2 miles; when it actually crosses the stern it would be about 4 miles off. If it moves as shown for target C, or near to that, it definitely poses a risk of collision and must be monitored closely so that appropriate action can be taken. As stressed in the text, however, it is often difficult to ascertain the actual projected path and CPA for a distant target, especially without a stabilized radar display (north-up or course-up). The top screen shows a head-up display; the bottom screen shows a north-up display. With north-up or course-up displays, we must always think relative to the heading line, not the top of the radar screen.*

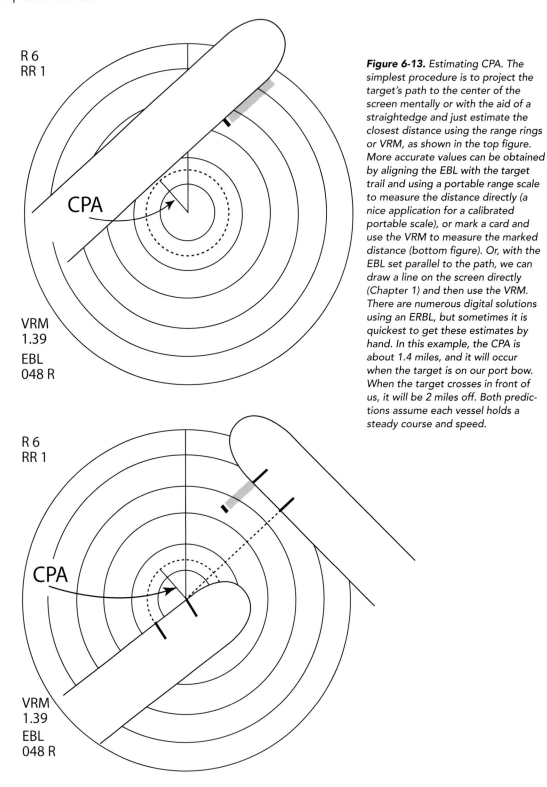

R 6
RR 1

CPA

VRM
1.39
EBL
048 R

R 6
RR 1

CPA

VRM
1.39
EBL
048 R

Figure 6-13. *Estimating CPA. The simplest procedure is to project the target's path to the center of the screen mentally or with the aid of a straightedge and just estimate the closest distance using the range rings or VRM, as shown in the top figure. More accurate values can be obtained by aligning the EBL with the target trail and using a portable range scale to measure the distance directly (a nice application for a calibrated portable scale), or mark a card and use the VRM to measure the marked distance (bottom figure). Or, with the EBL set parallel to the path, we can draw a line on the screen directly (Chapter 1) and then use the VRM. There are numerous digital solutions using an ERBL, but sometimes it is quickest to get these estimates by hand. In this example, the CPA is about 1.4 miles, and it will occur when the target is on our port bow. When the target crosses in front of us, it will be 2 miles off. Both predictions assume each vessel holds a steady course and speed.*

estimate the CPA. If you conclude that these distances are safe, then in many cases you are done—except for continuing to watch to see that nothing changes—assuming that each vessel maintains course and speed. If anything changes, the evaluation must be done again. You should watch every passing vessel until you are well separated and on safe courses. This brings up the next step of determining the time of passing.

STEP 6. In most passing situations it pays to compute the time of CPA. That is, how long do you have from your present observation time until the time of closest approach? If you have computed the target's SRM and measured its present distance from you, the time to CPA is simply that range divided by the SRM. If the target vessel is crossing your bow, you may also choose to compute the time of crossing, which will be somewhat before the time of CPA, unless it is a beam target.

Though you can calculate these times from range and SRM, it is often adequate to estimate them from the wake trails already showing on the radar screen. If you are using a 12-minute trail, for example, and note that the target is about one trail length from crossing your heading line, then you know that the target will cross ahead in about 1 x 12, or 12 minutes, as shown in Figure 6-14. The time of CPA in this example would be about 6 minutes after that.

STEP 7. If the target is still tracking down the EBL, you are on a potential collision course and must be prepared

to maneuver. Depending on the circumstances, one or both of you will have to maneuver. We cover related rules for maneuvering in Chapter 12. The key issue here is that you should not maneuver before knowing for certain what is taking place. This is one of the main reasons for sighting traffic targets visually as soon as possible. In clear weather, you can usually tell the *aspect* of the vessel (which way it is headed relative to you) from a visual sighting sooner and more precisely than you can with radar. Vessel aspect is discussed further in Chapter 11.

As we will see in Chapter 12, one of the requirements of the *Rules* is that you do not maneuver on the basis of "scanty radar information." Not knowing the relative course of an approaching vessel is definitely scanty information. This is especially crucial for head-on

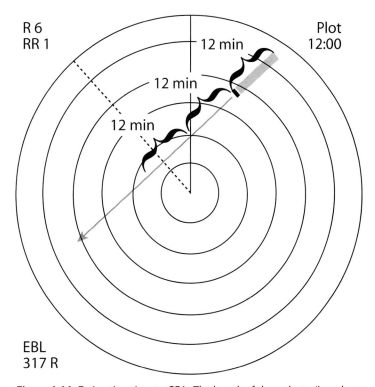

Figure 6-14. Estimating time to CPA. The length of the wake trail can be used as a time interval for predicting crossing times or CPAs. A portable range scale or marks on a card can be used to transfer the distances. In this example, the wake is 12 minutes, so the target will cross in front of us in about 12 minutes and will pass the CPA another 6 minutes or so after that.

targets in clear weather. For example, if you simply turn right before establishing the actual course of a target approaching from ahead, you might be turning toward the path of a vessel that would otherwise pass safely on your right side. Generally speaking, in clear weather you will be able to tell the course of a vessel while there is still plenty of time to maneuver safely and according to the rules.

In restricted visibility, on the other hand, the rules are different, and they generally call for earlier maneuvers. See the Rule 19 discussion in Chapter 12.

In clear *or* restricted visibility, it may be prudent to use your VHF radio on low power to attempt to contact the other vessel if you have any doubts about the passing. With your radar observations already made, you are in a position to be precise in your communications. For example, "Large vessel 4.7 miles on my starboard bow, this is the sailing vessel . . .," or some similar appropriate wording. The hailed vessel now knows precisely where to set its radar range to look for you if it has not already seen you. Related procedures, maneuvering guidelines, and a few sea stories are presented in Chapter 12. As a preview of that chapter, note that in fog, observing and maneuvering by radar alone, the *Navigation Rules* do not distinguish a sailing vessel from a power-driven vessel for this interaction. A ship learning of your position this way will most likely activate its ARPA computations (Chapter 8) to evaluate the interaction. These will require at least a minute or so for rough estimates, and up to 3 minutes for accurate values—presuming they have a steady echo from you on their radar screen, meaning you are not being obscured periodically by wave echoes.

NORTH-UP VERSUS HEAD-UP IN TRAFFIC OBSERVATIONS

Throughout the above discussion we have tried to word the observations in a manner that applies to both head-up and north-up modes, as well as course-up mode. In particular, we have described target motion relative to the heading line rather than to the top or bottom of the screen. The traditional terminology of up-screen or down-screen targets becomes confusing when the heading line is pointed to the southeast, as it might be when operating in north-up mode. See Chapter 7 for a more general discussion of the north-up option.

In a steady situation when you are not changing course, it is sometimes easier to decipher relative motions from a head-up display. But this advantage becomes compromised when you maneuver to avoid collision or to open up a passing distance. In head-up mode, when you turn one way all the targets move the other way, and their respective trails show a large kink at the turning point. The beauty of north-up mode with regard to evaluating collision risk is that the target trails remain constant as you turn. When you turn, your heading line turns on the screen but the land and the moving targets with all their trails remain unchanged. The picture is said to be *stabilized*, because, with the use of the required heading sensor input, the orientation of the radar images can be compensated for changes in vessel heading. With a stabilized display, you will be able to interpret the wake directions much more quickly, especially in a sailing vessel at sea in big waves. This can be a big advantage when evaluating collision risk in some conditions, because you also do not have to wait as long for target trails to rebuild themselves after you turn in order to see the effect of your maneuver. Figure 6-15 shows a situation with three vessel targets on the screen before and just after a right turn of 60° in both north-up and head-up display. Figures 6-16 and 6-17 show similar maneuvers with land on the screen and the new target trails developed after the turn.

When using north-up mode, it is important to evaluate target motions based on how they move relative to your own heading line. It is obviously important to maintain unambiguous communications with those in the pilothouse

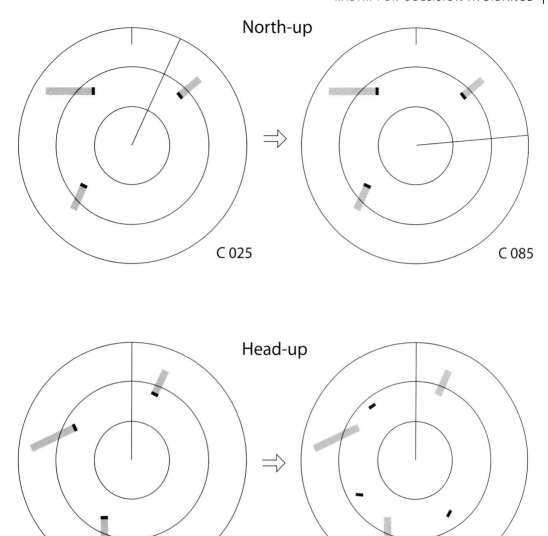

Figure 6-15. *Radar screens just before and just after a 60° right turn in north-up and head-up display. There are three vessel targets in sight, and no land. As time passes after the turn, the trails will rebuild from the positions shown.*

about the display mode on the radar. The pictures look and behave differently in the two modes. Once again, the common radar terms *up-screen* and *down-screen* always refer to motions relative to the heading line. This will come into play in Chapter 11 when we discuss Rules of Thumb for predicting target behavior in response to our maneuvers.

Course-up mode behaves essentially like north-up mode except that the user has the freedom to place the present heading of the vessel at the top of the screen in place of true north. It is often an excellent compromise for those used to navigating with head-up alone, offering both the virtues of a stabilized display—target images do not shift and smear in response to

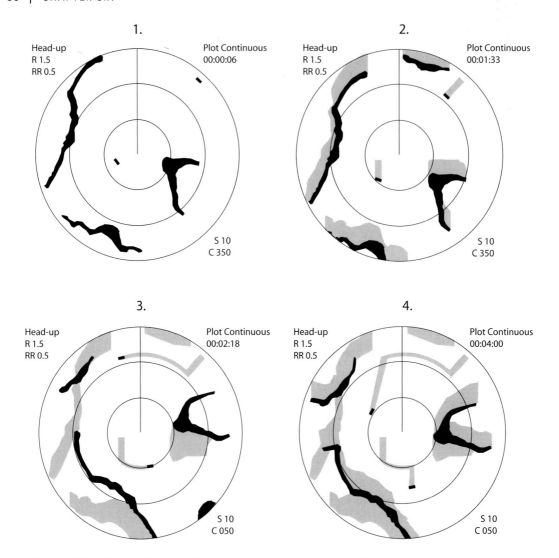

Figure 6-16. *Behavior of target trails in head-up display mode. Screen 1 shows two targets just 6 seconds after turning on the Plot option. After 1 minute, 33 seconds (screen 2), we see clear trails from each target as well as that of the land. The port quarter target has a trail length matching that of the land and it is moving straight down the heading line. It must be either a buoy or vessel that is not moving. The starboard bow target is a definite threat with a CPA near zero. Its trail is slightly longer than the buoy, so its SRM is slightly larger than our speed. Referring to Figure 6-13, we see that we have about 3 minutes left (plot clock time of about 00:04:00) before we will be in close vicinity to this target.*

After watching for a total of about 2 minutes, we turn 60° to the right and then see screen 3 a bit later. In head-up mode, all the land turns with us (the opposite way) and we can see a trail marking our turn. (The amount of the turning trail that might be visible depends on how fast we turn.) Holding a steady course of 050, we see the new trails develop (screen 4). The buoy is still moving straight down the heading line, but now on our starboard quarter.

Note that the DRM of the target before our turn was about 230 R, and that after its big shift to the left, its new DRM is about 195 R. Our turn opened up the CPA to about 0.5 nm. In Chapter 11 we discuss Rules of Thumb for predicting this general behavior and procedures for making predictions.

We could have restarted the Plot option after making the turn to clean up the screen, but that may not be a good choice if we are watching other approaching targets at the same time. Compare this display with the north-up mode in Figure 6-17.

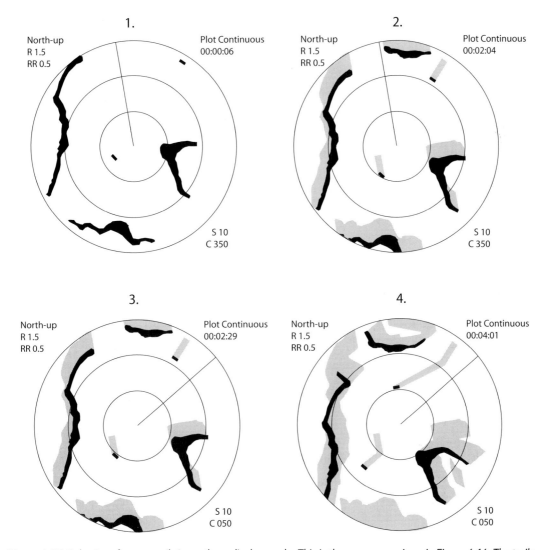

Figure 6-17. *Behavior of target trails in north-up display mode. This is the same scenario as in Figure 6-16. The trails of both targets and land are actually the same, except that the large shift in the picture at the turn is gone. This is the big advantage of north-up mode. Screens 1 and 2 are identical to 6-16 except that the picture is rotated to put north at the top, and our heading line is now pointed to our heading of 350. (We were also on 350 in head-up mode.)*

Things are much different, however, when we make the turn at about 2 minutes into the plot. Right after the turn, screen 3 is essentially identical to screen 2 except that the heading line now points to 050, reflecting our 60° turn to the right. The bearing to the buoy again shifts from port quarter to starboard quarter, but it does not move on the radar screen. The subsequent buoy trail at this point will also turn to maintain its straight path down the new heading line. The target trail will also shift slightly to reflect its new relative motion. The land all remains in place, and target trails shift directions without large, distracting shifts in position. With several targets on the screen, it can sometimes take a while to reidentify all the targets you see after a large turn in head-up mode. This problem disappears with north-up and course-up displays.

A course-up display would behave the same way as this one, except that the heading line might be more verti-cal if the course-up mode had been recently engaged. If the course-up mode were engaged, and then a 10° turn to the left was made (regardless of actual heading), the scenario would look identical to what is shown here.

Note that in either display mode, if we are moving and see a target moving straight down the heading line and then we make a big turn and it is still moving straight down the heading line, then it must be dead in the water.

normal heading variations—and the value of having relative bearings to vessels and landmarks correspond with what you see around you.

One issue to keep an eye on is the stability of the stabilizing system itself. In course-up or north-up modes, all target wakes are oriented relative to your heading line. In normal operation they behave in a predictable manner, even if the resulting pattern is complex (Figure 6-17). But if the heading sensor loses communication with the radar for any reason, or sends a false heading, then the heading line temporarily shifts and the wakes get drawn in for a few sweeps in the entirely wrong place. This generally calls for resetting the plot clock and start-ing new trails. Since the trails are crucial to evaluating risk of collision, if this happens too frequently, a technician should check out the system.

In any event, it takes practice to get used to thinking along the heading line for those whose experience is mostly with the head-up mode. The same quandary can occur in tight-quarters radar navigation in general, regardless of traffic concerns. When you sail with others, they might determine the display mode in use, and certainly when you replace equipment you will be faced with the newest technology. Other aspects of these display mode options are presented in Chapter 7.

PART 2
BEYOND
THE BASICS

Part Two contains more details and special topics. Some of Part Two depends on basics presented in Part One; other material is independent information, added for completeness.

Installation, Specifications, and Performance

In this chapter we distinguish between the technical specifications of the radar unit that determine its performance and the features that affect its use. Broadly speaking, today's most basic radar unit has most of the advanced features and options—such as north-up display, GPS interfacing, electronic range and bearing lines, zooming, mini-ARPA, and others discussed below and in Chapter 8—that were only found on advanced ship radars a few years ago.

This means that when you invest in a higher-end radar unit, you are really paying for better performance rather than new features. Here we cover a few radar beam specifications that significantly affect performance, and other options that might influence your choice among radar units.

Most radar units could be installed and configured by an industrious boatowner willing to follow instructions. But if there is any instrument for which you might seek assistance from a professional electronics technician, radar is the one. A system that includes assistance with installation, alignment, and initial internal adjustments is definitely one to consider. This chapter also includes notes on installation that should help with communication and collaboration with professional installers. There are pros and cons unique to every vessel on these matters, so background on the basic issues is helpful.

Note that you do not need an FCC station license for your radios or radar unless:

1. the vessel carries more than six passengers for hire; or
2. the radio operates on medium or high frequencies (SSB); or
3. the ship sails to foreign ports (including Canada and Mexico); or
4. the ship is larger than 300 gross tons and is required to carry a radio station for safety purposes.

If your vessel is in any of these categories, contact the FCC (see the References section).

INSTALLATION
Antenna Mounting Options

One issue that arises when adding radar to a vessel is where the antenna should be mounted. The height of the antenna is an important factor in how far the radar can see, so within reasonable limits your first choice would be to mount the antenna as high as possible. This is a good guideline for most powerboats, but on a sailing vessel you could mount the antenna too high on the mast, compromising radar and sailing performance, if elevation is the sole consideration.

The main difference between a high antenna on a powerboat versus a sailboat is the stability of the location. If a radar is mounted 50 feet high on a power-driven vessel, then the vessel must be fairly large and chances are the radar antenna will remain vertical and roughly 50 feet high throughout its operation in most seaways. If you mount a radar antenna 50 feet up the mast on a sailboat, then the radar will be going on a roller-coaster ride when you are going to weather in a seaway, which could cause increased stresses on both the antenna components and the rigging. Actual effects on stability and sailing performance are discussed below.

All installations should have a clear view of the horizon in all directions and be positioned so the emitted radar beam itself is above the normal locations of crew and passengers. For powerboats, a cabin top or instrument arch is the obvious choice. For a sailing vessel, the choice is usually between a mast or backstay mount versus a post or arch mount. Various options are shown in Figure 7-1.

Sailboat owners should also consider the op-

tion of a gimballed mount or one that can be manually tilted so the radar beam remains parallel to the horizon when the vessel heels. Some related issues of mounting are discussed below; the main issue of heeling angle effect on radar performance is discussed in Chapter 8.

The antenna can be mounted higher on a sailboat when on the mast or backstay, but the gain in radar range must be balanced by performance. Also, when considering the height factor, keep in mind that the radar range depends on the square root of the antenna height and is not directly proportional to the actual height (Chapter 3). An antenna mounted on a post 16 feet above the water has a radar range to the horizon of 4.8 nm in standard atmos-

Most Common Installation Problems

According to radar repair departments, some 50 percent of all installation problems come from radar antenna cable damage during the installation: premade cables that were taken apart and then not put back together properly; or cables damaged by pulling them through areas that pierce the cable, causing shorts in the cable components. These cables come in fixed lengths and you may be tempted to shorten them or remove a connector to lead it more easily.

(A related, more general issue to keep in mind is to use extreme care when using a sharp blade to cut loose electronics cables from plastic ties to replace or rerun them. It takes just a microscopic nick into the cable to reach the shielding. If the shielding is thus minutely exposed, the cable will work fine for some period of time, but if exposed to salt water it will quickly corrode and ruin the cable from within. It might take just long enough to get you into the middle of the ocean . . .)

The next most common radar installation problems are setups and interfacing with other equipment. Radars are so packed with features these days that it can be a challenge for users new to electronic interfacing to follow the conventions on signal format and compatibility, not to mention connector types, NMEA sentence structures, and so on, especially when combining units from different manufacturers.

Another common installation problem can often be traced to inadequate power management on the vessel. If the ship's batteries get overcharged, they can send surges to the radar that can damage the unit. Modern electronics require careful power management.

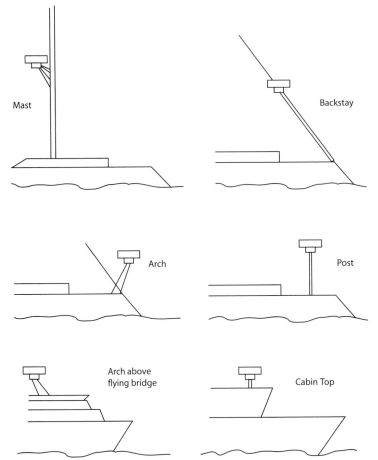

Figure 7-1. *Antenna mounting options for sailboats (mast, backstay, arch, post) and for powerboats (arch, cabin top). Backstay mounts can be forward or aft of the backstay.*

to those with high-performance racing yachts. To obtain the most competitive advantage in local racing (Chapter 11), the yacht should have as good an antenna as possible, so it will not have the lightest, smallest unit. For example, on a 40-foot racing yacht with carbon fiber mast, a quality radar antenna could weigh 20 percent of the entire mast weight. On a typical cruising boat or recreational racer, this will not be the case, and chances are other factors will determine where the radar is placed.

To get a quantitative idea of the effect on sailing performance, we contacted Robert Perry Yacht Designers. They kindly agreed to run their velocity prediction program on a typical 43-foot racing yacht (23,000 pounds displacement) with and without radar on the mast. It was suggested that the post mount was effectively moving weight to the quarter, which would not affect computed performance, and in fact might even help performance in some cases. Thus comparing no radar and a mast radar would be a reasonable comparison of the two mounting options.

Computations were done for 30 pounds and 50 pounds at both 20 feet and 30 feet, and there was hardly any difference in the results, so we chose to use the extreme of 50 pounds at 30 feet for the final comparisons. This overestimates the specifications in both height and

pheric conditions. If you mount it on the mast 30 feet above the water, the range is only 6.6 nm, so you would gain only 1.8 nm in radar range to the horizon.

An obvious question at this point is how or why the radar can claim a 16- or 24-mile range when the radar beam hits the horizon at 4 to 6 miles off? The answer is that it will be seeing things that stick up above the horizon, such as an 80-foot-tall ship or a 500-foot-tall coastal bluff. For more on this, see Chapter 3.

The full effect on sailing performance of mounting a radar antenna high on the mast is not easy to quantify, and is mostly of interest weight—a modern 2-foot radar dome with mount, bolts, and cables would weigh about 30 pounds—but it is still a reasonable basis for this computation.

The radar raised the vertical center of gravity by 0.8 inch on this vessel, which led to a speed reduction of about 0.03 kt when sailing to weather in winds above 14 kts. This translates into about 2 seconds per mile in a handicap rating computation. That is certainly not anything a cruising sailor would care about, but a racing sailor might. Bob reminded me of the basics: "If everything else is equal, the crew without socks will win the race." Factors the velocity program cannot compute, for example, include the effect on the pitching moment, and the effect of extra windage and weight aloft on mast stress in high winds or fast rolling seas. The heel-angle limit of positive stability decreased slightly from 122° to 120°, which was not a surprise since putting 50 pounds at 30 feet up the mast on this boat would take about 205 pounds more

lead in the keel to regain its original righting moment.

In short, actual numerical arguments against a high mast mount are not very strong, even for a racing yacht, but it seems there are few virtues that would override potential drawbacks. Numerical values of how the elevation of the antenna might limit the minimum detectable target range are presented later in this chapter. A radar on a post in the starboard quarter might be the best option for many sailing vessels that do not have an antenna arch installed. The cost is likely comparable to a mast mount if the mast has to be pulled for the installation. The post height would only need to be high enough to ensure that the vertical beam angle remains safely overhead of crew positions located near the antenna, as illustrated in Figure 7-2. Ten feet or so above the deck might be a common average. The post could also be used to mount other antennas and it allows for manual or electric leveling of the antenna, if de-

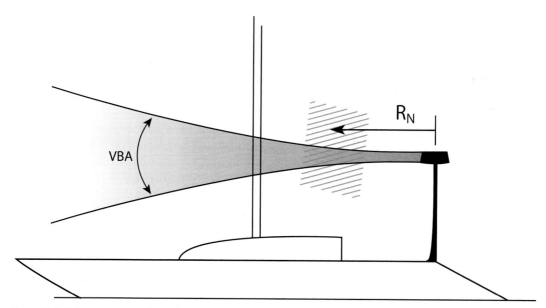

Figure 7-2. Schematic view of a radar beam across a vessel from an antenna of a given height. The approximate profile of the beam can be estimated from a scale drawing of the boat using some estimate of the range to the end of the near field (R$_N$), where the beam starts to diverge, together with the vertical beam angle (VBA) of the antenna. The latter is between 20° and 30° (see your antenna specifications); the former can be estimated from the width of the antenna (Figure 7-21).

sired. Sample mounts are shown later in Figure 8-4.

Powerboaters also want to keep in mind crew or passenger locations when installing the radar. Regardless of our thoughts on radiation safety (discussed below) we see many installations that are simply too close to the crew by any standard, not to mention cases where entire portions of the horizon are blocked out by obstructions.

Sailors who choose to use mini-ARPA for automatic tracking of target vessels (discussed in Chapter 8) should consider some form of antenna-leveling mount. The ARPA system requires clean, sharp, and stable targets. If a target is lost for just one or two sweeps, there will be a time delay to acquire the target again and analyze its motion. A gimballed antenna or one you can mechanically tilt as needed will be more successful for this application, especially on a smaller sailing yacht.

Backstay mounts are another option for sailboats. These are usually third-party products (i.e., not sold by the radar companies themselves) and vary significantly in price by model and manufacturer. In some cases, a high-end gimballed backstay mount may cost almost as much as a low-end radar. They are often mounted higher than post mounts and lower than mast mounts. It is definitely an attractive option for a sailing vessel, but one that should be researched by interviewing both manufacturers and users of the products to investigate their operation in the conditions you intend to use them. Backstay mounts are mostly all gimballed, whereas mast mounts are rarely gimballed, although options to do so are available. Post or arch mounts can be fixed or gimballed, or you can devise some scheme of leveling the antenna manually when you tack the boat. We have seen the latter arrangement done with electric trim-tab controllers, or mechanical plates that rotate and are pinned in place by

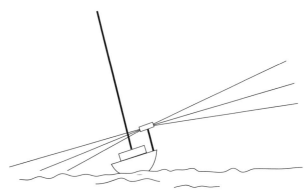

Figure 7-3. *When a sailing vessel is heeled over, an unleveled radar can miss some sweeps to weather and see more sea clutter to leeward. Due to the motion of the boat, however, targets are rarely lost completely.*

hand. Chapter 8 includes a discussion of heeling on radar performance. Figure 7-3 illustrates the concern at hand.

When mounting on the mast, you cannot avoid some shadowing as the unit will be in front of the mast. This is generally not a problem when the mast is narrower than the width of the antenna. The blind spot will be rather narrow and covered by the normal motion of the vessel along its course. You should be careful, however, about mounting it in line with the spreaders (or any other *horizontal* obstruction), since this would indeed block out the aft signal.

When mounting on a post or arch and you have the option of placing the unit on the port or starboard side, the starboard side might be better if there is any shadowing present. The starboard bow quadrant is generally the area you might want to monitor most carefully. Vessels coming from this quadrant often are the stand-on vessel, so if your view across the bow is compromised in any way, you should rig for the best view to starboard. In most configurations, this is a minor issue.

If your installation is on a planing powerboat with some bow rise to your trim at cruising speed, then you might consider installing the unit on a wedge to have it level at cruising trim.

Figure 7-4. Sample radar installations. The top and middle are on a sailing vessel, in the cockpit, under the dodger, and at the nav station. The one under the dodger is a removable, waterproof repeater that can also be used for full radar controls. The bottom shows a mount at the wheel of a powerboat. This mounting offers good viewing in varying light conditions and comfortable operations. It is to the right of the wheel, so others can view and operate the radar without interfering with the helmsman. See also Figure 3-12.

Installers are familiar with this issue and commercial mounts are available. It will enhance the performance when going fast and not hurt it when going slow.

Control and Display Location

The location of the radar unit within the nav station or pilothouse also deserves careful consideration. Since radar has a central role in vessel navigation, it deserves a central place in your console of navigation instruments and readouts. Figure 7-4 shows sample installations.

It is best to have the radar placed so that when you look at it, you are looking at the bow. This is usually not an issue in the typical powerboat pilothouse, but it can be a problem in the often cramped nav stations of sailing vessels. In any vessel, navigation is always simpler when you are properly oriented with your radar. The nav station can face any direction, and in sailboat nav stations it often faces the side. You will become accustomed to this, but if you are designing from scratch, you may have more options than those who are adding radar to an existing nav station. I have navigated on several large sailing vessels with the nav station facing aft or abeam, and in my experience, when you get tired it takes longer to figure out which way to look for targets with this radar orientation. Remember that the advantage of the basic head-up display mode is that the heading line is straight up on the screen, parallel to the centerline, *and pointing in the direction you are heading*. When you orient the radar so that this no longer applies, you lose this basic convenience, and with it the opportunity for a quick reality check if the more sophisticated display modes should become confusing. (North-up, course-up, and true motion modes, discussed below, typically have the heading line pointing in some diagonal orientation on the radar screen.)

The elevation and orientation of the radar unit is more controllable in most installations.

It is best if you are comfortable when viewing and operating the instrument. Often an overhead mount or one above your line of sight offers good use of space and a convenient viewing angle, but it should be tested before being permanently installed. Be sure it is comfortable to look at and adjust over an extended period of time. If the elevation is just slightly off, it can be uncomfortable to view and operate. Remember, radar is an instrument that you will often use for studying details, adjusting the picture, measuring bearings, and sometimes looking for faint or hard to discern features. I have seen some installations that seemed fine at the dock, but once underway there was nothing to hold onto while rolling about in a seaway and trying to adjust and read the radar.

If there are two people sharing navigation duties, then it is common to have one at the helm and one at the radar. But be aware of possible problems. For example, I have seen a very elaborate navigation station that was ideal for single-handing. All the instruments were within convenient view, wrapped around the helmsman's seat with the radar centrally located. But when the helmsman was at his station, no one else could see the radar! This arrangement was not good for shared nav duty, and could limit both the safety and enjoyment of a voyage.

Powerboaters who mount the radar in the pilothouse also have to take compass distance into account. A large cathode ray tube (CRT) radar can create a compass disturbance that extends out several feet, limiting the location of the radar unit. The radar cable running under the dash or chart-table shelf could affect instruments above it, even though the unit is some distance off. Check the radar manual for compass-safe distances for all components of your radar installation. If in doubt, use a small handheld compass to investigate the magnetic fields near the radar unit. This is not usually an issue for sailors, since, in most sailboats, the radar is located at the nav station belowdeck and the main steering compass is in the cockpit.

Sailors do have the issue of actually seeing the radar (down at the nav station) while steering the boat from the wheel in the cockpit. This remains an issue to be solved. For sailboat navigation in close quarters or traffic that requires radar work, it is definitely convenient to have two people who can share the helm and navigation roles.

For those who want to prepare for solo sailing, there are options. I have used two styles of radar mounts that were on large pivot mechanisms that allowed the radar unit to rotate for viewing from the nav station or from the cockpit. In one case the rotation put the radar screen in front of a large port light in the bulkhead facing the helmsman; the other rotated the face of the unit directly into the companionway. In both cases, the radar could be seen from the wheel but, in my opinion, neither was a very satisfactory solution since the radar viewing was compromised in both positions.

The best solution might be one of the new waterproof units or repeaters that can be mounted in sight from the wheel of a sailboat or on the flying bridge of a powerboat. Currently, some repeater displays can cost as much as a primary radar unit, but this is changing. Most small-craft radar units are waterproof, so mounting the unit on a cabin top under the dodger of a sailing vessel is a good solution for a helmsman-navigator. Others can sit next to it for more careful inspection and there are hand-held remote controls the helmsman can use underway to change the Range, adjust the Gain, and so on. When the unit includes charts as well (Chapter 8), the issue of comparing chart and radar images is also accommodated in this outside location.

Another option is the new PC-based radar unit, where the signal from a radar antenna is overlaid on an electronic chart. In this case, the problem is setting up a PC screen so it will be protected from the weather and viewable from the wheel of a sailboat or flying bridge. There are an increasing number of options on the market, as discussed in Chapter 13.

And finally there is the consideration that applies to all types of displays (CRT or LCD, see next section): can you read the screen in bright daylight from your chosen installation location? This may take some well-deserved testing if there is any doubt. It is a potential issue with any CRT as well as any LCDs, except possibly some of the latest, high-end models. Even inside a pilothouse at some times of day on some headings, this could be an issue that needs to be addressed. Special shades might be called for, or variable monitor angles. Installations outside on an open bridge or in the cockpit of a sailing vessel require special care in this regard. It would be very disappointing to discover a problem after the cables have been run.

SPECIFICATIONS
Screen Type: LCD versus CRT

After deciding to install radar on your vessel, the next step is choosing the type of display. There are strong feelings about screen choice floating around among existing users, but many of these opinions may be a bit out of date. There is definitely a difference in how they look and function, and the new LCD units have a very broad range of specifications.

There are two basic types of displays available to small-craft operators. One is the more traditional CRT display, which typically has a black background with bright-green radar images. Up until about 1990, this was the primary option. The newer option for radar display is LCD, or liquid crystal display. We go over the differences below, but we must note immediately that LCD technology is changing rapidly. Differences that were prominent five years ago are not as prominent now, and will certainly be less so in the future. In the not too distant future there will not be any CRT options available for new radar units.

In light of today's options, you should not choose a radar based on screen display alone;

you must also consider the unit's features, size, power consumption, interfacing capabilities, and price. Users may well find that certain enhanced options in one model outweigh the issue of display alone. Figure 7-5 summarizes properties of the two types of display.

Some years ago, it might have been appropriate to compare these as raster scans (for LCD) versus analog displays (for CRT). You might still see this terminology in some radar publications but it is no longer appropriate for modern radars. These days, both LCD and CRT are considered raster displays, meaning the radar image is not painted directly onto the screens in a rotating continuum of positions (analog) but instead is created and stored briefly within the electronics of the unit as a digital bitmap and then displayed in rasters, or rows of pixels, similar to computer images. The radial sweeps are still visibly going around the screens, but the pictures in both LCD and CRT displays are actually drawn very rapidly in horizontal sweeps from top to bottom of the screens.

The difference in radar display options these days is more like comparing an (older) desktop computer monitor (CRT) to that of a laptop computer display (LCD) or the new flat-panel desktop monitors. The practical distinctions are resolution, color depth, and luminosity, day and night visibility (bright enough to see with the sun shining on the screen and dim enough at night to not interfere with night vision), as well as the physical size of the unit, its power requirements, and cost. And since LCD technology is advancing so rapidly, chances are what we say here could soon be outdated—in five or six years there likely will not be any more CRTs on the market for any application. Many business offices are already in the process of exchanging their standard workhorse CRT computer monitors with flat-panel LCDs. The new monitors are much nicer to work with and take up less space, and it won't be long till they are superior to CRTs in every regard.

Color versus Monochrome Display. The question of color versus monochrome display extends beyond the radar itself in most cases, since the display is often shared with charts and the depth sounder. The charts and depth sounder are definitely best in color, and more information can be conveyed on the radar screen with a color display. Confining the question to radar alone complicates the issue. The combination of brilliance, contrast, and hue controls allows for a very flexible design of the screen presentation. It is easy to set up distinct differences in the display for day and night use, and it is easy make the echo trails very distinct from actual live targets. But is it a matter of personal choice as to whether this flexibility adds to or distracts from your radar usage. It is likely that when relying on the chart and depth sounder functions of a combined unit, it would be worth adapting to the virtues of the color radar, but for a unit with radar alone the monochrome might be preferred by some navigators. Color displays are generally more expensive at present, but this is likely to change with time.

Besides the option to make unique and beneficial color schemes, you can also adjust the various options into almost unusable color patterns. If that should happen, there are always the default settings to fall back on. With your own unit there will be time to learn the optimum settings, but this may not be something to dive into when visiting on someone else's vessel!

Radar Beam Specifications

The invisible electromagnetic radar beam that sweeps around the horizon every few seconds has a very specific shape and frequency pattern. Basic knowledge of this beam structure helps us understand the capabilities and limitations of radar observations, which in turn can help with more effective radar operation.

We have already discussed one basic aspect of the radiation pattern—the signal is line of sight. While it does bend vertically very slightly over the sea horizon due to refraction, it does

Figure 7-5.

COMPARISON OF CRT AND LCD MONITORS FOR RADAR APPLICATIONS

Property	CRT	LCD
computer analogy	like an older desktop monitor or TV tube	like a laptop monitor or flat-screen TV
quality range in radar applications	narrow; most behave about the same way	very broad; newer designs have much better resolution, brightness, contrast, and especially backlighting than older ones
unit size for same viewing area	large, almost cube-like in shape	smaller, much flatter
weight	heavy	light
target intensity determined by . . .	number and brightness of pixels	number and color of pixels
waterproof	generally not waterproof	can be waterproof
viewing angle	wide; can be seen from the side	monochrome are narrower, best seen head-on; new TFT units have excellent viewing angles
static electricity	can be extensive	very little
magnetic disturbance	can be extensive	generally less, but some models need clearance as well
power consumption	large relative to older LCDs	total radar use will be just slightly less, but standby power savings will be better when monochrome monitor is left on; however, new backlit TFTs can draw even more current than CRTs
bright daylight viewing	can be poor	generally good in newer units; backlighting is the key—above 800 nits is good
nighttime viewing	excellent; has high contrast in normal to low light	good in newer units, poor in older ones
colors	color and monochrome	color, multiple shades, and monochrome
contrast adjustment	excellent	good in newer units, poor in older ones
viewable screen area	standard	slightly larger than CRT standard in new units, smaller in older units
cost	more than low-end LCDs	less, in general, but may be more for state-of-the-art units
trends	was historically the standard, but on the road to extinction; will not be produced after 2010 for any application	used more and more and likely the standard in the near future as technology improves

not bend horizontally around corners. Another basic behavior of radiation we have relied upon is the fact that it reflects back enough power for detection whenever it strikes an object.

It is technologically impressive. A beam of focused radiation is sent out into space (from a device the size of a breadbox), as much as 20 miles or more, and then whenever it strikes a reasonably large object, enough of the radiation packet is reflected all the way back to the sending antenna that we can detect it and time its transit interval. The returning signal is millions of times weaker when it gets back than when it left, but it is still enough to detect and analyze with sophisticated electronics. It makes us appreciate the radar antenna as much for its detection and amplification capabilities as for its transmission prowess.

The choice of microwave radiation (3 cm wavelength) for radar, as opposed to radio waves (up to a thousand times longer), or visible laser beams (more than a thousand times shorter), has to do with a physics issue and an engineering issue. The physics issue is that radiation has to interact with matter in the right way, meaning good transmission through air along with good reflection from solids. Radio waves have excellent transmission in air, but many solids are essentially transparent to their passage and are not good for reflection. Very short wavelengths, on the other hand, reflect nicely from solids, but are rapidly absorbed in the air. This restriction brings us into the microwave range. The engineering issue is that the radiation beam has to be well focused in order to be used for bearing discrimination. These two issues limited the range to a fairly narrow band of practical wavelengths, and then federal and international regulatory agencies codified the specific limits.

Regarding the engineering challenge—focusing electromagnetic waves into a narrow beam—you need either short wavelengths or large antennas. Considering equipment sizes compatible with typical vessels and the desire

to orient within a degree or so, we end up restricted to radiation in the microwave range. For 3 cm radiation, for example, an antenna 5 feet wide can focus a beam into 1.5°. More of this important relationship is covered in the next section.

Shorter wavelengths could be focused even more, but as the wavelength gets lower, physics comes back into play. Microwave absorption in the atmosphere increases very rapidly for lower wavelengths, so the overall efficiency falls off. There are in fact sharp peaks in the atmospheric absorption of microwave radiation just below and above the selected wavelength.

The main carrier frequency of the radar radiation is 9,345 MHz (megahertz = 10^6 cycles per second), corresponding to a wavelength of 3.2 cm. For any electromagnetic wave, the frequency and wavelength are related by the constant speed of light, $c = 3 \times 10^{10}$ cm/sec = 186,000 miles per second.

frequency (Hz) = c (cm/sec)/wavelength (cm)

and

wavelength (cm) = c (cm/sec)/frequency (Hz)

Microwaves used in ovens, for example, have a frequency of 2,450 MHz, so their wavelength = $3 \times 10^{10}/2.450 \times 10^9$ = 12.2 cm. One-centimeter microwaves used in communications have a frequency = $3 \times 10^{10}/1$ = 30,000 MHz or 30 gigahertz. The overall microwave band is usually thought of as 30 cm to 1 mm wavelengths, corresponding to 1 to 300 GHz in frequency. We might note that the radar band we are discussing (9,300 to 9,500 MHz) is called *X-band radar*. Some ship and shore stations also use, in addition to X-band radar, *S-band radar*, which has a wavelength of about 10 cm with a frequency in the range 2,900 to 3,100 MHz. This type of radar can have a longer range (70 miles or more), but it requires much larger antennas for a focused beam and generally a much higher power requirement. S-band radar is less sensitive to interference from rain and waves, but it has less reflection sensitivity to small targets. Generally ships will switch to their X-band units when navigating inshore or within range of small targets. All small-craft radar units use the X-band frequency corresponding to 3 cm wavelength.

For radar applications, it is more convenient to think of the wave speed (c) in terms of c = 328 yards per microsecond. A microsecond is one millionth of a second, and in 1 microsecond a radar pulse moves 328 yards, which is the same speed as our VHF radio waves, or light from a lightbulb, or X-rays from a dentist's office. All electromagnetic radiation moves at 328 yards per microsecond.

Three centimeters is a good wavelength to focus, transit the atmosphere, scatter, and return. But it cannot radiate in a continuous beam like light waves from a lightbulb. It needs to go out in separated pulses that can travel out, reflect, come back, and be counted before the next pulse goes out and before the radar antenna rotates even a fraction of a degree. Another need for pulse structure is to pack as much energy as possible into each beam pulse so we can look for reflected echoes from large distances away. Output power and radar range are discussed in the next section.

There are two basic aspects to the structure of a radar beam as it moves out across the water. There are the physical dimensions of the beam itself (1° to 6° horizontally and 20° to 30° vertically) and there is the electronic pattern of the electromagnetic wave within this physical shape, as illustrated in Figure 7-6. The physical structure is easy to picture; the electronic structure can only be imagined. The operational implications of the beam dimensions—and details of its shape near the antenna—are discussed in following sections, but for now we are just describing the characteristics of the beam.

Small-craft radars use different pulse structures depending on the range used. Specific val-

ues for various brands are listed in the sample radar manuals on the Radar Resources CD; typical values might be:

PULSE VALUES

Range	Pulse Length	Pulse Rate	Pulse Period
short	0.1 μs (33 yd)	2,100 Hz	486 μs
medium	0.3 μs (98 yd)	1,500 Hz	667 μs
long	1.0 μs (328 yd)	600 Hz	1,667 μs

A pulse pattern is also illustrated in Figure 7-6. The medium-range pulse is on for 0.3 μs and off for 667 μs. If you think of the leading edge of the pulse moving out from the antenna at a speed of 328 yd/μs, we have a pulse that is about 100 yards long, with a space between pulses of about 100 miles.

For a target 12 miles away, that pulse will go out and get scattered back in a roundtrip time of 146 μs, then the next pulse goes out another 520 μs later. In other words, on a microsecond scale, a radar beam is more like a gun shooting bullets at the targets than a hose spraying water on them.

Another way to physically picture what is taking place is to consider that the antenna is rotating typically at the rate of 24 rpm (revolutions per minute), or one revolution every 2.5 seconds. If a typical small-craft radar's horizontal beam width is 4°, then from the time the leading edge of the radar beam strikes a target until the trailing edge of the beam leaves the target will be about (4/360) x 2.5 seconds = 0.028 sec. For the medium-range pulse rates, there are 1,500 pulses per second emitted, or 0.028 x 1,500 = 42 pulses emitted during the time the beam passes that target. Each of these pulses hits the target because each pulse covers the full extent of the wave front (4° x 30°), but it does not mean that we get a return echo from each one. That issue is discussed more in the next section.

One last crucial feature of the radar beam is the quality of its focus. The critical dimension is the horizontal one, parallel to the horizon, as opposed to the vertical profile of the beam. The large vertical extent of the beam helps ensure that we maintain contact with targets as we roll in a seaway, but the precise shape and vertical extent of the beam are generally not crucial to routine operations. The horizontal focusing, on the other hand, is crucial to several aspects of radar operation. It affects the precision of bearings taken, the ability to separate two close targets on the radar screen, and other behaviors of the images at both distant and close ranges. These subjects are covered individually in following sections.

The first point to bear in mind is that the actual definition of the horizontal beam width is relative. When the specifications say, for example, horizontal beam width (HBW) = 4°, there is not a sharp cutoff in the radiation intensity at exactly 2° either side of the center of the beam, but rather the intensity falls off rapidly from the peak value and diminishes to some specified level at HBW/2 away from the center (Figure 7-7). In most cases, HBW is defined in

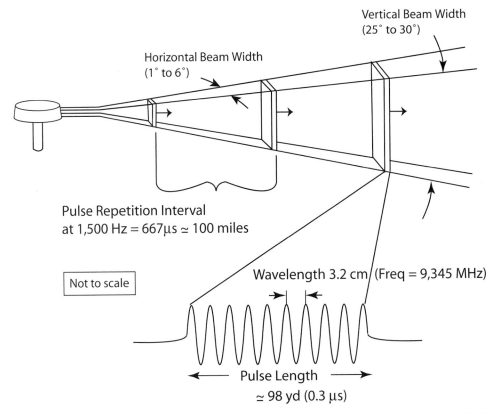

Figure 7-6. *Structure of the radar beam (not to scale) away from the antenna. The top portion shows the physical structure of the beam, which is confined to a conic region a few degrees wide and some 30 degrees tall. The actual boundaries of intensity are not sharp, as shown, but diminish at the edges (see Figure 7-7). The beam itself is not continuous, but is made up of a series of pulses (wave packets) that are very far apart relative to their own dimensions. The example shows a radar emitting 1,500 pulses per second. Each pulse goes out and is scattered back (if it strikes a radar target) long before the next one goes out. Radar pulses travel at the speed of light, as does all electromagnetic radiation. For distant targets, the pulses strike the target as very tall, thin vertical walls of radiation. The structure of the beam close to the antenna is discussed in Chapter 12.*

terms of the half power or 3 db level, which means that about 95 percent of the main beam power is within the specified limits, but there is still some intensity in the wings of the main beam. This can mean that observed target widths might show up on the radar screen somewhat wider than we would expect on the basis of published HBW, especially at lower ranges for smaller antennas.

The second point to bear in mind is that beyond the main beam not being wholly contained within sharp boundaries, the total emitted radar intensity is not wholly contained within a single main beam. The vast majority of the intensity is in the main beam, but there are also unavoidable weak side lobes of intensity that can make themselves apparent when interacting with large targets at close ranges. As with the focusing of the main beam, the wider the antenna, the more these unwanted side lobes are suppressed. An 18-inch antenna might have side-lobe suppression down to –20 db (power ratio of 1:100) whereas a 4-foot antenna might have these side lobes suppressed to –30 db (power ratio of 1:1,000), which is a factor-of-10 improvement in radiated power suppression over the smaller antenna. Side-lobe radiation is illustrated in Figure 7-8 and its influence is discussed further in Chapter 9.

Power Output

Most small-craft radar units come in either a roughly 2 kW or 4 kW peak output power option depending on the maximum range of the unit. Ship radars, on the other hand, might be rated as high as 10 to 25 kW peak output power. This does not mean that any of these radars actually consume that much power. A typical small-craft radar might consume some 30 to 50 watts when running in normal mode, and maybe as low as half to a third of that when operating in Economy or Watch mode, discussed in Chapter 8.

The peak output power is, however, a measure of the strength of the very short pulses of the actual radar beam. It is the initial power content of these pulses that is called the peak output power. It is, in a sense, being stored slowly during the off time of each pulse cycle and is then released in a burst during the pulse itself.

The peak power output ultimately contributes to the maximum usable range of the radar, because the usable intensity diminishes with distance from the antenna; the more you start with, the farther you can reach for echoes.

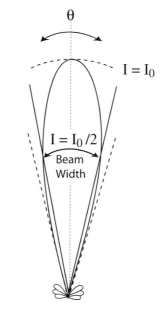
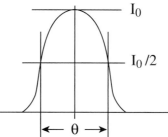

Figure 7-7. *Horizontal beam width defined. The convention used in radar and other radio applications is to call the beam width the angular width of the beam at the points where the beam intensity (power per unit area, I) drops to 50 percent of its peak value (I_0). The angle theta represents the bearing spread of the beam about its direction of propagation. The top view is looking down on the beam; the bottom view is a cross section of the beam. Note that with this definition, there is some small amount of main beam intensity outside this range, not counting the weak side lobes. Horizontal radar beam widths are typically 1° to 6° depending on the width of the antenna, whereas vertical beam angles are typically some 20° to 30°, more or less independent of antenna dimension.*

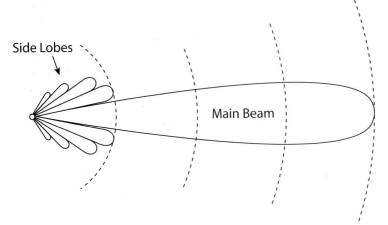

Side Lobes

Main Beam

Figure 7-8. Side lobes on a radar beam. Radar beams are not perfectly focused but emit some weak intensity to either side of the main beam. In this schematic representation, you can think of the dotted circles as the effective ranges of intensity. If a given target is just detectable at 16 miles off, then it would begin to give back reflections from side-lobe echoes when it is within 4 miles of the antenna at the same Gain setting. Higher-end radars with larger antennas have more focused beams with fewer side lobes.

It is not just losing intensity from absorption or scattering in the air, but like all electromagnetic radiation patterns, the energy is spread over a wave front that expands with distance from the source. Like a balloon being blown up, the surface area of the balloon ($4\pi r^2$) is increasing as the square of the radius. The energy per square cm of wave surface of the radar beam is decreasing as the square of the distance from the antenna. Double the distance from the antenna, and the signal intensity drops by a factor of 4, as illustrated in Figure 7-9.

With radar, the issue of signal intensity versus distance off is more complex, since we rely on detecting the returned echoes, not the ones being sent out. When the radar pulse hits a solid target we tend to think of it as scattering like billiard balls and either heading back to be detected or heading off in some direction not to be detected, which is a useful way to imagine the interaction. On the other hand, when it comes to issues of intensity, it is more realistic to think of the incident radar pulse as being completely absorbed by the target, transferring all of its energy to molecules of the target,

which are then agitated to the extent that they radiate the same signal back out in all directions. In this sense, reflection is a matter of absorption and reemission.

With that physical picture in mind, we can understand why the intensity of the returning echoes does not decrease as just distance squared, but rather as the fourth power of the distance off. The reflected signal decreases in intensity on its return to the antenna as the distance squared from the reflecting surface, but the very intensity that is available to be reflected at that distance was diminished from the original source by the same distance squared. So, we have the intensity of returning echoes decreasing with distance off as the square of the distance squared, which is distance to the fourth power.

What this means is that the maximum range of a radar (assuming everything else is equal) is very dependent upon the peak power output. In this simple picture, to double the usable range of a radar requires increasing the available power output by a factor of 16. Put another way, if you double the peak power output, you only increase the maximum range by about 19 percent (4th root of 2).

That is the basic relationship between power and maximum range, but that leaves us with an apparent quandary when looking at published specifications of various models of small-craft radars. We see lower-end units with maximum ranges of 16 or 24 nm that have peak output powers of about 2 kW, and we see the next group up the scale has ranges of 32 to 48 miles with peak output powers of 4 kW. It appears from these specifications that you double the maximum range if you double the power!

The key lies in the phrase mentioned earlier, "assuming everything else is equal." Everything is *not* equal in these two classes of radar units. The 4 kW units have significantly larger antennas with much more focused beams and more sophisticated antenna receivers and amplifier circuitry. In short, they have a lower threshold for echo detection and are thus more efficient. The 2 kW units would indeed work to a range as large as these 4 kW units if they had the same antennas and electronics, but they would be some 16 times less efficient with lower power output. Put another way, if you changed the power output from 2 to 4 kW on the lower-end

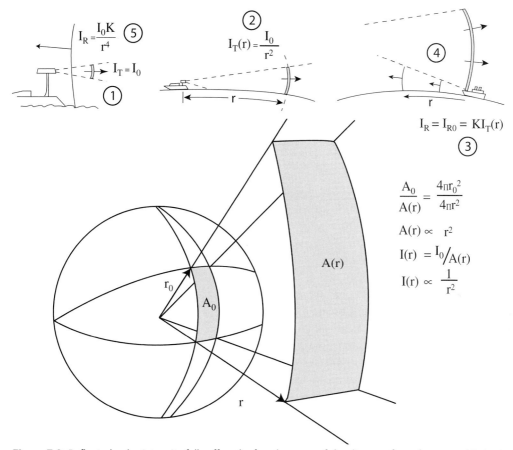

Figure 7-9. Reflected pulse intensity falls off as the fourth power of the distance from the source (r). A transmitted beam intensity of I_0 (watt/m²) is emitted in a tight beam, but begins to diminish in intensity as the surface of the pulse increases in size as it spreads outward **(1)**. The rate of decrease is $1/r^2$ as shown **(2)**. The pulse strikes a target that then effectively reflects back some portion (K) of the pulse (I_{R0}) as a new source of radiation **(3)**, which in turns begins to diminish at the same rate for the same reasons as it returns back toward the antenna **(4)**. The pulse has returned after traveling back the distance r **(5)**, having been reduced by a factor of K/r^4, which depends on the nature of the target and its distance off. Reflected beam intensities are many millions of times weaker than the initial transmitted pulse.

The bottom illustration shows why pulse energy per unit area decreases as $1/r^2$. Since the angular boundaries of the pulse surface (say 4° horizontal by 30° vertical) is the same for both spheres, the area of the pulse surface (A) is proportional to (∝) the area of the full spheres ($4\pi r^2$). The intensity of the pulse per unit area therefore diminishes with distance from the source by $1/r^2$, because the same amount of energy is distributed over an increasingly larger area.

units without changing anything else, you would still not gain much in useful range because their performance is limited by other design factors.

The overall radar system is a package, determined in large part by the specifications of the antenna. It is correct, though not quite valid, to say you want the higher power unit to achieve the larger ranges. It is better to say you want the higher quality unit to achieve the larger ranges, which will include higher output power as part of the package.

To appreciate the sophistication of the radar receivers, note that the same unit can detect echoes from a ship at 0.125 mile away as well as 10 miles away, in which case the returned signal intensity is weaker by a factor of millions.

So far we have discussed the nature of the radar beam when it is well away from the antenna, on its way out to interacting with targets. Close to the antenna, where the beam is still on the boat in many cases, the shape of the beam and its power distribution are different. This is mostly a concern in the area of radiation safety, so it is discussed in that section, below.

Bearing Resolution and Antenna Width

As mentioned in the previous section, the angular width of the radar beam in the horizontal plane is determined by the width of the radar antenna. The wider the antenna, the narrower the beam. Typical values are shown in Figure 7-10. A 2-foot antenna—in a radome or in an open array—produces a beam that is about 4° wide, and a 4-foot antenna produces a beam that is under 2° wide. As a rule, you should use the largest antenna that is consistent with the installation on your vessel, since the horizontal beam width (HBW) determines the bearing resolution that can be achieved with the radar. The exception would be those larger vessels in the "small craft" category that do have room for a 6-foot antenna, but find that a 4-foot antenna and associated radars adequately meet their needs.

The finite beam width on the radar has sev-

eral important implications for routine radar operation. First, the HBW determines whether two adjacent targets at the same range will appear separated as distinct targets on the screen or as just one large target. A beam that is, say, 4° wide cannot resolve two targets at the same range that are within 4° of each other from your perspective. For two targets to appear separated, the beam has to go between them without hitting either one. If one side of the radar beam is sending back echoes from the right side of the first target at the same time it is sending back echoes from the left side of the second target, then you have an uninterrupted source of echoes, so these will appear as one large target on the radar screen, as illustrated in Figure 7-11.

As another example, suppose you have a 24-inch antenna with a beam width of 4° and you are approaching an opening in a breakwater

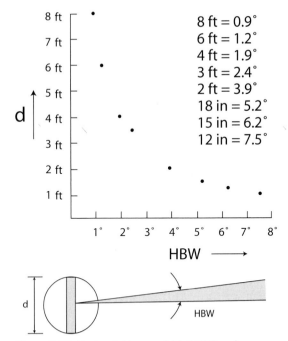

Figure 7-10. *Horizontal beam width (HBW) and antenna width. The HBW decreases as the antenna width increases for both open-array antennas and those enclosed in a radome. Typical values from specific units (according to radar manuals) are also shown. Actual beam widths for the smaller antennas may be somewhat larger than indicated by these data.*

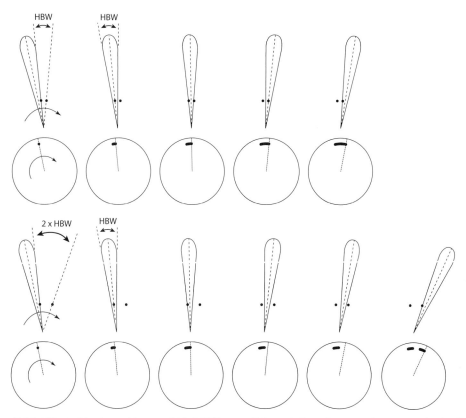

Figure 7-11. *Effect of horizontal beam width (HBW) on radial resolution of targets. As soon as the leading edge of the radar pulse strikes a target it starts sending back echoes and continues to do so until the pulse leaves the target. If two targets at the same range are equal to or less than HBW apart, they will appear as a single target, as shown in the top part. The bottom part shows two well resolved targets separated by twice the HBW. This is an important factor to keep in mind when looking for a channel or breakwater opening from some distance off. It also affects bearing precision as shown in Figure 7-13. Refer back to Figure 3-11 to see how this influences land images on the radar.*

from seaward. The entrance is 100 yards wide. How close will you have to be to that entrance to see it as an opening on the radar? With a 4° radar beam, this is equivalent to asking when the difference in compass bearings to either side of the entrance will be more than 4°. When that happens, your beam will pass through it without giving signals from either side and you will see the entrance start to open up. This is unlikely to be a very clean separation at just 4° because that is where the beam just fits, and it may in fact be slightly wider in actual practice, but at, say, 2 x HBW it should be a nice, clean opening.

One way to make a quick estimate of the theoretical "range to first resolve" is to use this formula:

$$\text{Range to first resolve,}$$
$$D = K1 \times (57 \times L)/HBW,$$

where L is the width of the entrance and HBW is the horizontal beam width in degrees. K1 is a "reality factor," which for now we will just call 1.0, meaning the formula works as given. You will most likely find that K1 has to be less than 1, meaning you have to get closer to resolve things.

In the above example, L = 100 yards and HBW = 4, so D = 57 x 100/4 = 5,700/4 = 1,425 yards, which is 0.71 nm (since 1 nm = 2,000 yards, approximately). If you have a radar with a 2° HBW, then the breakwater entrance will show up on the radar from farther off—at a distance that separates the sides by 2°. From the equation, D = 5,700/2 = 1.4 nm off.

This formula computes how far off you have to be to have two objects, separated by a distance L, appear to be HBW degrees apart. Chances are, you will have to go 1.5 or 2 beam widths inside the opening before it appears nicely resolved. That would correspond to K1

= 0.7 or K1 = 0.5 in the above equation. Examples are shown in Figure 7-12.

In that example, we might call the last view at 1.39 miles off as barely resolved, so with the target width of 0.063 mile and a HBW of 2°, we see that this unit has an effective K value of 0.77. For your own specific radar, you might group the constants together for a simpler formula:

$$D = K2 \times L,$$

where $K2 = (K1 \times 57)/HBW$ can be determined

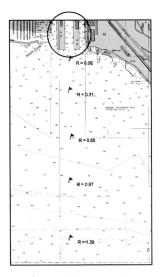
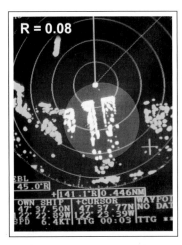

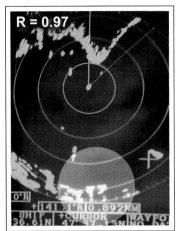
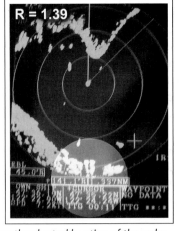

Figure 7-12. *Bearing resolution as a function of distance off. The top left shows the charted location of the radar snapshots, each of which is labeled by its range to the end of the piers. This 4-foot radar antenna has a nominal HBW of 2°. The two piers are 2.6° apart at 1.39 miles off, so the observation is consistent in that these remain barely resolved at this distance. At just farther off, however, the opening would not be apparent. A smaller antenna would show the piers closing to one image much earlier.*

from individual measurements as $K2 = D/L$. In the example shown, $K2 = 1.39/0.063 = 22$, so for this unit we have $D = 22L$ for all further measurements. If we approach a channel entrance that is 0.1 mile across, we would expect to see it barely resolved at some $22 \times 0.1 = 2.2$ miles off. A little practice with this approach—along with radar picture optimization—should yield a working relationship for your unit that will expedite interpreting radar images.

There is also a chance that the actual practical HBW that you have is not quite as good as the published specifications might imply. As mentioned in the previous section, radar beams are not sharply defined in space, but tend to fade from full intensity to no intensity over some distance. The horizontal beam width is defined as the angle at which the intensity drops to 50 percent of its peak strength. That leaves some intensity at angles larger than the nominal HBW as well as the small contribution from side lobes—the amount depends on how well the beam is focused, which in turn depends on the width of the antenna (see Figures 7-6 and 7-7), and these wings of the beam might generate enough reflections to visibly broaden any target to more than the expected HBW. I have worked with some radars that supposedly had a HBW of 6°, yet minimum target angles were consistently almost 10° wide. Also, some radar specs quote a HBW *and* a bearing resolution, where the bearing resolution is a degree or two wider. In this case, we would use the bearing resolution in the equation above as a starting point on gauging our minimum distance off for resolving two targets.

I highly recommend that you carry out a similar observation with your own radar. Find an appropriate opening (or two nearby objects) and then sail away from it and note the radar picture at various distances off. Then compare what you learn with what you get from the formula above. You will easily learn for your own system what a proper working value of K will be in the equation. From this, you can develop your own guidelines such as: I must be within 15

times the separation in order to see the opening resolved. This is the same reasoning you would use to estimate when two nearby islands would appear separated instead of as one large target.

When you practice optimizing the resolution of two features, be sure the radar picture itself is optimized first. Put the objects on the smallest Range that shows them on the screen (so they appear as big as possible), then adjust the Gain and Brilliance to be sure you have a sharp picture. Sometimes slightly reducing the Gain will make a sharper distinction between two nearby objects.

Closely related to the angular resolution issue is the operation of taking radar bearings for navigation using the EBL or cursor. Since the beam has a fixed width equal to the HBW, essentially all targets are at least this wide on the radar screen. That is, a single buoy will start emitting signals when the leading edge of the beam hits it and will stop emitting signals when the trailing edge of the beam leaves it. The buoy will appear on the radar screen as 4° wide, if that is your HBW, even if it is a long way off and does not subtend an angle as big as 4°—a buoy 6 feet in diameter at 0.5 nm off, for example, only subtends an angle of about 0.1°.

The implications for bearings should be clear. For targets like buoys, where we can clearly see both sides of a small, symmetrical target, we can assume the proper bearing to the target is halfway between the right and left sides of the radar blip. The same is true for all prominent, more or less symmetrical targets—take the bearing to the middle of the radar image as the proper bearing.

Taking a bearing to the edge of an island or headland, sometimes called a tangent bearing, is another matter. In this case, we know the target was emitting echoes before and after the center of the beam passed over the edge of the target. It sent echoes continuously until the trailing edge of the beam passed over the target. So when we want a precise bearing to a tangent, we have to correct for one half of the HBW. The finite size of

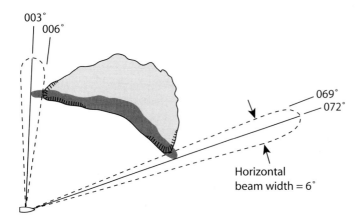

Figure 7-13. *Correcting a radar bearing for horizontal beam width. The dark region of the picture is the radar image we observe for this island overlaid onto a chart sketch of the island. Every target on the screen is expanded in the radial direction by half of the horizontal beam width as shown. In this example if the EBL read 072° to the right edge of the island's radar image as shown, we would plot this on the chart at a bearing of 069°. This is an important correction for units with small radar antennas and hence larger HBWs (see also Figure 7-10).*

the radar beam has smeared out the radar image of the target, as shown in Figure 7-13.

If the tangent bearing is to the right side of the object, then we have to subtract HBW/2 from the measured EBL or cursor bearing in order to get the proper bearing. If it is a bearing to the left side, then the beam started to send echoes before its center crossed the tangent, so you have to add HBW/2 to the observed EBL bearing. When making this correction, however, it is important to use the proper effective HBW for the correction. Only using the value from the published specs may not be correct. If your specs call for a HBW of 6° but your own measurements show it to be 10°, then the correction should be 5°, not 3°. Chapter 10 discusses applications of this correction to position fixes based on radar bearings. The section above on radar beam specifications discusses the definition of HBW that may be related to this issue. It is not defined as a sharp cutoff angle; there is some intensity beyond it.

Another interesting point is that some antennas can be too good for some applications. A 6-foot antenna, for example, would have an HBW of about 1°, not the 6° we have discussed for smaller radars. With the small antenna, a nearby buoy would show up as a target 6° wide. Nice and bright and easy to spot. But this same buoy would only be 1° wide when seen from the bigger antenna, which is a dot on some range scales. This consideration of prominent detection of close targets has led some owners of larger vessels to add a second, smaller radar to help with navigation among close targets, a point which is further discussed below. Figure 7-14 compares a close view of a buoy on some different radar sets.

Minimum Range

The smallest range scales on most small-craft radars are either ⅛ mile (0.125 nm) or ¼ mile (0.25 nm), with generally the lower lowest range corresponding to the units with the lower maximum range. A radar with 16 or 24 nm maximum range would tend to have a 0.125 mile minimum range, whereas a 36- or 48-mile radar might go down to only 0.25 mile as smallest displayed range.

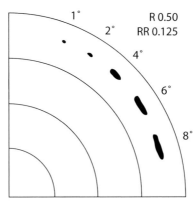

Figure 7-14. *Minimum target width is determined by the horizontal beam width as shown in Figure 7-10. Here is how a close buoy might appear on radars with various antenna widths, from a 6 ft antenna (about 1° target width) down to a 1 ft antenna (7 or 8° target width).*

In the radar manual's technical specifications of minimum range, however, they are not referring to the minimum displayed range, but rather to a practical limit to the closest object that can be detected based on the characteristics of the radar antenna and associated electronics. This can be an important operational issue when navigating in very close quarters such as a marina or a narrow channel in thick fog. The beam property that matters for this is the pulse length, because the pulse length determines how long the antenna is in the Transmit mode before switching to the Receive mode.

The pulse length of the radar, which changes with range settings, is usually specified in microseconds (μs), but for now we need to know how long the pulse is in space. Since the pulse travels at a speed of 328 yards per microsecond, half of the pulse length in distance is 164 yards multiplied by the pulse length in microseconds. A radar cannot detect any object that is closer to the antenna than half its pulse length, because reflected signals from a target that distance off or closer would be coming back to the antenna from the front edge of the outgoing pulse before the back edge of the pulse had left the antenna, in which case it would not yet be switched from Transmit to Receive mode.

So the minimum "theoretical" range is just 164 yards multiplied by the pulse length of the range scale in use, which at low ranges in small-craft radar is typically 0.1 microsecond, implying a theoretical minimum range of about 16 yards. In actual use, however, you would never see targets that close for two reasons, one of which you cannot control and one you can. Inherent in every unit is a fixed recovery time for the antenna to make the conversion from Transmit to Receive, and there is also some extension of the range due to the near-field projection of the beam from the antenna. Very little has been published about either of these effects, but, depending on models, these effects together appear to add some 10 to 20 yards to the minimum range, so that typical quoted values in radar specifications might be more on the order of 25 to 35 yards. You cannot improve on the specified value—meaning you cannot hope to see closer than that—but you can end up with a rather higher minimum range depending on your choice of antenna location.

When it comes to minimum range, antenna location is crucial, both with regard to elevation and obstructions. The limited vertical beam angle means the higher the antenna is, the farther off the beam will be when it hits the water. A beam emanating from a 40-foot-tall antenna first hits the water at about 60 yards from the base of the antenna (see Figure 7-2 and the table below). It will see things closer that are raised some height above the surface, but the main point is this geometric factor could easily increase the minimum range above the quoted specifications for some installations.

When choosing the elevation of the antenna, you might consider the trade-off between distance to the horizon (R_{max} in the table below) compared to the geometric minimum range (R_{min}). Note that since one dependency is linear and the other is a square root, you lose on minimum range faster than you gain on maximum range as you raise the antenna height (H). The formulas are:

$$R_{min} \text{ (yd)} = H\text{(ft)}/\tan(12.5°) = 1.50 \times H$$

and

$$R_{max} = 1.22 \times \sqrt{H\text{(ft)}}$$

RANGE AND ANTENNA HEIGHT

H (ft)	R_{min} (yds)	R_{max} (nm)
6	9	3.0
9	13.5	3.7
12	18	4.2
18	27	5.2
24	36	6.0
32	48	6.9
40	60	7.7
48	72	8.5

At antenna elevations above 20 feet or so, you may be compromising the optimum minimum range, depending on the specific model and antenna. Other factors, however, may have more influence on the choice of antenna location, as discussed earlier in this chapter.

Obstructions near the antenna and side-lobe production cause proportionally more effective interference when looking at signals from very close objects. Also, when using the lowest ranges you are often moving very slowly on an even keel (such as entering or leaving a marina in the fog), which means you don't get to "see around" the obstructions on board since you are not yawing or rolling about as you proceed. Or put another way, you should be moving very slowly when navigating among targets within some 30 yards of you that you cannot see visually!

Even in open water, however, target detection at very close distances can be severely limited by sea-state echoes unless it is flat calm.

With the understanding that you may not achieve quite the minimum range quoted in the manual, it should also be said that modern radars do indeed work remarkably well on the lowest range. Even the most basic models generally work exceptionally well at the lower limit. In fact, in some cases, a lower cost radar might actually work better for very close targets than a more expensive model that works to higher ranges. That is why many commercial vessels will carry more than one radar, and have one that works better on lower ranges. In any event, if the goal is to have your radar work best at small ranges, then it would be valuable to keep the geometry issues in mind during the installation.

Numerical examples of minimum range observations are shown back in Figure 2-9. The extent of the effective minimum range for a particular installation can often be estimated from the radius of the sunburst pattern seen at the center of the screen when set to the lowest range—after tweaking the Gain and STC to optimize the display, although those may not be the best settings for any other observations. On the other hand, even though you might be able to "tune out" that sunburst pattern with Gain and STC, or other special controls, you still will not see any targets in that region.

Range Resolution and Pulse Length

As described above, it is the HBW that determines when two targets will be resolved in bearing. The result is, if the two are at the same range, but at slightly different bearings, we see them as separate targets if they are more than the HBW apart.

But what about two targets at the same bearing but at slightly different ranges? For example, a small vessel passing a buoy, or a tug and tow headed toward you, or a rock just offshore (as shown in Figure 4-6). In the case of bearing resolution, the limit was ultimately set by the width of the radar antenna and it was a fixed value for all range settings. In the case of range resolution, the subject at hand now, it is ultimately the pulse length that determines how well two targets on the same range can be separated. The main difference is that this range-resolving power is not the same for all radar settings, since the pulse length can change with the range scale, either automatically or by user selection.

The situation is similar to that mentioned when considering minimum range. As illustrated in Figure 7-15, two targets at the same bearing cannot be resolved unless they are farther apart than half the pulse length, which is:

$$\text{Minimum resolved separation (yds)} = 164 \text{ yds} \times \text{pulse length (µs)}$$

Generally we want the longest pulse length possible when looking for weak or distant targets, because the longer the pulse length, the more energy is being transmitted per pulse, and the chances of getting a reflection are increased. But when we can clearly see the target but cannot tell if it is one or two objects in line, then we do not want strong reflections but rather crisp reflections, and for this it is best to use as short a pulse as possible to resolve the two images.

With this in mind, radar units use different pulse lengths for different ranges, and in many cases also let the user decide on a long or short option. Typical pulse lengths range from just over 1 µs down to less than 0.1 µs. In these cases, the minimum resolved separation varies from 164 yards to 16.4 yards—a very large difference when it comes to resolving two close targets.

From an operational point of view, this means when looking for the best range resolution, first use the lowest range scale that will show the objects. This makes the images as big as possible on the outer area of the screen; all units use smaller pulse lengths for lower ranges. Then, secondly, if your unit offers the option for long or short pulses on that particular range, choose short. Also check the overall picture adjustment as mentioned in the section above on bearing resolution.

It is easy to see how a tug and tow 100 yards apart at 1.9 miles off would appear as one echo on the 4-mile range scale (pulse length = 0.8 µs, distance = 131 yds), but appear nicely separated as two targets on the 2-mile range scale (pulse length = 0.3 µs, distance = 49 yds).

PERFORMANCE

NMEA Interface

Most shipboard electronics can share the data stream of information from multiple instruments and display various user-selected outputs on various consoles. Shared data usually include GPS position and related derived data such as range and bearing to active waypoint, course over ground, speed over ground, velocity made good, cross-track error, and so forth (see glossary), as well as compass heading, depth, and even wind speed and direction, magnetic variation, and barometric pressure. For radar applications, the heading input is the most important, but the GPS data can also offer convenient radar display options. The use and availability of these external inputs is an important factor to keep in mind when designing a new nav station.

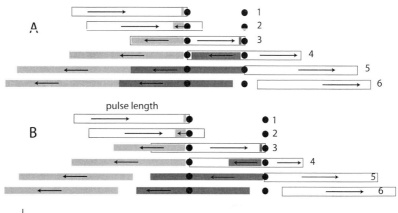

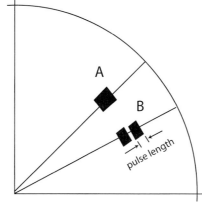

Figure 7-15. *Range resolution is limited by pulse length. Two targets at the same bearing separated by less than one half of the pulse length will appear as one target, because returning echoes from the far target will reach the close target before the close target stops sending its echoes, as shown in A4. The two pulses return as a continuous signal (A6). For targets separated farther, as in B, the targets appear resolved because all echoes from the close target are gone before those from the far target reaches it.*

Lower ranges generally have lower preset pulse lengths, so moving a target to the outer edge of the screen by using the lowest possible range will often show an enhanced resolution. Be sure Echo Stretch (also called Target Expansion) is shut off when trying to resolve targets at the same bearing. Also note that you can turn the target B image into the target A image by having the Gain set too high. See Figure 4-6 for a direct observation of the effect of pulse length on range resolution.

The standard format for marine electronic data has been developed by the National Marine Electronics Association (NMEA). The goal is to make the outputs and inputs from all brands of instruments universal, so individual units can be interfaced regardless of brand. Whether or not this goal has been achieved with a particular choice of components is something that must be tested with the equipment at hand. Even if the digital and electronic format of the signals are compatible, you must still contend with cables, connectors, and other limitations that might be unique to one component.

As time goes by, another component of the instrumentation that is becoming more popular is an integrated computer, either permanently installed or using a removable laptop. Various navigation software programs are available that not only read the instruments and display the data in several boxes on the screen or on nautical charts, but can also be used for setting up waypoints, routes, and various other navigation data that can then be sent to the instruments themselves, including the radar. Several companies now offer software that can overlay the radar images directly onto the active electronic chart of the region. This option is discussed in Chapter 13.

Heading Sensor

If you have a fluxgate compass available (heading sensor) that can provide compass heading data to the radar, then there are several radar display mode options that some navigators prefer over the basic head-up mode. This input also allows for several other useful features. You can either buy a special compass made specifically for your radar or perhaps use one from another part of your instrumentation, such as the autopilot. Most radar manufacturers make an optional digital (fluxgate) compass for this specific purpose and some radars will also accept the input from other brands of digital compasses. If you already have a digital compass installed, then it is worth checking if your radar

can accept compass input. The heading input is a valuable aid to any modern radar and many of its advanced functions rely upon it. A compatible heading sensor is highly recommended.

The backs of many radars have two inputs, one labeled "Compass or Gyro" and the other labeled "GPS or NMEA." The NMEA signals are pretty standard, but the compass inputs may be more specialized to the radar brand. In some cases, the output from the digital compass can be input into a GPS unit or other NMEA device that is linked to the GPS. In this case, you might be able to get the compass heading data into the radar via the NMEA input even when the digital compass is not directly compatible with the radar. In some units, this may be the only way to input the heading data. The trend of several manufacturers (Chapter 13) is to link all instruments together along a single network. These two approaches are illustrated in Figure 7-16.

All radar features that take advantage of compass input depend on the input being correct! If this input is not correct, the great advantages of these features can turn into detriments that can lead your navigation astray. Unless the input is a gyro compass—unlikely in the typical small craft we are concerned with in this book—it is important to remember that even though the electronic compass does not look like your standard magnetic compass, it nevertheless is one. It converts the magnetic field measurements into digital output, but it is still dependent on the magnetic fields around it, just like any compass.

Be sure to check the manual to see how you can read the output of the compass independent of the radar, and periodically check that it is correct compared to your standard steering compass. Fortunately, almost all modern digital compasses include an automatic means of checking and correcting for moderate deviations. The manuals explain how to "swing the ship" at some slow steady rate, meaning to slowly turn in a large circle according to the instructions. Simple computers inside the compass electronics then compute the deviation curve and correct for it.

You should know where this compass sensor is located and be sure to keep extraneous magnetic materials away from it. Most come with guidelines on installation, but many come to new owners already installed. The specifications, calibration, and monitoring are especially important when used with mini-ARPA options. When you plan to use one of these options, you may need a heading sensor with higher specifications, especially frequency of data points, than required for basic navigation. In other words, your autopilot compass with an output of 3 cycles per second might not be acceptable for a radar with mini-ARPA functions, since it needs to know the heading 10 times a second, according to some standards. See the related discussion in Chapter 8. Also, any system that might involve an overlay of the radar images onto an e-chart presentation (Chapter 13) may also require a 10 Hz NMEA input of the heading data.

Heading sensors are especially valuable in a sailing vessel, which will often be steering by the wind rather than by a compass course, or for any small vessel when exposed to a seaway that swings the heading around. When the vessel heading is swinging about it is difficult to keep a precise radar track of vessel target locations, which in turn makes collision avoidance and other evaluations more difficult. In some units, a radar feature that requires heading data might actually operate without a heading sensor by using the GPS value of COG. The COG tells you which way you are actually moving as opposed to which way you are pointed. Although that might seem better, in most cases it is not. Radar bearings, orientation, and computations are relative to the centerline of the vessel (your heading), so in those areas or times when you might be in current moving in quite a different direction from the way you are headed, you can get confusing output from the radar computations if you use COG for what should be vessel heading. Applications where this COG substitution might take place include lollipop waypoints; north-up, course-up, and true motion display modes; and some ARPA systems. On the plus side, without a heading sensor, this substitution lets new users see how these special functions work, even when not optimized, which gives them a better justification for the extra expense of the heading sensor. It is fair to say, that with all the valuable information you can obtain with the use of a proper heading sensor, it is well worth the investment, and generally not a good idea to substitute COG for this data. Some ARPA applications simply do not permit it.

Since modern radars with a heading sensor allow for so

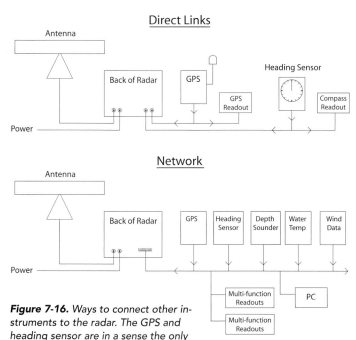

Figure 7-16. *Ways to connect other instruments to the radar. The GPS and heading sensor are in a sense the only real contributors to radar function, but in modern radar units all NMEA data can be displayed in various data boxes on the radar screen, which in turn can be used as a GPS or e-chart plotter as well.*

much flexibility in setup options, we should keep in mind the logical selections. Without a heading sensor, all bearings from EBL or cursor readout will be relative. In course-up or north-up mode, you could in principle set bearings to be relative, true, or magnetic. In most cases, the logical selections would be: head-up, relative; north-up, true; and course-up, magnetic. But flexibility is there for individual choices, although generally it is much simpler to change display modes than it is to change bearing units, since the bearing unit control is usually deeper in the menu structure.

Some of the latest models of handheld GPS units actually include a fluxgate digital compass. These units already export NMEA data for location, waypoints, course, and speed, but as of now do not yet export this compass heading. If they choose to add this output, there might be new opportunities for a portable heading sensor input. With a proper mount that kept the unit in line with the centerline and level with the horizon, yet was still exposed to enough sky for satellite reception, you might be able to rig a cost-effective plug-in for the radar that provided both the GPS and the heading data from a single unit, which could also be removed for handheld use away from the vessel. We must wait and see how this technology evolves. (There must also be some big improvements on either the circuitry or some form of gimbal. As it is now, some are way too sensitive to being held *precisely* level for accurate reading.)

North-Up Display

With a heading input to the radar, the radar knows the magnetic heading of your vessel at all times—pro-

viding, of course, that it is properly calibrated. With your magnetic heading known, the radar can compute your true heading as soon as it knows the magnetic variation, which it can get either from the GPS input or from a direct manual input from the operator. True heading = Magnetic heading ± variation. The radar knows how to figure out where true north is relative to the heading line on the radar. Note that all modern GPS units compute the magnetic variation based on a location and date (you do not need actual connections to a satellite to get variation). If you get stuck with very old charts, then you might want to check the GPS to see what the proper variation is at present. In some cases,

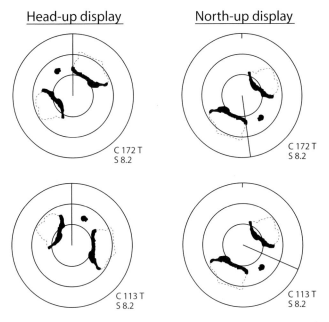

Figure 7-17. *Head-up and north-up radar displays compared. Both modes show the screen just before (top) and just after (bottom) the turn illustrated in Figure 7-18, which includes a chart plot of the turn (A in Figure 7-18) as well as a horizon view before (B in Figure 7-18) and after (C in Figure 7-18) the turn. The heading of the vessel at the time is shown in the Course and Speed readouts in the bottom right corners. In both display modes, the heading line is pointed toward the indicated course. The difference is, in head-up mode the heading line stays vertical and in north-up mode it rotates to follow your turn. North-up display and course-up display (Figure 7-18) usually also show a north marker on the circumference of the screen. The dashed lines on the radar screens are imaginary outlines of the islands seen on the radar.*

the rate of change changes, so even applying the charted annual change corrections on an old chart will not yield the proper variation.

A simple application of this heading input to the radar is to allow the EBL to be optionally displayed in true, magnetic, or relative bearings for any display option, as discussed below. But the main advantage of this scheme is it allows the radar to run in what is called a stabilized mode, with true north remaining on the top of the radar screen at all times. When you choose north-up display mode, the entire radar picture rotates instantly during the next redraw of the picture so that the visible land within range around you is oriented north-up on the radar screen, and your heading line is pointed in the direction you are heading. If you are headed 205 M according to a properly adjusted compass, and the variation in the region is 20° E, then your heading line will be pointed due SW at 225 T on the radar screen.

This display mode has several nice features. For one it is oriented in the same way most navigators look at their charts. If you are comparing a dead reckoning (DR) plot with your radar screen, or looking at a GPS trail across an electronic chart (normally run in north-up mode as well) then you have a nice one-to-one correspondence in the orientation. An even more important feature of the display is its stabilization. When you turn in head-up mode, all the land and vessel targets around you shift the same amount in the other direction. With north-up mode, stabilized in direction to 000, the land and nearby targets will remain stable on the radar display and only your heading line will rotate with your turn. This makes both radar navigation and collision avoidance easier in many circumstances. Figure 7-17 illustrates the north-up display mode compared to unstabilized head-up display. There are more sample comparisons in Chapter 6 (Figures 6-15, 6-16,

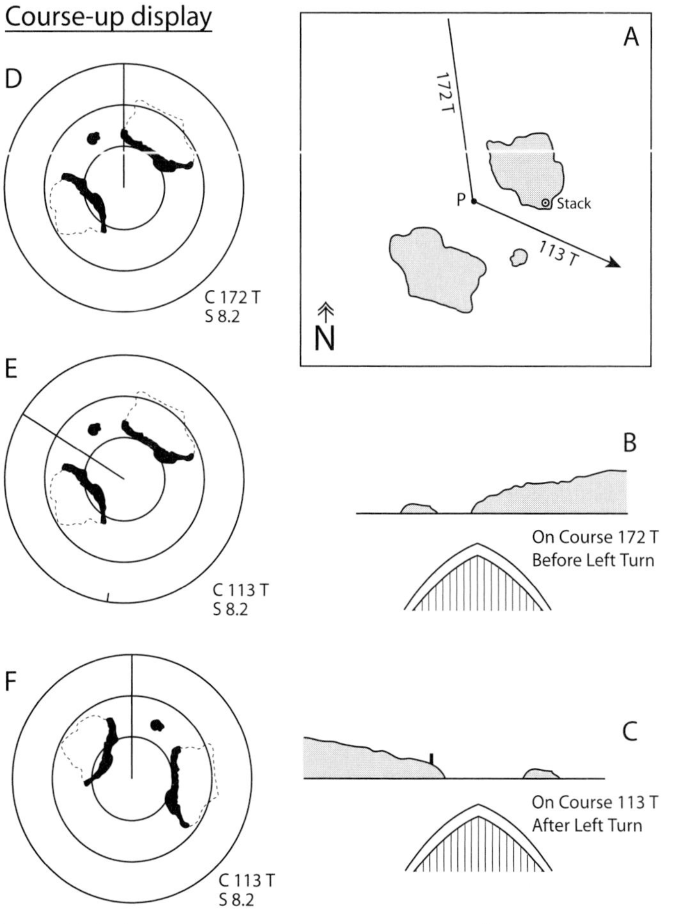

Course-up display

Figure 7-18. *Course-up view going through a turn. When centered on the present heading, course-up behaves as a stabilized head-up display. During the turn, the heading line rotates to the new heading just as in north-up, leaving the radar in an unusual orientation until it is recentered. D shows the radar before the turn, with the heading line at 172. After the turn (E), the heading line rotates to 113, leaving 172 at the top of the screen. Then when the course-up heading is recentered, the picture rotates to place the new course 113 at the top of the screen. The recentering takes place with a single button click.*

and 6-17). The compromise between these two modes is the course-up mode shown in Figure 7-18, and discussed below.

Remember that in north-up mode, as in head-up mode, the normal location of your vessel is the center of the screen, and the heading line points from there to the edge of the radar screen in the direction you are headed. We have heard that several new users of this function have been confused by this, especially when the radar center has been manually offset (Chapter 8) in the presence of overlapping display boxes and hidden range rings. In other words, a modern versatile radar offers enough options that you can set it up in a manner that would be difficult to interpret. See Figure 7-19.

Ship radars are usually run in north-up display all the time as it is well suited for integration with their ARPA and ECDIS (electronic chart display and information systems, discussed in Chapter 8). For recreational vessels, however, this powerful option is new and just beginning to be used. Without practice, this type of radar orientation does not seem as intuitive as head-up mode, and it is not unanimous among recreational and professional mariners that it is the best mode for evaluating risk of collision. Nevertheless, every user will soon agree that the stabilized display is

indeed a wonderful improvement over the shifting images of head-up mode, which makes the course-up display discussed below an attractive option.

Course-Up Display

Course-up display is a stabilized radar display mode that appears similar to head-up mode. It

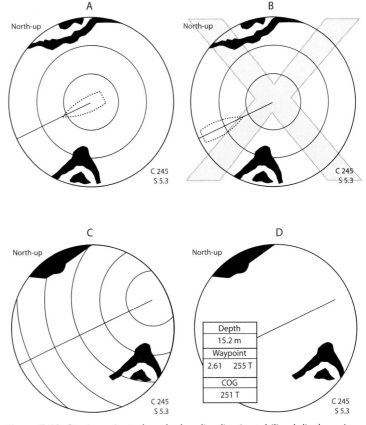

Figure 7-19. *Staying oriented on the heading line in stabilized displays. A shows normal north-up display with the schematic addition of a boat outline as reminder of which way our vessel is headed on the radar. B shows the wrong assumption about boat orientation. C is the same as A, but now the radar has been offset so more can be seen in the forward direction. Note that the range rings are a good reminder of where our vessel is located on the screen. D shows the same view but the operator has shut off the range rings and is displaying a data box, a common choice. It could lead to some confusion if a new crewmember viewed this setting without further explanation. It is always crucial when first looking at the radar to immediately check what the display option is set to, which is usually marked in a corner of the screen with HU, NU, CU, or TM. View C, for example, could also be the result of a true motion display without any offset at all.*

is essentially the same as north-up display, but the operator is not restricted to having 000 T at the top of the radar screen. At any time, the users can put their present heading at the top of the screen by simply pressing a button, regardless of which way they are pointed. If you are headed toward 225, for example, and then press the "Course-Up" button, the screen will appear to be in head-up mode, with 225 at the top of the screen. Now, however, the display is stabilized to 225. If you turn 10° to the right, the heading line turns 10° to the right, but the rest of the screen remains unchanged. Your original heading of 225 is still at the top of the screen, although your heading line is no longer in that direction, and all target and land trails remain as they were before you turned.

To many users, this display mode offers the best of both other options. It gives the relative locations of vessels and land like the head-up display, but at the same time the display is stabilized so that target trails and land do not move on the screen as your own vessel turns or yaws in a seaway. As your vessel yaws about your course line, you will see the heading line shift back and forth across the centerline of the top half of the radar screen, but land and other targets will not move and your desired course heading will remain at the top of the screen.

The course-up mode is different from the head-up and north-up modes in that it is an *interactive* display mode. The user needs to recenter the top of the radar after making course changes in order to maintain the course-up orientation, which is not required in the north-up and head-up modes—those orientations are unique, regardless of your actual numerical heading. In other words, after running along in course-up mode with your heading and heading line at the top of the radar screen, if you make a large turn in your course, then your heading line turns to the new course but the old course is still at the top of the radar screen. On your new heading, that previous orientation of the screen no longer has any significance. The so-lution is simply to press the Course-Up button again as soon as you are onto your new course. That will put the new course at the top of the screen and you will have a proper course-up display again, which appears like a head-up display. On most units, you recenter to the present heading by simply selecting Course-Up again, as if you were switching to it from another mode. Figure 7-18 illustrates the process.

If we do not follow up a large course change with a recentering of the course-up display, we end up with an unusual radar display that might be confusing to a new navigator. Knowledge of the bearing readout options (discussed next) is helpful for getting the mind aligned with the radar display or vice versa. In this regard, we should mention that most e-chart programs and GPS plotter displays will allow the chart picture to be presented in a course-up orientation, which would match the radar. Some navigators not accustomed to these new options might cringe at the idea of looking at charts any way but north-up, but times are changing. Safe, efficient navigation is not always tied to our traditional biases.

When or how quickly to recenter after a course alteration depends on the circumstances. When navigating in areas where you are well oriented with the landmarks and radar targets, and there is no traffic of concern in the area, you might recenter just after every turn, maintaining a more realistic head-up type of display (some units even have an automatic recentering option that can be engaged). But if you are watching traffic and evaluating risk of collision, it might be best in some circumstances to not recenter immediately after turning, because it might cause you to lose orientation with approaching traffic. If you recenter, the target wake trails would shift in response to your new orientation (much like they do in a head-up display), which means waiting longer to reestablish relative motion patterns. If you do not recenter immediately, you benefit from the stabilized display and the trails will remain continuous, even though they may turn somewhat if you have made a large turn.

When there is no traffic in the area but you have just turned into a waterway or around a corner and are not yet completely oriented relative to the targets you see on the radar, recentering is a matter of personal preference. Will it help you get oriented more quickly to be in a head-up mode immediately (then recenter), or will you orient more quickly by keeping the lay of the land fixed on the radar screen and observing your turn on the screen relative to the land (do not recenter immediately)? The course-up mode is interactive, and one you use to meet your present needs.

Several radar units offer options to the manual recentering of a course-up reference heading. Some have a user-selected or preset heading offset that will automatically trigger a recentering. If this offset is set to, say, 22.5° (the choice used in one unit), then if your heading changes by more than 22.5° the course-up reference will shift automatically to that new heading, otherwise only the heading line will shift. Likewise, some units allow you to have the course-up heading follow the course of the route leg being actively used by an autopilot. Such arrangements might be called "Auto Course-Up" or "Locked Course-Up." Another option is called "Waypoint-Up," in which the bearing to the currently active waypoint is automatically set at the top of the course-up display whenever you change active waypoints. These options are often linked to the charting or plotting functions included in the same electronics, and they obviously assume the GPS is interfaced to the radar. The actual functionality is different for different brands, and even sometimes for different models within the same brand of radar.

Having the course-up reference heading changed for you in some manner is rather like having the GPS automatically switch to the next waypoint when you pass within some criteria of the active waypoint when following a route. There are pros and cons for this extra help to the navigator. My own bias is to make all such changes manually rather than automatically, because that keeps you more in touch with the setup and what is going on. Practice with the options you have will determine what is best in various circumstances.

Relative versus Course-Based Bearing Readouts

The many options for setting up the radar screen require us to be especially careful about the meanings of the various digital bearing outputs. We can read the bearing to a landmark or vessel target on the radar screen with either the cursor display or by setting an electronic bearing line (EBL). When we read bearings, we get a number between 000 and 360. We are steering a course that is somewhere between 000 and 360 and at the same time the top of the radar screen can be oriented toward some course that is between 000 and 360, which may or may not be what we are steering.

In the days when head-up radar was used for all relative bearings, life was simple. The head of the vessel was always at the top of the screen and the bearings were always relative bearings, 000 to 360 clockwise. If you wanted to know an actual magnetic bearing to a light on a point of land, you would take the relative radar bearing from the EBL (say 330 R) and apply it to the present vessel heading (200 M) and essentially "compute" the magnetic bearing (330 + 200 = 530 − 360 = 170 M). This was the process whenever chart work or handheld bearing compass sights were correlated with radar sights. It still is needed in exactly the same way when running in head-up mode with relative bearings and still an option on the most modern radars.

Now you have the option to change just about any readout you choose. With a heading sensor, you can run the radar in head-up (unstabilized) mode, and instead of relative bearings on the EBL and cursor, you can elect to have actual course-based magnetic bearings.

This can be very handy for radar navigation or for correlating the bearings of a vessel target with radar observations and direct handheld compass observations. Then, there is none of the computing as done in the last example; the EBL would simply read 170 M. When running in head-up mode and you put an EBL on a target, however, it will move off the target whenever you yaw off the course you were on when you first set the EBL. In head-up mode, the EBL is a fixed angle off the heading line. When the heading line moves, the EBL moves. On the other hand, if you change to course-up mode, the screen stabilizes and the EBL can be operated two ways. Choose relative EBL, and it is again an angle relative to the heading line and its output will be labeled R. Choose course-based EBL, and it is relative to the top of the screen and will remain on a target as your heading line yaws about, and its output will be labeled M or T as you prefer.

In a sense, it is logical to run relative bearings in head-up mode and course-based bearings in north-up or course-up mode, but there are virtues of the opposite configurations as well. A clean solution might be to switch to all course-based bearings in all modes of operation. Then whenever you read a direction or bearing from the radar it will be the same as what the compass bearing to the object would be. This is convenient for using the cursor mode, since you can move around the radar screen directly measuring the range and magnetic bearings to various targets.

In summary, there are three basic types of display mode in use for small-craft radars: head-up, north-up, and course-up. In these labels, *up* means what is permanently at the top of the radar screen. In head-up, the top of the screen is the bow of the boat, regardless of what course it is on. In some units, that can only be marked on the screen as 000. No heading input is allowed and all bearings are relative. If your radar does accept a heading sensor, then the "up" can be either set permanently to 000 T or it can be set to your current course heading. Bearings and directions can then be read relative to the top of the screen (course-based) or relative to the heading line, which are called relative bearings. Different navigation styles and circumstances will call for different choices here.

Radiation Safety

In Part One we referred to one aspect of radar etiquette as not running the radar when in the close quarters of a marina, locks, or other setting where personnel would be exposed to the direct radar beam, even though they might be some distance off. The distinction between what might be called etiquette in this regard and actual radiation safety is one that is under debate in many forums—if not so much on the topic of marine radar, then at least with regard to microwaves from other sources such as cell phones, communications links, remote sensing devices, and so forth. And even if we might not be up to date on latest results from radiation science, we do know that the intense electromagnetic fields in the microwave oven in the galley can cook a chicken in a very short time. In other words, there are established effects. There are also established safety limits for exposure to microwave energy. However, because the potential exposure associated with radar is generally not known by the operator, there are fair questions to be addressed here.

The very use of the word "etiquette" implies the goal is not to offend someone's sensibilities on the issue, which does not really acknowledge any actual risk involved in a particular situation. A radar beam is a small but intense beam of electromagnetic energy as it leaves the antenna and, under certain circumstances, it is possible it could produce exposures that exceed contemporary safety standards and guidelines. Chances are that most exposures experienced away from the vessel would fall into the etiquette category, but up close to the antenna is another matter, especially if the beam is not rotating. All radar manuals state that the beam up close can be harmful and to avoid operations close to the unit. Some give specific instructions such as not looking directly at a transmitting antenna from within 1 meter of it, and so on. It is important to check that the unit is off before working on or near the antenna and to post notices at the controls if you are going to work on the unit. Some technicians remove the fuse to insure it is not turned on while they are working on it.

It is fundamental to not install an antenna in a location that would routinely expose skipper, crew, or passengers to the direct beam close to the actual antenna. Radiation safety standards are discussed at the Web sites of the World Health Organization (WHO), Health Physics Society (HPS), the International Commission on Non-Ionizing Radiation Protection (ICNIRP), U.S. Food and Drug Administration's Center for Devices and Radiological Health (FDA/CDRH) and the Federal Communications Commission (FCC). They are listed in the References. WHO's International EMF project provides in-depth coverage of all aspects of the subject, including a thorough list of scientific studies and an excellent set of guidelines for useful communications between parties who strongly disagree on the subject.

Microwave radiation exposure limits are generally expressed in terms of power density in watts per meter squared (W/m²) averaged over a 6 min or 30 min interval for workplace and general public exposures, respectively. The limits found in contemporary safety standards such as IEEE C95.1, the ICNIRP guidelines, or the NCRP recommendations range from 10 to 100 W/m² at the frequencies used for X-band radars (about 9.4 GHz).

The power output section earlier in this chapter explains that the emitted power density in the far field drops off as the square of the distance from the antenna, but in the near field where radiation exposure might be a concern, the power density remains roughly con-

MICROWAVE EXPOSURE LIMITS

Frequency Range (GHz)	General (W/m²)[1]	Occupational (W/m²)[1]
9.3–9.5 (X-band)	66.7	100[2]
1.5–100	10	50[3]
10–300	10	50[4]

[1] *General* refers to all individuals, ages, and health conditions, who may not have knowledge or awareness of any potential hazard, nor control over their exposure. These are averages over 6 minutes. *Occupational* refers to individuals with training who are aware of any potential hazards and how to avoid exposure if needed. Includes occupational situations with transient exposure. These are averages over 30 minutes.
[2] www.hps.org, FAQ #315, December 31, 2003 (IEEE and ACGIH). Specific to X-band radar, whereas the other two values cover broader ranges that include frequencies that may present higher risks.
[3] OET Bulletin 56, August 1999 (FCC/OET).
[4] *Health Physics*, April 1998, vol. 74, No. 4, p. 510 (ICNIRP).

stant with distance from the antenna and is distributed over a wave front roughly defined by the geometric profile of the antenna aperture. The distinctions between these two regions are illustrated in Figure 7-20. Estimates of their probable ranges are in Figure 7-21.

A rough computation can give some insight into the values involved. Consider the potential exposure from a radar with peak power of 2 kW and a horizontal beam width of 6°. Within a few meters of the antenna (the near field) the beam is roughly the shape and size of the rectangular array antenna. Assume that the antenna width (D) and height (h) are about 40 cm and 8 cm, respectively, which is typical for this class of radar. The maximum peak power density in the near field (S) is approximately four times the peak power put into the antenna (P) divided by the area of the antenna (A = D x h), or S = 4 x P/A. The factor of 4 accounts for reflections and in-phase addition of electric field coming from different parts of the antenna. This is a conservative estimate of the *maximum* power density used when considering radiation exposures.

For this antenna we have S = 4 x 2,000

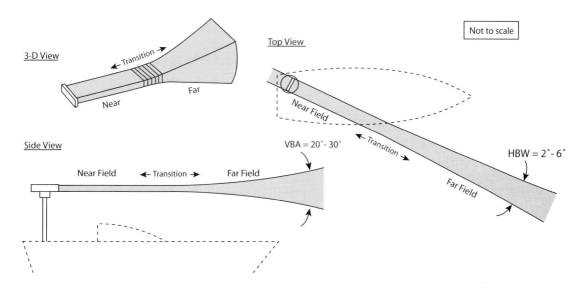

Figure 7-20. *Schematic shape of the radar beam near the antenna. Throughout the region called the near field the beam has a profile that approximately matches the profile of the antenna itself. Farther off in the far field, the beam begins to diverge to the angular specifications given in the manual. These two regions blend together in what is called the transition zone. The actual distances from the antenna that mark the boundaries between these zones are difficult to predict precisely, but estimates are given in Figure 7-21. The figures are not to scale. Boat outlines are only for orientation; they could be relatively much longer in some cases.*

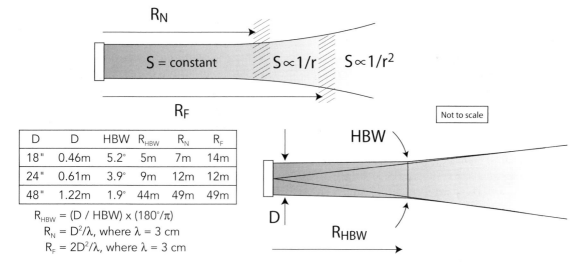

D	D	HBW	R_{HBW}	R_N	R_F
18"	0.46m	5.2°	5m	7m	14m
24"	0.61m	3.9°	9m	12m	12m
48"	1.22m	1.9°	44m	49m	49m

$$R_{HBW} = (D / HBW) \times (180°/\pi)$$
$$R_N = D^2/\lambda, \text{ where } \lambda = 3 \text{ cm}$$
$$R_F = 2D^2/\lambda, \text{ where } \lambda = 3 \text{ cm}$$

Figure 7-21. *Estimates of the boundaries of the near field (R_N) and far field (R_F) radiation patterns from typical small-craft marine radar antennas. It must be stressed that these are estimates based on other antenna designs and generally accepted approximations. The estimates depend on the antenna width (D) and the radar wavelength (λ), as shown. The values could vary by a factor of 2 or more on specific units. For the purposes of estimating radiation exposure, the power density (S) within the near zone is considered constant; within the transition zone it diminishes as 1/r; and then in the far field it begins to drop as $1/r^2$. For comparison, the distance from the antenna of width D that subtends an angle equal to the horizontal beam width (HBW) is also shown (R_{HBW}). Note that these field lengths are in meters, so even with the uncertainties present, typical radar beams remain fairly localized within the dimensions of small-craft vessels. The figures are not to scale.*

watts/320 cm² = 250,000 W/m². This is the peak power density for each pulse. Radars operate by sending out a short pulse, waiting for reflection of the pulse to return, and measuring the time it took the pulse to reach the target and return; consequently, the transmitter operates only a small fraction of the time that the radar is on. The ratio of the length of the pulse to the interval between the start of one pulse to the start of the next is called the *duty factor* (pulse length/pulse interval). The duty factor for typical small-craft radars is about $\frac{1}{3,000}$ (average of typical settings, presented earlier). Thus the average power density is $\frac{1}{3,000}$th of the peak power density, so the effective average power density within a few meters of the antenna (at the same height as the antenna) is roughly 83 W/m², still assuming that the beam is stationary with the antenna not rotating.

For this small radar and this average duty cycle, this is below the limits of some safety standards and above those of others. However, the average power density would be lower when the antenna starts rotating, because the time the narrow beam illuminates an object as it sweeps by is only a small fraction of the time it takes for a complete rotation of the antenna. The stationary antenna value is still important, however, because such values could occur close to a transmitting antenna that is not rotating. On the other hand, at several meters from the same antenna while it is rotating, the average power density would be reduced by the duty factor of the rotating antenna, which is the ratio of the time for the beam to sweep by a point to the time it takes to complete a single rotation of the antenna (the ratio of the beam width to the scan width). For the radar described above, the rotation duty factor is 6°/360° = 1/60. Thus the average power density while the beam is scanning is $\frac{1}{60}$th of the above values, or 1.4 W/m², which is below the limits found in contemporary standards and guidelines. Once in the far field of the antenna (beyond some 5 to 10 m for the above antenna),

the beam begins to diverge and the power density decreases with the square of the distance. Thus the average power density at 20 m is one-quarter that at 10 m, and it continues to diminish at that rate as the distance increases.

Standing right next to a small rotating antenna within a radome—which by the way prevents you from knowing if it is rotating or not—you would not get the full $\frac{1}{60}$th reduction, because your body might subtend some 120° of the scanning range of the antenna on each sweep. In such a case, you could be exposed to levels higher than accepted standards even from a rotating small antenna. For any size radar, it is only good sense and prudence to not work close to a transmitting antenna, in line with the beam.

Microwaves are nonionizing radiation, and the consensus of the scientific community is that established biological effects are associated with tissue heating. X-band microwaves would only penetrate 1 cm or less into the body, so organs close to the surface with low internal cooling such as eyes and testes are the areas most sensitive to the exposure. However, the safety standards take this into account and exposure to levels of microwave energy below the limits found in these standards is presumed to be safe.

In summary, even the smallest conventional marine radar unit in normal operation could pose a radiation safety concern for exposure within a few meters of the antenna, especially when the antenna is transmitting but not rotating, which is not a normal operating mode. In this regard, a separate switch for the rotation motor that is not linked to the Standby/Transmit mode would be an arrangement that required special care with regard to radiation safety; that is, a unit that let you maintain transmission and still shut off the rotation motor. I have seen an installation like that; there was a simple toggle switch for the operator to shut off the rotation motor. I have been told that such arrangements were made on some older radar units on sailing vessels to lower power consumption while at the same time keeping the radar warmed up for quicker observations. Modern units shut off the rotation motor in normal Standby mode and would not call for this dubious arrangement.

Referring to the definitions in the table above, it would seem that prudent restrictions from the radar antenna site would be higher for passengers and untrained crew (general category) than they might be for vessel operators and trained crew (occupational category) who are aware of these issues. As for exposure from farther off from the antenna, that may boil down to a personal judgment. Clearly the larger the radar, the farther off you would want to guard against exposure. The above numerical example was for a small radar. Some radar manuals simply state the radiation can be harm-

ful, but then go on to only warn about very close contact. It would be prudent to consider the shape and intensity distributions in the near field versus far field when making this evaluation. The maritime industry seems to have made the judgment that distant exposure from a rotating antenna is safe, based on the fact that the intensities are way below the recommended exposure levels set by various agencies, as sketched above.

Those wishing more data and discussion can find it in the references sited above. To put specific intensity levels on specific units at specific distances, with specific duty cycles, the rough calculations presented above could be used as a starting point. Larger antennas have significantly larger near-field ranges and power densities.

CHAPTER 8

Special Controls and Features

The fundamental radar controls for optimizing and viewing the screen were covered in Chapter 2. Here we go over the more specialized ones that are used less frequently. However, when they are needed, they can be very valuable.

SPECIAL CONTROLS
Echo Stretch

The Echo Stretch (ES) radar option enhances the size of target echoes. It can be useful when looking for or following a small target vessel or buoy, especially when farther out on the radar range. Turn it on, and all targets become larger. It widens them along the arc about the center of the screen, and some radars allow for echo stretching in the radial direction as well. Their width and depth are distorted, but generally the range to the closest edge of the echo is left unchanged. The ES option should normally be set to Off and only used when needed. Remember that it also stretches out the land images—indeed, one application of the control is to help locate distant land as it first becomes visible on the radar. When taking bearings or ranges for accurate fixes, or looking for narrow entrances, it should be turned off. Echo Stretch is illustrated in Figure 8-1. Echo Stretch is similar to increasing the pulse length without changing the range; both operations tend to blend together two targets very close to each other on the same bearing.

In some units, Echo Stretch is called (Target) Expansion. Common on-screen abbreviations include ES, EXP, and ST. Some units have levels of Target Expansion (low, medium, and high). It pays to read the manual carefully on how Echo Stretch works on your specific unit. It can be a valuable function, especially to a larger vessel that might have a 6-foot antenna. With an HBW of just 1° or so, a buoy or other small target has a very small image on the screen, so the Target Expansion mode can help track these as needed.

Interference Rejection

The Interference Rejection (IR) control rejects interference from other radars broadcasting in your vicinity. This is not a common problem except in busy harbors or channels. Generally this control would be left in the Off position, but it could be left on with no deterioration in performance, except for the potential to distort observations of radar beacons (Chapter 4). The most common problem it solves is radar-to-radar interference that shows up as a large number of radial streaks on the screen, or as transient dotted curves that streak across the screen during individual sweeps. This control will generally shut these off completely. Interference and other unwanted echoes on the radar screen are discussed further in the Radar-to-Radar Interference section in Chapter 9.

Zoom and Offset

These functions appear on some modern radars, although their function and operation differ among models. Offset or Shift relocates your po-

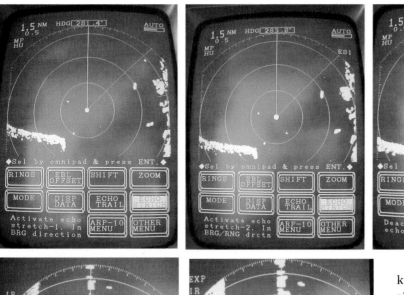

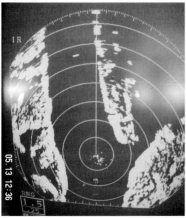
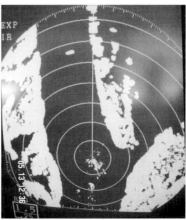

Figure 8-1. *Echo Stretch (ES) enhances target size. Some units have just one option, others have both bearing stretch (middle), and radial stretch (right). The top left has ES off; the top middle has bearing stretch on; and the top right has range and bearing stretch on. Note how the small target on the starboard quarter is enhanced. The bottom left shows a different radar in a different location with this function off. The bottom right shows it on. In this unit, the expansion options are set in a separate menu, then just turned on or off with one key. Notice how the channel that is 2.5 rings forward, just to the right of the heading line, is not resolved when Expansion is on. This function should be turned off when you are looking for details in the radar image. Both top and bottom radars have the range set to 1.5 nm. The top has a ring spacing of 0.5 nm, the bottom has 0.25. The bottom radar has the center offset for a farther look forward (see Figure 8-2).*

keep a wider look to the side opposite a shoreline when close to shore.

Zoom allows users to expand the range about the new center, also using the cursor position to determine the extent of the zoom. Generally these features are used to get a better look forward on a given range, although there are applications for using these features in other directions. Figure 8-2 shows several options. A new style on some units lets you set a small zoom window on the screen where you can watch details while still watching the rest on the screen on the normal display.

sition away from the center of the display so that you can concentrate on a specific region. Set a cursor to the new center and press a button to shift to it. A common application is to shift the center aft to get an expanded view in the forward direction, but it can be just as useful to

These can all be useful options for watching specific circumstances, but they do leave the radar set in an unusual display mode. This could lead to confusion in some cases, so it is important to convey to others how the radar is set and how to return it to normal display. On some units it is easy to switch into Zoom or Offset mode, but not obvious how to get back to normal. On your own unit, you will master this, but when sailing on another vessel with unfamiliar radar this can be a pitfall.

Guard Sectors and Alarms

Modern radars allow users to define a safety range ring using the VRM, and then engage an alarm that will sound whenever a target is detected within that ring. One use of these options is to watch for approaching traffic, but

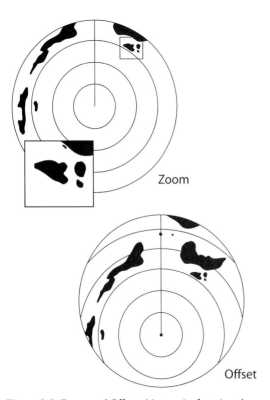

Figure 8-2. *Zoom and Offset. Most units function the same way with these features. Zoom activates a small index window that can be moved with the cursor or track device and its contents are expanded and presented in a new pop-up window. It is a good way to monitor specific regions or look for more detail without changing ranges. Offset lets you shift the center of the screen to have a longer look in a specific direction. The most common application is to look farther forward as shown here and in the bottom part of Figure 8-1, but you can also look back or to the side with this feature.*

you should test such arrangements extensively before relying on them for assistance. Read the manual on their use carefully, as the Gain and other options must be set properly. Also test what might or might not set off the alarm, and whether weak targets will trigger it—sometimes only strong echoes fire off the alarm, but on some modern units a bird will set off the alarm. The alarm sensitivity can be set on some units. The alarm can be set to go off when a target enters or leaves the guarded region.

More elaborate guard options allow for setting two rings to define a radial band sector that can be monitored, and with these you can also use the EBL to define radial sectors of the band to guard. Some units also use a cursor drag option to set the regions.

In typical small-craft radar operation at sea, it is not often you would want to monitor a sector of space around you, as opposed to a given radius around you, but it could be a valuable option for low ranges in the presence of sea clutter. Or, you might be anchored in a bay or harbor with a well-defined entrance that you want to monitor, and yet you do not want the traffic milling about to set off the alarm. Or, since the alarm can be set to go off if a target leaves the zone as well as when it enters the zone, you could also use it to monitor a vessel traveling with you to see that you stay in the intended formation. Tugboat skippers set a sector aft to include their tow to be sure that it stays where it is supposed to. When anchored, you could set it on a vessel moored to a buoy you want to tie up to, and set the alarm to go off when it leaves! Or, you could set an alarm at night when anchored to detect any approaching vessels that may be unlit. More advanced radar units employing automatic radar plotting (discussed later in this chapter), use sector alarms to define areas of automatic target acquisition.

The most common application of a guard sector might be to set a semicircular sector on the side of the vessel nearest the shoreline. This way if you get too close to the shore, the bright

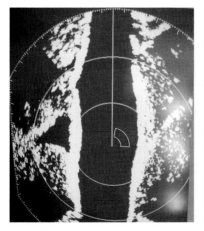
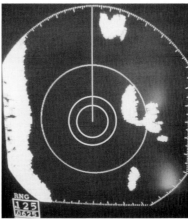

Figure 8-3. *Guard rings and sectors. The left screen shows a guard sector set on the starboard bow to warn if the vessel approaches too close to shore, while still leaving the port side unguarded so passing vessels do not set off the alarm. If the shoreline image enters the guard sector it will set off an alarm. The right screen shows a guard ring set at anchor. If the vessel swings enough to bring the guard ring into contact with the land, an alarm will sound.*

signal from the land will set off the alarm, but passing traffic on the other side will not enter the guard sector, as shown in Figure 8-3. Specific sector configurations that you might use often can be saved in some radar models and then recalled. Different models have different methods of defining the sectors, some of which are more intuitive than others.

Regardless of the application, you must test this option carefully and study the setup options to be sure that it works as desired before relying on it for any crucial data, and check that you can hear and identify the alarm. Most stock internal alarms I have heard are not loud enough to offer warning very far from the unit, or the alarm sounds just like the alarm on another instrument. Some units offer an inexpensive optional external alarm buzzer that would benefit anyone using alarm features when sailing shorthanded.

FEATURES
Watch Mode

Some radars offer a power-saving option, the Watch mode, that allows the radar to remain in Standby mode but still turn on automatically every 5 or 10 minutes to look for traffic. This option combined with guard rings, alarms, and trail recording might offer some level of warning for shorthanded operations. However, a proper watch is not kept by such arrangements alone. There is no electronic device that can be totally relied on to detect and warn you of risk of collision. Serious collisions have occurred involving vessels depending solely on such a system.

Once tested underway, this mode could be useful to sailors at sea with limited battery power as a supplement to nighttime watches. As for how often the radar should automatically turn on, consider a ship approaching from dead ahead at 23 kts. Add to this your speed of, for example, 7 kts, and you have a closing speed of 30 kts. Thirty knots is 2 minutes per mile, so if you can only see a ship well at 10 miles off on the radar (which might be the case for smaller radars), and you want at least 6 miles to think about it once detected, you need to look every 4 miles of closing distance, or turn on and take 10 sweeps or so every 8 minutes. A higher-end radar that could dependably see a ship at 20 miles off would yield a 26-minute period. But you could still miss small, fast targets. In any event, you would want to have the trails turned on as well as the Echo Stretch option discussed earlier in this chapter.

Heel-Angle Adjustments

Adjusting for heel angle is not a customary radar adjustment, especially for power-driven vessels, but it can be important for sailing vessels in some conditions. It is not part of the radar, but rather a mounting-method option for the antenna. If you will be sailing to weather in areas where you expect to see traffic—especially in regions where wind with fog is common—then you should consider an antenna rig that gimbals, or tilts, the antenna so it can be kept parallel to the horizon, or one that you can level manually. When you are heeled over, the windward side is not covered well by the radar sweep and the leeward side points more into the waves so that the sea clutter is greatly enhanced in some conditions (refer to Figure 7-3). Hence the value of some rig that compensates for the heel angle.

Level radar antennas are more common on racing sailboats than on cruising sailboats because weather, traffic, and point of sail are unchangeable facts in a race. The cruising sailor has more flexibility in these matters and might avoid some of the situations where a level radar mount is important.

There are several companies that produce gimballed units for mounting on the backstay or on the mast. Another option is to build a rig that lets you manually tilt the radar. I have seen these made from hydraulic trim-tab adjusters common on fast powerboats. These radars are not gimballed, but must be leveled at each tack by adjusting the trim of the antenna. Another solution is an antenna with a manual clamp that is released to manually level the antenna then clamped back into place, as shown in Figure 8-4. You will need to place a step to reach the clamp. Some designs use quick-release pins in place of pressure clamps. Be sure your rig will withstand the rigors of the ocean if you plan to go to sea with it. I have seen more than one radar antenna come out of a storm hanging by its cable. In either case, with manual rigs you tack the radar after you tack the boat.

A related issue concerns fast power-

boats. Some of these do not ride on an even keel, but have some significant trim by the stern even when on a full plane. In these cases, building in some permanent rake to the radar an-

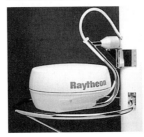

Figure 8-4. *Radar leveling options. The top shows one method of keeping a post-mounted radar antenna level when sailing to weather. This uses a quick-release clamp (top inset) and then the radar is tilted by hand. (This radar has been tilted and clamped for the picture.) The adjustments can be made while reaching up, without being in line with the beam, or you could make the adjustments while in Standby mode. The bottom left shows a gimballed mast mount, and the bottom right shows a gimballed backstay mount. (Bottom left courtesy Waltz Manufacturing. Bottom right courtesy Marine Services and Salvage.)*

tenna may be more efficient. See the discussion in Chapter 7 on radar mounts.

Lollipop Waypoints

With the GPS interfaced to the radar, there are several convenient options or displays available to assist with navigation, some of which are discussed in the next section. Here we mention one simple display, lollipop waypoints, that is extremely valuable and available on many units. It generally requires a heading sensor input to the radar for best performance, but it may work with GPS alone using the COG.

Once you select an active waypoint in the GPS, the GPS computes the range and bearing to that point from your present position. That information is then exported from the GPS to the radar. Since the radar then knows your location on the radar screen, it can display the range and bearing to your active waypoint on the screen. Usually this is done by extending a

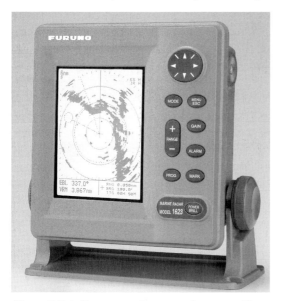

Figure 8-5. *Lollipop waypoint on a radar screen. The dotted circle marks the range and bearing to the active waypoint in the GPS. Without a heading sensor, this function assumes the heading line is oriented in the direction of the COG. Notice the simple layout of the controls on this unit. Most functions are operated via menu commands. Other models have even fewer controls on the main console. (Courtesy Furuno.)*

dotted line from the center of the screen out to the waypoint position, which is marked with a prominent circle (the stick and candy of the "lollipop"), as shown in Figure 8-5.

With your next waypoint clearly showing on the radar screen you have a nice visual confirmation of your navigation. If your waypoint is a buoy, you will expect to see a small target within the lollipop. If there is none—and you are indeed close enough to see a buoy on the radar according to the practical radar ranges given in Chapter 3—then you have to figure out why it is not there. If you see a small target off to the side of the lollipop that is behaving like a buoy (Chapter 6), then you know the buoy is probably not where it should be. In any event, you have gained valuable knowledge.

When you have a well-defined waypoint clearly marked with your lollipop, you have a continuous radar confirmation of your GPS position. The waypoint (buoy, rock, islet, headland) that is clearly showing and staying in your radar lollipop is proof that the GPS position is correct and that you are not being set off course. This technology is effectively providing the crucial radar check of the GPS that was recommended as standard procedure in Chapter 4.

The radar marks waypoint display, described in the next section, is a similar feature with similar benefits that does not use the lollipop display.

For these lollipop functions to work you need a heading sensor input to the radar. Most units will automatically substitute COG from the GPS input for the heading if you do not have a heading sensor. Heading sensors are extremely valuable, as discussed in Chapter 7, but they are expensive, $500 to $800, whereas the GPS connection is simply a wire. This substitution will work for many purposes, except when you are set in strong current that causes your COG to differ from your actual heading. That will cause the display to be in error by the set angle. Also, once you stop, the COG has no meaning, and although the lollipop waypoint display will still be in effect, it may be bouncing around the radar screen as the COG assumes random values.

When using this valuable radar function, remember that the waypoint shown on the radar is the active waypoint from the GPS, and some GPS units include the option to automatically shift the waypoint after passing within a certain radius of the point, which means the lollipop might suddenly shift on the radar screen. There are pros and cons to using the GPS option of automatically advancing the waypoints—it is a convenience in some cases but a definite distraction in others. I generally prefer to manually change waypoints when cruising to keep more control over the navigation. But I use the automatic option more often in racing, since everyone is usually busier at the time of mark rounding (where most of the waypoints are set) and you almost always pass precisely at the mark. But there are exceptions in both cases. The choice to use this GPS option deserves careful consideration in most cases.

On-Screen Nav Data

Other data from the NMEA interface (Chapter 7) that can often be shown on the radar screen include present Lat and Lon, COG, SOG, and course heading, as well as the range, bearing, and position of the active waypoint, and the time required to get there at the present speed of advance (called VMG on some units). Some displays also include depth, water temperature, and even a barometer trace. In short, since many new radars are wired in a network with other instruments, the radar display can be used as a remote or additional display of just about any navigation data flowing through the network.

Some of these displays are more of a convenience than a direct integration of GPS and radar, such as the lollipop display discussed above. A function that is much like the lollipop option is one that lets you select a mode that displays the Lat and Lon of the cursor position.

With this you can move around the radar screen and read off the locations of various targets. This might be a useful way to identify radar targets in some circumstances. It is certainly a nice way to identify a target vessel if, for example, you need to be certain you are speaking to the vessel you see on the radar. Generally, range and bearing is a quicker way to identify landmasses seen on the radar, since most e-chart programs have a similar option that shows range and bearing of the e-chart cursor relative to your present position. Typical navigation data output is shown in Figure 8-6.

Some mariners are reluctant to answer a radio call if they are not certain that they are the one being called, or are reluctant to call a radar target vessel if they are uncertain of its identity. The use of Lat-Lon output from the radar cursor can alleviate that problem. Just use the cursor to find the Lat and Lon of the target you want to call and use them to make your call more specific: "Calling the vessel located at . . ." If they did not answer before, they might now.

Remember, though, that convenient outputs can be a double-edged sword. In several radar models, the nav data display can be set up to show both your present position and the cursor position, often side by side, with identical formats. Most e-chart navigation programs have the same option. You must be careful in such cases to not read the cursor position when you want your vessel position. It is an easy trap to fall into; I recommend showing only one position at a time and manually switching back and forth as needed—in both radar displays and e-chart setups. (The same potential for error was mentioned in Chapter 1 for confusing the EBL/VRM readout with the cursor readout. Both have nearly identical formats.)

Another feature some models have is the radar marks option, which allows users with a GPS and compass input to actually plot marks on the radar screen based either on their relative locations as they move the cursor around, or set them according to actual Lat-Lon posi-

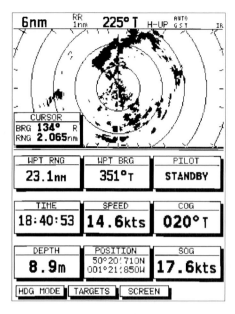

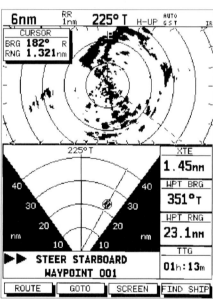

Figure 8-6. *Navigation data display on a radar screen. This unit divides the screen for the maximum display and then gives several options for nav data layout. It can also use individual pop-up windows for other data, such as the cursor data window. You can essentially design the screen however you like. Other units use bands of nav data across the bottom of the screen, and some replace the entire screen with navigation data when interfaced to a GPS. Generally LCD displays have more optional layouts than CRTs. (Courtesy Raymarine.)*

tions. This way, you can set a mark at your active waypoint or any waypoint you choose. These waypoints are not sent back to the GPS for routes, but offer a nice visual picture of where you are going or where you have been. There are numerous applications for this feature. Radars with this option usually allow you to set one at the present vessel position, which would be a valuable man-overboard marker. These radar marks are stored in the radar as Lat-Lon positions, so their range and bearing from you will change as you move, in contrast to a position marked by EBL and VRM, which is always relative to your present position. Some radar consoles also have full electronic chart systems (ECS) built into the same control unit. These are essentially two independent electronic navigation systems that are sharing the display screen, but they can also share actual data, as explained in the ECDIS section below. When present, they can usually be displayed either full screen, or share the screen half-and-half with the radar. They use vector chart displays and can be quite convenient, but they are not usually as versatile as PC-based charting programs.

ARPA

ARPA stands for *a*utomatic *r*adar *p*lotting *a*id. Like radar itself, its full name is almost never used. It is an electronic enhancement of marine radar designed to help evaluate risk of collision and trial maneuvers that might be called for. It has been used in ship navigation for many years. ARPA is regulated by the International Maritime Organization (IMO), which establishes the precise functionality, symbols, terminology, and quality-control criteria of the output.

ARPA is an internal computer interface to the radar screen that allows operators to acquire a target via touch screen or cursor click and monitor its motion. Then, using known values for your own vessel's heading, speed, position, COG, SOG, etc., the unit will compute and display all the interaction data needed to evaluate risk of collision. The output includes the CPA, time to CPA, projected position of the target, true speed and heading of the target, and so forth. It is, in principle, doing digitally all that we discuss doing manually in Chapter 11 (and more), and then continuously displaying the results on the radar screen. The computer can monitor up to ten targets simultaneously.

If one or more targets are passing too close, then you have the opportunity to execute a trial maneuver that will recompute all the CPA data to check that the proposed maneuver is a safe one. An ARPA radar screen is much more complex than a typical small-craft radar display, and its safe, efficient use takes special training.

When you contact a ship to clarify passing and include your present range and bearing, they will often report back to you the CPA and perhaps time of passing, if they have been monitoring you from their ARPA. If they have not spotted you before your call, the data you supplied will help them locate you and start a track. Generally it takes 2 or 3 minutes to acquire and plot a new target. The required time depends on your relative speeds and courses, as well as the quality of your echo.

The term *mini-ARPA*, or other variations of the name, is often used generically to mean that the radar has some but not all of the ARPA features. It might also imply that the derived information is provided, but that the overall system is not being regulated in the same manner as in ship navigation. The actual computations may well meet the IMO standards for accuracy and promptness, but the input from, for example, the heading sensor might not be calibrated to the precision required by IMO standards, or the ability to acquire targets of certain types in certain conditions may not meet general standards without special picture adjustment, and so forth.

In short, this is potentially a valuable aid to small-craft radar operation, especially for larger vessels with larger antennas, but one that must be used with special care, both in its operation and installation. It is fundamental that we understand the basics of the relative motion diagram (Chapter 11) before relying upon a computer calculation to inform us of the risk of collision.

Typical outputs from mini-ARPA systems in-

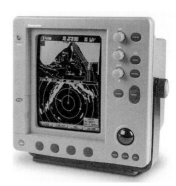

Figure 8-7. *Mini-ARPA and AIS displays. The radar screens look basically the same as normal, with the addition of new text areas that show vessel identification (AIS) and interaction data (ARPA). The vessel targets being tracked are marked with special symbols (see Figure 8-8). The top unit shows the ARPA display being shared with an e-chart display. The bottom shows an example of the "black box" design, where the screen and control console are separate units (other examples are in Figure 8-9). (Top courtesy Raymarine. Bottom courtesy JRC.)*

clude: true course and speed of the target, CPA and time to CPA, and projection vectors on each of the acquired targets that show their position in a user-selected time interval of 30 seconds to 30 minutes. Up to ten targets can be acquired simultaneously and these can be selected manually or automatically. Automatic

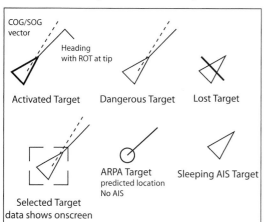

COG/SOG vector

Heading with ROT at tip

Activated Target   Dangerous Target   Lost Target

ARPA Target predicted location No AIS

Sleeping AIS Target

Selected Target data shows onscreen

Activated target. A target whose text data is being displayed on the screen. The symbol contains speed and course over ground vector, vessel heading, and rate of turn (ROT) indication.

Dangerous target. If an AIS target (activated or not) is calculated to pass preset CPA and TCPA limits, it will be classified and displayed as a dangerous target and an alarm will be given.

Lost target. If a signal of any AIS target at a distance of less than a preset value is not received, a lost target symbol will appear at the latest position and an alarm will be given.

Selected target. If the user wants detailed information of a target (activated or sleeping), he may select it. Then, the data received as well as the calculated CPA and TCPA values will be shown in an alpha-numeric window.

ARPA target. A target acquired by ARPA that does not have AIS. The symbol shows COG and SOG vector for user-selected time interval.

Sleeping target. A sleeping target indicates only the presence of a vessel equipped with AIS in a certain location. No additional information is presented until activated.

Figure 8-8. Typical symbols used in ARPA and AIS radar displays. Some mini-ARPA models use modifications of these. In each case, the symbol is overlaid onto the radar target once acquired.

target selection is done much like setting guard rings or sectors. You set the sector and instead of an alarm going off, it attempts to acquire the target for analysis. Practicing with alarm functions is a good way to practice target acquisition. After a sharp course alteration of your vessel, the target may have to be acquired again. Sample mini-ARPA and ARPA screens are shown in Figure 8-7, and Figure 8-8 shows the typical symbols used on such systems, which usually include AIS as well (Chapter 13).

Acquired targets can also be set up to leave special trails that show when the target has changed course or speed. These work well with strong, clean targets at optimum ranges. It may take special tuning or other picture adjustments to monitor all these features for multiple targets.

It is important to keep the basics in mind when using these features and output. The radar is simply solving the relative motion triangle as we do manually in Chapter 11. That solution requires your speed and heading from a knotmeter and compass. If these inputs are not correct, the output will not be correct. In this regard, your knowledge of how to check your digital compass and heading line alignment, and how to calibrate your knotmeter, are fundamental to the use of ARPA data.

It appears that some units substitute SOG for knotmeter speed and COG for heading whenever these latter inputs are not available. In current or strong winds the resulting ARPA data may not be precise. Always check that the GPS input to the radar includes the proper NMEA sentence for heading and knotmeter speed. Operator's manuals tell which sentences are needed. (NMEA data is a series of text lines called *sentences*. Each sentence type has a unique name, and some data appear in more than one sentence type.)

In most units, unlike other features that use the heading sensor and GPS input, the ARPA function is often an option (extra circuit board) that must be purchased separately. In short, a mini-ARPA radar may mean ARPA-ready radar. It will also require an additional input of knot-meter speed.

ECDIS

ECDIS stands for *e*lectronic *c*hart *d*isplay and *i*nformation *s*ystems. It is an integrated electronic navigation and safety system that is an increasingly popular choice for ship traffic and other commercial vessels. The centerpiece of the system is an electronic chart in vector format that includes multiple layers of all relevant navigation data such as lights, depths, notes, shipping lanes, buoys, hazards, bridge clearances, waypoints, routes, marks, and so forth, which can be called up and displayed as the user wishes. Besides convenient route layout and ETA computations, the electronic chart is integrated with the radar output so land images or targets acquired from ARPA or AIS (see Chapter 13) can be overlaid onto the electronic chart. Like ARPA, ECDIS is regulated by the IMO and the IHO (International Hydrographic Organization). So when we say a vessel has ECDIS, we mean that it has a very specific type of this system, with all the correct functionality and performance criteria established by these regulating agencies. As a rule, we would not refer to a yacht with full electronic charting interlinked to its radar as having ECDIS, even though it might indeed have all the functionality and sophistication of that aboard a passing ship. The more generic term, which does not have specific standards yet—but will likely soon, is electronic chart system (ECS). ECDIS must use official government vector charts, whereas ECS can use any type of digital chart.

Consequently, when it comes to electronic chart use on or in collaboration with small-craft radar, the manufacturers generally do not use the term ECDIS because of its official association, but the functions provided are very similar. Small-craft radar units would generally refer to these options as Plot or Plotter mode, or

possibly Navigation Chart mode, or they could use ECS.

We will not be covering the use of electronic charts, but should point out that this is a very common option when purchasing small-craft radar, and it will certainly grow in popularity.

In this basic mode, you might just view the radar and the electronic chart side by side. Instead of having the radar or the e-chart take up the full screen, you switch to a split-screen presentation showing both screens reduced but side by side. This can be a very instructive way to set up your navigation and monitor what is taking place. You see your position on the chart along with a trail of past positions, perhaps with a projector line that shows where you will be in 5 or 10 minutes (an ARPA-type function on the e-chart). These are standard e-chart options available on PC versions as well as the integrated models we are discussing here. Displayed beside the e-chart, you see a regular north-up radar display. This would not require an ARPA radar. Indeed, if you had this chart option without a heading sensor, the radar view might be head-up only. It is just a convenient dual display from two instruments. When set to the same scale it makes an especially nice comparison. Both displays have range and bearing cursors, so you can move the cursor around on the chart and then on the radar to compare and identify radar images. Figure 8-9 shows a radar and plotter sharing the display screen.

The next level of plotter-radar interaction might be when the radar involved has ARPA capabilities. This type of radar can generally export along its network the range, bearing, course, and speed of all acquired targets. This data can then be imported by the plotter function and the targets can be displayed on the e-chart. In this case, if you are not concerned about the land but only the traffic, you could close the dual view (chart next to radar) and expand the full screen to chart view and you will see an e-chart presentation that is enhanced by showing all the moving traffic around you. As long as the targets are properly acquired on your radar, they will move properly on your e-chart. This type of ECS might be called a mini-ECDIS.

In some units you can actually display the full radar image overlaid on the e-chart. In this case you would see land images and traffic targets, but if you did not have some ARPA features in the radar, you would be left to figure out the interactions and collision risks on your own. Sometimes the vector charts used in such devices do not contain much information about land contours, so a comparison with a paper or raster chart might be needed for more detailed understanding of the radar image, but more often than not, they provide very good confirma-

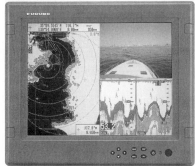

Figure 8-9. Multifunction display screens. Most displays of this type allow for one, two, three, or four panels of display. A depth sounder trace or table of navigation data are other common pages to show on the screen. (Top courtesy Simrad. Bottom courtesy Furuno.)

tion of your location relative to the land around you. A sample is shown in Figure 8-9 in a multifunction display. (In PC-based radars, you can overlay the radar image right onto a raster (bitmap) chart, or onto a topographic map, as well as a vector chart. See Chapter 13.)

True Motion Display

As the internal and shared workings of radar have become computerized and integrated with GPS and heading data, we see more sophisticated features of radar navigation made available on the most basic radar models. Another radar display option in this category is the true motion (TM) radar display, which makes the radar screen look much like the e-chart display mentioned in the example above. On the radar screen itself, the land images remain fixed and your vessel position, heading line, and range rings move across the radar screen. Your position is then in true motion and perspective relative to land and vessel traffic in range. It is just like viewing an electronic chart, but you are moving among the radar images of the land, not the chart outlines, as shown in Figure 8-10.

The picture recenters itself when your vessel reaches about two-thirds of the way to the farthest range ring. This puts your vessel back into the center of the screen (or to one side if you are off center) and you start moving again from there. Or you can choose to manually recenter the vessel at any time.

This display mode comes with various levels of sophistication and unless the inputs are correct, you could be easily misled by the results, especially when there are strong currents present. This display mode can be very helpful to identifying your situation relative to moving and stationary targets, but it is not recommended for collision-avoidance situations because it takes away the display of relative motion. As Van Wyck and Carpenter remind us in *The Radar Book* (see References), "relative motion is what runs over you." With true motion display, we are back to evaluating risk of colli-

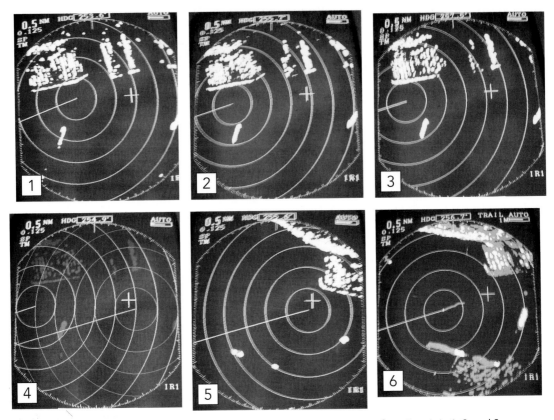

Figure 8-10. *True motion (TM) radar display. The screen shots are in sequence from 1 to 6. In 1, 2, and 3 we see our own vessel and associated range rings moving along the breakwater. When we reach the edge of the display, it automatically recenters (4) and carries on from there. In 5 we turned on a 1 min Wake option. Several minutes later in 6, we see trails from target vessels and land as well as from our own vessel. TM display is the only option that shows a wake trail from your own vessel.*

sion by eye alone or by plotting the relative motion diagram (RMD) backward. In relative motion, potential collision courses are obvious. In true motion, they are less so. With ARPA features, you could acquire the targets and evaluate them, but true motion displays exist on radars without ARPA. In these cases it would not be an optimum mode to use in traffic, because you cannot see very far ahead once your position has advanced toward the edge of the radar screen.

In some navigation circumstances, even in the presence of traffic, this display mode can be convenient for getting the quick radar view of

the world around you, but it takes practice and experience to sort out its optimum role in the various circumstances of routine navigation. It requires active GPS input as well as a calibrated heading sensor, otherwise you will see a very impressive display that could be quite wrong.

As a rule, when the various sophisticated display options (NU, CU, TM) start to get confusing, or you lose track of your orientation on the radar screen, switch back to head-up display, the quickest and simplest display to interpret since the heading line is straight up, parallel with the boat and pointed in the same direction.

CHAPTER 9

False Echoes and Interference

I n most cases, all persistent blips or echoes shown on the radar screen represent real objects that have sent back legitimate reflected radar signals. The range and bearing to the image tells us where the object is located. This is true often enough that we should generally assume that a target is real before considering other interpretations, such as false echoes and interference.

Luckily with radar, situations that lead to false or distorted echoes are easy to evaluate, so false echoes can be identified. The extent to which this issue affects general radar operation depends on the sensitivity of the unit, the antenna location, and the location of the vessel relative to land or other large radar targets. It can also depend on sea state and local weather conditions.

We already touched on this phenomenon when we discussed raising the Gain when adjusting the radar picture until a light background of speckles appears. The speckles referred to are not real targets, but electronic background noise. This interference is actually beneficial since it confirms that the Gain is working in the absence of real targets. Reflections from waves or rain are types of unwanted echoes we discussed in Chapter 2. In this chapter, we discuss the three most common types of interference and then add a section on unnatural propagation, which causes the radar to see either farther or not as far as we would expect in normal conditions.

SIDE-LOBE INTERFERENCE

Side-lobe interference (the common term for echoes received from side-lobe scattering) in small-craft radar operation is what occurs when you get too close to a target and do not turn the Gain down. You may not see the other types of interference discussed here very often, but everyone will see prominent side-lobe interference at some point. If not corrected, it can completely incapacitate a small-craft radar screen. (We emphasize small-craft radar here, because as mentioned in Chapter 7, larger antennas have significantly weaker side lobes, which cause less interference.)

As discussed in Chapter 7, the primary radar beam has weaker beams of intensity to either side of it due to imperfect focusing. For distant targets, the reflections from these side lobes are so weak that they do not interfere with the primary echo on the radar screen. But as we get closer to a large target, we will notice slight radial wings developing to either side of the main echo, and if we do not reduce the Gain, they will continue to grow in brightness and size, completely masking the true location of the primary target, as shown in Figure 9-1.

How far off this takes place depends on the initial Gain setting, and the target size, antenna size, and range. For example, you would certainly see this on an 18-inch antenna if the Gain were set for a crisp view of the side of a ship at 2 miles off, and then you drove to within a half

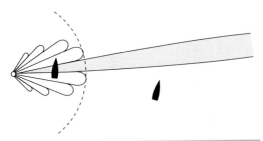

Figure 9-1. Side-lobe interference. The top figure shows how a distant vessel interacts with the main radar beam only, whereas up close the vessel can send back echoes from the weaker side lobes as well. The latter are emitted over wide angles, which smear out the target image. A sample is shown in the bottom photo, taken from a sailing vessel at sea. The vessel trace is already smeared out in this head-up display as our vessel heading swings about in the waves. As the target gets closer, its image starts to wrap around the range ring, a clear sign of side-lobe reflection. The Gain on this picture should have been reduced much earlier, if we were monitoring the radar for collision avoidance. In this case the image was accumulating unattended as we safely passed the ship visually. Another sample of side-lobe interference is shown in Figure 9-3.

ference begins occurring in conditions where it previously did not, it could be a sign that the antenna requires maintenance.

If your main concern on the radar screen is targets farther off and not the one causing large side-lobe interference, then it might be useful to try turning on AC Sea to remove the interference. This would not require you to turn down the Gain as much, which might degrade the sharpness of farther-off targets.

RADAR-TO-RADAR INTERFERENCE

The radar receiver is very sensitive and since all radars are operating on about the same frequency, radar-to-radar interference will occur. The interference signals are not synchronized with your broadcasts, so the unwanted signals show up as random streaks or dotted arcs that shoot across the screen. In crowded harbors or channels this interference can be distracting, though rarely will it actually interfere with your navigation. Turning on the IR function (Chapter 8) will eliminate this background. This feature is only used for this purpose. The shooting dotted arcs and fields of short streaks are easily identified (see Figure 9-2). They are transient and usually do not appear in the same place twice. IR can be left in the On mode with no deterioration of performance, although it is normally turned off. It should be tried periodically in congested waters to see if it helps reduce interference.

Note that in some radar units IR can prevent the detection of racon signals, discussed in Chapter 4.

As an aside, if you detect these radar interference streaks while at sea, it means another vessel has its radar on, even though you may not see the vessel visually or on the screen. In the few cases I have tested this, it seemed that you might be able to locate the direction of the traffic by noting the location of the sweep when the interference arc appears. The arc can appear anywhere on the screen, but it seemed to

mile or less of the target, or set for 6 or 8 miles off and then come within, say, 2 miles of the target. As a general procedure the Gain should be reduced when large targets approach; if you see side-lobe interference developing, it means you waited too long to reduce the Gain.

Side-lobe interference is more of an issue with smaller radar antennas. If side-lobe interme that the sweep always appeared in the same location where the arc appeared. In these cases, the arc only showed a few times over many minutes of watching and in all cases the traffic did not appear visually to confirm this observation.

GHOST TARGETS FROM REFLECTIONS

If your Gain and Tuning are adjusted properly, you are not likely to notice ghost echoes in typical small-craft radar operations very often, and if you do, they are not likely to interfere with your navigation. Look closely in the right conditions, however, and you will see them. On some vessels with structures in line with the antenna, they may be more frequent. Ghost echoes require the close proximity of a strong reflector either on your vessel or near it. The problem occurs when signals from your antenna reflect on a target after reflecting from the larger strong reflector near you. When the twice-reflected signals are then detected by

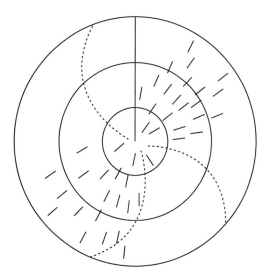

Figure 9-2. *Radar-to-radar interference appears as transient radial streaks or dotted arcs that flash across the screen during individual sweeps. The Interference Rejection control removes such interference very effectively. Note that both types of interference are shown on the same picture here, but you are most likely to see just one or the other in any given instance.*

your antenna, they appear to be marking a target where there is none; hence *ghost target.* Figure 9-3 shows prominent ghosts created by reflections seen when passing close abeam an anchored ship.

Reflections from your own vessel may sometimes be the source of the ghost if you have any structures in line with the antenna and not far from it. For example, say your initial radar beam reflects from an obstruction in line with the radar, then proceeds off the vessel to strike a large nearby target such as a steep shoreline or passing ship, and then some of this strong source of echoes hits the same obstruction again, and gets reflected back into the antenna. To the radar, these double-reflected echoes appear to be from a target in the direction of the obstruction at a range equal to the distance to the actual target—plus the distance to the mast, if that is significant, but if the mast is very far from the antenna it will not cause much reflection. (Deck cargo stacked high enough to reach into the radar beam is a potential source of these ghosts.)

Figure 9-4 shows a prominent example of reflections from a large mast on a fishing vessel, located 8 feet aft of the antenna. If you have this type of ghost, you will see it often when passing large targets, always in the same location, in line with the obstruction. For small-craft operations, it is unlikely that these ghosts would appear as an actual vessel target because the source of the reflections is not likely to be large, which means the only thing you could see reflected twice would be a very large target up close. These generate the dispersed images seen in the two figures.

Except for persistent cases caused by your own rigging—which might be more common on fishing vessels and other working vessels—this type of interference is more of a novelty than a practical consideration. Nevertheless, it is instructive to look for them as a matter of improving your skills as a radar observer. Gain and Tuning adjustments can usually suppress

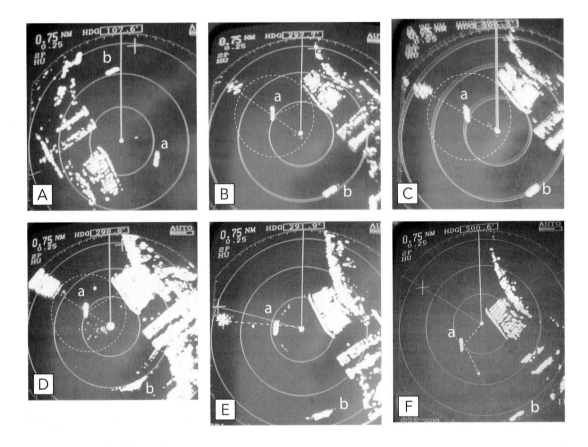

Figure 9-3. *Ghost targets from sources not on our vessel. In A, we have left the marina and see two anchored ships in the bay, marked a and b. Notice that there are no targets behind ship a. In B, we turn in the opposite direction to pass close abeam of ship a, and as we approach we begin to see ghost echoes behind ship a. Our radar beam has struck the ship, reflected off it, and then struck the breakwater. Echoes from the breakwater then strike the ship and are again reflected back into our antenna—all in a fraction of a second while the antenna is still pointed at the ship, as explained in Chapter 7. These ghosts will always appear in line with the primary reflector at a distance behind it equal to the distance between reflectors, as illustrated with a dotted circle centered on the ship. In C we increase the Gain to enhance the effect, and a bit later in D we increase the Gain even more (for the sake of illustration only). With this high Gain setting—obviously way too high—we now see the marina behind the ship, as well as side-lobe interference developing on ship b and the pier near it. Some sea clutter to windward is also now apparent. In E the Gain has been reduced, but being directly abeam the ship we see weak side-lobe interference on its image, and the ghost, though weaker, is still obvious. In F we have passed the ship, and reflections from it do not lead to any large target that might send back more ghosts. Ghost images need strong first and second reflectors. (If there were secondary reflections from ship b, they would be behind a, and off the radar screen under the letter F.)*

the ghosts without distracting significantly from other parts of the radar image.

ABNORMAL RADAR RANGES

In Chapter 3 we discussed how far the radar can see in normal atmospheric conditions. If you have ever seen a mirage, however, you will understand that in abnormal atmospheric conditions, we can see things that are not really there. I saw a very dramatic mirage in the Strait of Juan de Fuca once, in the late afternoon on an overcast, warm summer day, with calm wind. From the deck of a 70-foot sailing vessel, I could see a shimmering image on the horizon

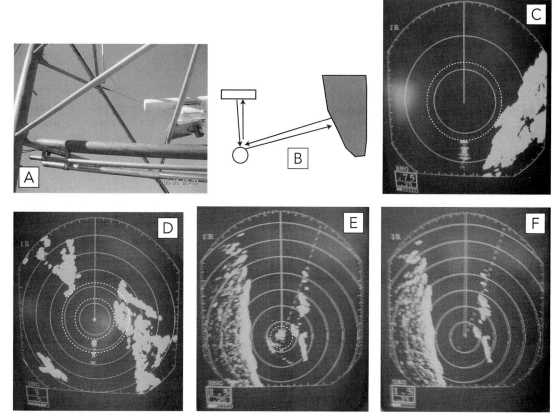

Figure 9-4. *Ghost targets from sources on our vessel. These behave essentially the same as those shown in Figure 9-3, except that since the first source of reflections is fixed on our vessel, they will always be in the same direction. A shows a 9-inch diameter mast located 8 feet aft of the axis of a 4-foot antenna (configurations such as this are often unavoidable on working vessels). B shows the source of the ghosts. The beam hits the mast and reflects off to strike a steep shoreline or passing ship, which sends echoes back to the mast and from there to the antenna. C shows an example from a shoreline just over 0.25 mile off the starboard side. D shows another example with ghosts from a shoreline about 0.6 mile off to starboard as well as another group from about 1 mile off to port. The obstruction is aft, so the ghosts always appear aft. The mast is close enough to the radar antenna so that the final distance to the ghost is essentially the same as the range to the secondary reflector. E shows still another example, with perhaps some additional ghosts from a large boom set on the port side. This picture had four tuning-bar segments showing. In F the tuning bar was reduced to three segments showing and the ghosts were gone, without degrading the rest of the picture. On this radar unit, the Tuning control is an effective way to minimize ghost images.*

that would periodically fade in and out, appearing to show a tug and tow, though oversized and distorted. When I took a step down into the cockpit, the image vanished. When I stepped back up, there it was. After several minutes or so, it disappeared completely.

Such mirages are examples of abnormal atmospheric refraction. They occur during temperature inversions and in other conditions.

For this reason celestial navigators try to avoid very low altitude sextant sights whenever possible. Seeing a distorted sun on the horizon or shimmering heat waves on pavement are similar effects.

The geographic radar range formula has a "fudge factor" to account for the refraction of radar beams, which carries the beam over the geometric horizon. This factor is slightly larger for radar than for visible light. Abnormal refraction can increase or decrease this factor, so that in some cases we see radar targets farther off than expected, and in other cases we do not see them when we think we should.

Abnormal radar refractions are more likely to be seen in certain locations. In cold, high-latitude waters, especially in the presence of warm ocean currents, conditions can lead to *subrefraction*, which can diminish practical radar ranges to 80 percent of their normal ranges. If you compute your geographic range to a tall coastline and expect to see it on the radar at 20 miles off, you might not see it until you are some 16 miles off in conditions of subrefraction. In waters near deserts or other warm landmasses, *superrefraction* might increase practical radar ranges by up to 40 percent of their normal values. If you expect to see a similar coastline at 20 miles off, it might come into view on the radar at 28 miles off due to superrefraction. Subrefraction is usually associated with the bad weather of lows, clouds, and rain; superrefraction is generally associated with the fair weather of high-pressure systems.

RAIN AND SQUALLS

Radar echoes from rain are not "false," but they can definitely be classified as interference, especially when looking for traffic in the rain zone. On the other hand, tracking the location, motion, and development of squalls on the radar can be quite a valuable aid to navigation, especially for sailing vessels. Ocean sailors have stated that observing and tracking squalls by radar is one of radar's most valuable features on tropical ocean passages. But we must not overlook its value to all small craft. I used radar once to maneuver around a massive squall just outside of Nassau, Bahamas, in a 63-foot powerboat. Later that afternoon while checking in at customs, a local vintage cabin cruiser about 30 feet long pulled into the dock with its entire cabin and most of its deck gone. It had somehow survived having its deck removed by

that same squall. It was confirmation enough that we were glad we had radar and maneuvered around the squall, even though we were delayed quite a bit getting in.

Monitoring squall activity can also be a good argument for longer-range radar units. We discussed earlier that in routine inland and coastal waters it is rare to use scales larger than 6 miles or so, except for the periodic look ahead for traffic or a distant landmark. One scenario where a longer range might be helpful is when putting down divers in tropical waters in seasons of frequent squalls. Since divers usually plan on a prearranged dive time underwater, your ability to scan 30 or 40 miles out onto the horizon with radar to look for heavy squall activity and motion could help with this planning, though you must always bear in mind that squalls can develop quickly from cloud formations that might not yet show up on the radar.

Radar sensitivity to squalls and heavy rain is a nuisance when looking for traffic, and a blessing when using it for weather observations. When looking for traffic, we must rely on the AC Rain control discussed in Chapter 2, which will usually work, except in very heavy downpours when radar observations can be completely blocked out. Squalls show up on the radar as fuzzy, white globs, roughly the size of the rain patterns (most often a few miles in diameter), whose intensity changes as the rain intensity changes. They move on the screen like a large, globular vessel. Typical speeds would be up to 10 or 15 knots. As the squall develops, it gets bigger and brighter, and as it diminishes, it gets smaller and weaker. See Figure 9-5. A large squall or cold front, on the other hand, can show up as a solid bright image extending clear across the radar screen. These may be moving or stationary.

The interaction of radar and rain is well documented due to its extensive use in weather observations. Radar detects raindrops not cloud droplets, which are too small. The strength of the echoes increases with drop density and

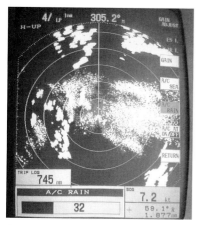

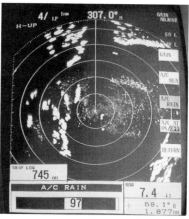

Figure 9-5. Squall images adjusted with AC Rain. The left screen shows two or three squalls that are masking real radar targets, even with some level of AC Rain applied (dialed at 32). When the AC Rain is increased to 97 (right screen), which is almost the max for this unit, the picture is much clearer and we see several well-defined targets. It is important to turn off AC Rain when it is no longer needed, or weak targets might be missed and optimum Gain settings will be difficult to achieve.

drop size, but drop size is the main factor in creating strong echoes. Drop size is almost directly proportional to rate of rainfall, and tropical squalls have the highest rate of rainfall. The brighter the image, the larger the drops, which implies heavier rains, which in turn can be used to judge the development stage of the squall.

As a rule, squalls come in groups, so if conditions are right for squalls, it's likely you will have a lot of them. There is more on squalls in Chapter 11, where we will see that rain is the key to judging the development stage of a squall. You can sometimes discern the difference between squalls with heavy rain and light rain and squalls where rain has not yet developed. If you see a squall on the radar without rain, then you must be seeing echoes from water in the cloud itself, not beneath it. Figure 9-6 illustrates the geometry. Typical tropical

squall ceilings are some 1,000 to 2,000 feet, which means that, on an even keel, you can see under squall clouds not yet raining that are within a mile or two, depending on cloud base and vertical beam angle. As you roll in the seaway, you will get glimpses of the higher clouds. Often, when the fuzzy image of the squall becomes noticeably brighter, you will see clouds start to produce rain.

When negotiating squalls for navigation you should temporarily shut off the AC Rain, which reduces the echoes from the squall, but as soon as you are looking for traffic within the

Figure 9-6. Which squall clouds are seen on radar? The radar beam must interact with water droplets to be seen on the screen. The closest squall here would show up well. The next one out would not because the beam is traveling under the water that is still being held aloft by updrafts. The third one could show up on the radar, even though from the deck we could see that it also is not yet raining. These are just guidelines that might help us interpret what we see. Squall clouds are transient—they not only move, but develop and diminish, which can appear like they are moving on the radar.

squall, you should turn it back on. In heavy squalls, AC Rain makes a big difference in the visibility on the radar screen. You might also experiment with short and long pulse options, if available on the range scale in use.

Also remember that when you are located within a rain pattern or looking beyond one for traffic, the overall efficiency of the radar is reduced. Rain is a very ef-

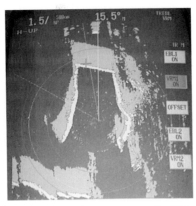 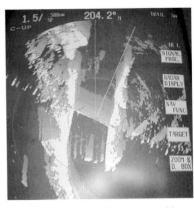

Figure 9-7. *Bridges seen on radar. This is actually the same bridge (Tacoma Narrows, Washington) approached from opposite directions. The left view employs a continuous wake; the right shows a gradient or multi-tone wake, viewed as we were just about to pass under it. Note that the bridge wake makes a very nice buoy trail.*

fective scattering target for microwaves, and much of the beam is lost when passing through large areas of rain. The maximum range as well as the sensitivity at large ranges will be reduced when viewed through a region of rain.

BRIDGES

The first bridge you see on radar will always be a surprise. It is usually not difficult to realize what it is, but you should anticipate the image and its consequences. The image will be a straight line across the waterway. The thickness of the line will vary, depending on the elevation of the bridge and its distance off. The first impression is that of a breakwater or very straight coastline, but a quick reference to the chart will reveal the truth. An example is shown in Figure 9-7. In any case, bridge images are clearly interference of sorts as they could mask traffic over quite a large area.

Besides convincing yourself that there is open water in the direction of a bright solid radar image—at night you would be driving straight into what appears to be solid land—you must think of a few special issues. One is that it might not be obvious from the radar image where the open spans are located. On some

bridges there are radar reflectors set up to mark the main channel, in others you can detect the pilings, and in others there is no way of telling without reading off actual distances on the chart. There is a USCG convention on bridge lighting that could be helpful at night: the pilings on fixed bridges are marked with red lights and the main channels under the bridge are marked with green lights, though not all usable small-craft channels are lighted. These special bridge lights might not be shown on the chart nor listed in the *Light List*.

Another factor to keep in mind, night or day, is that the wake trail of a target emerging from a bridge will appear too short at first. It will take the full time interval (3 minutes, for example) before you can evaluate the speed of a vessel emerging from under a bridge, even though all the other targets on the screen have long since established their 3-minute wake trails on the screen.

Also remember the possibility of detecting a bridge ghost as described above and in Figure 9-3, which would depend on bridge clearance, distance off, bridge structure, antenna type, and so forth.

CHAPTER 10

Advanced Navigation and Piloting

As mentioned earlier, if you have a GPS on your vessel and you want to know your specific chart location, the GPS will do the job. But there are many times when you only want to know where you are relative to the land about you, or just want a quick check of the GPS. For either of these applications radar is usually the best tool. However, both applications entail several basic precautions and procedures.

Remember: Radar is generally the most valuable aid to your navigation at night and in the fog, but that is not the time to learn how to use it! There is immense value in practicing these techniques in clear weather, without other pressing navigation issues at hand.

CALIBRATIONS

First and foremost, all related features and instruments must be properly calibrated. This process is often time-consuming, but it must be dealt with. Keep in mind that the calibration process may or may not be considered part of the normal installation by your electronics technician. If calibration is included, it is instructive to take part in this phase of the installation. There is often a second manual that covers installation that can be downloaded from the Internet if the first is lost.

The first step in calibration is to see that the radar's range, bearings, and heading line are set up properly. The heading line alignment is especially important, as it is fundamental to most radar applications and one that can be

off even after professional installation. The antenna can be mounted square to the centerline to within a few degrees visually or mechanically, but the last step in the alignment must be done electronically using special controls on the radar. When doing your own installation, remember that without this check, the alignment can be significantly off. In modern units, this step is often the main setting of the alignment, rather than a fine-tuning of the alignment as in older units. To check alignment, find a target dead ahead and see that the heading line points to it when the bow points to it. This can be done from a moored or anchored position which might give quicker results, but it is perfectly manageable underway. Furthermore, underway measurements offer more opportunities for checks and double-checks with different targets—a sample is given in the Performance Monitoring section in Chapter 13. Also check the EBL to see that the bearing to some well-defined target off to the side is what it should be as measured from a well-known position. The same check can be made with the VRM.

This process can be considered either calibrating the readouts or determining how accurately you can find your Lat-Lon position by radar alone. In any event, it is important to establish how accurately you can measure a range or bearing from a known position, so you have confidence in your results from unknown positions.

Bearing measurements from radar are always more accurate from a stabilized radar mode, but these still depend upon your reference compass (heading sensor) being correctly adjusted. Almost all electronic compasses include a semiautomatic means of calibration, as mentioned in Chapter 7. This process should be done at least once and compared to the course-up heading with the steering compass when steady on a heading near *each* of the cardinal and intercardinal compass headings (000 C, 045 C, 090 C, etc). Being correct (electronic compass equals steering compass) on one or two of these headings does not guarantee it is correct on others. Each heading must be checked. Protect your heading sensor location by making sure nothing iron or magnetic is stowed near it.

For ARPA applications, your knotmeter speed input must also be correct and calibrated for the collision avoidance outputs to be correct. However, a wrong knotmeter does not affect the position navigation we do with radar, as long as we are not doing a running fix. We can do running fixes with radar, but we have so many other options that this is not a likely choice. Detailed procedures for knotmeter calibration are included in the home study course listed in the Small-Craft Navigation section of the References.

FIX FROM MULTIPLE RANGES

A fix obtained by intersecting several radar ranges is the most reliable means for accurate position fixing from radar alone. Set the cursor or VRM onto the nearest edges of two or three conspicuous radar targets and record the ranges to each. Then construct circles on the chart centered on the objects sighted; the intersection of the circles is your position. The fix is not as convenient to plot on paper charts as the simple radar range and bearing fix, but it is almost always more accurate. On e-charts, however, it is very quick and convenient to plot using electronic range circles. Samples are

shown in Figure 10-1. This plotting method works, of course, regardless of whether you have GPS signals or not. The criterion for a strong fix is about the same as with compass-bearing fixes. We want the circles to intersect at angles of at least 30° or more, which means taking sights to targets that are at least 30° apart yields a good fix. Three targets 60° or 120° apart would give the ideal fix.

This technique calls for adding a new tool to the nav station, a drawing compass or dividers with pencil lead to draw the arcs. In an emergency you can punch two holes in a piece of cardboard with your dividers' point and use one hole for the dividers to hold down the center and put a pencil in the other hole to draw the circle. If the target is an isolated body such as a rock or islet, it is best to measure the range to the closest edge of the target rather than the center. The edge of the target may be better defined if the Gain is reduced slightly to make sure the image is as sharp as possible.

For any target, you generally take the range to the point nearest to you, but if you anticipate any uncertainty on where that point might be on the chart, take a radar bearing to the point and record that with the range. Then on the chart, find the point that is farthest offshore on the target in the opposite direction of your measured bearing and draw the arc from that point.

This technique can be practiced and mastered with the simulator on the Radar Resources CD.

RADAR RANGE AND VISUAL BEARINGS

The virtue of the radar range and bearing fix is its ease of measurement and plotting. No special tools are required for measurement and only traditional parallel rules and dividers are needed for the plotting. More accurate radar position fixing requires swinging arcs on the chart with a draftsman's compass or the use of

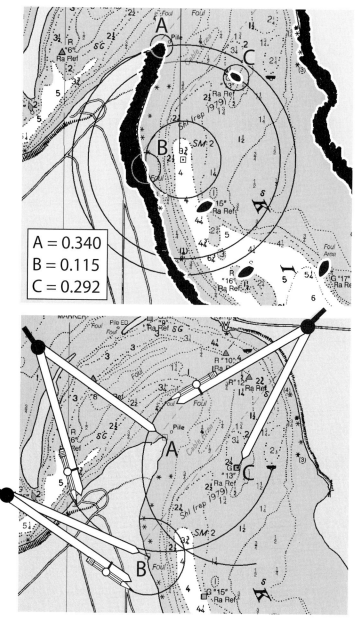

$$A = 0.340$$
$$B = 0.115$$
$$C = 0.292$$

Figure 10-1. *Three-range fix. The top view shows three ranges measured from the radar, with the radar image overlaid on the chart. A is to a point of land, B is to the nearest shore on the port quarter, and C is to a prominent radar reflector on a daymark. This harbor is lined with these radar reflectors, which are labeled "Ra Ref" on charts. They are excellent nav aids. The fix is established by plotting circles of positions from the reference points as shown on the bottom view. This can be done by hand on paper charts, or can be accomplished very quickly on e-charts by placing a mark on each of the reference points and then setting a range ring on each mark corresponding to its distance off. See also Figure 3-10.*

range circles in an electronic chart program, as described in the previous section.

One way to improve the accuracy of the radar range and bearing fix is to replace the radar bearing portion of the fix with a visual compass bearing to the target. Bearings made with a handheld compass must always be tested. Some locations on the vessel will give good bearings and others may not. In some circumstances, accurate bearings can be taken relative to the ship's heading using an inexpensive plastic sextant. For vessels that cannot use hand-bearing compasses, this technique would be worth learning both for navigation fixes and evaluating risk of collision. The sights require a landmark or light dead ahead to use as a reference for the horizontal sextant angle to the target in question. The bow itself could also be used without a landmark if the navigator could be on the centerline during the sightings.

More accurate than visual compass or relative sextant-angle bearings is a fix made from a radar range taken when in range with charted landmarks. Two objects on the horizon are said to be in range when they line up from your perspective. The line of position from two objects in range is one of the most accurate means of piloting. The use of natural ranges for a line of position are shown in positions D, E, G, and H of Figure 10-2, along with other examples of radar navigation along a coastline.

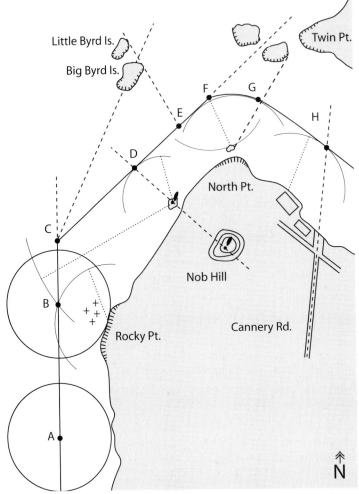

Figure 10-2. *Radar piloting. These are just several of numerous ways to use radar for piloting. At A and B we can use the VRM to pass safely around Rocky Point, at which time we can carry out a two-range fix with the islet off Nob Hill. At a predicted distance farther along (C), we should see Big Byrd Island at a predicted bearing, at which time we turn to the next course, which should have the heading line bisecting the two islands off of Twin Point. When we pass in range of the Nob Hill lights (D), we should be a predicted distance off the islet. When the Byrd islands are in range (E), we are preparing for our turn at F, which we monitor with the VRM as we round. At G the rock off North Point will be abeam and in range with the island off Twin Point, at which time we assume our new course into the channel.*

OPTIMIZING RADAR FIXES

Many aspects of optimum radar position fixing are the same as in other types of piloting with lines or circles of position. Close targets

are better than far, fixed targets are better than floating ones, and intersection angles greater than 30° are required for a good fix, although intersections greater than 60° do not significantly improve a fix.

When taking radar ranges or bearing lines for a position fix from a moving vessel, there is usually a preferred order in taking measurements that optimizes the accuracy of the final fix. This is necessary because we are moving off the first measured line as we switch over to measure the second line. Generally the navigator corrects for this motion between measurements when plotting the data by advancing the first observation to the time of the second to obtain a running fix. For more on plotting procedures, see the Small-Craft Navigation section in the References. The optimum fix is one with minimum correction needed in the advancing process, which is especially true in the common practice of simply ignoring the advancing process and accepting the resultant error as part of the fix's uncertainty.

The goal is to first take the measurement that is changing most slowly with time. When doing a fix with two bearing lines, for example, you would take the one closest to ahead or astern first, record the time, then take the one nearest the beam last, since that is the bearing that changes fastest with time. When using two range circles for a fix, on the other hand, the timing is usually just the reverse. The range on the beam—in the extreme case, the shore we are paralleling—changes slowly or not at all compared to the range to a target ahead or astern.

An especially convenient line of position is a natural range dead ahead or astern, because it can be accurate and independent of compass errors, and does not need to be advanced since we are moving along that line.

These considerations apply to any type of piloting observation; they are not unique to radar, except that range data used for piloting are much easier to obtain with radar than by other piloting techniques using sextant or bow angles. When using either a range or a bearing, stop to ask yourself what corrections might be needed. When recording a range to be used for a circle of position, make sure what you are seeing on the radar is really there. In some parts of the world, the height of the tide can dramatically change the location and shape of radar targets compared to what you might guess from a casual glance at the chart.

When taking a bearing line, ask yourself, "Why are radar bearing lines sometimes suspect?" One reason is that the output from the EBL or cursor is always the bearing relative to your heading. If you have a heading sensor input, then the bearing will be as good as that calibration, but if you do not have a heading input, then you must apply that relative bearing by hand to the magnetic heading of the vessel at the time of measurement. That means recording your vessel's heading each time you record the EBL, and possibly asking the helmsman to hold a steady course while you do your navigation, and so on.

In addition to getting the proper numerical value for the bearing, there is the always present effect of the horizontal beam width, discussed earlier. For bearings it would be best to

take those to the central part of a symmetrical target, rather than to a tangent. When taking bearings to a tangent, we must correct by one half the beam width as illustrated in Figure 10-3. If the beam width is 6°, for example, we would add 3° to left-hand bearings and subtract 3° from right-hand tangents. Practicing from a known position using paper or e-chart plotting will illustrate the point and show how to determine a correct bearing from the radar EBL values. For 4-foot antennas, on the other hand, this becomes a much smaller concern because the beam width is down below 2° or so, and we must correct by less than 1°.

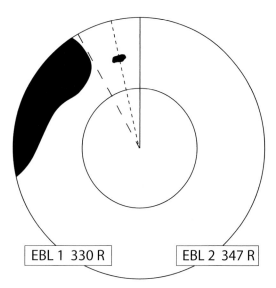

EBL 1 330 R   EBL 2 347 R

Figure 10-3. Correcting bearings for HBW. EBL1 (dashed line) measures the bearing to the corner of a headland, and EBL2 (dotted line) measures the bearing to the center of a buoy target. The buoy bearing of 347 can be plotted directly on the chart (after correcting for vessel heading) since it is to the center of the target. But we can see from the size of the buoy target itself (about 8° wide) that we have a significant beam width on this antenna. Before plotting the bearing line to the headland, we should subtract 4° to account for the beam width. The correct bearing would be 326°. This correction is most important for antennas smaller than 2 feet. See also Figures 7-10 and 7-13. For the smaller antennas, your actual beam width may be larger than predicted in the manuals. Use the EBL to measure the widths of several buoy targets to get a feeling for its practical value.

PARALLEL INDEXING

In prudent navigation, you do not want to rely on any single aid in areas where a mistake could lead to serious trouble. Crossing a river bar, or entering an island cut, or passing through narrow channels sprinkled with rocks and strong currents require special care. Many parts of the world have their special navigation challenges. Some of these challenges may have good navigation aids, either man-made or natural, but others have very few. If there is no current, no wind, and no swell, you can generally traverse such passages safely by simply going very slowly. But strong current, wind, or waves are usually the factors that rule out that option, and leave you with a challenge that takes special care and preparation.

For such passages, the GPS linked to an electronic chart with a predefined route of specific waypoints can be easily set up and is easy to follow graphically and digitally as you proceed. Radar offers the best backup for this approach—or the only method, if GPS signals are not available in the region. In the cases we consider now, we need special systematic radar planning, called parallel indexing. There are various adaptations. It is a valuable technique in tricky passages where dependable aids to navigation are sparse, but it can also be of use in simpler situations, as was described in the offset tracking example of Chapter 5.

In Part One we did not cover the use of north-up mode (NU) in any detail. Parallel indexing, however, is one radar piloting technique that is much better done in NU mode than in head-up mode (HU). It can be done in HU mode with ranges, as outlined in Figure 5-5, but it is more limited and requires more care than the use of NU mode. Another example of HU mode using an index range is shown in Figure 10-4. Note that an offset radar center can be very useful in this application. You can extend the view forward as you approach the index range to get aligned earlier, and then extend it

aft as you proceed along the range to keep the aft target in view longer.

If your index targets drift off the index line in HU mode, adjust your heading promptly back toward the line—which will shift at least one index target well off the index line temporarily—then go back on course promptly to put the targets back on the index line again, or to show that more correction is needed. In HU mode, it will be very difficult to just "crab" along the line correcting for current or wind; instead it will take prominent adjustments back to the line and then back onto your course to check the alignment. Whenever you are on course, however, you will know at a glance where you are relative to where you want to be; it is just not as easy to correct for errors as it might be.

This is in striking contrast to using this same method with NU, which will not only let small course adjustments be made to maintain alignment, but it can also be done with just one index target alone. A range is not required. The reason for the distinction is that in HU mode the targets shift when you turn, but in NU mode only the heading line turns. In NU mode, you can slowly adjust your heading to actually crab along the desired course.

Figures 10-5 and 10-6 illustrate this big distinction and point out another great advantage of the NU display (put another way, this is another justification for the extra expense of adding a heading sensor to your radar!). When you use a range in HU mode, you at least know when you are off course. But if you only use a single target in HU mode, you cannot safely determine that from the radar alone. You need either a range and HU mode, or a single target and NU mode.

The key to the problem with course corrections using HU versus NU displays is that *once you are off track, no one single heading adjustment will correct the problem, regardless of display mode*, and therefore the stabilized display (north-up or course-up) is required to keep track of where you are relative to the lay

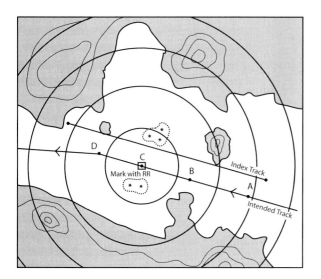

Figure 10-4. *Offset tracking using a range in HU mode (an expansion of the example given in Figure 5-5). HU mode requires a range for parallel index tracking, because a single index mark is not reliable in HU mode (see Figure 10-5). This sets some limits on its applicability as both targets making up the index range must be in view throughout the passage. Electronic charting or equivalent plotting on paper charts is the best way to plan the passage.*

Step 1. In the chartlet, select a working radar range from the hazard region (point C) that shows both targets.

Step 2. Plot the intended track, note the course heading, and measure the offset distance to the parallel range that will guide you along the track. Make a note of what will signal you to turn to the next course—in this case, abeam the islet at point D. The offset in this example is 120 yards (0.06 nm). (continued below)

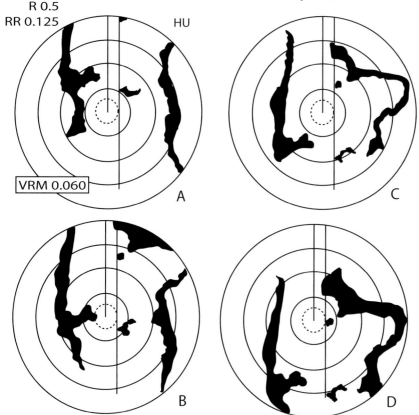

Step 3. Set the radar to the working range, set the VRM to the offset distance, and draw a vertical line on the radar screen at that offset, parallel to the heading line.

Step 4. Slowly approach point A, where the farthest index target will first appear on the screen, and maneuver to be on the right course with each target on the index line on the radar screen.

Step 5. Proceed on course, keeping both targets on the index line, as explained in the text.

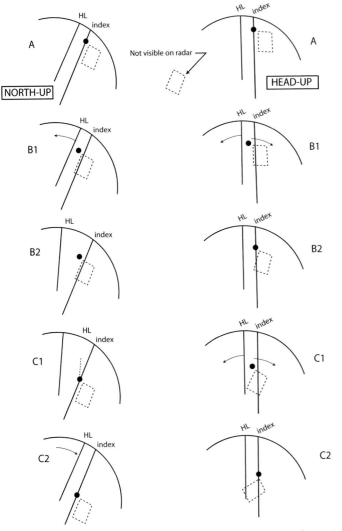

of the land (in this case an imaginary straight shoreline running through the index target, whose orientation is shown permanently on the NU display with the index line).

Figure 10-6 may shed more light on this distinction. Note that keeping the index target on the index line in HU mode does not guarantee that you stay a fixed distance off the hazard.

The purpose of parallel indexing is to have some radar piloting technique that lets you monitor your progress *continuously* (as opposed to a series of individual measurements and plots), as when you drive along a coast or shoreline, dragging the VRM along the shore to keep yourself at a fixed distance offshore. That process is a type of paral-

Figure 10-5. *Parallel indexing in the presence of current, using head-up versus north-up display modes as seen on the radar. Head-up mode is not a safe way to do parallel indexing with a single target. The dashed line marks the outline of an underwater hazard not visible on radar. See Figure 10-6 for a chart view of similar interactions. In the top figures (A), which show corners of a radar screen, if there were no current or leeway, the index mark would travel straight down the index line of the HU or NU display providing we held a steady course. With nothing pushing us off course, either display mode*

would work—a condition, however, that is not known in advance in some waterways.

To consider the effect of current, look at B1 in the NU sequence. We note we are getting set to the right, toward the shoal, because the index target is now inside the index line. Hence we turn left into the current and the heading line shifts to the left, but the index line remains in place. As we proceed on the new heading, the (stationary) index mark will travel straight down-screen, parallel to the heading line, or it may drift more if we have not corrected enough. Note that the task here is not to choose the proper crabbing angle to just offset the current. We are not where we want to be, so we must overcorrect to some extent to get the index mark back on the line. At C1, we have driven the mark back onto the index line, applying more or less correction as needed. At this time, we could come back onto course, or maintain whatever correction is needed to keep the index mark on the index line, which assures us we are passing the shoaling on the track we intended.

In a head-up display mode, on the other hand, shown on the right side, the radar operator's observations are quite different. At B1 we also know that the boat is being set toward the shoal and that a turn to the left is required, but it is difficult to keep track of the effects of these turns. When we turn left, the index mark rotates to the right, and then proceeds down-screen from there. Turning just enough to put the mark back on the line (B2) would typically not solve the problem permanently, and the mark would continue to slip inside the index line as shown in C1. Another turn to put the mark back on the line (C2) and we are further disoriented relative to the hazard.

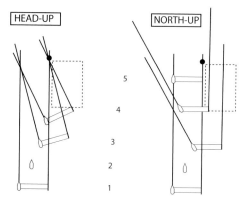

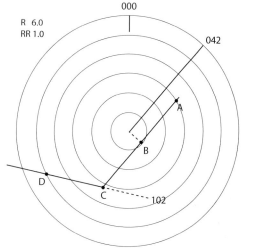

Figure 10-6. *Differences between head-up and north-up modes for parallel indexing in the presence of current. The vessel positions are plotted as they might appear on an e-chart presentation. Here the radar heading lines and index lines are overlaid onto the chartlet to show how the tracks might have been determined based on radar observations alone. The dotted lines mark an underwater hazard zone.*

lel indexing, but now we consider cases where there is no shore to drag the VRM along nor any convenient range to follow.

All forms of parallel indexing—and this term typically implies you are using NU mode—require drawing lines on the radar screen itself, either by hand or using electronic lines, or more often using electronic lines as guides to hand-marked lines. You can also draw the lines on a transparent overlay that is placed onto the radar screen for the passage. (If you use overlays, you can reuse them for the same passage in the future without redoing the layout.) The idea is to select a target that will be in view throughout the passage, and then mark the path of that target as it moves across the radar screen during a safe transit. Then drive the vessel so the index target follows the path. A simple example is shown in Figure 10-7, which shows the use of an islet for an index target to transit a region of unmarked shoals. It is the radar equivalent of following a route using GPS and monitoring your trail on an e-chart or plotter.

Remember that stationary targets always

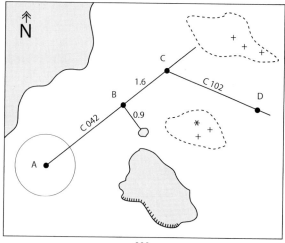

Figure 10-7. *Parallel indexing in north-up display mode. The chart shows our intended course NE and then SE between two underwater hazards. We identify the islet 0.9 mile to the right of the course as our index target. Once the target is on the radar screen (bottom), 3 miles off on the starboard side, we draw on the radar screen the exact track it will follow (A-B-C-D) as we proceed. We then drive to keep the index mark on its track. A floating EBL (ERBL) is very convenient for laying out the lines on the screen, which we then trace with an appropriate marker. At B, the target will be abeam. At C, we turn to course 102, and by keeping the target on the C-D line we will safely transit the hazard.*

move straight down the heading line, so your overall index line will always be a series of straight lines, and your index mark will always be moving down-screen, parallel to the heading line. When your index mark hits a bend in the index track, it is time to turn, after which the index mark will track straight down the new line segment.

When following your index mark through the passage, you will be keeping it on its line and the mark will have a wake like all other targets. It is helpful to mark the location of the index mark (and the time) periodically on the screen with a pen. This makes the radar's picture of your progress more dynamic and informative and also serves as a backup to the charted track.

The best index targets are grounded isolated targets (lights or islets) or the tip of a sharp headland or breakwater. Your target should remain a good one regardless of aspect throughout the transit. Also make sure you have selected the optimum radar range; your lines on the screen will not be correct if you change ranges.

This process can be practiced with the simulator. With real radar, it is much easier to set up once you are accustomed to using the ERBL as a guide for laying out the lines. The lines must be drawn properly on the radar screen, which takes some thought and double-checking. If you plan to use the same route to enter and exit a region, you might be able to draw the path on the radar screen of an appropriate index target on the way in and use that path to set up the track for the outbound route. A series of dots with an overhead projector marker will do the job. North-up display mode is generally the best for this application, but once practiced and understood, it has applications in head-up mode as well. E-charts that allow range rings on a movable mark make it especially easy to set up the indexing with assurance that the target will be in view where needed.

MAKING LANDFALL

In clear weather, with a typical small-craft radar, it is a toss-up whether you will see land first by sight or radar. If the landfall has high hills or mountains, and it is very clear, then most likely you would see it first by eye. But if it is night or the least bit hazy, cloudy, or rainy, then radar might be your first indication.

You might need to use the maximum range of your radar when making a landfall (discussed in Chapters 3 and 7). The height of your radar antenna contributes to when you first see land on the radar, but the shape and elevation of the land you are approaching is more crucial.

First compute the geographic range (Chapter 3). If the target is beyond the radar horizon of the antenna ($1.22 \times \sqrt{\text{antenna height in ft}}$), then you must guesstimate which elevations of coastal features might first appear.

For radar (and visual) identification, it is useful to use a highlighter marker to trace elevation contours, such as all 500-foot lines in yellow, all 1,000-foot lines in green, etc., to help you picture the lay of the land as it might appear from seaward.

British Admiralty Pilots dated earlier than 1980 include special tables of radar detection ranges for prominent landmarks along the coastlines covered in each volume. They include ranges when typically first seen on radar, ranges when seen clearly on radar, and ranges when close enough to identify the landmark by its target shape. Some targets do not have entries in all columns. The data are based on ship reports, so they are from higher antennas than are typically found on small craft, but they are still useful guides. These range tables have been discontinued in newer editions, presumably because much of the data are from outdated radar equipment and thus might be misleading in some cases.

Landmarks with the farthest radar ranges are typically in the 20- to 25-mile range (with a few at 30 miles), which should be detectable with the longer-range small-craft radars at about the same ranges. In clear weather, however, you would see tall peaks visually from much farther off than 25 miles, even though geographic radar range is actually slightly farther than geographic visual range due to different refraction values.

The point is that the eye can easily see a part of a hill above the horizon regardless of its shape, whereas radar needs an adequate exposed perpendicular surface to generate reflected echoes. In other words, some peaks can be well over both visual and radar horizons (taking into account both the landmark heights and the observer or antenna heights), and yet be visible by eye only. This is not a particularly unusual situation. It is not uncommon, for example, for a low-intensity navigation light located at a high elevation to be visible during the day from farther off than it can be seen at night. In *Light List* terminology, it would be a light with a geographical range larger than its nominal range.

In any event, when first detecting radar echoes from distant land it will be very difficult to make any positive identification of the coast or landmark. The echoes detected are likely from peaks or elevation contours well inside the coastline. If you mistakenly identify a radar image with the coastline that is actually a contour well inland, you could overestimate your distance off shore, which could be hazardous.

If you see land, for example, at 17 miles off and your antenna is 10 feet high, then work with this equation (from Chapter 3):

$$\text{Detected range (nm)} =$$
$$1.22 \times \sqrt{\text{antenna height in ft}}$$
$$+ 1.22 \times \sqrt{\text{target elevation in ft,}}$$

which we can rearrange to get

$$\text{Target elevation (ft)} = [(\text{detected range (nm)}/$$
$$1.22) - \sqrt{\text{antenna height in ft}}]^2$$

or in this example,

$$\text{Target elevation (ft)} = [(17/1.22) - \sqrt{10}]^2$$
$$= [13.9 - 3.2]^2$$
$$= 115 \text{ feet}$$

This is the minimum height the land must be to appear over the horizon, and then you need some elevation above the horizon to make a real target. If you arbitrarily add 20 feet for that, then you can say that for a landmark that shows up on radar at 17 miles from an antenna that is 10 feet high, you should look for elevation contours on land of at least 135 feet to identify what you are seeing.

Once you can establish range and bearing to three distinct targets, you can figure out where you are, but you will usually see land long before you can identify it. When you do get reasonable ranges and bearings it might be useful to transfer the potential target locations to a universal plotting sheet (as used in celestial navigation) to plot a fix. Since you can make these at any scale, it solves the problem of not having a convenient chart scale for this type of plotting.

When details of the images start to show up on the radar as you get closer, recall that bays and headlands will be filled in or rounded out according to the horizontal beam width as discussed in Chapter 7. It is very important to keep that effect in mind along with the obvious shadowing of higher land obscuring lower land behind it.

A more subtle effect may occur when approaching a sloping coastline. Without careful analysis, a radar target that looks like a coastline could actually be an elevation contour well inland running parallel to the coast; here, the coastline is actually below the radar horizon. Or you might see a raised street or row of tall buildings well inland over a beach.

Returning to the previous example of seeing land on the radar at 17 miles off at an elevation of 135 feet, suppose that the 135-foot elevation is 5 miles inland from the actual coastline and that you are traveling at 5 kts toward the shore. To make things really interesting, let's assume that the slope of the shore is such that the land is just below the radar horizon. In this case, for each mile you get closer to the beach, you see another mile of real target, so the coastline appears to be closing in on you at roughly twice your actual speed! In short, correlating the first

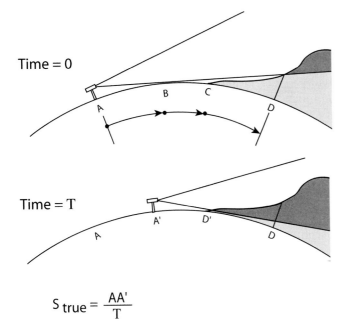

Time = 0

Time = T

$$S_{true} = \frac{AA'}{T}$$

$$S_{apparent} = \frac{AD - A'D'}{T} = S_{true} + \frac{DD'}{T}$$

signs of land on the radar with our GPS position is important. See Figure 10-8.

Remember, if it is raining your maximum range could be significantly reduced. For first observations of all distant targets, use long pulse length, turn on Echo Stretch, tweak up the Gain a bit, and watch carefully.

Figure 10-8. *Land rushing over the horizon. In the top part, the radar beam emitted from A skims the horizon at B, passes over the top of the true coastline at C, and reflects from an elevation contour at D. The apparent distance to the coastline is AD. In the bottom part, after moving toward the shore from A to A', lower land on the coast is now visible on the radar, and the apparent distance to the coastline is now A'D'. In such an approach, the true speed toward the shore is enhanced by the rate at which new land is exposed.*

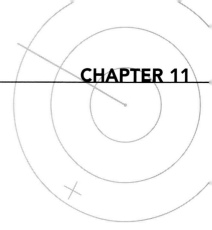

CHAPTER 11

Radar Maneuvering

I n this chapter we expand on the ideas introduced in Chapter 6 related to evaluating risk of collision and learning about approaching traffic in order to choose the best way to maneuver.

TARGET VESSEL ASPECT

One of the main tasks in radar observation of vessel traffic is to determine the other vessel's aspect, because that is what ultimately specifies which of the *Navigation Rules* apply to the encounter. *Aspect* in this sense refers to the orientation of the other vessel as you see it, which depends on its heading relative to yours and its relative bearing.

One way to specify aspect is to state what part of the target vessel you are looking at, such as head-on, port bow, starboard quarter, and so on. If a vessel were crossing in front of you from your left to your right, you would see first its starboard bow, then its starboard beam, and then its starboard quarter. Describing aspect in this way works for general communications, but it is not adequate for more precise specifications, such as predicting what lights we might see at night, or determining whether we are an overtaking vessel.

The more precise way to specify aspect numerically is to state what your own relative bearing would be as observed from the other vessel. Instead of saying the aspect is "starboard bow," you could be more precise by saying, "aspect is 30° green." This means that if someone on the other vessel looked at you, he would see you at a bearing of 30° to the right on his own bow. We use red or green to specify what side of the vessel we are looking at, as illustrated in Figure 11-1.

With this terminology, at night you would expect to see a white stern light for all vessels whose aspect is greater than 112.5° red or

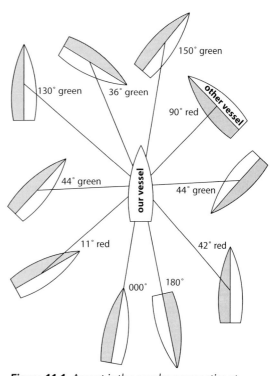

Figure 11-1. *Aspect is the angular perspective at which we see a vessel approaching or leaving. Defined as the relative bearing of our vessel as seen from the other vessel, it is measured from 0° to 180° and labeled* red *when we are on the port side of the vessel or* green *when we are on its starboard side.*

green, and you would expect to see red side-lights for vessels with aspect 000 red to 112.5 red. (In the real world we do not see vessel light changes at precisely the legal specifications, as some lights show through wider or narrower sectors than they should.)

We can combine this terminology with the wind analogy used to describe relative motion in Chapter 6. Whenever you see a crossing target, its true aspect will be aft of its apparent aspect as discerned from its direction of relative motion and relative bearing. Thus, if its appar-

ent aspect on the radar screen is 60° red, its true aspect might be 100°, 120°, or more, depending on its actual heading and speed. This can be very useful to keep in mind when figuring out what vessel lights you should look for on the horizon based on radar images. Though the apparent aspect might lead you to expect to see a red sidelight out there in the darkness, the true aspect might tell you to look for a white stern light instead.

On the other hand, for parallel targets, no matter where they are seen on the radar screen, after you figure whether they are headed toward or away from you (Chapter 6), their aspect will be just what you would guess based on their relative bearing. These points are summarized below and illustrated in the top part of Figure 11-2.

> ➤ **For parallel targets: true aspect equals apparent aspect.**
> **For crossing targets: true aspect is aft of apparent aspect.** ◄

The problem is, you do not know how far aft the true aspect will be for a crossing target. What appears to be an aspect on the bow could be one on the beam or almost all the way back on the stern. To solve this problem we need to solve the relative motion diagram, discussed next.

RELATIVE MOTION DIAGRAM

In Chapter 6 we distinguished between *parallel targets*, moving straight up-screen or down-screen (meaning parallel to the heading line), and *crossing targets* moving across the radar screen at an angle. Crossing targets will cross the heading line safely in front of us, pass safely behind us, or approach straight down the EBL, in which case they pose a definite risk of collision (Figure 6-12). As we saw, it is easy to figure the true speed and heading of a parallel target from the length of

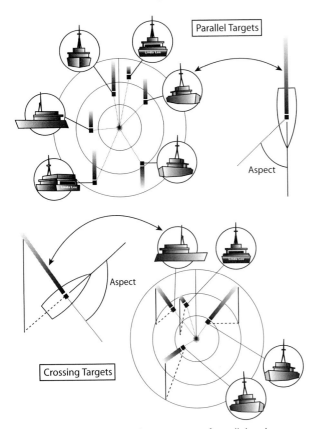

Figure 11-2. *Apparent and true aspects of parallel and crossing targets. The top view shows parallel targets with "binocular view" inserts showing what aspect you would see for each of the targets. The aspect of the vessel at 045 R is diagrammed to show that it is about 045 green, as might be expected. The bottom is a similar picture for crossing targets, but for these the apparent aspect is not the true aspect, which must be determined by solving a relative motion diagram. If you are not moving, trails for crossing as well as parallel targets indicate the vessel's true aspect.*

its wake trail alone, but we could not do the same simple analysis for a crossing target.

We have this knowledge: a target tracking straight down the EBL is an indication of a collision course, but we do not know if the collision will be with the bow, the beam, or the quarter of the approaching vessel. In other words, the simple observation that a target is getting closer to us with time does not tell us which way the other boat is headed or how fast it is traveling. This is fundamental information to be deduced from the radar, and we can obtain it by solving the *relative motion diagram* (RMD).

The principle behind the procedure is illustrated in Figure 11-3, which is similar to what we saw in Figure 6-4. Referring to the top part of Figure 11-3, if we were approaching a buoy just as a vessel passed it, we would see on the radar screen the vessel target move away from the buoy target as shown, and we would at the same time see the buoy moving down the radar screen due to our own motion.

The buoy wake is due to our motion. The target vessel wake is a combination of our motion and the target vessel's motion. We want to know the motion between the buoy target and the target vessel, because that represents the true motion of the target vessel regardless of our own motion.

In this case, draw a line between the buoy target and the vessel target and the length of that line would be the target's speed, and the direction of that line (buoy to target) would be the target vessel's true course. Or we can simply imagine a buoy trail where there is none and figure the target's true course and speed as illustrated in Figure 11-4.

The key to this process is knowing the length of the buoy trail for whatever speed you are running; this is your buoy trail, as explained in Chapter 6. If you see a real buoy or point of land on the screen, you can measure the length directly from that (all stationary targets on the screen leave the same trails in direct response to your motion) or figure the buoy trail length

from the time interval of the wake trails and your speed. When the time interval is 6 minutes, the trail length in nautical miles is ¹⁄₁₀ of your speed in knots (the six-minute rule), as explained in Chapter 6 along with other ways to compute the length.

Another key point to remember is that you should always draw the buoy trail line down-

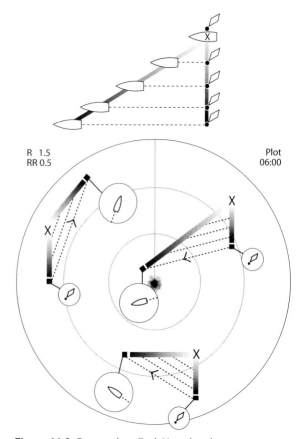

R 1.5
RR 0.5

Plot
06:00

Figure 11-3. *Buoy wakes. Each X marks where a target vessel passes a buoy. The top shows how the radar picture of this passing would occur; the line from buoy to vessel at any time represents the true motion of the vessel. The bottom part shows several examples of how such a passing would appear on the radar screen. In all cases, the line from final buoy position to final vessel position represents the true motion of the target vessel. In each case, this true motion is quite different from the relative motion of the target vessel that we see on the radar. This buoy trail concept is the key to understanding the relative motion diagram, which is nothing more than the triangle made up of buoy wake, target wake, and the line connecting them. The circular insets show the orientations of the target vessels.*

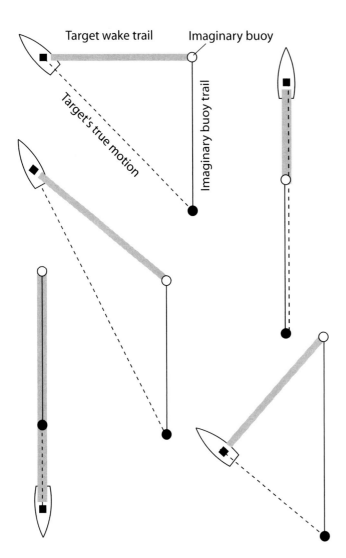

Figure 11-4. *Imaginary buoy trails. Imagine a buoy (open circles) at the origin of the target wake and then draw the buoy trail it would make straight down-screen, parallel to the heading line. The length of the buoy trail is how far we moved during the duration of the target vessel wake. If it is a 6-minute wake, the length of the buoy trail is just ⅒ of our speed. The ends of the buoy trails are marked with solid circles. The true motion of the target vessels is shown by the dashed lines from the solid circles to the preset locations of the targets. Note that we can also draw this diagram for parallel targets, as illustrated, but for these we do not need to make a diagram, as discussed in Chapter 6.*

screen from the back end of the target's wake trail, not from the target position at the time of the calculation. If you do not have Wake or Plot options of any kind, then remember that the buoy trail is drawn down-screen from the first target observation. The length of the buoy trail will be how far you moved between the first and second observations, and the true motion line should be drawn from the bottom of the buoy trail to the location of the second observation.

The down-screen direction is always relative to the heading line, so when using a north-up display mode, buoy trails are not vertical lines on the radar as they are in head-up mode. The difference is illustrated in several figures in Chapter 6. It is this difference between head-up and north-up display that leads some navigators to prefer head-up or course-up over north-up when it comes to interacting with traffic. In a head-up display the buoy trails are always vertical lines, no matter what your course is, but in north-up, buoy trails are parallel to the direction in which the heading line is pointed. The great advantage of having the target trails stabilized to your heading in the north-up mode would seem to outweigh this inconvenience in most cases—or you can switch to course-up and have the best of both worlds.

The actual plotting is often done most conveniently right on the radar screen, using the marking techniques discussed in Chapter 1, and shown in Figure 11-5. Wet-erase overhead-projector markers work well for this. With a little practice, however, you might find that you can figure out what you need by tracing through the plot process without actually drawing the line. That is, after laying off the distance of the buoy trail, plot a dot there, and then by eye or using a portable range scale, measure from the dot to the target to get the target's course and speed.

Regardless of how you choose to do the RMD plotting in the long run (options are given below), there is no substitute for some practice at traditional transfer plotting. This means measuring two values of range, bearing, and time from the first and second observations of a radar target (usually 6 minutes later), and then transferring or plotting these points onto a paper representation of the radar screen called a transfer plotting sheet, maneuvering board, or radar plotting sheet. A sample is shown in Figure 11-6, and printable versions are on the Radar Resources CD.

The relative motion diagram is then solved on the plotting sheet, along with other solutions such as CPA and time to CPA. It is often a way to get precise answers, but you must remember that the accuracy of the results still depends on how accurately you measured the data from the radar screen. For more sophisticated solutions such as course to steer for desired CPA (below), or to investigate the effects of your own or the target's speed changes, you must usually resort to careful transfer plotting for accurate results. The RMD, however, is still the most common problem in radar observing

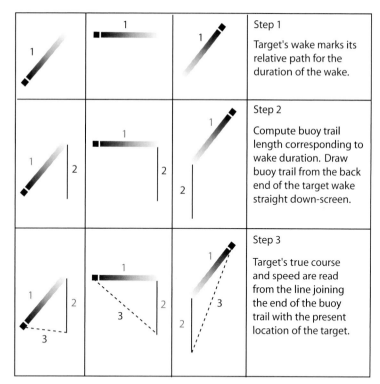

			Step 1 Target's wake marks its relative path for the duration of the wake.
			Step 2 Compute buoy trail length corresponding to wake duration. Draw buoy trail from the back end of the target wake straight down-screen.
			Step 3 Target's true course and speed are read from the line joining the end of the buoy trail with the present location of the target.

Figure 11-5. *Drawing a relative motion diagram. Examples are shown for a bow, beam, and quarter target. The plot can be made directly on the radar screen (Chapter 1), on a separate plotting sheet, or in an e-chart program.*

by far, especially for small-craft operations, and the more you practice this on paper, the easier it will become on the radar screen.

Looking into more modern options, you can also solve the RMD digitally using an electronic range and bearing line (ERBL) as illustrated in Figure 11-7. This will give precise values, but is not often required over the estimates you can obtain from reading the screen by hand with the aid of a portable range marker. Some units have a more convenient interface to the ERBL than others. In some units, switching from fixed to movable EBL reference (called *floating the EBL*) requires a menu option within another menu; on other units you just press a button, or you may have the option to set up a user-defined hot key for the operation. This approach is more valuable when the ERBL is easy to use.

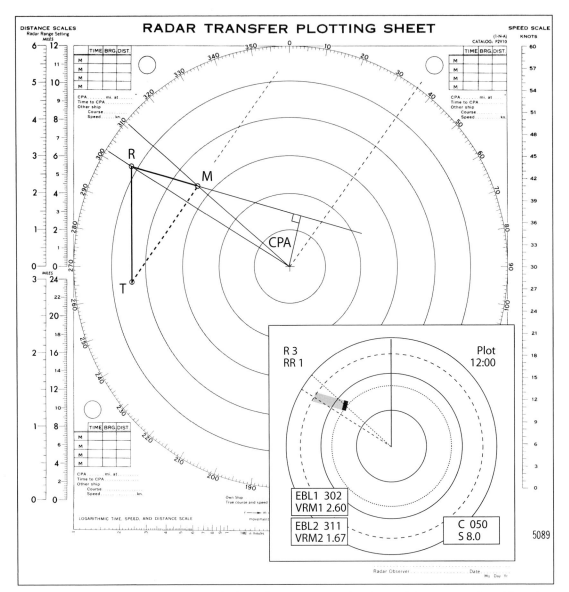

Figure 11-6. *A radar plotting sheet. Several values of a target's range, bearing, and time are transferred from the radar screen to sheets like this for solving the relative motion diagram and related problems. Plotting sheets are used mostly in schools and for practice. Underway the procedure of rapid radar plotting right on the radar screen is more common, but more complex radar maneuvers and analysis are much easier and accurate when done by transfer plotting. These sheets were once government publications but now are only available from commercial reproductions. There are several styles, but they typically include several scale options and nomograms for speed-time-distance computations. There are custom versions of radar plotting sheets on the Radar Resources CD that can be printed on conventional letter paper.*

The sample shown using the 3-mile scale is based on the radar data from the inset. R is the first data measured and M is the second, taken 12 minutes later. The line RT is the buoy trail. The plot is often called the RTM triangle, where RM represents the relative motion and TM represents the true motion. A careful plot of these data yields true course and speed of 8.1 kts on course 036 R or 086 T, based on the true course of 050. If all courses and speeds remain unchanged, the CPA will be 0.7 nm and will occur about 18 minutes after M was recorded.

This process is essentially what the ARPA functions discussed in Chapter 8 do automatically. But no matter how you solve the relative motion diagram, and even if you have mini-ARPA on board, it is crucial that you learn the process and practice it. Solving the relative motion diagram by hand is how you confirm that the ARPA is working correctly. The ARPA is reading your course and speed (essentially your buoy trail) from remote inputs. If these are not correct, it will not compute the right data for the interaction. With incorrect input, it could claim you are passing at a safe distance when in fact you are not. Periodically checking it by hand will add safety and confidence to your navigation, and allow you to take better advantage of the ARPA functions.

One of the key values of radar is being able to determine the course and speed of moving traffic. It makes a night-and-day difference in your comfort with radar operations and will add to the safety and versatility of your navigation. Figure 11-8 shows one example of deciphering the situation with a simple analysis. When transiting a fleet of fishing vessels meandering around fishing grounds in the fog or at night, you would have chaos on the radar screen without this basic understanding.

Along with the value of solving the RMD for discovering the aspect of a target vessel so we know what lights to look for at night, it can be valuable to know the true motion of a vessel when hailing it by radio. We shall see in Chapter 12 that the Rules of the Road require us to understand this analysis, because parts of Rule 19 require us to know whether or not we are overtaking a vessel in the fog that we see only on radar.

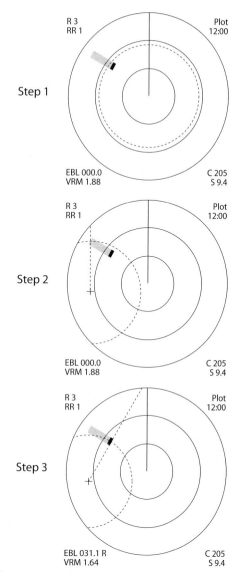

Figure 11-7. *Solving the relative motion diagram using an electronic range and bearing line (ERBL). The procedure is the same for head-up and north-up displays. The sample shown is a head-up display.*

Step 1. Set the EBL to coincide with your heading line (in head-up, this will be vertical) and set the VRM to the length of your buoy trail. In this example, at 9.4 kts in 6 min the buoy trail = 0.94 nm, so in 12 min it is 1.88 nm.

Step 2. Float the ERBL and place the intersection of the EBL and VRM on the tail end of the wake. Lock this ERBL reference position. In most units the VRM value set remains the same when you float it; if not, reset it to buoy trail length.

Step 3. Set the EBL and VRM to the current target position and read target course (EBL) and speed (VRM). In this example, the true course is 031 R (read from EBL) and the true speed is 8.2 kts. Recall this reasoning: in 12 min the vessel moved 1.64 miles (read from VRM), so in 6 min (a tenth of an hour) it would have moved 0.82 nm, and in a full hour it would have moved 8.2 nm, which is 8.2 kts. (See the six-minute rule discussion in Chapter 6.)

As shown in Figure 11-8, you actually do not know if you are overtaking until you solve the relative motion diagram.

When applying radar observations to sailboat racing (as discussed below), finding the course and speed of your competitors is the main task at hand, so this exercise is crucial.

On the Pacific Northwest and California coasts, there are still many boaters who have read the old books that recommend going 100 miles offshore and then turning south, primarily to avoid the traffic that includes both ships and fishing fleets. But with radar on board *and the knowledge of how to use it*, it is far safer and more efficient to go right down the coastline and deal with traffic rather than deal with the higher winds and seas offshore. Many of these boaters actually do have radar on board but are not comfortable with traffic interactions. The relative motion diagram is the key to that comfort. Every minute spent practicing will pay off.

The radar simulator included on the Radar Resources CD is an excellent way to practice the relative motion diagram. Figure 11-9 summarizes misinterpretations of the radar screen that are easy to make if you overlook the crucial significance of relative motion.

Historically, the relative motion diagram has

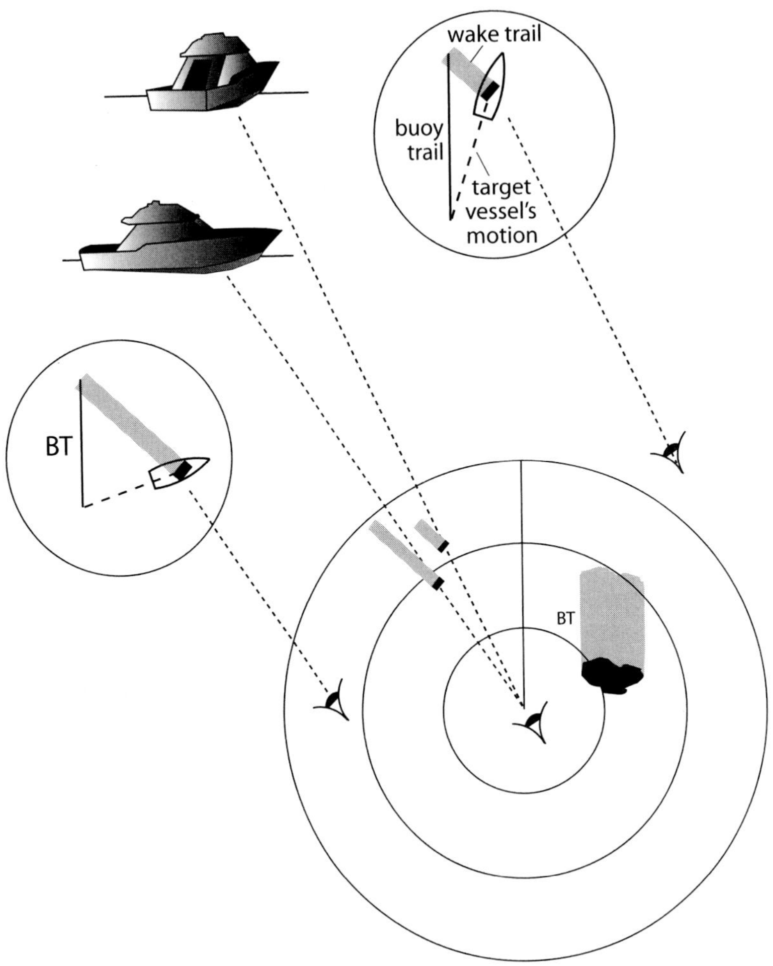

Figure 11-8. *Crossing versus overtaking. Two targets on the port bow appear to be approaching on parallel courses, with the leftmost one apparently moving faster, as we approach an islet on the starboard side. A quick application of the relative motion diagram, however, shows that one target is actually headed almost across our path and the other is headed away from us. If we saw these vessels visually, one would be a crossing vessel according to the Rules and we would be overtaking the other. At night, we would see well-separated masthead lights from one and only the stern light of the other. Note that it is very easy to get this RMD information in this case because we have the buoy trail of the land as a reference for completing the diagrams without any computations. As it turns out, the one with the short trail is actually moving faster than the other one, even though its speed relative to us (SRM) is lower.*

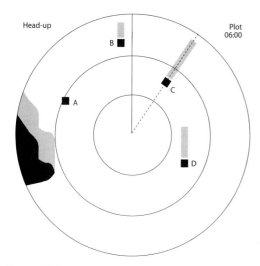

Figure 11-9. *Common misinterpretations of relative motion displays. A shows a target believed to be stopped that is actually moving at precisely the same course and speed as we are. B is a target that appears to be approaching slowly from ahead and should show red and green sidelights but is actually one being overtaken and showing a white stern light. C is a target approaching straight down the EBL that might be expected to show both its red and green sidelights with its masthead lights in line, but it is actually headed more perpendicular to our course line (aspect more aft); thus, we would see a red light only and well-separated masthead lights. D is a target that appears to be moving on a parallel and reciprocal course to ours but is actually a stationary target, such as a buoy or anchored vessel (wake length same as the land).*

been solved by transfer plotting, and Coast Guard licensing exams still require this type of plotting, but it is not used often in the wheelhouse. Ships use their ARPA solutions and other vessels solve relative motion problems right on the radar screen. But this relative disuse does not detract from the value of learning transfer plotting. It is, of course, the basis for all other approaches. In the next section we propose a new twist to the relative motion solution that might rekindle some interest in a new form of transfer plotting—although, again, we must stress that with practice, you can often find what you need by tracing out the relative motion diagram with your finger or a portable range scale right on the radar screen.

E-CHART PROGRAMS FOR VECTOR SOLUTIONS

The relative motion diagram is just one type of vector problem navigators face routinely. Two others are the wind triangle for discerning true wind from apparent wind and the current triangle used to figure course and speed in the presence of a current. Having described traditional radar plotting techniques above, here we examine a neat trick for solving any of these triangles right on the screen of any e-chart navigation software program, along with related radar applications. If you happen to use e-chart software near your radar screen, you may find this a handy solution when you want precision. With a little practice it is a fast and accurate way to solve all vector problems. There are numerous e-chart programs online that either offer a free demo period or are available for continuous free evaluation usage until an actual connection to GPS is required. Any of these will do the job. If you are unfamiliar with this technology, these free demos might be a good introduction to learning the power of this resource.

There are several approaches, and once you understand the underlying principles you will easily decide which works best with your software. (This section and the examples given are better understood after reading through the previous section on conventional solutions.)

The idea is to set up a fictitious route on any chart or plotting sheet, connecting three waypoints that represent the three corners of the vector triangle to be solved. Since all programs let you display the range and bearing of each leg of the route, you can then drag the corners (waypoints) to match the sides you know and read off the unknowns as illustrated in Figure 11-10. Choose the chart display scale to conveniently match your data from the radar. For distances or speeds you can use either 6-minute wake lengths, which are ⅒ the actual speeds, or the full speeds—whatever is most convenient.

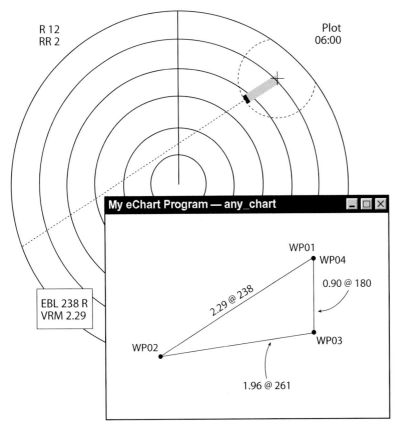

Figure 11-10. *Plotting relative motion diagrams using e-chart navigation programs. The principle works with any e-chart program. Our course = 047 T and our speed = 9.0 kts. Wake trails are 6 minutes long in a head-up display. From the radar screen (ERBL) we measure SRM = 22.9 kts (2.29 x 10) and DRM = 238 R for the target of interest.*

 Step 1. *Select Route Tool in your e-chart program and drop Waypoint 1 (WP01) anywhere on the open chart.*

 Step 2. *Watching the pop-up route-leg specifications from the e-chart program as you drag the second waypoint, drop WP02 at 2.29 miles from the first in direction 238. Use the plus key (+) to expand the scale to make the adjustments easier.*

 Step 3. *Put WP03 anywhere roughly due south of WP01.*

 Step 4. *Put WP04 right on top of WP01. Some programs will automatically close the route leaving three waypoints only—a nice feature for this application—but not all programs work this way. The resulting triangle is the relative motion diagram, with leg 2 equal to the target's true course and speed when we are finished.*

 Step 5. *Left-click and drag WP03 to make leg 3 exactly 0.90 nm at 000.*

 Step 6. *If the displayed route direction of leg 2 from WP02 to WP03 (the target's true course and speed) is pointing the wrong way, right-click anywhere on the route and select Reverse route.*

 Step 7. *Put the cursor on leg 2 to read off 1.96 nm at 261, which means the true speed of the target is 19.6 kts and its actual heading is 261 Relative, or 261 + 047 = 308 True.*

 Now that this triangular route is stored on your chart, you can use it for future relative motion solutions by just dragging the waypoints for the new data and using Reverse route as needed. The steps above work more or less the same for any e-chart program when in the head-up mode. They also work the same in north-up mode to read relative bearings. In north-up or course-up mode with course bearings, the procedure is essentially the same, but the diagram is oriented in the course direction rather than to 000. When done with the analysis, give the route a name such as "RMD" and then hide the route. It will remain in your permanent list of routes and can be shown and used again quickly. If your chart program has a plotting-sheet option in addition to regular charts, it might be best to draw the route on a plotting sheet so it can be used from any location; otherwise, it will be locked to the locations of the original drawing. Or just remember what chart you put it on. Or just draw it again—it is very quick.

A 1.6-mile wake means the SRM is 16 kts, so you could plot this as 1.6 nm or 16 nm on the e-chart, as long as you are consistent with all speeds in that triangle.

In the case of the RMD, to draw the triangle as just described you need to know the range and bearing between your first and second observation of the target's location. With an ERBL this is easy to obtain either from your marks on the radar screen or from the length and orientation of the target's wake. If after you draw the triangle, the route-direction arrows in the leg marking the true course and speed of the target are pointing the wrong way, just right-click the route and choose "Reverse route." (Most programs access this option in this manner.) Remember, the leg that marks your travel between observations (the buoy trail) is drawn from the first observation parallel to the heading line.

Figure 11-11 shows another approach, which uses individual lines for each component of the triangle starting with the raw data of range and bearing to the target sights. It does not require figuring the SRM and DRM ahead of time. The first line puts the first sighting onto the e-chart, the second line puts the second sighting onto the e-chart, the next line plots your buoy trail, and the final line is the target's true course and speed. This method is precisely the same as conventional radar transfer plotting except that you are using an electronic plotter instead of a plotting sheet and pencil. This method (and the earlier one), however, is much more accurate than you can achieve by hand using paper and pencil simply because you can zoom in to any level you choose and read out all segments and angles digitally. Once zoomed in, it is easy to see how much you would be off if your angle was in error by a fraction of a degree. On the other hand, this might be of more interest in solving textbook problems—in the real world the data you get from the radar to plot these diagrams will always be more uncertain than plotting electronically or by paper. Realistically, the

main advantages of this method are its speed and convenience.

From this style of electronic plotting you can go on to measure whatever else you care to about the interaction such as drawing a new course line extending from the first sighting to beyond the second sighting to determine the CPA and the time to CPA.

The key point to using these electronic tricks for plotting—just as with conventional paper or on-screen plotting—is to remember that all the line lengths must be for the same time intervals. You have the first sight (the tail end of the wake) and the second sight (the present target position at the front of the wake). You must make your own speed line (buoy trail) equal to the distance you traveled during that time period, and the line must be parallel to your heading line. This calls for slightly different procedures in head-up versus north-up modes, as outlined in the figures. As discussed in Chapter 6, if the time interval is 6 minutes or a multiple of 6, the math is easy using the six-minute rule, but any time interval will do as long as it is consistent.

The above e-chart tricks did not require a GPS to be connected to your PC, because no moving-map technology was involved. It did not interfere with your real-time charting operations if you were using them, but they were not required. Another e-chart application to radar observing that I have found useful does take advantage of the GPS connection showing your position moving across the chart. In this application, you transfer the observed target positions to the chart, each time plotting them relative to your own position at the time of observation—in effect setting up a type of true motion display discussed in Chapter 8. An example is in Figure 11-12.

To set this up, use the cursor mode from the radar to get range and bearing to a target at a specific time, and then use options on the e-chart program to place a mark at that same range and bearing from your present position.

Figure 11-11. *An alternative e-chart approach to solving relative motion diagrams. The key tool for this approach is a range and bearing tool (R/B), which will draw any line segment of a given length in a given direction on the chart. Some programs let you move the line once drawn, others do not. If your e-chart program does not have a dedicated R/B tool, then draw the line using the route tool by making a simple two-point route with the right range and bearing. It is just about as easy either way.*

We will use the same 6-minute observations we used in Figure 11-10, but we start with the ranges and bearings of the two sights and then complete the triangle, rather than making it all one route.

As shown on the EBLs and VRMs, the first sight (where the target was 6 minutes ago) was 10.1 nm at 044 R and the second sight (where it is now) is 7.9 nm at 040 R. Our course is 047 T and our speed is 9.0 kts, but since we are in head-up display our actual course does not matter.

Step 1. Draw a north-south line anywhere on the chart or plotting sheet, and starting at any point A on the line draw a line to point B to mark the first sight, R/B = 10.1 nm in direction 044 T.

Step 2. Draw a second line from A to C to mark the second sight, R/B = 7.9 mi in direction 040 T. (You should observe that the distance from B to C is 2.29 miles in direction 238 T, as used in Figure 11-10.)

Step 3. Zoom in on the scale and draw your buoy trail 0.90 nm due south from point B.

Step 4. Find the target's course and speed by drawing the line from point D to point C, 19.6 kts in direction 261. Usually the range and bearing of the line will appear automatically or whenever you hold the cursor over the line. Or right-click and ask for Properties.

With this approach, you can go on to extend the BC line ahead to see what the distance off will be when the target crosses your course line and also its CPA (2.4 nm). Time to CPA can also be computed as shown in Figure 6-14. This method can also be used in north-up or course-up mode.

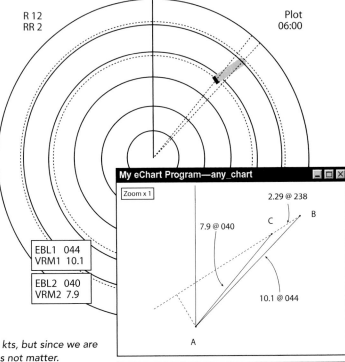

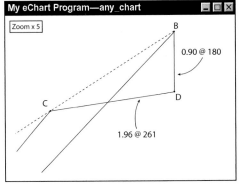

Label the mark with the time of observation. Repeat these observations every few minutes or so. Soon you have a plot of the vessel moving across your e-chart, from which you can determine its course and speed and relative crossing of your own course. With practice, this can be a fast way to plot and keep track of approaching traffic, and is especially useful for multiple targets. The tracks of the target vessels you plot in this manner are completely independent of your own motion.

Since a handheld GPS and a basic e-chart program can be very economical, this procedure can be thought of as an ARPA substitute. The exercise is, in any event, an excellent way to practice interrelating your radar and e-chart

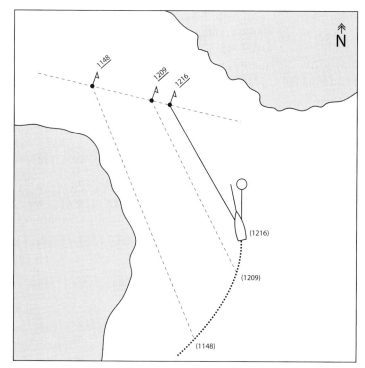

Figure 11-12. *Section of a GPS plotter used to record range and bearing to radar targets. Here the target has been marked three times using the Mark tool. The locations of your vessel at the times of the marks are also shown. The marks can then be labeled with the time of observation as shown. The boat icon marks your present GPS position, with a trail of past positions plotted. The times and places of where the earlier marks were set are typically not recorded on the plotter and are shown here just for illustration. Radar target positions can be measured instantly with the radar's cursor mode and then plotted very conveniently at the time of sighting with the e-chart's Boat-to-Cursor tool or any other range and bearing tool. The boat cursor itself also shows your heading line, and the line with a circle on it is a projected position display, in this case set to where you will be in 10 minutes if all remains the same. This vessel is being set to the right by strong currents, which is clear because it is not proceeding in the direction it is headed. Notice that you get a clear track of the target vessel with this type of plot, even though your own speed and course have changed significantly.*

outputs, and it will inevitably lead to a better understanding of the relative motion issues involved in radar observing.

RULES OF THUMB

Navigators thrive on rules of thumb and weather lore: "Do not rely on one nav aid alone"; "Plot your position on the chart often, marked with the time"; "East is least, west is best" (for magnetic corrections); "Look back often"; "Passing weather fronts bring a sudden veer in wind direction"; "Double the bow angle and distance off equals distance run"; "If it's on, take it off" (for sextant index corrections); "Strong winds come with the rain" (of squalls); "60 D Street" (for speed, time, and distance computations); and many more. Some are statements of fact, some are approximations, and some are just guidelines.

They have in common the goal of helping you remember proper procedure. Another sample is, "When in doubt, turn right." But not all mariners would agree with this. Some might prefer a different rule: "Do not turn until you know what the other vessel is doing." But if you have to maneuver to avoid a collision and do not have time for analysis, then the "turn right" guideline will comply with most *Navigation Rules* in most circumstances, and it helps contribute to improving your instincts, and in that sense is a useful "rule." There are endless examples. More dependable and specific guidelines for maneuvering according to the *Navigation Rules* are given in Chapter 12, in the form of a maneuvering diagram.

There are numerous guidelines or rules for radar to help analyze a situation. It is another way to state or summarize what we know from previous study. It is important, however, for you to know these rules and to have practiced them so you can predict the consequences of maneuvers based on radar observations alone. As always, if you can see the target vessels visually, the logic and results of your maneuvers are more easily understood.

The goal of these rules is to tell you how a target's DRM or wake trail will change under various conditions in response to your maneuver or to theirs. The underlying basis to the rules is that radar target trails should be straight patterns as long as everyone is holding a steady course and speed. Currents can make a steady target heading appear to be one that is changing. If you see an individual wake or trail that is bent or curved, it means something has changed; most likely either vessel has undergone some maneuver.

Another basic point to keep in mind is that if you maneuver, all moving targets on the screen will respond with a change in direction or length of their wake, though some will respond more than others. The rules below tell you how to guess which way they will move, but they do not tell you how much—although Maneuvering Rule 7 helps you guess which targets would respond most. These rules are based solely on your observation of the DRM relative to the heading line, which means specifically that they do not depend on you solving the relative motion diagram. They are often used in conjunction with the diagram or other vector solutions, but their main job is to give some answer to the question: If I do this, what will happen? They might help, for example, in deciding which way to turn when you have a choice, or whether to slow down.

Rules for When Your Speed Changes

MANEUVERING RULE 1. *When you slow down or stop, all target wake trails turn up-screen.*

This rule is illustrated in Figure 11-13. It is true in all display modes—keeping in mind the meaning of *up-screen*—and it is true for all moving targets on the radar screen. To help remember this rule, recall that the true aspect of a vessel is aft of its apparent aspect, and when you stop it will assume its true aspect, so when you slow down it will assume an orientation more toward that true aspect, which is a turn

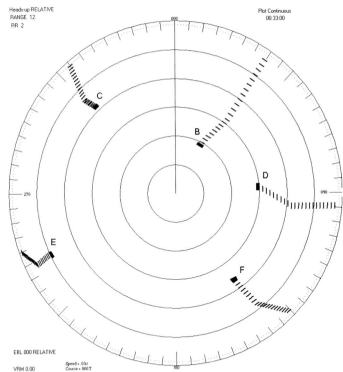

Figure 11-13. *When we slow or stop, all target vessel trails turn up-screen, in any radar display mode. This picture, captured from the Radar Trainer simulator, shows the effect for five targets approaching from different quadrants. Our original speed was 6 kts and our heading was 000, and then we stopped. The stop took place at plot clock reading 17:00, where the kinks in the trails are located, then the data accumulated for another 16 minutes to plot clock reading 33:00. Note that in all cases the directions of relative motion (DRMs) turned up-screen when we stopped. Note that in this example, the two targets E and F that were safely passing astern when we were moving are now on converging courses.*

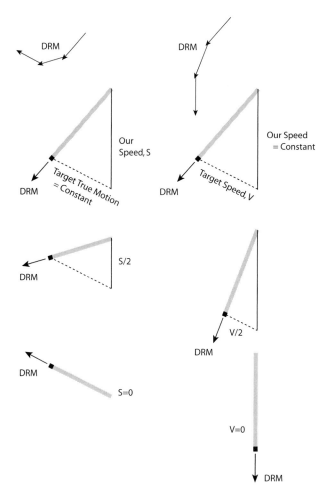

Figure 11-14. *Relative motion diagrams for speed changes. The left side shows why target DRM turns up-screen as we slow down. Once we are stopped, we are then seeing the true motion of the vessel. The right side shows why the target DRM turns down-screen when the target slows its speed. When it has stopped, its wake turns into a buoy trail reflecting our speed alone.*

up our heading line. When you slow down or stop, all target wake trails turn up-screen.

This is an important rule because when you see a target tracking straight down the EBL when you are moving, you know that if you stop, the target trail will curve up-screen and you will no longer be on a collision course. But you must be careful. You may be stopping in front of another vessel that would otherwise have crossed safely behind, but now his trail also curves up-

screen to point right at you. Nevertheless, this is a fundamental rule to know and use for a quick guess of the results of slowing down.

MANEUVERING RULE 2. *If you speed up, target wake trails turn down-screen.*

This is the reverse of the above rule. Figure 11-14 shows how both rules are a simple consequence of the relative motion diagram.

The rules are reversed when the target changes speed.

MANEUVERING RULE 3. *If a target slows, its trail turns down-screen and becomes shorter.*

MANEUVERING RULE 4. *If a target speeds up, its trail turns up-screen and becomes longer.*

Remember that if a target stops moving, no matter which way it is headed, it will start moving straight down-screen like a buoy would.

Rules for When Your Course Changes

Rules for what a target trail will do in response to your course changes are equally important, but they are more complex in that they depend on the radar display mode and the type of target. When you turn in north-up mode, the heading line turns with you, and the target does not move on the radar screen. It responds by turning from its present position. This is a big advantage over its behavior in head-up mode, where the heading line does not move and always represents the direction you are headed. When you turn 40° one way, a moving target will immediately rotate 40° the other way, and then show its turn in response to your new course. Thus, north-up and course-up modes present a continuous trail of target positions on the radar screen regardless of your turns, whereas in head-up mode there is a discontinuity in the target trails at each of your course alterations. (See the note in Chapter 7 about recentering a course-up display.)

MANEUVERING RULE 5. *In north-up or course-up mode, when you turn, the subsequent behavior of moving targets on the screen depends on whether they are down-screen or up-screen targets.*

MANEUVERING RULE 5A. *Down-screen targets turn the same way you turn.*

MANEUVERING RULE 5B. *Up-screen targets turn the opposite way you turn.*

These rules are illustrated in Figure 11-15 along with supporting diagrams in Figure 11-16. In other words, if you turn to your right, down-screen target trails will turn to their right and up-screen targets turn to their left; if you turn to your left, down-screen target trails turn to their left and up-screen targets turn to their right.

This may seem difficult to remember, but there is a trick that will help. In the next

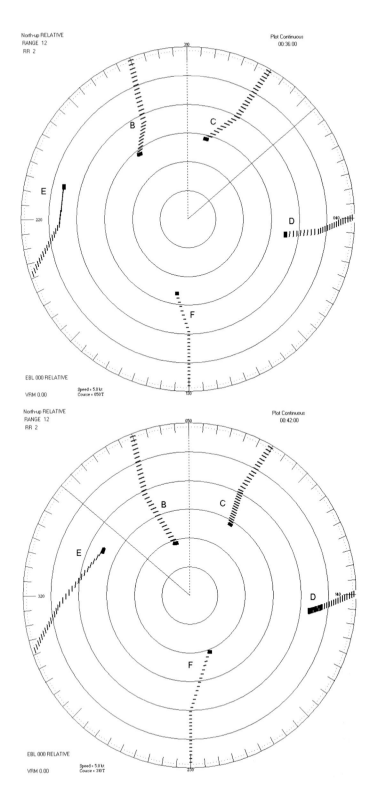

Figure 11-15. *Maneuvering rules. In north-up or course-up display mode, when you turn, the wakes of down-screen targets turn the same way you turn, but up-screen targets turn the opposite way you turn. The turn was 50° to the right in the top and 50° to the left on the bottom.*

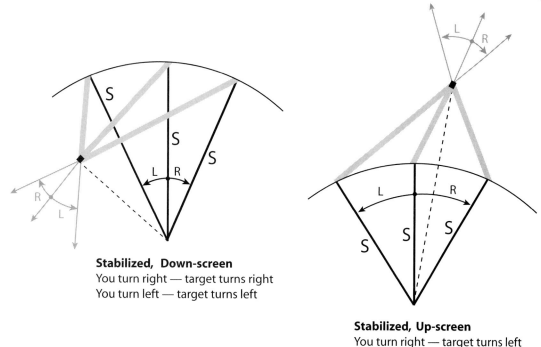

Stabilized, Down-screen
You turn right — target turns right
You turn left — target turns left

Stabilized, Up-screen
You turn right — target turns left
You turn left — target turns right

Figure 11-16. *Use of the relative motion diagram to illustrate Maneuvering Rules 5A and 5B for stabilized displays (north-up or course-up). Each picture is three diagrams, superimposed. Our speed (S) remains constant as we turn either right (R) or left (L), but the heading line turns with our turn. The true motion of the target vessel (dotted line) remains constant.*

For down-screen targets (left), our turn to the right yields a new DRM and SRM for the target, which produces a new wake trail for the target—it turns to the right from its original direction. Likewise, our turn to the left causes the target's wake trail to turn to its left.

For up-screen targets in a stabilized display (right) the opposite is true. Our turn to the right yields a target wake trail turn to the left of its original direction.

chapter we go over the important Rule 19d of the *Navigation Rules*, which tells you how to respond to approaching radar targets that you do not see visually. In a nutshell, when targets come toward you forward of the beam, Rule 19d tells you to turn right, but when targets approach from aft of the beam you turn away from them. In other words, for bow and head-on targets you turn right and they turn right (since they are seeing you approach forward of their beam). For stern and quarter targets, they turn one way (it's their choice), and you turn away from them. Loosely, then, down-screen targets turn the same way you do, and up-screen targets turn the opposite way. After finishing this chapter and the next, you might

return to this discussion to see if that reasoning helps.

MANEUVERING RULE 5C. *Beam targets (also called limbo targets) do not respond much when you when you make moderate turns.*

Targets moving perpendicular to your heading line are neither up-screen nor down-screen. According to the above rules, these should not turn when you alter course in north-up or course-up mode, and indeed, in practice, they do not change much for moderate course changes. But as your turns become bigger they will shift to become either up-screen or down-screen targets, and for subsequent turns behave as expected.

What can be said of their motion in either stabilized display is that if you look at the orientation of your heading line *before you turn,* then beam target trails will turn in response to your turn such that their new DRM is more up-screen relative to the location of your original heading line direction. In Figure 11-17 we leave the EBL in the orientation of the original heading line so that this part of the rule is more apparent. Figure 11-18 shows the related relative motion diagrams.

Again, Rule 19d helps you remember that these beam targets are special, since it tells you what to do for targets approaching forward and aft of the beam, but it does not say explicitly what to do for targets approaching right on the beam. In short, you have a way to remember that, as far as predicted turns are concerned, these are special.

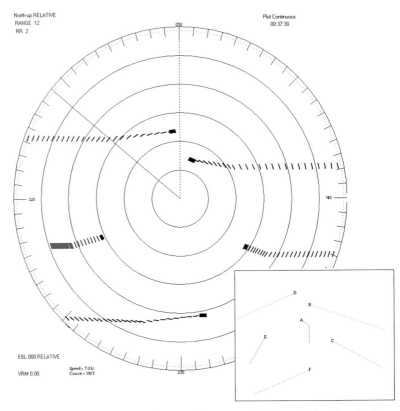

Figure 11-17. *Limbo targets (those moving perpendicular to the heading line) show little response to your turns in north-up or course-up displays. The radar trails in this simulated picture from the Radar Trainer program had been accumulating for the equivalent of 37 minutes with a 60° left turn about 12 minutes earlier. The overhead true view of the target courses is shown in the inset.*

Here is a summary of the maneuvering rules in north-up or course-up mode: down-screen targets turn right when you turn right and left when you turn left, whereas up-screen targets turn the opposite way. Beam targets, on the other hand, respond very little to your turns.

In head-up mode, these turning rules are different. They might be considered simpler or more complex than those of a stabilized mode, depending on your attitude. The very fact that they are different implies some level of complexity, but the rule can be worded in a simpler way. In any event, it is clear that when dealing with traffic interactions, it is best to decide which mode you prefer, and run in that mode. Switching back and forth can be confusing.

MANEUVERING RULE 6. *In head-up mode, all targets you are viewing—whether up-screen, down-screen, or limbo targets—turn left when you turn right, and turn right when you turn left.*

A target's turn, in head-up mode as in stabilized modes, refers to the direction of relative motion of its wake trail. But remember before they make this turn in DRM, which may be small or large depending on relative speeds, targets in head-up mode will always first make a well-defined rotation in their location on the radar

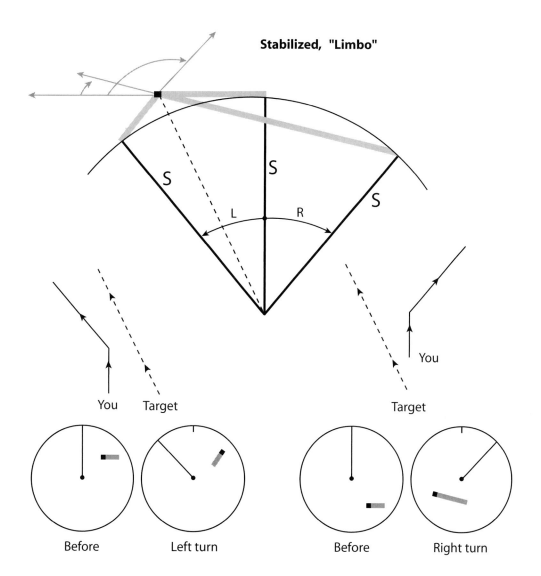

Figure 11-18. *Use of the relative motion diagram to illustrate Maneuvering Rule 5C for stabilized displays (north-up or course-up). The top is three diagrams, superimposed. Our speed (S) remains constant as we turn either right (R) or left (L), but the heading line turns with our turn. The true motion of the target vessel (dotted line) remains constant. A limbo target is one moving perpendicular to the heading line, regardless of our heading line orientation and regardless of where it actually appears on the screen. It is neither up-screen nor down-screen.*

For these targets it is difficult to predict the behavior of the target wake trail after our turn since it depends on the size of our turn and the direction we turn, toward or away from the target (hence the term limbo). For relatively small turns, the wake trail changes little, as can be demonstrated with this type of diagram. For any turn, however, it can also be seen that the subsequent wake trail direction will shift to an up-screen direction relative to its original direction, and the amount of turn depends on the direction we turn.

The bottom shows sketches of true motion plots above the relative motions that would be seen on the radar screen.

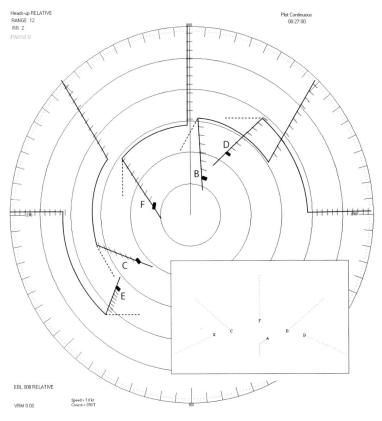

Heads-up RELATIVE
RANGE 12
RR 2
PAUSED

Plot Continuous
00:27:00

EBL 000 RELATIVE

VRM 0.00

Speed = 7.0 kt
Course = 050T

Figure 11-19. *Target response to a 40° turn to the right viewed in head-up mode. The targets rotate to the left, then turn to the left, according to Maneuvering Rule 6. The dotted lines show the original DRMs before the turn.*

I think of these targets as "turning back toward me." That is, judging from their original wake trails, the large rotation that occurs immediately upon the turn seems to put them safely away, assuming they would carry on in the relative direction they were moving before my turn; but in fact, the clearance is not so large because their new DRMs turn back toward me, canceling out part of the effect of the rotation.

Note, too, that with multiple targets present, we can turn to avoid one and end up in the path of another. Don't forget to look out the window! There can be a tendency to get stuck concentrating on the radar screen. Figure 11-20 shows a generalized relative motion diagram that helps explain the vector basis of this behavior.

is fairly prompt, the target will not have changed range from you, but just rotated. In head-up mode you must always keep this behavior in mind so you can keep track of targets as you turn. If you turn slowly, you can often see their wake trails spread out along the arc of the turn (as the image is painted every 3 seconds or so). But if there is a lot of traffic or other targets on the screen, the screen can get messy after a large turn and you might lose identification of the targets. You may have to restart the plot clock to clean up the screen. Avoiding this is one advantage of using a stabilized display mode, in which the targets do not rotate when you turn.

Several cases are shown in Figure 11-19. If you have, for example, a target approaching straight down-screen from dead ahead and you turn 40° to the right, then this target will immediately rotate 40° to the left and then turn to its left. It does not carry on

screen in direct response to your turn. If a target is 15° to the right of your heading line—which means it is 15° to the right of your bow—and you then turn 20° right, this target rotates to a position 5° to the left of your heading line, as you are now pointed 5° to the right of the target on the water. (In north-up or course-up mode, the heading line would just cross over the target and the target would not move.) If your turn

with the same straight down-screen DRM that it had originally, but has turned back toward you quite a bit. It has changed from a head-on target to a bow target. You are not as clear of it as you might have thought just after completing the turn. Indeed, as we shall see in Chapter 12, the recommended turn in the fog would be 60° to 90°. Generalized relative motion diagrams are shown in Figures 11-20 and 11-21.

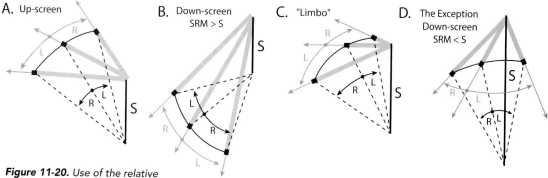

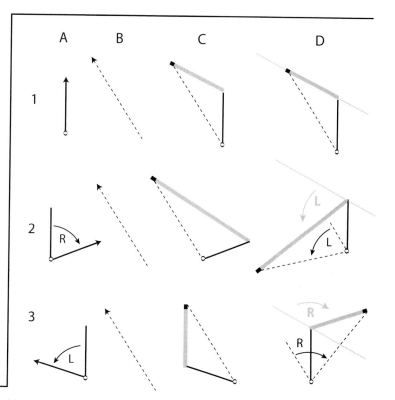

Figure 11-20. *Use of the relative motion diagram to illustrate Maneuvering Rule 6 for unstabilized (head-up) display. In each case there are three diagrams, superimposed—the initial central solution before we turn, and the two solutions representing turns to the left (L) and to the right (R). Our speed (S) remains constant as we turn and, in head-up mode, our heading line also remains unchanged.*

The target's true speed does not change when we turn, but in a head-up representation of the interaction, its course changes relative to our fixed heading line. From our head-up perspective, our turn is equivalent to the target vessel turning to a new course relative to ours, and that new course will turn, relative to our heading, in the opposite direction we turn. This latter point is illustrated in Figure 11-21, which further explains the background of these composite figures.

Figure 11-21. *Sample components of the composite diagrams shown in Figure 11-20. Column A shows our speed vectors before and after a right and left turn. Column B shows the constant speed vector of the target vessel. Column C shows the conventional relative motion diagrams for each of the cases. In column D, the diagrams of column C have been rotated to a common head-up orientation to show the relative direction changes.*

The results are consistent with Maneuvering Rule 6, but these special cases do not demonstrate the generality of the rule. To build the more general diagrams of Figure 11-20, we note from here that our turn in one direction causes the target vessel's direction relative to our heading to turn in the opposite direction. From this observation we can build the generalized diagrams of Figure 11-20.

This is just a vector representation of what we know intuitively without the drawings. If we are headed 000, for example, and a vessel approaches us on course 330, he is headed 30° to the left of our course. If we turn 30° to the left, the two vessels will be on the same course, and in a head-up display it will appear on the radar (after the initial rotation of its location) as if he turned 30° to the right. Likewise, if we turn 70° to the left, he will now be headed 40° to the right of our course, which we would learn from solving the relative motion diagram, although his actual wake trail would turn more than that, as viewed in relative motion and illustrated in the bottom right diagram.

It is valuable to keep this behavior in mind when running in head-up mode. The rule can be summarized as: When you turn right, targets rotate to the left and then turn to their left, and when you turn left, targets rotate to the right and then turn to their right—their turns being relative to their original wake directions. This is true for any target vessel actually headed toward you as you view them on the waterway. The end effect on radar observations is that the wake trails end up turning back toward you to some degree. Note that in head-up mode, beam targets are not in limbo, but respond the same as up-screen or down-screen targets.

Now the exception: Target vessels headed away from you that you are overtaking, or with whom you are on a relative course that will lead to an overtaking aspect, will have trails that do not behave according to the rule just described. These targets will have an SRM that is less than your speed. All down-screen targets with an SRM less than your speed are in this category. If their SRM is not much less than your own speed, they will typically show little change in direction in response to moderate turns on your part, but if their SRM is small compared with your speed they will tend to turn the same way you do, which is opposite to the rule for all other targets in head-up mode. To compare results from the two display modes, in stabilized display you have one rule for all up-screen targets and one for all down-screen targets, and a weaker guideline for limbo targets. In unstabilized (head-up) display, you have one rule that works for all targets, except that for down-screen targets with low SRMs it is reversed. Since the SRM is one of the very first things we must determine for any approaching target, this is typically something we will know ahead of time, before making decisions based on maneuvering rules.

MANEUVERING RULE 7. *The effectiveness of your maneuver (a turn or speed adjustment) in all display modes depends on* your speed

compared with the target's speed, *as well as its direction of relative motion.*

In other words, you have a new assessment to make. You must distinguish between *speed ratios* (your knotmeter speed compared to their knotmeter speed) and speeds of relative motion. They are obviously related, but they are two different things. Speed ratio means, for example, that if you are going 20 kts and he is going 10 kts, you are going twice as fast as he is. If you are at 3 kts and he is at 18 kts, he is 6 times faster than you, and so on. The resulting speeds of relative motion, on the other hand, depend on your relative orientations as you travel. Your speeds could be equal, but when headed toward each other you have a high SRM, whereas if headed nearly in the same direction you may have a very low SRM, as summarized in the following rules:

MANEUVERING RULE 7A. *If the target's speed is low compared with yours, the effects of your maneuvers will be large.*

MANEUVERING RULE 7B. *If the target's speed is high compared with yours, the effects of your maneuvers will be small.*

The conclusion is reasonably obvious: If you are moving much faster than an approaching vessel, you have more control over the passing than when someone is closing in on you at a much higher speed. The question then is how to use your general knowledge of the relative motion diagram to make these speed assessments.

You do not need precise speeds for this evaluation. The goal of these rules is to make sound judgments without solving the relative motion diagram. You only need estimates: roughly the same speed, roughly half as fast, roughly twice as fast, etc. You can make these estimates from the SRM and DRM alone in most cases. In fact, as mentioned earlier, it does not take much practice to make rough estimates of the true course and speed of a target just by tracing out the diagram on the radar screen, as shown in Figure 11-22.

Remember that it is always true of up-screen and beam targets that the longer their trail lengths, the faster they are moving. Their trail lengths are a measure of how much faster they are going than you, not just a measure of their absolute speed, so significant trail lengths mean they could be more difficult to maneuver around. When they show no trail or a very little one, they are maintaining about the same speed as you are, and your maneuvers will be more effective.

Down-screen targets, on the other hand, could be moving faster or slower than you. Those with very short trails (small SRMs), barely slipping down-screen, are headed away from you at a slower speed than yours. They could respond well to your maneuvers. Head-on targets with SRMs roughly equal to your speed are essentially dead in the water, so you clearly have a higher speed than they do and they will respond well to your maneuvers. Any bow or head-on target with an SRM much larger than your own speed is one with a higher speed than yours, so your maneuvers alone will not alter its DRM to the degree you might like.

The above conclusion—you have more control over slower targets than fast ones—helps you remember that when interacting with fast parallel targets you must make bigger maneu-

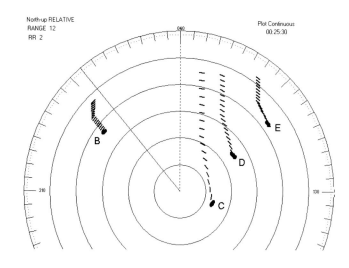

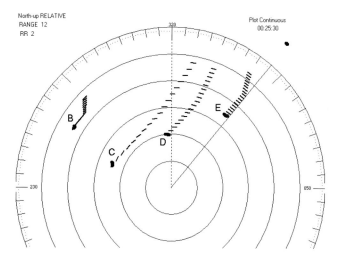

Figure 11-22. *Speed ratios and target response. The trails shown had accumulated for about 12 minutes, then we made a 40° turn to the right, and the trails accumulated for another 13 minutes in this continuous plot mode. Our speed is marked by the target B at 6 kts, since we know it is a buoy. From this we know the other three targets are headed toward us since their trails before the turn are all longer than that of B's trail before the turn. From inspection alone we can tell that E is a slow target (true speed 3 kts), C is a fast one (true speed 18 kts), and D has some intermediate speed (which if we solved for it we would learn is 9 kts). From this we can guess that E would have the largest response to our turn and C would have the least response, as indeed was the case.*

The bottom is the same example, but the three targets are headed toward 225 instead of 000. And the same conclusions apply. Note we can make this comparison because the targets have about the same DRM. If this were not the case, it would be more difficult to guess the magnitude of their response to our maneuver without solving the RMD. See Figure 11-23.

vers to see an effect on the radar screen, but it does not help in predicting the response of two targets approaching on rather different DRMs, as shown in Figure 11-23. A quick estimate of the target's true course and speed with the RMD may be needed to best gauge the effect of a maneuver.

MANEUVERING RULE 8.

If you turn toward or away from a moving target and its trail goes away, you have turned onto the same course as a vessel with the same speed as yours. You now have a buddy boat.

When you turn, take note of new trail lengths. If you turn toward a vessel headed toward you, its wake trail will get longer. If you turn more toward the direction it is traveling, its trail will get shorter, and so forth. Rechecking all the trail lengths after a maneuver is a nice confirmation.

MANEUVERING RULE 9.

When traveling with a buddy boat, you have the choice to join it without increasing speed provided it is aft of your beam.

The procedure is to note how far aft of the beam the vessel is, and then turn toward it by twice that amount; you will then be on a converging course with the vessel. In practice, it would be best to turn less than that until you cross its path, then resume your

original heading and slow down to rendezvous. If you turn more than twice the angle abaft the beam, you will pass astern of it and not be able to catch it at the same speed. This maneuver is illustrated in Figure 11-24.

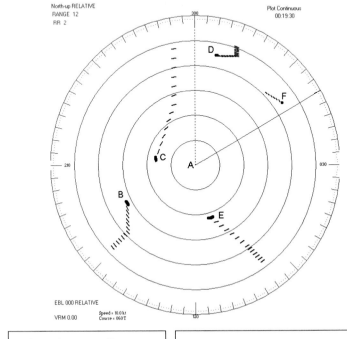

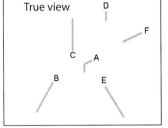

Tgt	S	SRM1	SRM2
A	10		
B	20	11.7	13.1
C	20	30.0	26.5
D	5	5.0	8.7
E	20	11.7	21.6
F	10	10.0	0.0

Figure 11-23. *Responses to our maneuvers are not always easy to predict from inspection alone. From our known speed of 10 kts we can conclude that D is slower (we are overtaking him) and C is much faster and headed toward us. We can guess rightly that following our 60° turn to the right, D will respond more than C, as in the case shown. The trails accumulated for 10 minutes before our turn, and 19 minutes after it.*

In contrast to those two head-on targets (C and D), the two quarter targets (B and E) on different DRMs are not easy to predict, even though they have the same SRM before our turn (SRM1 in the table). The inset (bottom left) shows the true view of all vessels moving throughout the maneuver.

Note that target F stopped moving completely after our turn, which means he has the same speed as we do and we have just turned to be on his same course. He is now a buddy boat, with the same course and speed, and his target on the screen will not change until one of us changes course or speed.

Valuable guidelines on maneuvering are in Chapter 12 in the section on Rule 19d. They are presented in the form of a convenient diagram designed by A. N. Cockcroft and J. N. F. Lameijer (Figure 12-7).

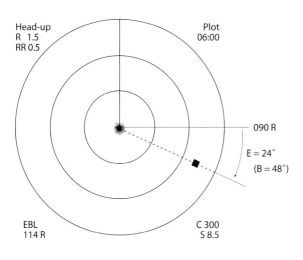

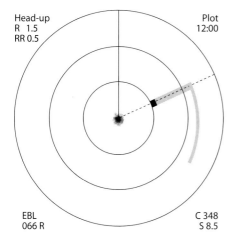

Figure 11-24. *To join a buddy boat traveling at our heading and speed and located at an angle E aft of our beam, we turn toward him by angle B = 2E for a perfect meeting course. In practice, it is best to turn somewhat less than that, then resume our earlier course and slow down when we cross his course line. If we turn more than 2E, we will not be able to catch him without increasing speed. Note that after the turn, the buddy boat has turned onto a collision course. (To prove this rule, note that the geometry is the same as that used to show that doubling the bow angle makes distance off equal to distance run.)*

SQUALL TACTICS

An important background discussion of squalls and radar was presented in Chapter 9. Here we add more details of squall behavior and some guidelines for maneuvers.

When using marine radar as a weather observer, you need to do everything backward: shut off AC Rain (you may need to keep some AC Sea), select a long pulse, and experiment with Gain, Brilliance, and Echo Stretch for the best squall outlines. You will also be tracking their motion using Wake or Plot trails. This will take some experimentation. Sometimes the trails are useful; other times, with a changing squall shape, they are less useful. Marking the squall outlines by hand on the screen (Chapter 1) might work best. And, as is the case in so many applications, a stabilized display using a heading sensor input dramatically improves your ability to track any target at sea, especially squalls. Figure 11-25 shows typical squall images on radar.

In the Northern Hemisphere, squalls usually move from a direction that is veered by some 15° to 30° or so from the ambient surface wind around them. If the wind well away from the squall, for example, is northeastly, blowing from, say, 035 toward 215 T, then squalls in that region would likely be moving in a direction toward about 215 + 30 = 245, as shown in Figure 11-26. In other words, if you see a squall precisely to windward, in the true wind direction of 035, then you would guess that the squall is not coming toward you at all, but will pass well astern. The squalls coming toward you are those located about 30° to the right of the surface wind direction, at about 065 or so, and even those will not get to you if you are moving at a speed close to that of the squall. Given the relative motions involved, it will be those even more to the

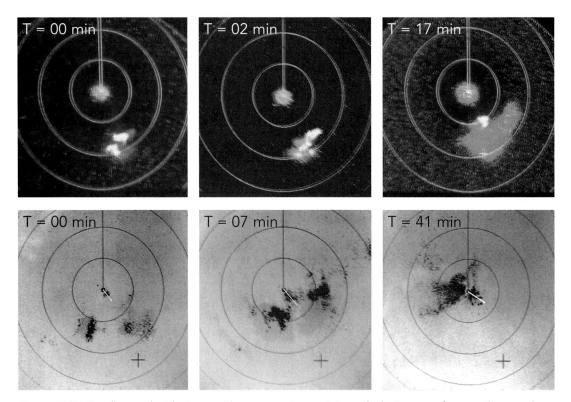

Figure 11-25. *Squalls on radar. The top row shows range rings at 2.0 nm; the bottom row, from another vessel, has ring spacing of 1.0 nm. Both vessels are on starboard jibe running before relatively small squalls. The brighter images are reflections from water drops; the lighter tones are plot trails of past squall positions. Both are in head-up mode. The times (T) of the screen shots are shown relative to the left figure in each row.*

The apparent squall motion to the right in the top middle figure is artificial due to a left turn of the vessel heading. Likewise, the large smear of the plot trails at T = 17 minutes is also due to heading changes during this time, as well as squall development, dissipation, and motion. A stabilized display mode would remove much of this uncertainty. Note that the squall did not catch the boat, which picked up speed when the advancing edge of the squall winds reached the boat, in this case at about 3 miles in front of the rain echoes. This is downwind sailing at about 10 kts. In 17 minutes, the squall has only gained about 1 mile on us. The size of the rain pattern has reduced. The Gain had been increased to emphasize the last of the rain pattern.

In the bottom sequence at T = 0 the wind was calm, but it picked up at T = 7 minutes to about 9 kts true, when the rain echoes were about 0.5 mile from the boat. In this sequence, however, there was no apparent rain on the horizon nor over the vessel. The wind increased to as much as 15 kts, but this was not enough to keep this vessel ahead of the squall, and by T = 41 minutes it was forward of the beam and the wind was nearly calm again. The squall on the right developed and then dissipated.

In the bottom sequence we have marked with a short line the direction of the center of the sea clutter, which is toward the face of the waves; when there is wind, this is usually the true wind direction. In both examples, the squalls were effectively running as parallel radar targets, which is consistent with them approaching from some 30° to the right of the true wind direction, since we were sailing with the true wind at about this angle off the stern on the starboard quarter.

right that make up a converging course. (In the Southern Hemisphere, this is reversed. The elevated winds that drive the squalls along are backed to the left of the ambient surface winds. The squalls to the left of the wind are coming your way.)

Knowledge of typical squall behavior helps you make guesses about squall headings. With radar, however, you do not need to guess—you can tell in a matter of minutes which way the squalls are moving. Furthermore, you have their relative motion, not just their true motion, which is what matters when it comes to maneuvering around them. These are especially valuable observations, because the squalls at hand might not be moving at all like they are supposed to be according to the textbooks!

It is, however, helpful to know from meteorology how squall winds are expected to behave and to correlate with their rain patterns. Strong winds come with the first onset of rain under the developing cloud. Before the rain, while the squall is developing, the nearby surface winds are pulled into the path of the squall, biasing all the wind directions under and near the cloud base to a direction more in line with the squall motion. Once the squall begins its downburst of strong gusty winds, the surface winds fan out from under the squall, with a strong bias forward. The downburst winds in front of the squall add to the motion of the squall itself, which makes them even bigger, but the downburst winds behind the squall cancel out the wind generated by the squall motion, leaving a large area of light, fluky winds. Woe to the racing sailor who rushes over to pick up the winds from a squall but misses getting in front of it and ends up behind it. He could end up flopping around in less wind than he had before he got there.

For both the racing sailor trying to harness a squall and the cruising skipper (power or sail) trying to avoid it, the first step is the same. Check the squalls as soon as they appear. You can learn what you need from the first ones you see on the radar. With that in mind, do not overlook the chance for this practice, even when you have no reason for squall maneuvering. If you see a relatively close squall on the horizon, check the radar to monitor its motion. As a rule, in a given time and place the squalls will move in the same manner. If you figure out the typical course and speed of the squalls early in the process, it will help with your other reasoning.

Once you see a squall moving on the screen, mark a line on the screen in that direction to see if others follow course. That is their direction of relative motion, not their true course, but their DRM is what matters unless you change course or speed significantly. You might find it interesting to solve the relative motion diagram for their true course and speed to compare with the present wind speed and direction.

The job of the racing sailor is to set up a converging course with the leading edge of the squall—to intercept its front edges, not its side, and definitely not its trailing edge. This may mean giving up on some close ones, and planning ahead for ones that are farther off. This is often called *rendezvous maneuvering*, which might be used in other contexts as well.

Figure 11-26 shows typical scenarios for vessels sailing downwind, which is the usual case of interest to racing sailors. Often one jibe will be on a near-parallel course to the squalls, so the trick is to jibe onto the course that heads you into the path of the squall, and then, once stabilized on that heading, study the squall's wake trail on the radar screen. Ideally you want to reach the squall's course line a few miles in front of it, then jibe back and wait for it to reach you. Whether or not it is best to cross over the front of it (if you have the option), depends on your desired course. The combined wind speed and direction will be somewhat different on the two sides of the squall's course line. This will be a matter of keeping records on what happens and applying what you learn to the next encounter.

If the squall trail is passing in front of you,

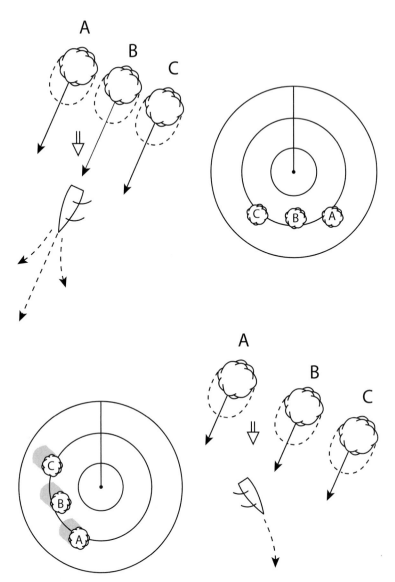

chances are you are not going to make it, and you might want to jibe back to avoid the backside of the squall. If the squall trail is aft of the EBL, you can either reach up to accelerate over to its line, or fall off and postpone the interaction. The DRM guidelines from the previous section might help with the reasoning, but there is no better way to practice this than with the Starpath Radar Trainer software simulator included on the Radar Resources CD.

And do not forget to look out the window! Important as this is when evaluating risk of collision with other vessels, it is even more important when playing tag with squalls—if they are visible. Squall trails on radar are often rather murky, whereas visual compass bearings to squalls can be very precise. If you can see the clouds you are maneuvering around, you will do a much better job by com-

Figure 11-26. *Squall motions in the Northern Hemisphere. In the tropics, squalls may move more in line with the wind direction, but at higher latitudes they tend to come from a direction veered from the ambient wind. The top shows examples of squalls that might catch us until we pick up speed from their winds, then push us along as a buddy boat with little relative motion, as indicated on the radar screen showing squalls with no wakes—or we may have to fall off and run with it. The squall winds may shift the wind one direction, but its main influence is to increase the wind speed, which moves the apparent wind forward, so we end up falling off. It is difficult to guess what will happen until we have gathered experience from several scenarios. If these two effects cancel, we might ride along more or less on the right course, but generally we are just going faster in whatever direction they happen to take us (dotted lines show potential course changes). More often than not, this is good in any case for a racing sailor, because squalls often occur when the wind is otherwise relatively light.*

The bottom shows squalls catching or passing us that do show wakes. The trick is to "go to school" on the first one to learn its behavior for our conditions. Subsequent ones are likely to behave in a similar manner. Radar observations can be a tremendous aid to the process. (Note this figure is oriented in the true wind direction, not a geographic direction.)

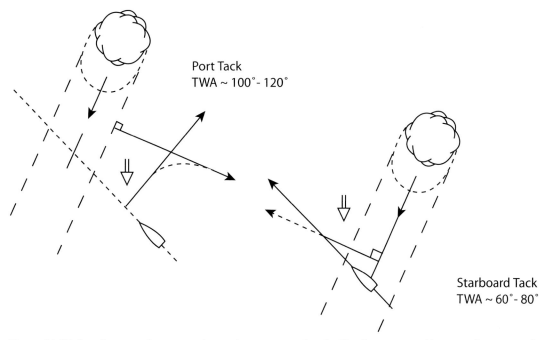

Figure 11-27. *Squalls to weather are rarely an advantage to sailors looking for more wind because they approach and pass rather quickly. Since ambient winds well away from the squall are usually moderate, tacking around them can be a useful avoidance maneuver. Under power, you can maneuver around them while watching the radar. Remember that strong, gusty winds can extend a mile or more in front of the leading edge of the squall clouds. Visual observations, when possible, are always a major asset to evaluating the radar images.*

In the left view, the boat has tacked and then fallen off to a course at about right angles to the squall's path, with rough estimates of the true wind angles (TWA) shown. In the right view, the boat has crossed the squall's path and fallen off to an approximately perpendicular course to increase the CPA with the leading edge of the squall.

bining compass bearings with radar observations.

When sailing to weather in the presence of squalls, there is rarely any virtue in seeking them out, and often value in avoiding them. Since you are on opposite courses they pass quickly, so even if more wind is desirable, it will not likely be worth the trouble of setting new sails. Tacking around them is likely the best solution (see Figure 11-27).

In contrast to a racing sailor, who might want to get in front of a squall, the cruising skipper who wants to avoid a squall should practice storm avoidance maneuvering to put maximum distance between himself and an approaching squall. The first step is to get onto the jibe that is away from the course of the squall, then monitor its wake as above. In most cases, that maneuver alone will do the job.

The optimum course to take for *maximum* separation is just forward of perpendicular to the squall's course, where the amount forward depends on your speed relative to that of the squall, as shown in Figure 11-28. That approach requires knowing the true heading of the squall, which can be either guessed from the wind direction or measured from relative motion diagram. An adequate approach in most cases is just to turn away from the squall until the DRM of the squall is running parallel to or away from your course. Squalls are very localized, so you do not have to miss them by much to be spared their strong winds. The exception might be right in front of one, where the strong winds can extend some several miles ahead of the rain and apparent cloud edge.

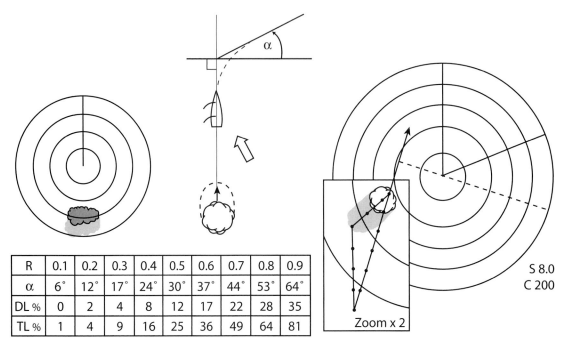

R	0.1	0.2	0.3	0.4	0.5	0.6	0.7	0.8	0.9
α	6°	12°	17°	24°	30°	37°	44°	53°	64°
DL %	0	2	4	8	12	17	22	28	35
TL %	1	4	9	16	25	36	49	64	81

Zoom x 2

S 8.0
C 200

Figure 11-28. *Storm avoidance maneuvering. To put the most distance between us and a squall—or to achieve maximum CPA with another vessel or squall—we head forward of the perpendicular to the target's true path by an angle alpha (α), where α depends on the ratio (R) of our speed to the squall speed. If our speed is 6 kts and the squall's speed is 10 kts (R = 0.6), we would choose α = 37°. With squall interactions we will not know its precise speed, so this is just a ballpark estimate. The table does show, however, that the closer our speed is to the speed of the squall (or storm), the more we might benefit from an optimum diagonal course. DL and TL are the distance lost (CPA) and time lost (TCPA) if we choose a perpendicular course versus the optimum diagonal course. In the example above, our CPA would be 17 percent smaller and the time to the CPA would be 36 percent shorter if we went perpendicular to the path rather than forward by the optimum amount. When on the optimum heading, the CPA occurs when the squall crosses our stern, which is not the case on any other heading. The right figure shows a converging squall with a crude relative motion diagram from which we can estimate (based on our own speed of 8 kts) that the squall is moving at about 12 kts in a direction about 20° to the right of our course. Here R = 0.66, so α is about 40°. To maximize our CPA, we would reason our new course as: right 20° to be headed in the same direction as the squall, then another 90° to be perpendicular to its path (a total of 110° to the right), and then forward of that by 40° to be on the optimum course, which would be a net turn of 70° to the right. That turn should put the squall on our starboard quarter with a DRM that is perpendicular to our heading line.*

SAILBOAT RACING WITH RADAR

Radar can be a most valuable aid to evaluating the performance of competitors in sailboat races. It is so valuable that it was banned from the 2003 America's Cup competition because the many options it offered to evaluate racing conditions went beyond the spirit of the racing rules. If one competitor has a custom radar designed to be optimized over the range of the race course, combined with a very sensitive custom ARPA system that computes and displays directly what a tactician wants to extract from a target vessel's motion (even for those targets not in the race!), it is easy to see why that boat holds an advantage over a competitor lacking such a system.

The beauty of radar is that you can tell—within minutes in some cases—whether a nearby vessel is just a tenth of a knot faster or slower than you at the moment, or if it is pointed just a few degrees higher or lower than you. The farther away the boat, the longer it takes to get these data, but the exercise is always valuable, and even on the edge of useful ranges (about 3 miles or so) it takes just minutes. Figure 11-29 shows an example generated from the Starpath radar simulator included on the Radar Resources CD, along with a few tips on interpreting the trails. The technique is simply to turn on the Wake trail option and solve the relative motion diagram for true course and speed as explained above. A heading sensor input and stabilized display mode are extremely valuable all the time, and sometimes mandatory for this application. (To push the limits of the radar's measurement ability, you want to give it all the help you can.) Refer to Figure 11-30 for various cases you might be looking at in a sailboat race.

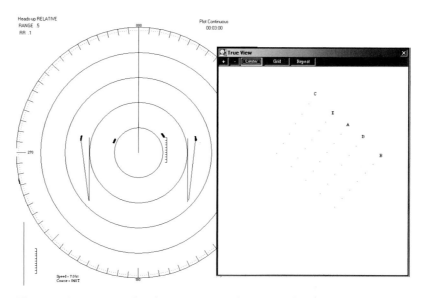

Figure 11-29. *Racing with radar. A is our vessel. B is 0.1 kt faster. E is 0.1 kt slower. D is sailing 5° lower at the same speed. C is sailing 5° higher at the same speed. This is a simulation of a 3-minute trail. In 6 minutes or longer, the definition would be much better.*

Figure 11-30. *Judging target true motion from short wake trails. If the plot clock has been running for some time, but the trails are still short, it means the target's true course and speed are not much different from ours. Here is how we might guess what that difference is.*

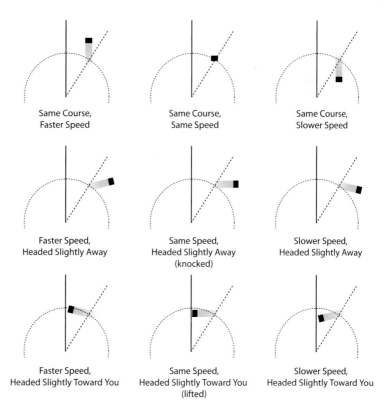

Same Course,
Faster Speed

Same Course,
Same Speed

Same Course,
Slower Speed

Faster Speed,
Headed Slightly Away

Same Speed,
Headed Slightly Away
(knocked)

Slower Speed,
Headed Slightly Away

Faster Speed,
Headed Slightly Toward You

Same Speed,
Headed Slightly Toward You
(lifted)

Slower Speed,
Headed Slightly Toward You

Any racer will appreciate the value of knowing a competitor's speed and heading. You might also use radar to determine wind directions at some distance from you. For this you need benchmarks. If, for example, there is a larger, faster boat in the fleet that points about the same as you do, you can use his wake trail on the radar as an indicator of wind shifts ahead. Some of these shifts can be seen by eye, but for others, and under some conditions (for example, at night), radar is your best bet.

In some cases you might not be able to get specific data, but even general information might help. For example, did your competitor jibe at night to go in toward the beach or is he still outside you? Or say you note that three vessels are way outside you and barely detectable on radar. You cannot measure their trail lengths accurately, but you can watch them over an hour or so to see if their relative positions are changing, or if any have decided to come back into the shore.

For racing applications it might be best to consider a gimballed mount or some leveling option for the antenna, because you will want to push the sensitivity of the reception and you will use it while going to weather in strong winds more often than a cruising boat might.

COURSE TO STEER FOR DESIRED CPA

You often choose to maneuver to increase the passing distance between yourself and an approaching vessel. That is, you detect a target and determine its closest point of approach (CPA), decide this passing is too close, and maneuver to increase (open up) that distance.

In clear weather, long before you are at risk of collision, you can maneuver this way according to the *Rules* regardless of who would eventually have right-of-way if you carried on. Once you are nearer to risk of collision, then presumably you would only do this when you are the give-way vessel and you choose to give way more than your present course provides, but you do not want to go farther out of your way than safe navigation calls for. If you are the stand-on vessel you should hold course and speed until you have safely passed the other vessel.

In this type of encounter you should already know the speed and direction of relative motion of the approaching target from its wake trail or from two or more observations of range and bearing. If you did not know these you would not know that you needed to maneuver to increase the CPA.

You can maneuver to achieve the new CPA either by changing course while maintaining the same speed (the most common choice), or changing speed while maintaining the same course, or a combination of both.

In clear weather, the *Navigation Rules* recommend the first option. In fog, that recommendation is not specifically given, but the obligation to maneuver applies more often; since there is no stand-on vessel in the fog, we are called on to use some form of this analysis more frequently. Rule 8b discourages the third option in any condition of visibility unless the combination gives a clear indication of your intentions to the other vessel. These points are discussed further in Chapter 12.

As a practical matter, when widely separated, you might just guess how much to turn, execute the turn, and then check the CPA again. In some cases that might do the job, but the problem with the "guess and tweak" method is that you might confuse the other vessel, who is watching you on his radar. And if you try to make this guess and maneuver too early, before you really know what your relative courses are, then by the time you do get close enough to see what is really taking place, you may have made things worse.

Generally it is best to wait until you are certain of the relative courses involved, then make a decisive, conservative turn. The maneuvering diagram discussed in Figure 12-7 offers good guidelines for the magnitude of the turn in various encounters. The graphical procedure

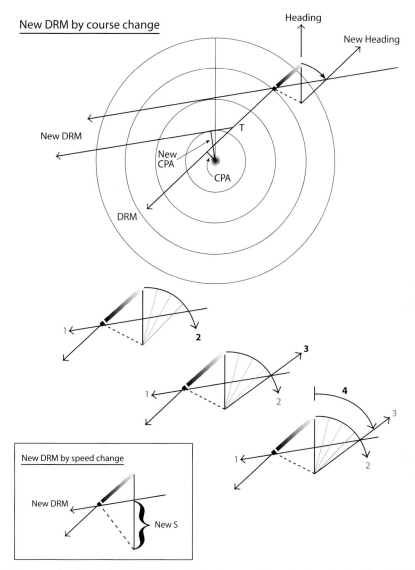

New DRM by course change

Figure 11-31. *Maneuvering for desired CPA. This solution is generally worked out by transfer plotting, but it can be estimated right on the radar screen with practice.*

Step 1. Choose a point along the target's present DRM where you wish to turn to change the CPA, and draw in the new DRM that will accomplish this. In the example, you choose to turn at point T to have a CPA of one range ring.

Step 2. With parallel rules, move the new DRM line to the present position of the target, and swing an arc of your buoy trail over to intersect the new DRM line.

Step 3. Draw your new heading line through that intersection, and measure the angle between present heading and this new heading.

Step 4. When you reach point T, turn to your new heading.

The inset shows how to accomplish this shift in DRM by reducing speed without a course change. Reduce the length of your buoy trail (your speed, S) to match the desired DRM. In the example, you would reduce your speed to about two-thirds of your original spseed to achieve the same shift in DRM—if your speed were 9 kts, you would drop to 6. Remember it is the bottom segment of your old buoy trail that marks your new speed; the target's course-and-speed line remains unchanged.

for setting a course to achieve a specific CPA is presented in Figure 11-31. You will not need to do this often, but practicing with a few solutions will help build your intuition on the size of the turns. You can also gain this experience and test your results using the radar simulator on the Radar Resources CD. The problem can also be solved on any e-chart software, as shown in Figure 11-32.

ERBL Solution

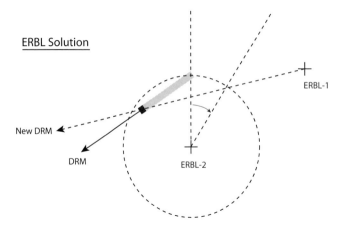

eChart Solution

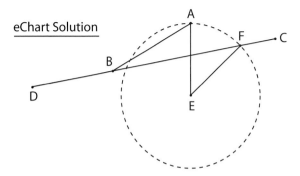

Figure 11-32. *Electronic maneuvering solutions. The top view shows an ERBL solution. This is quickest with two ERBLs, but can be done with just one with a few marks on the screen.*

Step 1. Set EBL-1 to mark your desired DRM (first centered on the target), then move center but leave EBL-1 passing through the target.

Step 2. Set VRM-2 to your buoy trail length, and then move it to the tail end of the target wake.

Step 3. Rotate EBL-2 to intersect EBL-1, and then the value of EBL-2 is your new heading to achieve the desired DRM.

The bottom view shows an e-chart solution.

Step 1. Measure range and bearing of the target wake with ERBL (Figure 11-10).

Step 2. Draw the measured wake (AB) on the e-chart, and then draw the desired DRM (line CD) passing through point B.

Step 3. Draw your buoy trail (AE) and on the waypoint or mark E place a range circle with radius AE.

Step 4. Draw the line EF that marks your new heading line and read off the direction of EF as your new heading to achieve the DRM of choice.

CHAPTER 12

Radar and the *Navigation Rules*

The book of *Navigation Rules: International–Inland* is in many ways the most important book in navigation. Every prudent mariner should know it well. The *Rules* constitute a remarkable document with an immense assigned task—the prevention of collisions between a vast array of vessels in a vast array of circumstances: vessels barely visible at 100 yards to vessels the size of horizontal skyscrapers; drifting without power or traveling at 80 knots or more; following unmarked lanes or crisscrossing open waters; in all conditions of weather, clear or fog, calm or storm; and often with no common language between their drivers.

Despite this enormous assignment, they do the job. Collisions can virtually always be traced to a violation of the *Rules* on the part of *both* vessels involved, so from a purely statistical point of view, you are unlikely to be involved in a collision if you, yourself, obey the *Rules* in all circumstances. The key to avoiding collision is a thorough understanding of the *Rules* and how to apply them, including what to do if an approaching vessel does not obey the *Rules*. A complete copy of the *Navigation Rules* is included on the Radar Resources CD.

Radar is covered in the *Rules* more than other navigation instruments because it is the tool mariners rely on most in reduced visibility, and the one that might be used to justify operating at higher speeds than they would if they did not have radar. The *Rules* help you understand the limits of the tools you use for any decision related to collision avoidance. The References include a section on the *Rules*; below we are sometimes paraphrasing what has been determined in various court cases as presented in those references. In the discussion that follows, we state the related rules in full, and emphasize with italics the text of the rule that relates to radar (there are no italics in the Rules themselves). After that, we explain how the emphasized text relates to radar.

An important point to remember when studying the *Rules* is the structure of Part B, Steering and Sailing Rules, which covers right-of-way and related issues in various encounters. Note that although the term *right-of-way* is not specifically used any longer in the International Rules, it still has the intended meaning in most circumstances, and is used here to reflect the distinction between stand-on and give-way vessels, vessels instructed "not to impede" or "stay clear of," and so forth—providing, of course, that the context does not call for more specific usage.

Part B is in three sections: Section I—Conduct of Vessels in Any Condition of Visibility, Section II—Conduct of Vessels in Sight of One Another, and Section III—Conduct of Vessels in Restricted Visibility. Those new to the *Rules* often overlook these distinctions and think that Section II rules always apply. But when in fog or interacting with targets on the radar screen that you cannot see visually, you are working under Section III *and* Section I rules. Thus, when maneuvering in accordance with a rule in Section III, that maneuver should also meet the rules of Section I.

RULE 2. RESPONSIBILITY

(a) Nothing in these Rules shall exonerate any vessel, or the owner, master or crew thereof, from the consequences of any neglect to comply with these Rules *or of the neglect of any precaution which may be required by the ordinary practice of seamen,* or by the special circumstances of the case.

(b) In construing and complying with these Rules due regard shall be had to all dangers of navigation and collision and to any special circumstances, including the limitations of the vessels involved, which may make a departure from these Rules necessary to avoid immediate danger.

Explanation of Rule 2

" . . . *or of the neglect of any precaution which may be required by the ordinary practice of seamen . . .* "

This is a catch-all clause, but it has been investigated in the courts many times. Note that exceptional performance, experience, or knowledge is not addressed here, but rather the "ordinary practice of seamen." Knowledge of compass use fits into that category, as does the effect of tides and currents. Knowing that large ships underway are not very maneuverable is an example of ordinary knowledge that is related to radar usage.

The existence of radar on board and its appropriateness in the fog or at night is another example,

as is maneuvering in the presence of another vessel before knowing what the other vessel is doing. Having someone on watch rely on radar for watchkeeping without proper instruction would not be classified as ordinary practice.

This rule reminds us that we must rely on, and are obligated to be familiar with, the rudiments of good seamanship to safely navigate a vessel.

RULE 5. LOOK-OUT

Every vessel shall at all times maintain a proper look-out by sight and hearing *as well as by all available means appropriate in the prevailing circumstances and conditions* so as to make a full appraisal of the situation and of the risk of collision.

Explanation of Rule 5

" . . . *as well as by all available means appropriate in the prevailing circumstances and conditions . . .* "

This rule requires you to use radar as part of

Figure 12-1. *A true story, told to us at a boat show, except that the captain's actual thought was phrased rather differently . . . and someone also needs a copy of the* Navigation Rules!

the lookout or watchkeeping in the fog or at night, or in any conditions where you cannot see well otherwise, because it is very clearly an "appropriate means."

This is a distinctly different requirement than requiring use of radar to evaluate collision risk. Evaluating collision risk requires the navigator to know how to interpret what he or she sees on the radar, but this requirement applies to anyone keeping watch. The lookout, who does not always have the responsibility to interpret and make decisions about approaching traffic, can just detect traffic and then find the right person to analyze the situation.

It seems reasonable that crewmembers who have watchkeeping responsibilities should be given at least the minimum training required to use radar according to this rule.

RULE 6. SAFE SPEED

Every vessel shall at all times proceed at a safe speed so that she can take proper and effective action to avoid collision and be stopped within a distance appropriate to the prevailing circumstances and conditions.

In determining a safe speed the following factors shall be among those taken into account:

(a) By all vessels:
  (i) the state of visibility;
  (ii) the traffic density including concentrations of fishing vessels or any other vessels;
  (iii) the maneuverability of the vessel with special reference to stopping distance and turning ability in the prevailing conditions;
  (iv) at night the presence of background light such as from shore lights or from back scatter of her own lights;
  (v) the state of wind, sea and current, and the proximity of navigational hazards;
  (vi) the draft in relation to the available depth of water.

(b) Additionally, by vessels with operational radar:
  (i) the characteristics, efficiency and limitations of the radar equipment;
  (ii) any constraints imposed by the radar range scale in use;
  (iii) the effect on radar detection of the sea state, weather and other sources of interference;
  (iv) the possibility that small vessels, ice and other floating objects may not be detected by radar at an adequate range;
  (v) the number, location and movement of vessels detected by radar;
  (vi) the more exact assessment of the visibility that may be possible when radar is used to determine the range of vessels or other objects in the vicinity.

Explanation of Rule 6b

"Additionally, by vessels with operational radar . . . "

The issue of safe speed comes up often in court cases. A common problem is a vessel that believes its radar watch is so good that it can justify traveling at normal high speeds in reduced visibility. Obviously, if this is being discussed in a court, the belief was wrong.

The *Rules* single out the precautions that must be made in radar watches. Again this is from Part B, Section I, which are rules that apply in all conditions of visibility.

"... (i) the characteristics, efficiency and limitations of the radar equipment ... "

This section of the rule is to stress to operators and masters that they cannot use a radar watch as justification for high speed in the fog without careful consideration. It is a broad warning emphasizing that you need to know how radar works and that unless you do, you might make wrong conclusions about present traffic and your speed.

Under "characteristics" you might include

the knowledge of warm-up times of the radar, what the screen should look like, how to optimize the picture, common types of false echoes, behavior in rain or waves, maximum target ranges for various types of targets, blocked regions, or more common issues like having the AC Sea turned up too high, which could block out close, weaker targets. Under "efficiency" you might include the effects of different pulse lengths, open array versus radome antennas, and so on. Under "limitations" you might include the reflective difference between various surfaces and aspects of targets, small versus large targets, resolving power limitations, range being limited by rain, etc. For sailing vessels well heeled over, if your radar antenna is not leveled, then you should be aware that your radar view to weather is limited.

This rule is about using radar to determine safe speed, so the primary concerns are those elements of radar operation that tell you where the traffic is or what the visibility might be, as opposed to analyzing the specific motion of that traffic to determine collision risk.

"... (ii) any constraints imposed by the radar range scale in use ..."

Obviously distant targets will be missed if you are viewing only the closer ranges. But equally important is that a small target can be missed when viewing the larger ranges. It is always important to switch back and forth on the range scales to check both regions efficiently. See related discussion in the explanation of Rule 7b.

"... (iii) the effect on radar detection of the sea state, weather and other sources of interference ..."

In bad weather and rough seas the radar is less dependable for detecting small targets, and maybe even larger targets in very bad conditions. There are picture adjustment options to help with this (see Chapter 2), but in severe cases it is still a problem. A severe rain squall or hailstorm, for example, can almost shut down the dependability of radar observations. Like-

wise, choppy seas can severely hinder detection of small targets on the lower ranges.

"... (iv) the possibility that small vessels, ice and other floating objects may not be detected by radar at an adequate range ..."

See related discussion in the explanation of Rule 7b. Typical ranges to small targets are listed in Chapter 3. This caution means simply that you might not see a small target by radar alone in time to maneuver around it. Note that this is one of two places in the *Navigation Rules* that imply the *Rules* are intended to prevent collisions with "things" as well as vessels.

The word *collision* implies the unintended striking of two vessels underway. An underway vessel striking an object other than a vessel un-

Figure 12-2. The Navigation Rules, *a USCG publication available at most marine supply stores, is in many ways the most important book in navigation. A complete electronic copy is included on the Radar Resources CD.*

derway (moored vessel, iceberg, dock) is called an *allision*. The USCG maintains separate safety statistics for these two types of accidents.

"... (v) the number, location and movement of vessels detected by radar ..."

The implication here is that a vessel that detects a large number of vessels moving about in various directions should slow down when passing through or by them. Examples are fishing fleets or yacht races. It is simply too difficult, even with modern ARPA, to track and evaluate a fleet of weak targets milling about in all directions.

I have seen this rule violated more than once, so I can tell you that simply sounding your whistle is no compensation for excessive speed in these conditions. Furthermore, Rule 8f (iii) (see below) applies, even if the large fleet of vessels is in fact illegally impeding the speeding vessel's passage.

Remember that a safe speed in one situation may not be safe after a target vessel changes course or speed. If a target maneuvers so as to increase the risk of collision, or significantly increase its rate of closing, then your present speed may no longer be safe, even if the other vessel's maneuver was not consistent with the *Navigation Rules*. Put another way, if you are sounding the danger-warning signal a second time, you should be slowing down at the same time.

"... (vi) the more exact assessment of the visibility that may be possible when radar is used to determine the range of vessels or other objects in the vicinity."

This part of the rule is an important reminder that with radar you can often determine the effective visibility. When a vessel or buoy first appears, note its range from the radar. Or when passing some object, note its radar range when it is no longer visible, and in the future you will know when to expect subsequent radar targets to emerge from the fog.

The state of the visibility can, of course, change with time, and is often different in different directions or elevations, but this remains valuable information in part because the steering rules change when a vessel is in sight.

Furthermore, if you have an estimate of the visibility, you can assess the extent of the region about you that you can see, and therefore make more reasonable estimates of what is a safe speed. The earlier parts of this rule emphasize the limits of radar in making this evaluation, and when the visibility is low these limits are even more crucial.

RULE 7. RISK OF COLLISION

(a) Every vessel shall use all available means appropriate to the prevailing circumstances and conditions to determine if risk of collision exists. If there is any doubt such risk shall be deemed to exist.

(b) *Proper use shall be made of radar equipment if fitted and operational, including long-range scanning to obtain early warning of risk of collision and radar plotting or equivalent systematic observation of detected objects.*

(c) Assumptions shall not be made on the basis of scanty information, *especially scanty radar information.*

(d) In determining if risk of collision exists the following considerations shall be among those taken into account:

(i) such risk shall be deemed to exist if the compass bearing of an approaching vessel does not appreciably change.

(ii) such risk may sometimes exist even when an appreciable bearing change is evident, particularly when approaching a very large vessel or a tow or when approaching a vessel at close range.

Explanation of Rule 7b

"Proper use shall be made of radar equipment if fitted and operational ... "

Rule 7 is from Part B, Section I, which includes those rules that apply to all conditions of visibility. In other words, the rule says proper use of radar "shall" be made night or day, rain or shine, in the fog, near the fog, or completely out of the fog.

Shall means *must*; it is not an option. If you have it, you must use it whenever there is any doubt about risk of collision, which there always is when you first see a vessel on the horizon headed toward you by sight or by radar. The term "proper use" implies you should know how radar works and how to use it.

If you can tell there is absolutely no risk of collision by watching an approaching vessel for some time, then you are not obligated to start any sort of radar plot. But in some cases even when a vessel is in clear view, it is easier to track the vessel with a radar plot. A quick trip to the radar to set a proper scale and start a plot can prove valuable even with vessels in clear sight. The rule simply states that if you have *any* doubt, you must track it.

"*. . . including long-range scanning to obtain early warning of risk of collision . . . *"

This means that at night or in the fog, when you cannot see far by eye, you should be frequently checking the higher ranges to see if anyone is headed toward you. On smaller radar units, this means the 12-mile range, as you will not see much beyond that, unless you are looking for land. See discussion of maximum radar range in Chapter 3.

Remember the warnings of Rule 6b on checking all radar ranges, and the word "proper" in Rule 7b. When local visibility is poor, you cannot just set the radar to a high range and leave it. You must frequently check the lower ranges to scan for small targets.

A small target might not be visible at all on any range from more than 3 or 4 miles off, and at the same time not be visible even at 1 mile off if you are looking for it on the 12-mile range. On all radars, the resolution is better on lower scales.

The normal procedures on a radar check is to look carefully at a few sweeps on the higher scales, then do the same on the lower scales. In rough seas, this can take some time as the screen can be cluttered with reflections from waves and may need picture adjustment on each scale. At the lower ranges you need to adjust the AC Sea to optimize looking for targets. This often involves an interplay between AC Sea and Gain.

It is my experience that the various styles of radar alarms on typical small-craft radar may not be dependable for making these observations and warning you adequately in all cases (see discussion in Chapter 8). It is usually important that they are set up with the proper picture adjustment, and it may be difficult to optimize these settings if you have no targets in sight on the screen. If you intend to use alarms for any purpose, it is best to carry out a thorough test of their operation and run them as often as possible so you can test their behavior.

"*. . . and radar plotting or equivalent systematic observation of detected objects.*"

This is a key phrase in the *Navigation Rules* about the use of radar. Remember, it applies to all conditions of visibility—in short, to all uses of radar involved in the evaluation of collision risk. The wording of this rule likely came about before the advent of Plot and Wake options on small-craft radar. You have to assume that this "radar plotting" does not simply mean turning on the Plot or Echo Trail option.

"Radar plotting" here almost certainly refers to making some evaluation of the relative motion diagram. In the simplest case, is a target headed toward you, pointed at you, or are you overtaking it? The next level of evaluation is determining the true course, speed, and aspect of the target vessel. These points are all covered in Chapters 6 and 11.

The "systematic observation," on the other hand, could clearly be met by engaging an automatic echo plot function with associated timer and then placing an EBL on the target position. It is my experience, however, that there will be cases where the interaction is so critical that writing the actual observations (range, bearing, and time) in the logbook or a corner of the chart seems more than justified.

Think of the case of a vessel closing from ahead at two or three times your speed. Remember too, that if someone inadvertently changes the radar range, the trails could be erased. If such an event contributes to anxious moments, it will be little consolation that this was not your error. Your error was failing to recognize the possibility of losing this record, and the consequences it might have. Some of the latest models of radar maintain a memory of trails on the screen that show up on any range you select. This is indeed a nice feature if you are compiling a list of things to look for.

Explanation of Rule 7c

" . . . *especially scanty radar information.*"

The scanty information is typically radar conclusions made from either too far off or not long enough a time. This rule is about evaluating risk of collision, which would call for some action. If this action is taken without proper evaluation, it could lead to trouble.

It is crucial that some form of "systematic observation" be made on the proper range. In head-up display mode, the trail or wake of an approaching target smears out as your own vessel yaws in a seaway. This is an issue with small antennas that have large horizontal beam

widths. See Figure 12-3. When viewed from far off, the direction of relative motion cannot be determined precisely, so you do not know if the vessel is going to pass safely to the right or left. A turn to the right without proper confirmation could interfere with what would have been a safe starboard passing. A stabilized (north-up or course-up) display mode can improve this type of radar observation significantly.

Careful plotting and visual observation are crucial in this interaction as well as radio contact if in doubt. When possible the target should be monitored by sight as well as radar. More often than not you can tell the aspect of a vessel from a distance more precisely with binoculars and compass than you can with radar. Night vi-

Figure 12-3. *Unstabilized radar trails can be misleading when viewed from a distance. This ship passed the sailing vessel quite safely 1 mile off in midocean in clear weather. Had this been in reduced visibility, however, radio contact would have been called for quite a bit earlier, because with this head-up, unstabilized radar with an 18-inch antenna, and under sail in waves, the track of the ship even at 4 miles off could not be safely evaluated.*

sion binoculars are a tremendous aid to this evaluation during twilight and night. Those who have used them for this application swear by them.

RULE 8. ACTION TO AVOID COLLISION

(a) Any action taken to avoid collision shall, if the circumstances of the case admit, be positive, made in ample time and with due regard to the observance of good seamanship.

(b) Any alteration of course and/or speed to avoid collision shall, if the circumstances of the case admit, *be large enough to be readily apparent to another vessel observing visually or by radar;* a succession of small alterations of course and/or speed should be avoided.

(c) If there is sufficient sea room, alteration of course alone may be the most effective action to avoid a close quarters situation provided that it is made in good time, is substantial and does not result in another close quarters situation.

(d) Action taken to avoid collision with another vessel shall be such as to result in passing at a safe distance. The effectiveness of the action shall be carefully checked until the other vessel is finally past and clear.

(e) If necessary to avoid collision or allow more time to assess the situation, a vessel shall slacken her speed or take all way off by stopping or reversing her means of propulsion.

(f) (i) A vessel which, by any of these rules, is required not to impede the passage or safe passage of another vessel shall, when required by the circumstances of the case, take early action to allow sufficient sea room for the safe passage of the other vessel.

(ii) A vessel required not to impede the passage or safe passage of another vessel is not relieved of this obligation if approaching the other vessel so as to involve risk of collision and shall, when taking action, have full regard to the action which may be required by the rules of this part.

(iii) A vessel, the passage of which is not to be impeded remains fully obliged to comply with the rules of this part when the two vessels are approaching one another so as to involve risk of collision.

Explanation of Rule 8b

" . . . be large enough to be readily apparent to another vessel observing visually or by radar . . . "

This rule applies in all conditions of visibility and even to those vessels that do not carry radar. When you maneuver, your maneuver should be visible to the other vessel observing "by radar." This calls for large turns, at least 30° and preferably 60° or more, depending, of course, on the presence of other nearby traffic or obstacles (e.g., "if the circumstances of the case admit").

If you use speed adjustments, you must generally make a 50 percent or more change in speed for your change to be readily apparent to another vessel, and your change should be made as rapidly as safely possible. Speed changes are often difficult to discern even when viewing the vessel visually. On radar, it will take a time interval of at least as long as the wake trail time to see the new trail length. The interval plot option (Figure 2-7) reveals speed changes more quickly, but that option is not as convenient for general operations. Practice (with real radar or the simulator) by setting up a wake trail on a buoy, then cut your speed in half and see how long it is before you can discern your new speed from your own radar. A course alteration, in keeping with Rule 8c, on the other hand, starts a bend in the wake trail immediately (bearing in mind the Rules of Thumb in Chapter 11).

Remember too, you can always stop. A collision course situation that develops when you are moving and a target is approaching diagonally will appear on the radar screen as a relative motion plot aimed straight toward you. If you stop, or make a significant speed reduction, the target's relative motion trail will curve up-screen (Chapter 11, Maneuvering Rule 1) and the collision threat will be alleviated. (When you are the stand-on vessel in clear weather, you are instructed to hold course and speed, but Rules 8e and 17b give you the option and obligation to maneuver as needed to avoid collision. In the fog, on the other hand, there is no stand-on vessel or associated rules that would inhibit you from stopping.) With more than one vessel present, it is of course important to not stop in front of a second vessel. During clear weather this is an obvious observation, but when viewing by radar alone it may not be. See Figure 12-4.

The Starpath Radar Trainer program is an excellent way to practice the degree of turning that can be seen on another radar and the simple practice of stopping in a collision situation (if consistent with the *Rules* in effect). You will see that in some cir-cumstances a target's turn of 30° or even 40° can sometimes be difficult to detect for some period of time.

RULE 19. CONDUCT OF VESSELS IN RESTRICTED VISIBILITY

(a) This Rule applies to vessels not in sight of one another when navigating in or near an area of restricted visibility.

(b) Every vessel shall proceed at a safe speed adapted to the prevailing circumstances and conditions of restricted

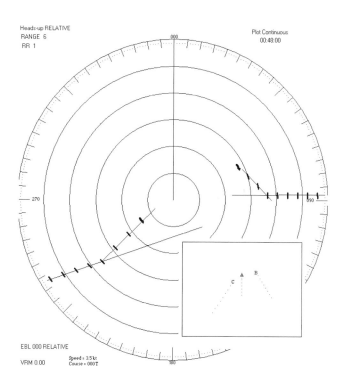

Figure 12-4. *Reducing speed to avoid collision risk. We have two targets approaching from either side. The beam target on the starboard side poses a risk of collision, but when we reduce speed by a factor of 2 (from 7 kts to 3.5 kts) that target pulls safely ahead of us. When making such a maneuver, however, we must be aware of other targets in the vicinity. The port quarter target was passing safely 1.5 miles astern of us before we reduced speed, but at our new speed this is now a converging target. Both targets are overtaking us, so the proper maneuver would depend on the condition of visibility, besides being an example of special circumstances of having more than two vessels involved.*

visibility. A power-driven vessel shall have her engines ready for immediate maneuver.

(c) Every vessel shall have due regard to the prevailing circumstances and conditions of restricted visibility when complying with the Rules of Section I of this Part.

(d) *A vessel which detects by radar alone the presence of another vessel shall determine if a close quarters situation is developing and/or risk of collision exists. If so, she shall take avoiding action in ample time, provided that when such action consists of an alteration of course, so far as possible the following shall be avoided:*

   (i) *an alteration of course to port for a vessel forward of the beam, other than for a vessel being overtaken;*

   (ii) *an alteration of course toward a vessel abeam or abaft the beam.*

(e) Except where it has been determined that a risk of collision does not exist, every vessel which hears apparently forward of her beam the fog signal of another vessel, or which cannot avoid a close quarters situation with another vessel forward of her beam, shall reduce her speed to the minimum at which she can be kept on her course. She shall if necessary take all her way off and in any event navigate with extreme caution until danger of collision is over.

Explanation of Rule 19d

This is the most important rule for radar observers in conditions of restricted visibility, which applies to all vessels, power and sail. It can be summarized as follows: On the radar screen, if a target that you cannot see visually is closing in on you from forward of the beam, turn right. If it is approaching from aft of the beam, turn away from it. You will turn right in all cases except for starboard quarter targets.

(Specific suggestions for when to turn and how much to turn are given at the end of this chapter.)

"A vessel which detects by radar alone the presence of another vessel . . . "

The rule applies when any target is first detected anywhere on the radar screen—forward, aft, port, or starboard.

It also states that you do not see the target visually, but this is also implied because this rule is in Section III, which applies to vessels in or near conditions of restricted visibility. Remember this rule applies when you are near fog as well as in it. You could have clear skies and not see a vessel in a fog bank several miles from you.

Whether or not you have heard the vessel is another matter (it says radar "alone"). If you have heard a vessel you cannot see, there are specific rules (Rule 19e) for that situation. Furthermore, you cannot always be certain that the vessel you detect on radar is the one you hear, especially if there is more than one target present.

" . . . shall determine if a close quarters situation is developing and/or risk of collision exists."

"Close quarters" is a key concept in the *Navigation Rules*, but one the *Rules* leave undefined, as they do with other key concepts such as "proper watch" and "do not impede," since their definition depends on the circumstances. "Close quarters" is generally thought of as the safety zone you need to maintain so you can maneuver on your own to avoid a collision, regardless of what the other vessel might do suddenly and unexpectedly. It is your safety space or zone. The radius of your safety zone depends on the circumstances. Passing at slow speeds in a narrow channel, it could be several yards. In the fog with a fast-moving ship approaching, this zone is measured in miles, not fractions of a mile. It could also be thought of as the minimum CPA you will accept as safe passing. Note that generally you know if a radar target is most likely a ship. If you see a vessel target at 8 or

10 miles off with a small-craft radar, then it is a ship. You would simply not see smaller vessels. And as it gets closer it will become a very large, bright target. This rule, however, applies to all vessel targets. The type of vessel does not matter, sail or power, large or small.

Your first job is to track the vessel ("systematic observation") to make an evaluation as soon as possible of its direction of relative motion, as described in the risk of collision section of Chapter 6. You should anticipate an early maneuver for any CPA that is approaching your determination of close quarters for the situation at hand.

If you are in a sailing vessel, for example, dealing with big waves and strong winds, then you must figure into this close quarters evaluation what type of wind shifts might be expected and how you might respond with course changes. A power-driven vessel might not understand these constraints. This is a proper concern for ocean-racing yachts that might be under spinnaker in strong winds and big seas within a region of dense sea fog. Your status as a sailing vessel does not play any role in this rule. Radio contact is always valuable in these conditions.

"If so, she shall take avoiding action in ample time . . . "

Note the crucial distinction in the wording here compared to interactions in clear weather. You are not maneuvering to avoid a collision when risk of collision exists, as in clear weather, but rather you are maneuvering to avoid the "development" of close quarters or collision risk itself. It is a clear call for earlier, more conservative actions. This rule is an acknowledgment that radar alone is not a good way to evaluate rapidly developing close quarters situations, and therefore if radar is all you have to go by, you should maneuver early.

It is also important to remember Rule 7c—assumptions should not be made on the basis of scanty radar information—which applies to all evaluations of risk of collision. In other words, you need to make whatever systematic observations are required so that you can indeed determine if risk is developing. To just see a target and maneuver is both wrong and dangerous.

" . . . provided that when such action consists of an alteration of course . . . "

The rule then gives explicit instructions that cover all cases.

" . . . so far as possible the following shall be avoided:

(i) an alteration of course to port for a vessel forward of the beam, other than for a vessel being overtaken . . . "

Part (i) tells us you that you should turn right for any vessel approaching forward of the beam.

The exception is when you are overtaking the approaching target, which means the first thing you need to know is whether or not you are an overtaking vessel. On a clear night it is easy to know you are overtaking, because according to the definition of overtaking you would see only a white stern light on the vessel you are overtaking. With radar observations alone, which is the domain of this rule, it is not always such a simple deduction.

For parallel targets moving down-screen from ahead this is simple to figure. If their SRM is less than your speed, you are overtaking them. On diagonal approaches, you must evaluate the relative motion diagram, as was illustrated in Figure 11-8, which showed two very similar target trails, but one was a crossing vessel and one was an overtaken vessel (see also Figure 11-9, which illustrates other common misinterpretations).

Figure 12-5 illustrates the criteria for overtaking—approaching the target from more than 22.5° aft of the target's beam, and how this can be evaluated from radar wakes.

Rule 8 gives you guidelines for avoiding risk of collision when overtaking. It tells you your obligation is to make an early and prominent maneuver to stay well clear. The target being overtaken will in turn see you on his radar approaching up-screen from aft of his beam. His job will then be to decide if close quarters is developing, and if so, to turn away from you. When overtaking, however, you should maneuver early enough that he would

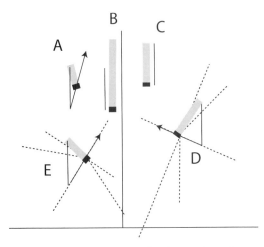

Figure 12-5. *Overtaking in radar observations. According to Rule 13, a vessel is "deemed to be overtaking when coming up upon another vessel from a direction more than 22.5 degrees (two points) abaft her beam." From a radar perspective, this means an overtaken target must be a down-screen target in approximately the forward quadrant of the screen that is approaching on a near constant bearing with a true speed less than ours. Candidates that are parallel targets (near the heading line) are easy to spot, as they have a wake length less than our buoy trail (shown as a thin line next to the wakes of targets A, B, and C.*

A has a wake about half our buoy trail, so it is definitely being overtaken. We are gaining on it at about half our boat speed and well onto its stern. B is actually headed toward us, closing with an SRM of about twice our boat speed. C is dead in the water (wake length equals buoy trail). If it is a vessel underway (i.e., not anchored, not moored, and not aground), then we are overtaking in clear weather depending on what way it is pointed when we come up on it. In reduced visibility, it is simply an obstruction that we should go around. Target D is a crossing target according to the rules; at night we would see only its red sidelight and masthead lights. It is not being overtaken. Target E, on the other hand, is being approached from more than two points aft of the beam, so it is being overtaken. At night we would see only its white stern light.

not be concerned about close quarters developing. Specific maneuvers are discussed in the next section.

" . . . *so far as possible the following shall be avoided:* . . .

(ii) an alteration of course toward a vessel abeam or abaft the beam."

Part (ii) of this rule tells you that you should turn away from any target approaching from abaft the beam. If it approaches from the port quarter, you turn right; if from the starboard quarter, you turn left.

Note that a target approaching from the starboard quarter is the only circumstance that calls for a turn to the left. All other cases call for a turn to the right.

In principle, the response to a vessel approaching from dead astern could be a turn in either direction, but see the suggestions and notes below for a preference that might be useful.

Note the distinction here between navigation in sight and not in sight. When you are being overtaken in clear weather, you are instructed to hold course and speed. But when you see someone overtaking you by radar alone, and he is headed toward a CPA that might involve risk of collision, then you must turn away from him.

An even more notable distinction involves a vessel crossing from the port side. In clear weather, a power-driven vessel approaching from the port side of your power-driven vessel would be the give-way vessel. You would be the stand-on vessel and should hold course and speed (Rule 17). It would be wrong in the fog, however, to treat or anticipate that target as a give-way vessel. Likewise a sailing vessel should not assume any rights over presumed power-driven–vessel targets when operating by radar alone. There is no right-of-way in the fog. Everybody has instructions on maneuvering.

The situations are shown in Figure 12-6. Situations 1 and 2 are consistent with clear-weather situations, but situations 3 and 4 are

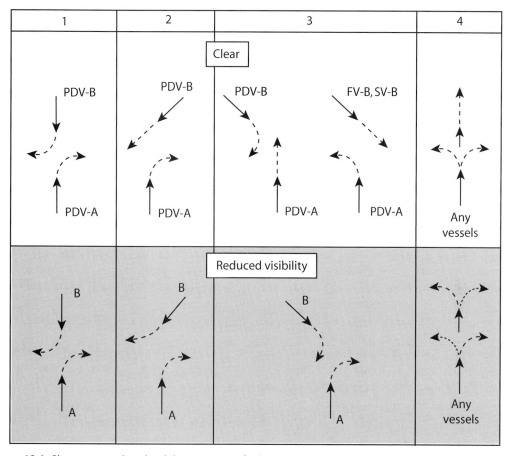

Figure 12-6. *Clear versus reduced visibility maneuvers for head-on, port, and starboard bow approaches, and overtaking. In clear weather, Rule 15 tells us (situation 1) both to turn right—the only case in clear weather where there is no stand-on or give-way vessel. In situation 2, B holds course and speed and A turns right when both are power-driven vessels (PDV). In situation 3, A holds course and speed and B turns right, or if A is a PDV and B happens to be a sailing vessel (SV) or a vessel engaged in fishing (FV), then A has the option to turn left, although would not be required to if A could stay clear by some other maneuver. When overtaking (situation 4), the overtaken vessel holds course and speed. In reduced visibility, however, when navigating by radar alone, there is no stand-on or give-way vessel in any encounter. Vessels meeting forward of the bow (as deduced from radar observations) are each instructed to turn right by Rule 19d, unless overtaking, in which case, as in clear weather, the overtaking vessel may pass on either side. The difference is that the overtaken vessel must now turn away from the overtaking vessel, rather than hold course and speed—assuming, of course, in all of these interactions that risk of collision could develop if they did not maneuver. (The reduced visibility maneuver of situation 2 is shown from the perspective of both radars in Figure 12-8.)*

not. In clear weather you would hold course and speed, or even turn to the left for an approaching port-bow vessel with right-of-way (meaning higher rank in the Rule 18 list of responsibilities between vessels). In the fog, however, interacting according to Rule 19d, you should always turn right for any vessel approaching from forward of the beam, from either side.

You turn right under the assumption that the other vessel will also be obeying the *Rules* and will be turning right as well, so both of you have jointly moved to open up the separation between you. The reduced visibility maneuver of situation 2 is shown from the perspective of both radars in Figure 12-8.

If the approaching target does not maneuver according to the *Rules* and your own maneuver did not provide adequate clearing, then you have to slow down or stop, because Rule 8e still applies, and nothing in Rule 19d prevents you from stopping. In the next section specific maneuvers are discussed and presented in a convenient maneuvering diagram. In most cases the suggested maneuver is large enough to clear the other vessel even if it does not do its part in the maneuver.

In summary, when you cannot see the radar targets visually that you see closing in on you from forward of the beam, you turn right, and expect them to turn right. Your right turn will be a large one, with specific suggestions given in the maneuvering diagram in the next section.

If you set an EBL on your original course, you can generally come safely back on course when the target crosses your original heading, but naturally all passing must be monitored until you are safely sailing off in different directions.

THE COCKCROFT-LAMEIJER DIAGRAM

The *Navigation Rules* tell you which way to turn in all encounters, and they tell you to do it early, and to make it large enough to be detected by the other vessel's radar, but they do not say specifically how much to turn, or when. A. N. Cockcroft and J. N. F. Lameijer in their book *A Guide to the Collision Avoidance Rules* (see References) have presented what they call the Course Alteration Diagram, which answers these questions very specifically for vessels interacting under Rule 19d. It is a summary of those maneuvers for each range of encounters that most effectively increases the separation of the vessels at passing. A version of their diagram along with instructions on its use are presented in Figure 12-7. This design is somewhat different than the original, but the content is intended to be the same.

Careful study of this diagram answers many of the difficult questions a navigator is confronted with when interacting with traffic in the fog, and in some cases in clear weather. Needless to say, they are guidelines, not rules. Rule 2b is a specific reminder that you must always respond to the actual circumstances at hand and to any special circumstances that may apply—in short, there are indeed no fixed rules like those presented in this diagram or others that might apply to all circumstances you might run across. A frequent example of "special circumstances" is the presence of more than two vessels in the interaction—and if both are converging on you from diagonal courses while you are underway, stopping could be the best solution.

An example of the use of the diagram as viewed from the radars of both approaching vessels is shown in Figure 12-8.

There are two apparent exceptions in the diagram to the literal application of the *Rules*. The first has to do with vessels approaching just forward of broad on the starboard beam, and the second has to do with close vessels overtaking from just left of dead astern. The proposed maneuvers in those regions are in apparent conflict with a literal reading of Rule 19d, and thus merit some discussion.

First, Rule 19d refers to three relative bearing regions: "forward of the beam," "abeam," and "abaft the beam." According to Bowditch, "abeam," is defined as "A line approximately at right angle to the ship's keel—opposite the waist or middle part of the ship." There is then a distinction between this approximate direction or range of bearings on the beam and the very specific (though rarely used) term "broad on the starboard beam," which is precisely 090 R. The diagram extends this "approximate" span of "abeam" to about two points forward of 090 R.

This is picking at terms that might allow for a broader interpretation. The key issue is more the question of turning toward a vessel that

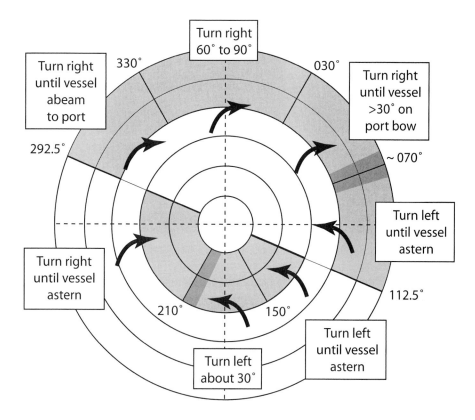

Figure 12-7. *Course alteration diagram adapted from* A Guide to the Collision Avoidance Rules *by A. N. Cockcroft and J. N. F. Lameijer (see References). It graphically presents suggested course alterations to avoid the development of collision risk in response to targets detected by radar alone (Rule 19d), keeping in mind the other applicable rules of Section I of Part B.*

The diagram is presented here in the form of a radar screen with rings spaced at 1 mile. The magnitude of the turn depends on where the target is coming from on the radar screen. The boundaries of the regions are marked by radial lines with their approximate relative bearings. It is presumed that the target has been tracked from first detection and that it does pose the potential for a close quarters situation, meaning it is approaching on a steady bearing and the adequacy of the CPA is uncertain.

Turns made for targets approaching from above the diagonal line in the drawing are called normal turns, and it is proposed that they be made preferably in the range of 4 to 6 miles off. Turns for targets below the line are called escape action, because to a vessel approaching in these regions, we would appear forward of the beam on its radar, and according to the diagram it should have turned at 4 to 6 miles off and we would not have had to maneuver at all. The escape turns preferably should be taken when the target is less than 3 miles off. These regions for taking action are marked with shaded range rings. After turning to starboard for a vessel on the starboard side, keep that vessel to port when resuming course.

Note these are the suggested turns when altering course from the proposed ranges. For targets approaching near the beam, a large and prompt reduction in speed is generally the most effective way to avoid a close quarters situation.

As a practical example of the diagram, if we see a target approaching from 045 R to within 4 to 6 miles range, we would turn to the right until that target appeared aft of 330 R (30° to the left of our heading line)—a 75° turn. That vessel would see us approaching at 315 R, and it would turn right until we appeared on his port beam—a 45° turn.

Examples viewed from the radars of both vessels are shown in Figure 12-8, including the cases where only one vessel maneuvers according to the diagram.

Refer to the text by Cockcroft and Lameijer for more details on this diagram and related discussion.

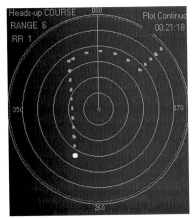

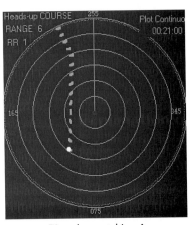

Only A maneuvers
True View from overhead

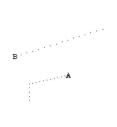

A's radar, watching B
as A maneuvers, B holding course

B's radar, watching A
as A maneuvers, B holding course

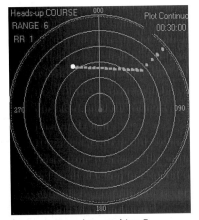

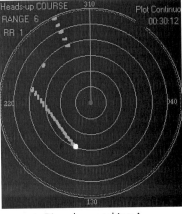

Only B maneuvers
True View from overhead

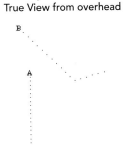

A's radar, watching B
as B maneuvers, A holding course

B's radar, watching A
as B maneuvers, A holding course

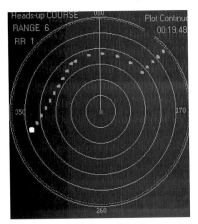

Both A and B maneuver
True View from overhead

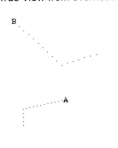

A's radar, watching B
as both vessels maneuver

B's radar, watching A
as both vessels maneuver

may in fact be closing in on you from a course heading not much different from your own—even if the relative motion approach is from 10° or 20° forward of 090 R, the true course of the approaching vessel could be similar to your own. You know that if and when he sees you, he will be turning to the right, because on his radar you will be approaching from well forward of his port beam. A turn away from him in this case would create a larger CPA than turning toward him since you would be both turning in the same general direction. The diagram proposes that a large turn away from the vessel (putting it on your stern) would be a safe "escape" maneuver in this case, and putting this option in the diagram implies that this might be better than a turn to the right. Assuming "abeam" = 090 R exactly, a literal reading of the rule would have you turn to-

Figure 12-8 (left). Application of the Cockcroft and Lameijer maneuvering diagram for a starboard bow target. Three examples of maneuvers in response to the same encounter are shown (top, middle, and bottom rows). The left column is vessel A's radar, the middle column is vessel B's radar, and the right column is the true view of the interaction of each row. In each case, vessel A detects target B approaching from 050 R and vessel B detects target A approaching from 340 R. The radars are set to range = 6 nm, and ring range = 1 nm, in head-up mode.

According to the diagram in Figure 12-7, A should turn right at about 4 miles off until B is at least 30° on its port side, which it does. B also has instructions for turning right in this encounter, but in this example B fails to turn. The results are shown in the screen captures, made with the Starpath Radar Trainer simulator. In head-up mode, when A turns right, target B rotates left, and then turns left as shown. We see that A's maneuver alone has opened up the CPA to about 1.5 miles.

In the middle row, A fails to maneuver, but B does turn according to the diagram (60° to the right for a target at 340 R), which puts A just forward of his port beam after the turn, which then proceeds to "turn back toward him" as discussed in Chapter 11. His turn in this case opened the CPA to 2.5 nm.

In the bottom row, both vessels maneuver according to the diagram (as they should according to Rule 19d) and the resulting CPA is 3 nm.

ward the vessel if it were approaching from 080 R or so.

Nevertheless, even with this reasoning at hand, this type of beam approach can present the operator with a dilemma when there is no time for such analysis, in which case stopping or significantly reducing speed would be the best maneuver, as shown in Figure 12-4.

The second apparent exception to the literal reading of Rule 19d is the diagram's suggested escape maneuver of turning to the left for a close vessel overtaking from just left of astern. Note first that this is an escape maneuver in that the vessel overtaking you should have seen you approach from ahead on his radar and should have turned either right or left well in advance, at 4 to 6 miles according to the authors. In other words, a vessel overtaking can go to either side of you in the fog, but they really should do so early enough that you do not even consider them a risk. In the case where they do approach closer, you might assume that this overtaking vessel did not see you at that distance and is now clearly headed in a direction that would lead to risk of collision.

Rule 19d calls for a turn away from the vessel to the right, but the authors suggest that in this case a large turn to the left would be not only appropriate, but preferred. One reason for this is that if this vessel does suddenly detect you approaching from ahead on his radar screen, his most likely turn would be to the right. If you also happened to be turning right at this time, neither of you have gained separation. Again, all circumstances are different, and here we are considering overtaking situations with a presumably low closing speed.

As a further note on this situation, as you first see a vessel approach from the port stern, you know that he has the right to pass you on either side. So you might well give him the opportunity to close in somewhat, waiting for him to make his decision. You might also expect him to indeed turn to the right as he gets closer in to cross your wake, since that passing generally ends up with a shorter interaction period. That is, if he turned left to pass you on a parallel course on your port side you would be traveling together for a longer period as he slowly pulled ahead far enough to go back onto course across your bow.

Another factor is that if he indeed did not see you on his radar screen until he was close in, and did not have time to compute your speed of relative motion, then he does not know if you are approaching from ahead or if he is overtaking you. If overtaking, he can turn right or left, but if closing from ahead he should turn right. In this situation he would most likely turn right.

With him likely to turn right in closer situations, your "escape" to the left could be a better maneuver.

In short, the diagram points out two narrow regions and circumstances where you might take advantage of the phrases "so far as possible" and "shall be avoided" to consider alternative safe maneuvers. The keys would be to do a quick evaluation of the relative motion diagram to determine the speed and aspect of the target and then to picture the underlying true view motion that is taking place beneath the relative motion seen on the radar. It is a case where the true motion radar display (Chapter 8) could be useful.

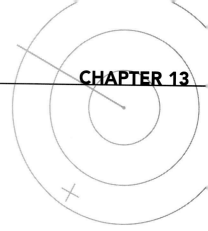

CHAPTER 13

Looking Ahead

There are inevitable developments in radar on the horizon, following in the wake of evolving hardware and software technologies. Some developments are more in the bells-and-whistles category—such as color displays, integrated instrument displays, multiple remote readouts, waterproof units, lower profile instruments with flatter screens, more functions on the radar screen, and so on—but others are much more fundamental and likely to have a more profound influence on navigation practice. We have already touched on one important area—screen brightness and resolution; the better you can see the targets, the more you learn from them. Radar has come a long way from the days when you had to press your face into a hood to see anything, to now, when you can sit on a flying bridge in bright sunlight viewing the radar and other video displays from some distance away . . . at least this is the goal that is well in sight with many units. We will take a look at a few others briefly that are already in various levels of implementation. Each of these features or systems are well established now, though not yet widely used.

PC RADAR

Several companies have developed systems available to recreational mariners that allow radar images to be overlaid directly onto an e-chart image viewed in a personal computer. These are different from the ECS-type overlays discussed in Chapter 7, since they were for vector chart displays internal to the same unit or for running on a PC integrated with the nav system. Here, the radar image is exported from the radar unit and imported into a stand-alone computer running a PC-based electronic navigation program. These programs might be running any type of local chart in the system. The radar images are geo-referenced for proper location and scaling and then overlaid on the chart. The PC can be one for personal use that you "share" with the boat.

When correlating the radar image with the chart, this type of display is ideal, because the chart underlying the images can show available detail and elevation data. Standard vector charts of most radar-plotter combinations do not have much detail on the shape of the land, and it is that land data that determines what we see on the radar. With such a system, you can overlay a topographic map or aerial photo onto a marine vector chart and then put the radar image on top of that. There are also accurate 3-D models of both land and bathymetry available for most parts of the United States as well as selected waterways worldwide, which are included in some e-chart programs. A radar overlay on these 3-D displays as shown in Figure 13-1 shows precisely how intervening landmasses create the radar images you see, although new building construction, ships at moorings, and so on can still generate surprises.

The main advantage of the overlay option is having complete confidence in what the radar targets are and where you are relative to them.

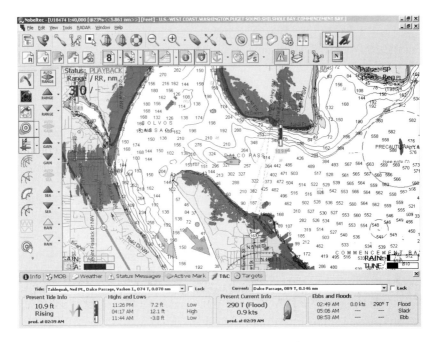

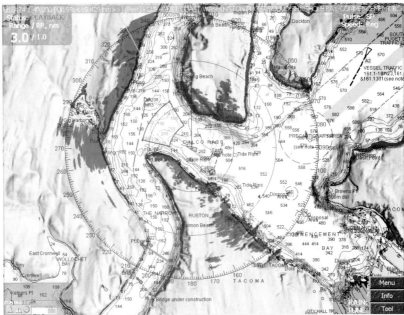

Figure 13-1. *Radar overlay onto vector charts. These screen captures are from Nobeltec's Visual Navigation Suite ECS software showing their Insight Radar image (dark regions) overlaid onto a vector chart. The top also shows real-time tide and current data on the same display. The bottom displays the radar rings, and has activated a relief map presentation of the charted lands. This type of display is ideal for learning about radar shadows. We can clearly see the radar image being blocked by the rise in the terrain. Once the radar targets have been properly identified and we are well oriented in our present position, we can switch to either pure chart view or pure radar view for a simpler picture, which might be better for watching for new traffic or first indications of current set, and so on. This system runs in the Master mode; the radar is operated from the PC.*

The disadvantage is that sometimes both the radar images and the target images are compromised when superimposed. Sometimes colors can conflict, and details from either data source can be obscured. So even with this powerful display option, for some applications you may need to revert to either chart or radar data to solve your immediate navigation concerns.

In some models, the radar image must be obtained from a specific antenna and that signal can only be viewed and controlled on a PC running the required program, in which case all radar settings and operations are done from the PC (called "Master" mode). Those models do not have a separate radar display other than the PC. Other models export the same signal that is being viewed on a conventional radar display unit. These offer all the normal radar options plus an export of the signal that can be viewed on a remote PC screen running a special charting program. Presently, some of these models offer viewing but not control of the radar from the PC, which is called "Slave" mode, others offer both Slave and Master mode. Some companies offer a way to take most existing radars already installed and convert them to a simultaneous PC display combined with ECS. These can be run in Slave or Master mode. Another radar overlay using PC software is shown in Figure 13-2.

Figure 13-3 shows a similar radar overlay on a chart-plotter display, an option offered now by most suppliers of radar plotter combinations.

The radar–PC interface is a well-established technology already, and meeting the needs of many mariners. Features and operations from various models and brands are certainly going to change, merge, and improve with time. For mariners who do not like computers in their boat operations, this is not attractive. But for the many who are taking part in electronic charting and various other aspects of ECS, this is clearly the future. When the two systems are properly correlated, there is no better way to be

Figure 13-2. *Radar overlay onto raster charts. This screen capture is from Xenex Navigations's WinHorizon ECS software. The radar image taken from the roof of a building is overlaid onto a Canadian raster chart of the area, an exact electronic reproduction of the official paper chart. The darker images are the radar. Although it does not show well in this grayscale graphic, the radar images in this system have different shades of green for different intensities of reflected signal. This system can be adapted to most existing radar systems as an add-on ECS display option to the main radar screen in either the Slave or Master mode.*

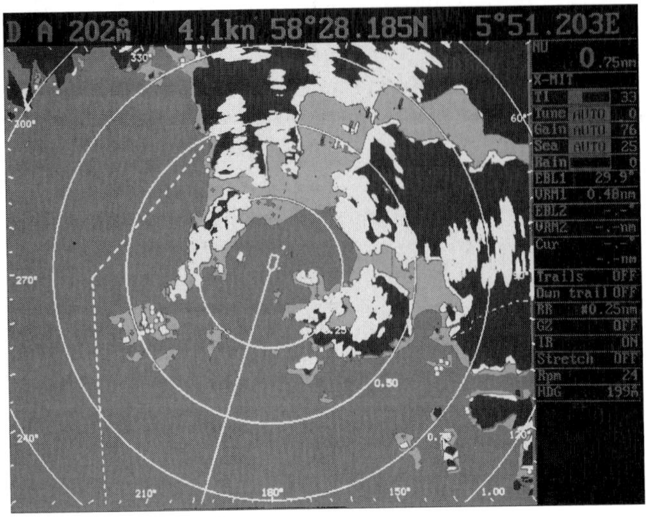

Figure 13-3. *Radar overlay onto chart plot display. This display is from a Simrad radar, showing the radar images (white in this picture) overlaid on a vector chart. The land is black and the water is gray; the shallower water is lighter gray. The actual data are, of course, in color, and users can usually adjust the color schemes. The vector format allows the user to turn on or off the various data layers to meet the needs at hand. Most manufacturers of radar plotter combinations offer this overlay option.*

confident of your position than when you see the radar images precisely outlined on the chart surrounding your GPS position.

This interface to a laptop PC also offers another way to have flexible remote displays of navigation data. With simple network wiring, a skipper can have a full readout of pilothouse navigation data in his private cabin, which in turn can be easily relocated to the saloon, bridge, or afterdeck as needed. You will need a high-powered computer for the job, and you should not count on multitasking other computer applications with the navigation computer while underway. In principle the networking could all be wireless, which brings us to the next topic of the future.

AUTOMATED IDENTIFICATION SYSTEM (AIS)

In the not too distant future, GPS will become an aid to collision avoidance much as radar is now. The technology is called *automated identifica-*

tion system (AIS). In this system, your GPS position, course, and speed will be automatically broadcast to all vessels around you via short-range radio signals. Any nearby vessel receiving the signal will in turn be broadcasting its position and motion, which you will receive (see Figure 13-4). The combined data can be displayed on an electronic chart on each vessel along with an automatic analysis of your interaction. It is a very promising development and will inevitably be used by all vessels and likely highway traffic as well. It has in fact been underway and being tested for several years now. But like all safety-critical high technology, it will be some time before it is available to the public. For now, we have radar, long tested and dependable, for the crucial task of collision avoidance.

Standards were developed for this system by the IMO in 1997. It is mandated for ship usage by some commercial vessel categories already, and will be broadly required by others after December 31, 2004. When it will become available for small craft is unknown, although all marine electronics companies are preparing for this now. As valuable as AIS promises to be, however, it will never replace radar, which shows nearby land, exposed rocks and logs, as well as where *all* vessels are located, not just vessels required to have AIS. AIS does, of course, have a crucial role to play in harbor security and related safety systems, and it will indeed enhance the use of conventional radar as outlined in Figure 13-5.

TRENDS

In just about any endeavor these days, the more you know about computers the better off you will be when it comes to interacting with the latest technologies. It is no different in boating, even though professional mariners are sometimes reluctant to allow new technology to replace long-tested and trusted procedures. But the "computer revolution" is a fact of modern life, and radar is in the vanguard of this change.

Radar screens on even the most basic units look more and more like computer screens, with many knobs and buttons being replaced with menu selections and cursor operations. The new "black box" design used by several companies epitomizes the trend. The display screen looks just like a computer screen and the separate control panel looks just like a high-tech keyboard. It may be foreign looking to those who have used radar for a generation or more, but it is a natural and expected interface to those who have grown up with daily computer use. For many in the middle of this transition, there is no choice but to retrain, and for this a positive attitude, rather than one of resistance and resentment, is most successful.

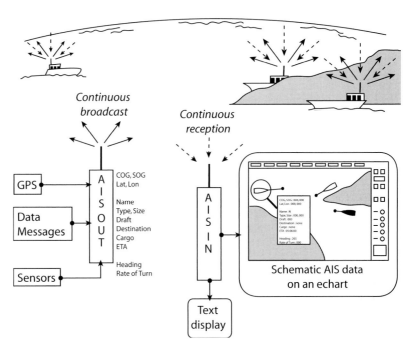

Figure 13-4. *Schematic outline of the automated identification system (AIS). Onboard navigation information is continuously broadcast and received from each AIS-equipped vessel within VHF radio range. Some vessels use a pure text display of the AIS information, rather than the ECS presentation. This information can enhance radar interpretation as outlined in Figure 13-5.*

Figure 13-5.

HOW AIS WILL ENHANCE FUTURE RADAR USE ON AIS-EQUIPPED VESSELS. SOME OF THESE ARE IN THE WISH-LIST CATEGORY; OTHERS TAKE EFFECT AS SOON AS AIS IS IMPLEMENTED.

1. AIS can find and communicate with targets hidden behind land or around corners and then plot them on an e-chart as if seen by conventional radar.
2. A radar echo can be identified by vessel name and vessel class rather than just a blip on the screen.
3. Target interactions (ARPA computations of CPA, TCPA, etc.) can be improved because the target vessel is broadcasting performance data such as ROT (rate of turn), as well as COG and SOG.
4. Extended radar range is obtained since VHF communications reach out farther than typical radar ranges and thus passing arrangements in tight quarters can be made long before the vessels meet.
5. Target intentions will be more clear, and will help with maneuvering decisions, because its route, ETA, cargo, draft limitations, etc. are broadcast along with other AIS data.

The trend in all navigation instrumentation is toward interfacing and integration. On the positive side, you can end up using the same display unit for many functions. The radar screen also shows the e-charts, with routes and waypoints laid out, your moving position controlled by the GPS, and a moving display of your depth sounder trace. You might even press a button to monitor all the engine variables on the same screen, or switch to a live camera view in various directions from the vessel. Click another button to show the tides and currents. Click another button to display the wind speed and direction, or even a weather map overlaid onto your active e-chart. Then you can choose whatever combination of data you wish to see on the screen, in two-, three-, or four-panel displays. But you must have patience when it comes to learning what the new features mean and how to operate them. Sometimes even the most basic radar operations are no longer intuitive.

Then, since the data are all on a network, it is practical to display this again from another location, even from a fully waterproof monitor, which is visible in bright sunlight. There is much virtue to such a system.

On the negative side, you might say that if

Patience

"If everything else fails, read the manual." This used to be a joke among those who prided themselves on figuring things out without the manual. If they could not figure it out, they would blame the engineers for designing an interface that was not "intuitive."

Things are different now with the latest generation of radars. Even the simplest function can sometimes be elusive, no matter how much experience you have with computers or other systems of electronics. There are just too many options and too many different designs of how to access them.

It pays to have patience, and take some quiet time on the boat, with no distractions, in front of the instrument with the manual and a notepad at hand, and maybe your favorite beverage. Start with the most basic things: where is the Gain, how do I turn on and use the EBL, is there more than one EBL, how do I switch them, and how do I shut them off. Then progress on up to the ERBL, manual versus automatic functions, how to operate FTC and STC, what sort of tuning options are there, and so on. And as you learn the system, make yourself a cheat sheet in your own words on how to do what you want to do. It will take some time, but it will be worth it. It is very frustrating to try to learn these things underway or with other people about.

It won't be long until you have it all sorted out, and then you might likely conclude that for all the things it has to do, the engineers have indeed figured out an efficient way to run the instrument. You may even begin to think of it as intuitive!

If you know you will be sailing on a new boat, it might be worth learning the brand of the radar. Most manuals are online, so you can download the appropriate one and prepare ahead of time on how to use the radar, and then impress your friends with your "intuition."

one thing breaks, everything breaks, and to some extent that might be true. It is a design challenge of the modern electronics industry to address that important issue, since the integration is taking place. Maintaining proper communication between networked systems is a common problem in modern marine electronics, as it is in every business office that uses computers.

And at some point you might experience that other consequence of complex computer-controlled electronics—they can crash, meaning the screen locks up and the keys and buttons do not respond. Six or seven years ago, it was essentially unheard of for a radar to crash, but it can happen in new models now, though it is a rare occurrence. As with a computer, you can usually solve the problem by turning it off, waiting about 10 seconds, and then turning it on. If this does not do the job, then check the manual for a master reset button or reset key sequence. If you must reset, your initial setup and internal tuning may be reset as well, which could mean you will not be obtaining optimum values of range and bearing, and image sharpness may not be optimized until the unit is calibrated again.

Also like computers, most radar models have periodic updates available for the internal software that controls the units. It pays to remember this and ask your sales representative about it. Typically there is no charge for the update; you may or may not need to send the unit to the factory.

In the future you will be more likely to buy all of your instruments from the same manufacturer, because that is the best way to make sure they all interface smoothly. On the other hand, there is another important trend that seems to counteract the requirement to deal with only one electronics source. One of the stated goals of the industry and various national and international organizations is toward standardization. The NMEA standards discussed in Chapter 7 are the leading example. In principle, one

company's device should be compatible with another company's device. Even though the data are consistent due to these standards, there is not a universally accepted protocol for the actual networking of the data. We will have to wait and see which trend wins out: standardization allowing mixing of brands, or proprietary interfaces that inhibit mixing and focus users toward single-brand nav stations.

One trend in the direction of single-brand nav stations taking place with several companies is modular options for all components of the navigation system—part of the "black-box" concept. A stand-alone radar unit is becoming a thing of the past. You might, for example, have a choice in display units from less-expensive, smaller monochrome units, on up to very large, daytime-bright color displays. To feed this display unit, then, you might choose a radar module from a list of various specifications, and then separately select an antenna with various specifications. Then add a depth sounder from several choices, e-chart options, wind instruments, etc. The GPS input is another module, but generally there are fewer user-selected options since most GPS units provide the same features. It is like buying a new computer, and selecting the components you want to optimize, rather than just buying model A or model B.

One aspect that seems to be evolving in all brands is a more common use of international symbols (Figure 2-3) and terminology. This is a positive step. The more options we have, the more important it is to establish consistent terminology.

PERFORMANCE MONITORING

Once your radar system is installed and calibrated and you have some experience using it, it is time to start a simple program of performance monitoring. An analogous program for other instruments might be looking at the depth sounder and the GPS before pulling away from the dock. With a GPS input to an e-chart, it is typically a simple matter to zoom in to check the GPS position and at the same time display an electronic tide reading for your location, from which you can check that the depth sounder is reading properly. As you pull out from the dock and drive along the breakwater, you can check that the compass reads correctly. These are all simple, valuable checks you can make without special effort.

For radar, you want to monitor the heading-line alignment, heading-sensor calibration, resolving power, and tuning. You can check the heading line every time you see some small but conspicuous radar target dead ahead, such as a buoy or light structure. In head-up mode or with EBL set to 000, the target should be right on the heading line. It is an easy check that should be made often. The heading-line alignment can also be checked when traveling along a long, straight dock, breakwater, or shoreline, as shown in Figure 13-6.

While traveling along this same close, long, straight target, you should also note whether it is indeed a straight image on the radar. If the internal timing has drifted off some, then a long, close, straight target will tend to bow in or out slightly from a straight edge. This is sign that the internal tuning and timing should be adjusted. Radar has the potential for remarkably accurate measurements of range and bearings, but to obtain this optimum accuracy, the unit must be adjusted properly upon installation and then the performance must be monitored.

The heading-sensor calibration can be checked, at least for consistency, using the steering compass. Generally you have three compass outputs at hand in any modern nav station: the steering compass, the heading-sensor output, and the COG from the GPS. The COG is not a heading, but in still water with no wind, it is another valuable data point. The prudent navigator will keep an eye on all three, expecting that the first two always read the same.

Resolving power and tuning are interrelated, and the check of these is much more subjec-

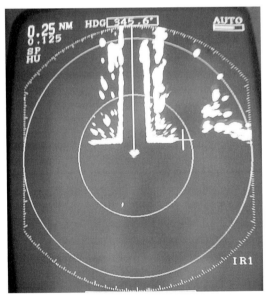
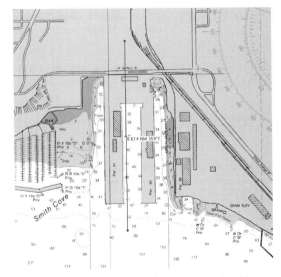

Figure 13-6. *Checking heading-line alignment and heading sensor calibration. By noting that you are indeed in line with the docks from visual sighting you see that the heading line alignment is correct, but the observation that this heading is on bearing 345.6° M according to the heading sensor indicates an error in the sensor calibration. The actual heading of the dock according to the chart should be 359° T – 18.3° variation East = 340.7° M, and 345.6° – 340.7° = 4.9° error. The heading sensor needs calibration.*

tive, but if this check shows any deterioration, it likely means the unit needs service. Tuning bar or digital tuning level settings might help quantify the observations. The idea here would be to choose any distinctive radar image that you see frequently, such as the approach to your marina, the entrance to some channel, the view of an islet and surrounding buoys, etc., and then to monitor the quality of that image each time you see it. Try to establish reasonable criteria, such as the crispness of the images, separation of close targets, tuning levels, and background noise. This observation will not only monitor the performance of the unit, but it might simply indicate that the settings have been left in some configuration you did not expect.

If you use an e-chart overlay option, then several of the above checks might be done with one view of the overlay of your test region. If the quality of the overlay changes, then something has changed in either the radar, the heading input, or the chart display program, which can be tracked down by testing each system separately. The e-chart overlay also offers an internal consistency check of the heading-line alignment and sensor calibration. With a calibrated sensor, the heading line will be drawn on the e-chart right across the target you see in front of you.

AC Rain. A name used by some radar models for the FTC control, which is used to remove unwanted echoes from rain patterns. See also *fast time constant, clutter, anticlutter,* and *rain clutter.*

AC Sea. A name used by some radar models for the STC control, which is used to remove unwanted echoes from waves. See also *sensitivity time control, clutter, anticlutter,* and *sea clutter.*

alarms. Audio or visual signals that can be set on radar to notify users when a target has approached within a user-set range limit *(guard ring)* or within some specific guard sector. They can also be used to signal when a target leaves the guard sector. Optional attachments exist for some units that convert simple beeps and flashing lights to real noise makers.

anticlutter (AC). Electronic circuits designed to remove clutter from radar images, primarily from precipitation *(rain clutter)* and from sea state *(sea clutter).* An important operational distinction between *AC Rain* (also called FTC) and *AC Sea* (also called STC) is that the former is effective over the full range of the radar, whereas the latter is effective only out to a limited range of a few miles. See also *fast time constant* and *sensitivity time control.*

apparent wind. The wind speed and direction you observe from a moving vessel as distinguished from the *true wind.* Apparent wind directions are usually specified in *relative bearings.* See also *wind triangle.*

aspect. The angular perspective at which we see a vessel approaching or leaving. It is defined as the relative bearing of our vessel as seen from the other vessel. It is measured from 0° to 180° and labeled "red" when we are on the port side of the vessel or "green" when we are on the starboard side.

automated identification system (AIS). An integrated system of GPS receiver, display module, and short-range radio transceiver. Vessels equipped with AIS continuously broadcast their position and present motion along with their identity and intended route, while receiving the same signals from other vessels in the region. The accumulated data from all vessels can be presented on an *electronic chart system* (ECS) so relative courses can be easily evaluated. The system is typically used in conjunction with ARPA and ECDIS. Some AIS systems, however, are text based without out an ECS display since that meets the AIS carriage requirements. See also *automatic radar plotting aid* and *electronic chart display and information system.*

automatic frequency control (AFC). The electronic circuit in a radar that controls the auto tune function. See also *Tuning.*

automatic radar plotting aid (ARPA). A computerized function of modern radars that can track, determine, and analyze interaction data for vessel targets on the radar screen. Such data might include CPA, time to CPA, true course and speed, relative course and speed, and so on. Targets being tracked typically show a vector of projected motion. The term "ARPA" is often considered to be restricted to systems that meet the standards of the IMO, whereas other implementations of this functionality use modifications of the name. ARPA-enabled units require a heading sensor and some require an optional ARPA plug-in card. On small-craft radar this function is often referred to as "mini-ARPA," "ARP," or some other slight variation of the name to distinguish it from the certified IMO standards, which are not always pertinent to small-craft installations.

beam target. A *crossing target* whose *direction of relative motion* is perpendicular or nearly perpendicular to the *heading line,* sometimes called a *limbo target.* Compare to *quarter target, bow target,* and *head-on target.*

bearings. Here used to mean the direction to a target determined from the radar using the *electronic bearing line* or *cursor.* Without a *heading sensor,* these would always be *relative bearings,* otherwise they could be true, magnetic, or relative. Modern radars often allow for any choice here, regardless of display mode, *stabilized* or *unstabilized.*

bearing to CPA (BCPA). The direction to a target vessel as it passes at its *closest point of approach.*

black box radar. A new terminology that implies the radar system is made up from user-selected modular components, such as antenna, radar module (the black box), display, and control console. The latter are looking more and more like computer keyboards, and the displays more and more like computer screens in this design approach, which is gaining popularity in *electronic chart systems* and other navigation instruments as well.

blind pilotage. A British term meaning navigation by instruments alone, which is called for in low visibility or at night in unlighted waters. Radar is clearly a key component of the process.

blind sector. A sector on the radar screen in which radar echoes cannot be received because of an obstruction near the antenna that blocks the signal.

blip. See *target.*

bow target. A *crossing target* with a *direction of relative motion* of about 095 R to 175 R or 185 R to 265 R, seen anywhere on the radar screen. That is, if you imagine yourself in front of one of these targets, it would be approaching somewhere on your port or starboard bow. Compare to *quarter target, beam target,* and *head-on target.*

Brilliance. A radar adjustment that controls how bright targets and other screen features appear.

buddy boat. Refers to a vessel moving with exactly the same speed and course as your vessel. The radar target of this vessel will not move on the screen as long as each of you maintain course and speed; its range and bearing remaining constant, speed of relative motion equals zero.

buoy trail. The wake or plot trail made by a buoy on your radar screen, or more generally the trail left by any stationary target. This trail length is an important observation as it is effectively plotting your own motion on the screen. Any target with a longer trail has a relative speed faster than your speed, and any shorter trail has relative speed slower than you. Actual numerical values can be estimated from the lengths of moving-target trails relative to any buoy trail. All stationary targets seen on the radar will have the same trail length. Without any actual buoy trails on the radar screen, you can compute the length of the buoy trail as discussed in the text.

The phrase "your buoy trail" means the trail length a buoy would make on your radar screen regardless of whether or not there is an actual buoy in range. In this sense, it is used as a reference length for judging the speeds of relative motion of all targets.

cathode ray tube (CRT). The picture tube of one type of radar screen. Cathode ray is the nineteenth-century term for a beam of electrons. A radar's CRT works (very roughly) the same way a TV screen does. A beam of electrons impinging on the phosphor of the screen is focused and deflected to match and display the information obtained from the radar's microwave analysis. The front face of the CRT that contains the radar targets is called the PPI *(plan position indicator)* or sometimes just the *radar screen.* See also *liquid crystal display.*

close quarters. A separation distance between two vessels that is crucial to the application of the *Navigation Rules,* but not specifically defined within the *Rules.* A good working guideline is to think of it as the space you need about you in order to maneuver on your own to avoid a collision, regardless of what the other vessel might do suddenly and unexpectedly. Passing slowly in a narrow channel it might be yards; passing high-speed traffic in the open ocean it is more likely measured in miles, depending on conditions.

closest point of approach (CPA). The minimum distance between you and an approaching radar target vessel that will occur as the target passes if no course or speed changes are made. This distance can be determined (anticipated) from radar observations while the target is still some distance away and used to evaluate risk of collision. This is a fundamental concept in radar usage. This distance is distinguished from the usually larger distance off that occurs when a vessel crosses your course line dead ahead or astern.

clutter. Unwanted radar echoes reflected from heavy rain, snow, waves, etc., that may obscure relatively large areas on the radar screen. See *anticlutter.*

course. See *true course, course over ground, direction of relative motion,* and *heading.*

course over ground (COG). The actual direction or track a vessel is following across the chart, as opposed to its present heading or desired course. This is usually determined for our own vessel by *GPS,* but it can also be determined from a series of position fixes obtained by radar or other means. The COG of a target vessel can be determined from the *relative motion diagram*. See also *true course*.

course-up display (CU). A *stabilized radar* display mode similar to *north-up display* but with a user-selected heading at the top of the radar screen. This display mode requires a *heading sensor*. See also *north-up* and *head-up*.

cross-track error (XTE). The distance you are off of your desired track to the right or left, when navigating a route by *GPS*.

crossing targets. Targets moving on the radar screen in a direction that is diagonal to the orientation of the *heading line* as opposed to *parallel targets*. A crossing target moving *down-screen* is called a *bow target*. Moving *up-screen*, they are called *quarter targets*. A crossing target moving perpendicular to the heading line is called a *beam target* or *limbo target*.

cursor. A crosshair or similar icon on the radar screen that can be positioned by track ball, pad, or keys. Range and bearing to the cursor position can be displayed as it is moved around the *radar screen* for quick navigation readouts. Other functions use the cursor position as well, such as *Zoom*, *Offset*, setting *guard sectors*, or positioning an *electronic range and bearing line*.

dead reckoning (DR). Keeping track of or determining your position using only your shipboard records of course and distance sailed from a known location.

differential GPS (DGPS). An electronic nav aid that is an enhancement of normal *GPS* with an additional signal that removes a degree of uncertainly in the position accuracy. DGPS positions are more accurate than unmodified ones, but its enhancement of the accuracy of course and *speed over ground* are usually more significant. Modern GPS, however, is generally accurate enough for practical navigation without this enhancement.

direction of relative motion (DRM). The direction a radar target moves toward as it crosses the radar screen. This direction depends on the target's course relative to yours, as well as its speed relative to yours. This is a fundamental concept in radar observing. See also *speed of relative motion*.

down-screen. Motion of a radar target in the general direction that is opposite to the way the *head-*

ing line is pointed. In *head-up* mode, the heading line points straight up, toward the top of the radar screen, and these targets are indeed moving down the physical screen, but in *north-up* mode, the heading line could be pointed in any direction (your heading at the time) and thus down-screen targets could actually be moving toward the top of the physical screen. The use of this valuable terminology requires us to think of the top of the radar screen as always that part at the tip of the heading line. Down-screen targets are further classified as *bow targets* (moving down-screen diagonal to the heading line) or *head-on targets* (moving down-screen parallel to the heading line). See also *up-screen*.

e-chart. An electronic (digital) chart as opposed to a paper chart. It is a computer file representation of a nautical chart used in *e-chart navigation*. There are two basic file formats, *vector charts* and *raster charts*, which look and behave quite differently.

e-chart navigation. The process of navigating with an *electronic chart system* (ECS), using any form of moving-map technology, wherein the present GPS position of the vessel is continuously adjusted on an electronic image of a nautical chart as the vessel moves through the waterway. There are numerous software and hardware options and numerous forms of electronic charts. It is a trend in modern electronics to integrate some form of e-chart navigation with the radar unit. See also *e-chart* and *electronic chart display and information system*.

echo. See *target*.

Echo Stretch (ES). A radar control option that stretches out the size of the radar *targets* so that weaker targets can be enhanced and monitored or located at a distance. Also called "Expansion."

electronic bearing line (EBL). An electronic means of measuring the radar bearing of a target with a rotating radial line on the radar screen. You can adjust the position of the line until it overlaps the target and read the bearing from numbers on the radar screen. This is a primary working tool of radar navigation and collision avoidance. It is usually controlled by buttons or by a *cursor*. See also *variable range marker* and *electronic range and bearing line*.

electronic chart display and information system (ECDIS). A *vector chart*–based *electronic* *chart system* (ECS) certified by the IMO to be used in commercial shipping. They are typically enhanced with overlays of navigation safety information, along with radar, ARPA, and AIS inputs. The main distinction between ECDIS and ECS is the former must use official government produced charts, whereas the later can use any form of digital chart. Also in some cases, ECDIS can replace the requirement for paper charts, whereas ECS cannot. See also *automatic radar plotting aid* and *automated identification system*.

electronic chart system (ECS). Any combination of hardware and software used for *e-chart navigation*, using any form of *e-charts*. Standards for ECS are under consideration in several agencies. See also *electronic chart display and information system*.

electronic range and bearing line (ERBL). An option on some modern radars that allows the reference point of the EBL and VRM to be moved to any place on the radar screen. With this option the range and bearing between any two points on the screen can be measured, as opposed to conventional EBL and VRM that makes all measurements relative to your own vessel location. It has numerous convenient applications. Its use is sometimes referred to as *floating* the EBL or VRM.

Expansion (EXP or ST). See *Echo Stretch*.

false echoes. Apparent radar targets and other images (echoes) on the screen that show up on the screen but are not real radar targets. They are artificially caused by some interaction of the radar beam with other nearby objects. There are several types of false echoes and it is important to understand the potential of these and their sources.

far field. That region of the radar beam adequately removed from the antenna where the beam is expanding to match the *horizontal beam width* and *vertical beam angle* and the power density is falling off as $1/r^2$. See also *near field* and *transition zone*.

fast time constant (FTC). An electronic circuit designed to reduce undesirable rain clutter and other applications to improve the radar picture. It reduces the sprinkle of rain echoes on the screen and tends to clip the far edges of other targets as well. See also *rain clutter*.

float. A term used by some manufacturers to mean the reference point for the EBL and VRM can be shifted off of center to any user-selected place on the screen. The origin of the measurements is thus said to be floating. See also *electronic range and bearing line*.

Gain. The radar control that determines the amount of signal amplification applied. It is one of the key controls in picture adjustment. See also *tuning*.

GPS (global positioning system). A U.S. satellite navigation system used as the primary means of electronic navigation by most vessels worldwide. With GPS equipment on board, accurate position, *course over ground*, and *speed over ground* are available continuously. GPS output data can often be *interfaced* to the radar and displayed on the radar screen.

guard rings. User-defined range rings that can be used to set alarms to signal whenever a target enters or leaves a defined region. Modern radars offer the option of setting angular guard sectors as well as guard rings.

heading. The actual direction a vessel is pointed at any moment, as opposed to the course it is attempting to steer or its actual *course over ground*.

heading line. A line on the radar screen from the center to the outer edge that marks the dead ahead direction of your vessel at the moment. For *head-up* radar this is always a vertical line to the top of the screen, but in *north-up* and *course-up* radar this line will point in the direction of your heading and rotate on the screen as your vessel turns to a new course. On most radars, this line can be temporarily hidden to look for weak targets dead ahead. Also called "heading flash" or "ship's heading line." For purposes of radar target classification, it is useful to think of this line as also extending backward to the opposite edge of the radar screen. Thus you can think of targets aft of you as also moving diagonal or parallel to the heading line.

heading sensor. An electronic compass that sends a continuous digital readout of the vessel's heading to the radar. In small-craft radar this is usually a fluxgate magnetic compass; in ship radar it is more often a gyro compass.

head-on target. A *down-screen, parallel target* seen anywhere on the radar screen with a *direction of relative motion* of about 180 relative to the *heading line* orientation. If in front of you, they are either targets headed toward you, or ones you are overtaking, or any target dead in the water. Their *speed of relative motion* determines which type of target it is.

head-up (HU). A radar display mode wherein the present heading of the vessel remains at the top of the radar screen regardless of your actual *heading*, and it is labeled 000. In this mode, bearings around the edge of the radar screen are marked in *relative bearing* units. This is the most basic and most common type of radar display used on small-craft radars. See also *stabilized radar*.

horizontal beam width (HBW). The angular extent of the radar beam in the horizontal plane, usually 4° to 6° or even larger on typical small-craft radars and about 2° to 1° on radars with 4-foot or wider antennas. Horizontal beam width is a function of both the transmitting frequency and the width of the antenna. In small-craft radar it is determined primarily by the width of the antenna. This angle determines horizontal bearing *resolution*. See also *lobe*.

interfaced. Two electronic instruments are said to be interfaced if they are hardwired together and share information. The interface can be uni- or bidirectional. Radars are often interfaced to gyro or magnetic compasses *(heading sensor)*, to *GPS* units, or other devices. As time goes by, these connections might also become wireless links as well.

Interference Rejection (IR). A radar control that electronically reduces interference from other radars seen on your radar screen.

knotmeter speed (S). Speed of a vessel through the water, as opposed to *speed over ground*, which is the actual speed the vessel is progressing "across the chart."

limbo target. Another name for *beam targets*, first introduced by pioneering radar instructors Max Carpenter and Wayne Waldo of the Maritime Institute of Technology and Graduate Studies in Linthicum Heights, Maryland, which reflects the fact that it is difficult to predict the behavior of beam targets in response to your maneuver when viewed in stabilized display modes, hence they are in limbo. (When viewed in head-up mode, on the other hand, these targets are not "in limbo.")

liquid crystal display (LCD). The type of graphic display used on laptop computers and many marine electronic displays, including radar. It utilizes sheets of polarizing material with a liquid

crystal solution between them. An electric current passed through the liquid causes the crystals to align so that light cannot pass through them. Each crystal acts like a shutter, either allowing light to pass through or blocking the light. Monochrome images usually appear as dark gray images on a light gray background. A high quality color LCD uses *thin film transistor* (TFT) technology, also called "active matrix technology," where each *pixel* is controlled by transistors. These can produce color images as sharp as traditional CRT displays.

In most applications the backlighting of the display is a key issue to ease of viewing, and also a key factor in power consumption. Light output from LCD screens is measured in *nits*. In the not too distant future, all radar screens (and computer screens) will be LCD (flat panel) types. See also *cathode ray tube* and *radar screen*.

lobe. The boundary of the volume inside which the transmitting radar beam intensity is everywhere greater than a chosen value; usually depicted by drawing its cross sections in the horizontal and vertical planes. See also *vertical beam angle*, *horizontal beam width*, and *side lobes*.

lollipop waypoint. The style used by several radar models to mark the active GPS waypoint on the radar screen. It is surrounded by a dashed circle (the "candy") at the end of a dashed bearing line (the "stick").

magnetron. The electrical component of a radar unit that produces the high-intensity pulse of microwave radiation transmitted from the antenna. It has two terminals, plus and minus. One terminal is a hollow cylindrical block of copper with cylindrical cavities in its wall, which is situated between the poles of a strong permanent magnet. When a square-wave direct-current pulse is applied to the terminals, it breaks into rapid oscillations for the duration of the pulse, the frequency of which is governed by the dimensions of the device. It is the only device capable of producing high-powered electrical oscillations at microwave frequencies. The device was invented independently in England and Japan in 1939. The design was crucial to the practical implementation of microwave radar, which took place in the United States shortly after that. Pioneering work on the development and implementation of radar at other frequencies was ongoing in England during this period.

maneuvering board. The name given to radar plotting sheets used to solve the *relative motion* *diagram* and other radar problems. They generally consist of concentric circles marked off in range and angle. Sometimes *nomograms* are presented to allow for speed-time-distance computations. Sample U.S. government products are NIMA Publications 5090 and 5089. Printable custom versions are on the Radar Resources CD.

Navigation Rules. The set of rules, regulations, and laws that govern the interaction of two vessels approaching each other, as well as light and sound signal specifications and other matters of safe navigation. There are international, national, and regional rules. A complete copy in e-book format is included on the Radar Resources CD.

near field. The region of the radar beam near the antenna where the beam has a profile approximately matching the face of the antenna, before it has begun to expand out horizontally and vertically. The power density throughout the near field is approximately constant. See also *far field* and *transition zone.*

nit. A unit of measurement of luminance (visible light intensity), where one nit equals one candela per square meter (cd/m^2). Nits are used to describe the brightness of video displays, such as LCD and CRT screens. Typical laptop monitors might have a luminance of some 150 to 200 nits, and flat-panel LCD displays are typically 200 to 300 nits, whereas marine displays are typically some 800 or so nits for dependable daylight viewing.

nomogram. A graphic aid used on navigation plotting sheets that consists of several lines marked off to scale and arranged in such a way that by using a straightedge to connect known values on two lines an unknown value can be read at the point of intersection with another line.

north-up (NU). A radar display mode wherein true north (000) remains at the top of the radar screen regardless of your vessel's heading. Your own heading is marked on the screen with the heading line oriented toward your actual course. This display requires a *heading sensor* input to the radar. In north-up display, when your vessel turns, the land targets remain stationary and the heading line shifts to your new course and moving vessel targets continue on their path relative to the fixed land. See also *head-up, course-up, true motion display,* and *stabilized radar.*

Offset. A radar display option that allows a shift of the center of the display to a user-selected location. A common application is to shift the center of the display aft, for a longer look forward.

open array. A radar antenna that is not covered by a radome. Most radar antennas wider than 2 feet are of this design as opposed to some small-craft radar which are encased in *radomes.*

parallel indexing. A radar piloting technique using *north-up* display mode in which you draw on the *radar screen*—or on a transparency to be held on the radar screen—the path you expect a prominent isolated radar target to follow as you proceed along your chosen route. As long as the indexing target remains on the index path, you know you are in the right position.

parallel targets. Targets moving on the *radar screen* parallel to the *heading line,* meaning they do not get any closer or farther from our line of travel as time passes. Parallel targets moving *up-screen* are called *stern targets,* moving *down-screen* they are called *head-on targets.* A special case of parallel target is one that is not moving at all on the radar screen as we proceed, which is a target with the identical course and speed we have (a *buddy boat*). See also *crossing targets.*

pixel. A single square element of a raster-scan *radar screen.* A typical radar screen might be made up of an array of somewhere between 240 x 320 pixels on up to higher resolutions of some 800 x 600 pixels, or even higher. Video display technology is improving rapidly these days.

plan position indicator (PPI). A somewhat outdated term for the active front face of the radar that shows the targets. A plan view of an object is the general term for the top view, looking down, which is schematically what this is intended to represent—a chartlike view of what is around you. This term is now more often referred to as the *radar screen* even though modern radar screens typically include much more data than just the radar image itself.

Plot. Often used to describe a trail of radar target images left on the radar screen behind a moving target. This trail or trace maps out the past locations of that radar target. This is an extremely valuable option for evaluating risk of collision. See also *Wake.* Not to be confused with a plotter option, which more often means sharing the radar display with a e-chart view of past GPS positions, waypoints, etc.

portable range scale. Any device constructed by the operator to help interpolate the spacing between *range rings* on the *radar screen* so it can be used to measure distances anywhere on the radar screen. Tick marks on an envelope would be a simple one. Printable scales that can be used for this are on the Radar Resources CD.

projected path. Most radar analysis is based on projecting the past track *(Plot)* of a target forward to evaluate risk of collision. This process makes the crucial assumption that course and speed of your vessel and that of the target will not change —and that current or leeway also do not change.

pulse length. The time duration, measured in microseconds, of a single radar pulse. The radar beam is made up of successive pulses, which are separated by the *pulse repetition interval.* The pulse length could also be expressed in yards, taking into account its duration and the speed of the microwaves, equal to the speed of light. A 1-microsecond pulse length would correspond to a pulse 328 yards long.

pulse repetition interval. The time between successive pulses in a radar beam, often expressed in terms of pulse repetition frequency or pulse rate. A pulse rate of 1,500 Hz means 1,500 pulses per second, which means each pulse consumes $\frac{1}{1,500}$ seconds or 667 microseconds. For a 1-microsecond *pulse length*, there are some 666 microseconds between each pulse.

quarter target. A *crossing target* with a *direction of relative motion* of about 005 R to 085 R or 275 R to 355 R, seen anywhere on the radar screen. That is, if you imagine yourself in front of one of these targets, it would be approaching somewhere on your port or starboard quarter. Compare to *bow target, beam target,* and *head-on target.*

racon. An active *ra*dar bea*con* located on a buoy or other structure that transmits back to your radar a signal that identifies it on your radar screen whenever it is struck by your radar beam. These are very valuable aids to navigation as they are unmistakable when triggered. The signals appear as bright, broad (5° or so) signals on your radar, often divided into sections to represent a Morse code letter. The radial length of the signals can be a mile or more, and if seen for the first time up close at night in the wheelhouse alone, they can be startling.

radar (*radio detection and ranging*). An electronic navigation instrument that measures the *range* and *bearing* of land masses and vessels in your vicinity by sending out a rotating beam of microwave pulses and detecting the pulses reflected back from them.

radar etiquette. Used to refer to the good practice of checking with the person in charge before adjusting radar, and not running the radar in marinas or locks where people may be exposed to the radar beam.

radar horizon. The farthest distance a radar beam reaches before being interrupted by the sea surface. It is 15 percent farther than the geometric range to the physical horizon from the antenna height due to refraction, and it is 5 percent farther than the optical or visual horizon in standard conditions because microwaves are refracted more than visible light. Given standard atmospheric conditions, the distance to the radar horizon in nautical miles equals 1.22 times the square root of the height of the antenna in feet. If the radar is to detect a target beyond the radar horizon, then that target must have adequate elevation and reflecting area extending up above the radar horizon. See also *shadow.*

radar marks. Waypoints or other Lat-Lon positions that can be selected, stored, and displayed using radar. The use of radar marks is not available on all radar models.

radar screen. Generic and common name for the front face of a radar's CRT or LCD. Also known as the PPI *(plan position indicator)*, especially on older units, although the latter refers more often to just the central radar target data, whereas the radar screen usually implies all of the display on the screen such as control settings, Lat-Lon position, and other derived functions from a GPS interface.

radiation hazard. Microwave pulses sent out by a radar antenna pose potential health risks to people exposed to them. Most radar manuals present guidelines for safe application and installation.

radome. The plastic enclosure that covers the radar antenna. An uncovered antenna is called an *open array.* Radomes are more common on smaller vessels, especially sailing vessels that must protect the antenna from lines and sails.

rain clutter (AC Rain). Radar interference caused by reflections from nearby precipitation.

Also, the electronic filter used to remove or diminish this interference (also called *fast time constant*).

range. As used in radar applications, the distance (in nautical miles) from your vessel to a target vessel viewed on the radar screen. It can also refer to the maximum range setting of the radar screen. See also *range rings* and *portable range scale.*

range limits. There are fairly well defined limits to the effective range of any radar installation and these are not equal to the maximum range scale that can be selected. They are determined primarily by the height of the antenna and the height and size of the targets.

range resolution. The minimum distance apart that two targets at the same bearing can be and still appear as separate targets on the radar screen. It is numerically equal to about one half of the *pulse length*. Since pulse length sometimes changes when switching ranges, the range resolution can depend on range setting. The pulse lengths used on specific ranges are presented in the manual, and sometimes they can be selected in a setup menu.

range rings. On the radar screen, the circles that mark fixed ranges. On the 6-mile range, for example, range rings are typically shown at 1.0 mile intervals. Some modern radars let users select the ring spacing. See also *portable range scale.*

rapid radar plotting. A method of solving radar problems (primarily the *relative motion diagram*) by plotting directly on the radar screen using appropriate markers or an *electronic range and bearing line,* as opposed to *transfer plotting.*

raster. A two-dimensional, rectangular, *pixel* grid used to present digital data or radar echoes on a CRT or LCD screen. Also used to refer to the format of an image, such as raster or vector. A picture of a circle is a raster image; the formula for a circle or a set of digital coordinates that make up a circle would be called a vector image. *E-chart* navigation uses both *raster charts* and *vector charts.* All radar images are raster images.

raster chart. A type of electronic chart made from a bitmap image of a paper chart scanned into a computer. Viewed on the screen it is identical to the paper chart, which is an advantage over *vector*

charts to navigators accustomed to the look and detail of paper charts, but they have the disadvantage of being large files, and they do not offer the display versatility of vector charts. Raster charts can only be viewed in a compatible software program. Topographic maps and aerial photo maps viewable in some e-chart programs are always raster charts.

refraction. The bending of the radar beam in passing obliquely through regions of the atmosphere of different densities.

relative bearings (R). Directions relative to the ship's heading. Dead ahead is 000, starboard beam is 090, dead astern is 180, port beam is 270. A target with relative bearing 330 R would be 30° to the left of the bow. In *head-up mode,* all bearings are measured in relative units.

relative motion diagram (RMD). A vector plot of the relative motion of a target vessel and your own vessel used to determine the *true course* and *true speed* of the target from the observed values of its *speed of relative motion* and *direction of relative motion.*

rendezvous maneuvering. The radar maneuver of setting a course to intercept another moving target. The problem can be solved graphically or analytically. It is the opposite of *storm avoidance.*

resolution. The resolving power of a radar, meaning its ability to show two close targets as separate echoes. Resolution in range and in bearing are governed by two separate factors, *pulse length* and *horizontal beam width.* It is an important concept when it comes to identifying land masses or close vessels.

Rules. See *Navigation Rules.*

S-band radar. A radar employing microwaves with a 10 cm wavelength, corresponding to a frequency of 3,000 MHz. It is used for long range (open ocean) radar on ships. S-band radar is less sensitive to interference from rain and waves, but has a lower sensitivity to reflections from small targets (reflection is inversely proportional to the square of the wavelength). Small-craft radar do not use S-band microwaves, but instead use *X-band radar.* Ships also use X-band radar for navigation inshore or close to smaller targets.

sea clutter (AC Sea). Radar interference caused by reflections from nearby waves. Also, the electronic filter used to remove or diminish this interference (also called *sensitivity time control*).

sensitivity time control (STC). An electronic circuit designed to reduce undesirable *sea clutter* and other applications to improve the radar picture of nearby targets. It is effectively an additional *Gain* reduction at close ranges.

shadow. That region behind an obstruction that the radar beam is blocked from reaching. Isolated objects or terrain within the shadow behind the obstruction may show on the radar if they rise above the obstruction, but anything below that will not appear on the radar screen. If the terrain behind the obstruction rises above it within the range that is in view on the radar, then echoes will appear again marking the end of that shadow.

side lobes. Weak segments of emitted radar beam intensity to either side of the main beam. An ideal beam would have no side lobes, since reflections from these parts of the beam do not yield proper bearing results. Larger antennas have more efficient side-lobe suppression. See also *lobe* and *side-lobe interference*.

side-lobe interference. A common type of unwanted radar reflection (interference) caused by target reflections from side-lobe emission. It shows up primarily for close targets and is more pronounced for smaller radar antennas. The effect is to smear out the target image in an annular pattern centered on the primary target location.

six-minute rule. The common trick used in radar analysis to quickly compute distance run in 6 minutes (speed divided by 10) and the speed made good in 6 minutes (distance times 10), which is based simply on the fact that 6 minutes is ¹⁄₁₀ of an hour.

speed. See *true speed, speed of relative motion, knotmeter speed, speed over ground*.

speed of relative motion (SRM). The speed at which a radar target moves across your radar screen, which is its speed relative to you. This observed speed depends on the target's course relative to yours, as well as its actual speed. This is a fundamental concept in radar observation.

speed over ground (SOG). The actual or true speed of a vessel from point to point on a chart. This is usually measured by GPS, but can be determined from any two position fixes spanning some time interval.

stabilized radar. A computerized display function of radar that uses a *heading sensor* input to maintain the locations of targets on the screen in specific orientations. The user-selected orientation of the display is either *north-up* or it can be set to the present heading of the vessel *(course-up)*. In these display modes, the location of a target on the screen is independent of *heading* alterations of your vessel and so the plotted *trails* of moving targets more closely represent their true motion. See also *true motion display* and *unstabilized radar*.

Standby mode. Means the radar is on and warmed up, but the unit is not transmitting. This is a power-saving mode, also sometimes used for transiting close quarters in locks or channels.

stern target. An *up-screen, parallel target* seen anywhere on the radar screen with a *direction of relative motion* of about 000 relative to the *heading line* orientation. If behind you, they are targets overtaking you. Their *true speed* is equal to their *speed of relative motion* plus your own speed.

storm avoidance. Here used to label the radar maneuver of setting a course to put the maximum CPA between yourself and another moving target. It is the opposite of *rendezvous maneuvering*.

sweep. A 360-degree rotation of the radar beam or simulated radar beam. The sweep period is typically 2 to 3 seconds on most radars. Computer-simulator sweeps might be slower depending on the computer speed and computations made during each sweep.

target. The blip or echo seen on the *radar screen* that marks the position of the object sending the reflected microwave signals back to your antenna. A radar target can be a vessel, buoy, landmass, or other objects in range, such as low-flying aircraft, prominent wakes, logs, etc. Depending on target size, blips usually first appear as tiny, faint line segments for distant targets that grow into huge, bright smears for close, large objects. For purposes of target identification and evaluation of collision risk, targets are classified in various ways such as *parallel targets, crossing targets, up-screen* or *down-screen*, and so forth. See also *trail*.

thin film transistor (TFT). A technology used in high-end LCD displays in which transistors are built into each *pixel* within the screen. This means the current that triggers pixel illumination can be smaller and therefore can be switched on and off more quickly. Also called "active matrix."

time of CPA (TCPA). The actual clock time of the *closest point of approach*.

time until CPA (dTCPA). The time interval between some specified time (usually that of the last observation) and the time of *closest point of approach*. In navigation notation, an interval is often marked with a *d*, e.g., "dLat" is an interval of latitude. Some references use MCPA for this concept, which stands for minutes to CPA.

trail. The history of a target's motion on the radar screen. Modern units show this with various display options. See also *Plot* and *Wake*.

transceiver. A radio frequency device that both transmits and receives, such as a VHF or single-sideband radio. A radar antenna is a transceiver as well—the same physical device both transmits and receives the microwave signals.

transfer plotting. The method of solving radar problems such as the *relative motion diagram* using graphical methods and in particular by doing this on plotting sheets *(maneuvering boards)* after transferring the pertinent data from the radar screen to the plotting sheet. Transfer plotting can also be carried out electronically on e-chart software programs.

transition zone. That region of the radar beam where it is making a transition between the *near field* and the *far field* properties. Within the transition zone the power density is decreasing approximately as 1/r.

true course (TC). The actual course of a vessel (its COG) as opposed to its *direction of relative motion* detected for that vessel on an observer's radar screen. This usage of true course is common in radar discussions, but it is unfortunate that it is not consistent with the more common use of the term, which implies a direction specified relative to true north. In this radar jargon, the "true course" of a vessel could be expressed in *relative directions*, true directions (commonly used on ships with gyro compasses), or in terms of magnetic directions, which are more often used in small-craft navigation. The choice depends on which units we use when we determine the vessel's true course by solving the *relative motion diagram*.

true motion display (TM). A *stabilized* display option that uses the GPS input as well as a head-

ing sensor input to move your vessel position across the radar screen leaving the landmasses and other stationary targets in fixed positions. It is like viewing an e-chart with your vessel moving relative to charted features, but in this case it is your *heading line* and *range rings* that are moving relative to the radar images. True motion displays are always in the *north-up* orientation.

true speed (TS). The actual speed of a vessel (its SOG) as opposed to its *speed of relative motion* that would be detected for that vessel on an observer's radar screen. A target's true speed is determined from the *relative motion diagram*.

true wind. The actual speed and direction of the wind as we would observe it from a stationary vessel. True wind directions are always specified as the true direction the wind is coming from. See also *apparent wind*.

tuning. General name sometimes loosely used for selecting the optimum radar control settings of Gain, Brilliance, Tuning, filtering, and others, so as to obtain the best picture on the radar screen. Since one of the several controls is actually called Tuning, it is best to avoid this generic use of the term, and reserve "tuning" for adjustment of the *Tuning* control.

Tuning. A radar control that tunes the receiver frequency to that of the incoming echoes to optimize the reception. Radars include both manual and automatic tuning options. The more precisely the Tuning is set, the sharper and stronger the ultimate signals. When manual tuning is available it is done while watching targets on the screen or a related bar-graph meter (tuning bar), similar to those used to tune a radio. The auto-tune function on a radar is called *automatic frequency control* (AFC). Manual tuning is sometimes a readily accessible primary control and in other units it is part of the setup controls.

unstabilized radar. This is the name used for traditional radar without a *heading sensor* input, as opposed to radar with a north-up or course-up displays, the latter of which are referred to as *stabilized radar*. In unstabilized radar (conventional *head-up* display), if the vessel heading yaws in a seaway, the recorded positions of targets on the radar screen also shift proportionally, which ultimately smears out their target *trails*. This is typical small-craft radar behavior, so the term "unstabilized" is a bit misleading. It is more useful for ship navigators whose radars typically have been stabilized for many years now.

up-screen. Motion of a radar target in the general direction that the *heading line* is pointed. In *head-up* mode, the heading line points straight up, toward the top of the radar screen, and these targets are indeed moving up the physical screen, but in *north-up* mode, the heading line could be pointed in any direction (your heading at the time) and thus up-screen targets could actually be moving toward the bottom of the physical screen. The use of this valuable terminology requires us to think of the top of the radar screen as the tip of the heading line. Up-screen targets are further classified as *quarter targets* (moving up-screen diagonal to the heading line) or *stern targets* (moving up-screen parallel to the heading line). See also *down-screen*.

variable range marker (VRM). An electronic means of measuring the radar range of a target with an expanding *range ring* circle. To operate it, adjust the radius of the circle until it touches the target and read the range from numbers on the radar screen. This is a primary working tool of radar navigation and collision avoidance. It is usually controlled by buttons or by a *cursor*. See also *electronic bearing line* and *electronic range and bearing line*.

vector chart. An electronic chart that is created in real time by the software displaying it using data from the computer file of the chart. Shorelines, depth contours, and other curves on a vector chart are made up of point-to-point line segments. At normal display, curved lines appear smooth, but when zoomed in for higher magnification, the line structure becomes apparent. Overlays of various data such as depths, lights, buoys, color schemes, navigation notes, and so on can be displayed permanently or hidden, and special information on aids can be shown on demand with a mouse click. Vector charts have the advantage of small file size, fast, versatile, interactive displays, and they are easily updated with Internet down-

loads. Some vector charts can be viewed on any PC with the appropriate software; other versions are proprietary to specific hardware. See also *raster charts*.

vertical beam angle (VBA). The angular extent of the radar beam in the vertical plane, usually in the range of 20° to 30°, more or less independent of antenna size.

Wake. In radar application, the term used by some radar brands to describe a plot trail behind a target that has a fixed lifetime on the radar screen, such as a 6-minute wake. Target wakes or other target *trails* are the key feature of a radar for evaluating risk of collision. See also *Plot*.

warm-up period. Radars do not become active the moment they are turned on, but require some 1 or 2 minutes to warm up before being ready to transmit. It is an important delay to keep in mind. See also *Standby mode*.

wind triangle. A vector triangle, whose three sides are your boat speed, the apparent wind speed, and the true wind speed. Generally the first two sides and the angle between them (apparent wind angle) are known, and the triangle is solved, graphically or by computation, for the true wind speed and true wind direction.

X-band radar. A radar employing microwaves with a 3 cm wavelength, corresponding to a frequency of 9,500 MHz. This is the typical beam specifications used in all small-craft radar. Ship radar equipment usually also includes a unit employing *S-band radar*.

yaw. One of several vessel motions in a seaway, this one being the oscillation left and right of the vessel's heading about the desired course.

Zoom. A radar control that expands the range about a user-selected point on the screen. Some include a zoom window that shows a small insert covering the zoom region overlaid on the main radar display. Zoom is not available on all units, and is rare in older ones.

AC	anticlutter		**HBW**	horizontal beam width
AFC	automatic frequency control (auto tuning)		**HU**	head-up display
AIS	automated identification system		**Hz**	Hertz (cycles per second)
ARPA	automatic radar plotting aid		**IHO**	International Hydrographic Organization
B	bearing		**IMO**	International Maritime Organization
BCPA	bearing to closest point of approach		**IR**	Interference Rejection
C	compass course label or course (in general)		**kts**	knots
			kW	kilowatt
cm	centimeter		**Lat**	latitude
COG	course over ground		**LCD**	liquid crystal display
COLREGs	International Regulations for Preventing Collisions at Sea		**Lon**	longitude
			m	meter
CPA	closest point of approach		**M**	magnetic course or bearing label
CRT	cathode ray tube		**MHz**	megahertz
CU	course-up display		**min**	minute
db	decibel		**ms**	millisecond
DGPS	differential GPS		**MV**	motor vessel
DR	dead reckoning		**mW**	milliwatt
DRM	direction of relative motion		**NIMA**	National Imaging and Mapping Agency
dTCPA	time until closest point of approach		**nit**	nit (unit of light intensity)
EBL	electronic bearing line		**nm**	nautical mile
ECDIS	electronic chart display and information system		**NMEA**	National Marine Electronics Association
ECS	electronic chart system		**NU**	north-up display
ERBL	electronic range and bearing line		**PC**	personal computer
ES	Echo Stretch		**PDV**	power-driven vessel
EXP	Expansion (Echo Stretch)		**PPI**	plan position indicator
FCC	Federal Communications Commission		**R**	range or relative bearing label
FTC	fast time constant		**RMD**	relative motion diagram
FV	fishing vessel		**ROT**	rate of turn
GHz	gigahertz		**RR**	range ring
GPS	global positioning system		**s**	second
h	hour		**S**	knotmeter speed

SOG	speed over ground	**TFT**	thin film transistor
SRM	speed of relative motion	**TM**	true motion display
SSB	single sideband	**TS**	true speed of a radar target
ST	Echo Stretch	**VBA**	vertical beam angle
STC	sensitivity time control	**VMG**	velocity made good
SV	sailing vessel	**VRM**	variable range marker
T	true course or true bearing label, or time	**W**	watt
TC	true course of a radar target	**XTE**	cross-track error
TCPA	time of closest point of approach	**μs**	microsecond

Navigation Rules

Allen, Craig H. *Farwell's Rules of the Nautical Road*. 8th ed. Annapolis, MD: Naval Institute Press, 2004. A classic treatment from a sea captain's perspective.

Cockcroft, A. N., and J. N. F. Lameijer. *A Guide to the Collision Avoidance Rules: International Regulations for Preventing Collisions at Sea*. 5th ed. Oxford, UK; Boston: Newnes, 1996. This is one of my favorite treatments of the *Rules*, but there are many other excellent discourses on this important subject, each having its own special value. Only a few samples are listed in this section.

Healy, Nicholas J., and Joseph C. Sweeney. *The Law of Marine Collision*. Centreville, MD: Cornell Maritime Press, 1998. Covers intricacies of the laws themselves as well as the cases that established them.

Holdert, H. M. C., and F. J. Buzek. *Collision Cases, Judgments and Diagrams*. London: Lloyd's of London Press, Legal Pub. and Conferences Division, 1984. Specific court cases analyzed and illustrated.

Starpath School of Navigation. *Nav Rules Plus!*. Seattle: Starpath Publications, 2002. A PC software training tool and resource. Includes discussion of each rule along with annotated questions from the USCG database on license exam questions.

U.S. Coast Guard. *Navigation Rules: International–Inland*. Washington, DC: U.S. Government Printing Office. The official print copy of the *Navigation Rules*. It is recommended that all mariners have at hand a printed copy of these *Rules* for both study and reference. Inexpensive bound versions are available at all navigation supply stores or from many sources online. A complete, searchable and printable e-book copy is included on the Radar Resources CD.

Radar

Bole, A. G., and W. O. Dineley. *Radar and ARPA Manual*. Oxford, UK: Heinemann Newnes, 1990. Covers all aspects of ship radar. Often used as a text or reference book in merchant marine training schools.

Carpenter, Max H., and Wayne M. Waldo. *Real-Time Method of Radar Plotting*. Centreville, MD: Cornell Maritime Press, 1975. This original publication is still in print. It is more of a workbook version of *The Radar Book*, still used in radar schools. These authors developed many radar teaching techniques still in use today. Much of their work on radar plotting was adapted for use in NIMA Publication 1310, *Radar Navigation and Maneuvering Board Manual*.

Corenman, Jim, Chuck Hawley, Dick Honey, and Stan Honey. *Radar Reflectors*. 1995. An in-depth comparison of several popular units carried out at SRI, International. The full paper is online at www.ussailing.org/safety/Studies/radar_reflector_test.htm.

National Imagery and Mapping Agency. *Radar Navigation and Maneuvering Board Manual*. Pub. 1310, 7th ed. Washington, DC: U.S. Government Printing Office, 2001. Reproduced by several private companies, but also available as free e-book download from http://pollux.nss.nima.mil/pubs.

Starpath School of Navigation. *Radar Trainer*. Seattle: Starpath Publications, 2003. PC radar simulator and tutorial. A time-limited working copy is included on the Radar Resources CD, and a full commercial version of the program is available for purchase at a discount, as explained on the CD.

Van Wyck, Samuel M., and Max H. Carpenter. *The Radar Book*. Centreville, MD: Cornell Maritime Press, 1984. A book on plotting techniques, with many examples and practice problems. This book is out of print, but is still used in radar schools.

Wylie, F. J., ed. *The Use of Radar at Sea*. 5th rev. ed. London: Hollis & Carter, 1978; Annapolis, MD: Naval Institute Press, 1978. The classic treatment of all aspects of radar usage, intended for ship operators. It is out of print and out of date in some respects, but still a wealth of information on practical radar usage.

Seamanship and Small-Boat Handling

Maloney, Elbert S. *Chapman Piloting and Seamanship*. 64th ed. New York: Hearst, 2003. The classic treatment of these subjects. The minimum one-book library for all powerboat owners.

Rousmaniere, John. *The Annapolis Book of Seamanship*. 3rd rev. ed. New York: Simon & Schuster, 1999. Popular and thorough treatment similar to *Chapman*, but with emphasis on sailboats.

Small-Craft Navigation

Brogdon, Captain Bill. *Boat Navigation for the Rest of Us: Finding Your Way by Eye and Electronics*. 2nd ed. Camden, ME: International Marine, 2001. Teaches navigation the modern, practical way by combining electronic aids like GPS and radar with commonsense visual piloting skills and simple chartwork.

Burch, David. *Inland and Coastal Navigation: A Complete Home Study Course*. Seattle: Starpath Publications, 2004. Includes online resources and direct instructor contact, available in paper, CD, or both. CD version includes e-chart training components.

Eyges, Leonard. *The Practical Pilot: Coastal Navigation by Eye, Intuition, and Common Sense*. Camden, ME: International Marine, 1989. Offers a practical approach to small-boat piloting that is popular with many mariners, and overlooked in many textbooks.

Sweet, Robert J. *GPS for Mariners*. Camden, ME: International Marine, 2003. Explains the buttons, screens, and menus of your GPS receiver, and how to make the best use of this crucial tool.

Electronic Aids to Navigation

Automatic Identification System (AIS), www.navcen.uscg.gov/enav/ais/default.htm. Extensive resources are compiled at www.uais.org.

Electronic Chart Display and Information Systems (ECDIS), www.openecdis.org. ECDIS is covered in detail.

Global Positioning System (GPS) is described at the USCG Navigation Center listed next. There are extensive useful links and practical information at http://gpsinformation.net.

USCG marine communications and related links to electronic navigation are at the USCG Navigation Center at www.navcen.uscg.gov/marcomms.

Government Resources

Canadian Hydrographic Service, www.chs-shc.dfo-mpo.gc.ca/pub/en. Provides up-to-date, hydrographic publications necessary for safe and efficient navigation for navigable waters of Canada.

Federal Communications Commission, FCC Commercial Radio Operator License Program, http://wireless.fcc.gov/commoperators/wncol.html. Describes who needs a commercial radio operator license.

International Maritime Organization (IMO), www.imo.org. A United Nations agency aimed at safer shipping and cleaner oceans.

NOAA Electronic Navigational Charts, http://chartmaker.ncd.noaa.gov. A resource for all aspects of nautical charts and related publications.

Ocean Prediction Center, National Weather Service, NOAA, www.opc.ncep.noaa.gov. Provides weather and sea-state analysis, forecasts, and warnings.

U.S. Coast Guard (USCG), www.uscg.mil. A starting point for finding documents and other information of general interest to the maritime community, including *Notices to Mariners*, *Light Lists*, and other data.

Radiation Safety

International EMF Project, World Health Organization, www.who.int/peh-emf/project/en. A clearinghouse for information on the effects of electromagnetic field radiation. The site contains scientific studies and public discussion, with extensive references.

Radio Frequency Safety, www.fcc.gov/oet/rfsafety. A quote from the Federal Communications Commission (FCC) Web site: "At the present time there is no federally-mandated radio frequency (RF) exposure standard. However, several non-government organizations, such as the American National Standards Institute (www.ansi.org), the Institute of Electrical and Electronics Engineers, Inc. (www.ieee.org), and the National Council on Radiation Protection and Measurements (NCRP) [www.ncrp.com] have issued recommendations for human exposure to RF electromagnetic fields."

Two informative papers are:

"Questions and Answers about Biological Effects and Potential Hazards of Radiofrequency Electromagnetic Fields." FCC Office of Engineering and Technology Bulletin No. 56 (www.fcc.gov/oet/rfsafety).

"Guidelines for Limiting Exposure to Time-Varying Electric, Magnetic, and Electromagnetic Fields (up to 300 GHz)," from the International Commission on Non-Ionizing Radiation Protection. *Health Physics*, vol. 74, no. 4, pp. 494–522, 1998. Gives specific values for X-band radar range in Table 5, which have been adopted by most countries (http://www.icnirp.de/documents/emfgdl.pdf).

For the latest detailed information, see papers and FAQs at the Health Physics Society site (www.hps.org) and do a search on "radar" or "microwaves."

Radar Sources

Furuno USA, www.furuno.com.

Japan Radio Company (JRC), www.jrcamerica.com.

Nobeltec, www.nobeltec.com.

Raymarine, www.raymarine.com.

Simrad, www.simradusa.com.

Xenex, www.xenex.com.

INDEX

(continued from CD-ROM-1)

The full version also includes an extensive tutorial on radar navigation and collision avoidance with many practice exercises set up and linked to the simulators. These are not available in the trial version, although the Help files included in both versions explain how to use the products.

	Trial Version	Full Version
Chart view and radar view	yes	yes
Built-in Help files	yes	yes
EBL and VRM	yes	yes
Set vessel traffic	yes	yes
Compute CPA data	yes	yes
Jump to other vessel	yes	yes
Control vessel traffic	yes	yes
Control course and speed	yes	yes
Chart regions covered	1	14
Time limit	30 days	un-limited
Number of runs	5	un-limited
Simulators included	RT3	RT3 + RT2a
Tutorials	outline only	full text and links
Practice exercises	outline only	many
Demo traffic patterns	1	many
Control sea state	no	yes
Cursor mode for EBL/VRM	no	yes
Separate CPA computer	no	yes
Rule 19d animations	no	yes
Online discussion groups	no	yes
Online exercises	no	yes
Instructor-graded online quizzes	no	yes

The regular packaged price of the full Radar Trainer program including access to online courses and resources is $159 plus shipping. You can purchase this full package from the link on the CD and begin to use the full product immediately using the "Purchase full version" link on the main menu page for $134 total. The serial number will be provided automatically when you place your purchase online.

Starpath Demo Tours

This section offers brief overviews of the several marine training software products available from the Starpath School of Navigation. These include the Radar Trainer, Weather Trainer, and Chart Trainer, as well as Nav Rules Plus and Bowditch Plus. The Radar Trainer tour is a good way to review the content of the full version of the program. The trial version and the full version are compared on each of the Radar Trainer menu pages.

Utilities

Many of the products on this CD are presented in the portable document format (PDF). To view and print these documents, you will need to have the (free) Adobe Acrobat Reader program installed on your computer. Links within the Utilities folder let you test to see if you have this already, and if not to install a copy from the CD. We also use the Microsoft HTML Help format for presenting the demo tours and the Help files within Radar Trainer. This too can be tested from the Utilities folder—this would likely be an issue only for older computers.

Tech Support and Updates

Updates, notes, additions, and tech support for this CD and its content can be found at www.starpath.com/radarbook.

Radar for Mariners covers all aspects of practical radar use, but there is no substitute for practice when it comes to radar operation. The Starpath Radar Trainer PC radar simulator has been recognized worldwide as the most effective means available for mastering the fundamental tasks of radar navigation and collision avoidance—at home and at your own pace.

This free trial version will familiarize you with the Radar Trainer and enable you to practice the skills presented in the book.

Trial Period

The trial period begins the day the program is run for the first time (it does not start when you register the program) and ends after 30 days or five sessions, whichever comes first. (The run number is incremented each time the program is opened using the desktop icon or link in the list of Programs under the Start button.) After that, the program will not open again.

Note: Use of the freeware on this CD, such as the Rules of the Road text, plotting aids, annotated screen shots, and the sample radar manuals, is unlimited. Further, such use does not initiate the trial period for the Radar Trainer. Only your first run of the Radar Trainer trial version does that.

Because the free trial period is limited, you may find the use of the simulator more beneficial after becoming familiar with the radar operations described in the book. The primary value of the simulator is to practice the crucial tasks of radar navigation (*Radar for Mariners* Chapters 1, 3, 4, 5, and 10) and collision avoidance (Chapters 6, 11, and 12). The Radar Trainer does not simulate radar picture adjustment and tuning. That subject is covered in detail in Chapters 2 and 8 of the book. All radar images in the simulator are presented with the tuning optimized,

without user controls for these adjustments.

Before running the program you can take a tour of its content at any time using the Starpath Demo Tours link to get an overview of what it includes.

System Requirements

The Radar Trainer will run on any Windows operating system, Win 98 or newer, including Win XP. The screen resolution must be set to 1024 x 768, or higher, and the font size set to small or normal.

If needed, you will be presented with a notice when you first run the program that these settings must be adjusted. These settings can be checked and adjusted from links under the Start button (Start/Settings/Control Panel/Display/Settings). If land does not show up on the radar screen, then go back to the Settings and increase the color quality to the next higher level.

Registration

The trial version must be registered to operate in your computer. The free registration process provides the numeric KEY that unlocks the program in your computer. The KEY will be unique to your computer; if you install the program in another computer, you will need to register it again to receive a KEY for the new computer.

Installation

Start by clicking link "(1) Install Trial Version." This will begin the process and then present you with the CODE that is unique to your computer. Record this CODE, as it is required to obtain the KEY.

To obtain the KEY using your specific CODE, you have several options. The quickest and easiest method is to use the Internet for immediate registration. This can be done at www.starpath.

com/register. Once there, select Radar Trainer Demo as the product to register. Enter your CODE and receive the KEY immediately. It will also send you a copy by e-mail. The online process requires an e-mail address. Note that you can obtain the KEY in this manner from any computer that is connected to the Internet. You do not need to register from the same computer you are installing to. You can, for example, install onto your home computer, record the CODE, and obtain the KEY from an office computer or from a friend or family member's computer.

If you happen to be online with the same computer you are installing to, a link appears during installation (at the bottom of the same window that presented the CODE) that may take you straight to the proper Web page and also transfer your CODE to the form. This button is activated after you press the Readme button. If that direct link does not work (this depends on your configuration), then the link on the page marked "(2) Register Trial version online" should take you to the proper page to complete the process. If neither of these shortcuts works, log onto the Internet in your usual manner and navigate to www.starpath.com/register.

If you do not have an Internet connection, you can call 206-783-1414 (10 a.m. to 5 p.m. Pacific Time, weekdays) with your CODE at hand to receive a KEY that way. If after hours or if your call is missed, then leave a message with your contact information along with the CODE and you will get a return call with the KEY.

Once you have your KEY, enter it in the space provided (below where you were given the CODE) and the installation will complete itself. If the installation process has been closed, just start it again and then enter the KEY.

Tech Support and Updates

Links to tech support for the trial version as well as updates on the content of this CD and general news about *Radar for Mariners* can be found at www.starpath.com/radarbook.

Uninstall

After the trial period has expired it would be best to uninstall the trial version. It cannot be run again, so it is just taking up hard drive space that could be recovered. If you choose to purchase the full version, it is a completely separate product that does not remove or replace the trial version components.

INSTRUCTIONS FOR PURCHASING AND INSTALLING THE FULL VERSION OF THE STARPATH RADAR TRAINER

This CD also contains a complete copy of the Starpath Radar Trainer program, which you can install directly from the CD. It includes all Help documents and related files. The content is identical to that delivered in Starpath's consumer package. There is no paper manual provided in either format, as none is required. All information on the use of the program is contained within it. Tech support and answers to frequently asked questions are also available at www.starpath.com/support.

To install the program you must first purchase a serial number. This is available to readers of *Radar for Mariners* at a discounted price of $134, which is $25 less than the standard retail price of the packaged product ($159) and $15 less than the download price of the product ($149).

There are two ways to purchase a serial number that can be used to register the discounted copy of the program on your CD:

1. Use link *(1) Purchase Serial Number Online*, which will take you directly to a special

discount page for the product and provide the serial number immediately.

2. Or, if you do not have Internet access, you can *call 800-955-8328* to reach the Starpath order desk, and someone there will log on and place the online order for you and give you your serial number.

After you have purchased your serial number, go to link *(2) Install Radar Trainer* to begin the installation process and obtain your product CODE.

With your serial number and CODE in hand, you can go to link *(3) Register Radar Trainer* to obtain the KEY that will unlock the program in your computer.

As with the trial version, the KEY is unique to your computer. If you choose to install the program onto another computer, you must obtain the KEY for the second computer and register it to obtain a new KEY for the second computer. The product can be registered a total of three times.

Your copy of the full Radar Trainer program along with your copy of *Radar for Mariners* are the two required materials for your participation in the Starpath online course in marine radar if you wish to take part. The course includes Lecture Notes, Practice Exercises, Discussion Groups, and Quizzes graded by an instructor.

SIMULATOR INSTALL QUESTIONS

Q. I pressed the Buy Online button that appears in the trial version, but that does not take me to the discount purchase offer. Where do I find the discount purchase?

A. The discount is available to *Radar for Mariners* readers through the special link provided on the Radar Resources CD. With that link you can purchase and receive your serial number automatically. Without an Internet connection, you can call the Starpath order desk at 800-955-8328 and they will execute the online order for you and give you your serial number.

Q. When I start the trial version I get an error message that says "This program requires a screen resolution of at least 1024 x 768." What do I do about this?

A. You must increase the screen resolution using the control at: Start/Settings/Control Panel/Display/Settings. Use the slider bar there to increase the resolution to 1024 x 768.

Q. When I start the Radar Trainer there is no land on the radar. What is wrong?

A. The color quality level is not high enough in your display settings. Go to Start/Settings/Control Panel/Display/Settings and increase the color quality by one level.

Q. I changed the date on my computer and now the trial version does not work. How do I fix this?

A. Unfortunately, there is no way to correct this. It is important to follow the install instructions and not change the computer date once the trial version is in progress. There is no way to reactivate a trial version in a particular computer once it has expired.

Q. Will the Radar Trainer run on a Macintosh computer?

A. Yes, providing you are running a Windows emulator program in the Macintosh. There are several versions of Windows emulators or virtual Windows programs available.

RADAR RESOURCES CD-ROM

This CD-ROM contains several products intended to enhance your study of radar and to introduce you to the Starpath Radar Trainer simulator and tutorial, which is an excellent supplement to the information presented in *Radar for Mariners*.

Radar Resources

Sample radar manuals of popular small-craft models from four leading companies are reproduced here with permission from the manufacturers. Reading radar manuals is an excellent way to learn about available features and the various solutions on how to implement them. Most companies have their manuals available for Internet download.

Annotated screen shots show various uses of radar with color screen captures and notes on the application at hand.

The *Navigation Rules* is a complete e-book copy (PDF—portable document format—see Utilities folder) of the U.S. Coast Guard printing of the *Navigation Rules*, both International and U.S. Inland. You can study the text on-screen or print it out for later reading.

Radar plotting aids are PDF presentations of graphic tools (discussed in the book) that help interpret the radar screen and evaluate the data obtained. Note that the link must first open Acrobat Reader before displaying the document you selected. This can take a moment for the first one. If you do not have Acrobat Reader installed, please refer to the Utilities folder on the main menu page of the CD.

These plotting aids include *portable range scales* for reading distances on a radar screen (see instructions in the book); *plotting sheets* for solving relative motion diagrams and for other problems such as determining a target's closest point of approach (CPA) and time to CPA; and *parallel index sheets* to be printed and then photocopied onto transparencies. The latter can then be cut to fit the profile of your radar screen or computer screen when working with the simulator. (The technique of parallel indexing is discussed in the book.)

Radar Simulator

The Starpath Radar Trainer is a realistic interactive radar simulator for personal computers running a Microsoft Windows operating system. It is designed to let you practice and master radar navigation and collision avoidance. It includes various waterways for practice along with a detailed tutorial. With it you can set up any vessel traffic scenario you choose or use the preset ones provided.

A time-limited trial version of the program is available free of charge on this CD (maximum use is five sessions or 30 days from the first session, whichever comes first) so that you can become familiar with the product, and use it to practice radar operations described in the book. (For more on the Radar Simulator, see the Instructions for the Free Trial section below.)

The CD also contains a complete copy of the full, unlimited program, which is available for purchase at a discounted price.

Comparison of the Full and Trial Versions

The trial version is essentially the same as the full version except that the number of land regions is limited and there is no RT2a simulator, which is customized for quick and efficient collision avoidance studies in open water. You can place and interact with traffic using the land-based RT3 simulator, but it is more efficient and there are more examples in the full version.

(continued on CD-ROM-2)